Reading the *Odyssey*

Reading the *Odyssey*

SELECTED

INTERPRETIVE ESSAYS

Edited with an Introduction by

· *SETH L. SCHEIN* ·

PRINCETON UNIVERSITY PRESS

PRINCETON, NEW JERSEY

Library of Congress Cataloging-in-Publication Data

Reading the Odyssey : selected interpretive essays / edited with an
introduction by Seth L. Schein.
    p. cm.
Includes bibliographical references and index.
ISBN 0-691-04440-6 (cl)—ISBN 0-691-04439-2 (alk. paper)
1. Homer. Odyssey. 2. Odysseus (Greek mythology) in literature.
3. Epic poetry, Greek—History and criticism.   I. Schein, Seth L.
PA4167.R43 1995
883'.01—dc20   95-10938

This book has been composed in Galliard

• *TO THE MEMORY OF HOWARD N. PORTER* •

· CONTENTS ·

THIS BOOK is intended for those who read, study, and teach the *Odyssey* in translation or in the original Greek. It includes ten essays by leading scholars that seem to me valuable for their interpretive approaches to the poem. Of these essays, one is new (Slatkin); the others were published between 1948 and 1988, though two appear in revised and expanded versions (Felson-Rubin, Nagler) and five in English translation, three for the first time (Hölscher, Reinhardt, Vernant, "The Refusal of Odysseus").

The ten contributions reflect five major interpretive concerns of modern *Odyssey* scholarship: the poem's programmatic representation of social and religious institutions and values; its transformation of folktales and traditional stories into epic adventures; its representation of gender roles and, in particular, of Penelope; its narrative strategies and form; and its relation to the *Iliad*, especially to that epic's distinctive conception of heroism. Some of the essays address one or more of these topics in general terms; others focus on a single episode, character, pattern of dramatic action, or element of style or diction. In my Introduction, I have tried briefly to indicate the background of the poem and to suggest fruitful lines of interpretation, some of which are developed in greater depth and detail in one or more of the ten essays.

Several of these contributions originally appeared in books and journals that are out-of-the-way and hard to find even for classical scholars. One aim of the present collection is to make them more readily available and, by juxtaposing them with the more accessible and the new pieces, to allow all the essays to engage in fruitful dialogue with each other. To some extent, they already do so. For example, Hölscher's concern with the transformation of folktale into epic is deeply influenced by Reinhardt's study of the transformation of folk-motifs into thematically relevant adventures and of "story" into dramatic "situation." In different ways, both Felson-Rubin's "Penelope's Perspective" and Nagler's "Dread Goddess Revisited" are concerned with Penelope and femininity in the poem, though the former essay is perhaps more interested in what might be called Penelope's psychological style and in the narratological implications of this style than in representations of gender and social roles. On the other hand, such representations are the central interpretive concern of Nagler's essay, which studies them in light of archetypal, Indo-European poetic themes.

Felson-Rubin's narratological concerns link her piece with Slatkin's essay on the interpretive significance of the overall narrative structure of the *Odyssey*. At the same time, Slatkin's interest in the representation and self-representation of Odysseus as a particular kind of hero, in a special, self-conscious relation to traditional heroic values and song, connects her discussion to Segal's "*Kleos* and Its Ironies in the *Odyssey*" and Pucci's "The Song of the

Sirens"—two pieces that also address Odysseus' and the poem's distinctive and self-conscious heroic themes, diction, and style (and that refer to each other in their notes). Similarly, Vernant's "The Refusal of Odysseus" and "Death with Two Faces," while focusing on specific episodes of the poem, situate these episodes in its overall narrative and thematic structure and view them as illustrative of its distinctive values; they owe much to Vidal-Naquet's wide-ranging essay and are fruitfully studied together with the essays of Pucci, Segal, and Slatkin. Originally I planned to include another half-dozen pieces on various literary, social, and historical topics, but that would have made the book too costly for much of its intended audience. I hope the loss in scholarly range and variety is offset by the gain in concentration and coherence.

I am grateful to the authors, editors, and publishers of previously published articles for permission to include them in this volume (for details, please see the list of Acknowledgments); to Vincent Farenga, Harriet Flower, and Simon Richter, who translated essays by Vernant, Reinhardt, and Hölscher, respectively, especially for this volume; to Kay Flavell and Andrew Szegedy-Maszak, who translated from French and German several of the essays I intended to include but could not find room for. I am grateful also to the many other colleagues and friends who discussed the contents of this volume with me, read drafts of my Introduction, and improved it by their criticism. For their advice and encouragement I wish to thank in particular Jenny Strauss Clay, Lillian Doherty, Nancy Felson-Rubin, Sheila Murnaghan, Gregory Nagy, Charles Segal, Laura Slatkin, Froma Zeitlin, and the anonymous Readers for Princeton University Press. I also wish to thank Jeffrey Carnes for the General Index and my former Research Assistants, Susan Brockman, Elizabeth Pittenger, and Susan Thomas, for practical help and numerous substantive improvements. At Princeton University Press, Joanna Hitchcock (at the inception of this project) and Lauren Osborne and Licia Wise (at its conclusion) were exceptionally helpful and supportive, and Marta Steele was an alert and instructive copy editor. I am grateful to the Academic Senates of the University of California at Davis and the University of California at Santa Cruz and to the Research Foundation of the City University of New York for their financial support.

I would like to thank my wife, Sherry Crandon, and our son, Daniel, for the patience and support that enabled me to complete this project.

I dedicate this collection to the memory of my teacher, the late Howard N. Porter, with whom I was lucky enough to study the Homeric epics in a series of unforgettable, yearlong courses at Columbia University in the early and mid-1960s. Howard was a brilliant reader of the *Odyssey* and an inspiring teacher; many of the ideas and interpretations suggested or developed in my Introduction go back to his classes.

• ACKNOWLEDGMENTS •

I AM GRATEFUL to authors, editors, and publishers for permission to reprint or translate the following essays used in this volume, which originally appeared in the publications listed below:

U. Hölscher, "Penelope and the Suitors" ["Penelope vor den Freiern"], *Lebende Antike. Symposium für R. Sühnel* (Berlin: Erich Schmidt Verlag, 1967), 27–33.

P. Pucci, "The Song of the Sirens," *Arethusa* 12 (1979), 121–32.

K. Reinhardt, "The Adventures in the *Odyssey*" ["Die Abenteuer der *Odyssee*"], *Tradition und Geist: Gesammelte Essays zur Dichtung*, ed. C. Becker (Göttingen: Vandenhoeck and Ruprecht, 1960), 47–124 [originally in Reinhardt, *Von Werken und Formen* (Godesberg, 1948), 52–162].

C. Segal, "*Kleos* and Its Ironies in the *Odyssey*," *L'Antiquité classique* 52 (1983), 22–47.

J.-P. Vernant, "Death with Two Faces," tr. J. Lloyd, *Mortality and Immortality: The Anthropology and Archaeology of Death*, ed. S. C. Humphreys and H. King (London: Academic Press Inc., 1981), 285–91 [originally "Mort grecque, mort à deux faces," *Le Débat* 12 (1981), 51–59]. Copyright © 1981 by Academic Press Inc. (London) Ltd.

J.-P. Vernant, "The Refusal of Odysseus" ["Le Refus d'Ulysse"], *Le Temps de la réflexion* 3 (1982), 13–19.

P. Vidal-Naquet, "Land and Sacrifice in the *Odyssey*: A Study of Religious and Mythical Meanings," tr. R. L. Gordon, rev. A. Szegedy-Maszak, *The Black Hunter: Forms of Thought and Forms of Society in the Greek World* (Baltimore and London: The Johns Hopkins University Press, 1986), 15–38 = *Myth, Religion and Society: Structuralist Essays by M. Detienne, L. Gernet, J.-P. Vernant, and P. Vidal-Naquet*, ed. R. L. Gordon (Cambridge: Cambridge University Press, and Paris: Editions de la Maison des Sciences de l'Homme, 1981), 80–94, 244–50 [originally published as "Valeurs religieuses et mythiques de la terre et du sacrifice dans l'*Odyssée*," *Annales E.S.C.* 25 (1970), 1278–97 = *Problèmes de la terre en grèce ancienne*, ed. M. I. Finley (The Hague: Mouton, 1973), 269–92 = *Le Chasseur noir: Formes de pensée et formes de société dans le monde grec* (Paris: François Maspéro, 1981), 39–68].

Of the remaining essays in this volume, M. N. Nagler's "Dread Goddess Revisited" is a revised and greatly expanded version of "Dread Goddess Endowed with Speech," *Archaeological News* 6 (1977), 77–85; N. Felson-Rubin's "Penelope's Perspective: Character from Plot," is a revised and greatly expanded version of her essay with the same title in *Homer: Beyond*

Oral Poetry: Recent Trends in Homeric Interpretation, ed. J. M. Bremer, I.J.F. de Jong, and J. Kalff (Amsterdam: B. R. Grüner Publishing Company, 1987), 61–83, and also of Chapter 2 of her book *Regarding Penelope* (Princeton: Princeton University Press, 1994). In the final pages of the Introduction, I have drawn on my essay "Female Representations and Interpreting the *Odyssey*," in *The Distaff Side: Representing the Female in Homer's Odyssey*, ed. B. Cohen (New York and Oxford: Oxford University Press, 1995), 17–27.

Translations of Homeric texts are either by the authors of the various essays (Nagler, Schein, Vidal-Naquet) or are taken from R. Lattimore, *The Odyssey of Homer* (New York: Harper and Row, 1965) and *The Iliad of Homer* (Chicago: University of Chicago Press, 1951) (Felson-Rubin, Hölscher, Pucci, Reinhardt, Segal, Slatkin, Vernant). The line numbers of translations and citations of the *Odyssey* refer to the standard *Homeri Odyssea*, edited by P. von der Mühll, in the *Bibliotheca Scriptorum Graecorum et Romanorum Teubneriana* (Stuttgart: B. G. Teubner, 1946; 3rd edition 1962, reprinted 1984), or to volumes 3 and 4 of *Homeri Opera*, edited by T. W. Allen, in the Oxford Classical Texts series, 2nd edition (Oxford: Oxford University Press, 1917–1919). Translations and citations of the *Iliad* refer to volumes 1 and 2 of *Homeri Opera*, edited by D. B. Monro and T. W. Allen, in the same series, 3rd edition (Oxford: Oxford University Press, 1920).

Because some of these articles have been published previously, no attempt has been made to achieve consistency from article to article in the spelling of Greek proper names, which therefore varies throughout the book, according to author preference. Minor copyediting has been done, however, to assure other consistencies of style throughout.

Reading the *Odyssey*

Introduction

SETH L. SCHEIN

THE *ODYSSEY*, together with the *Iliad*, has usually been thought of as the earliest work of Western literature. As such, its narrative form, its hero, and its social and moral values have been artistically and ethically paradigmatic. For the Greeks and later Western readers alike, it has served as a model and a mirror of both individual and cultural self-definition.

Actually the *Odyssey* is not an early work. Rather, like the *Iliad*, it is an end product of a Greek poetic tradition that may have been as much as a thousand years old by the time the epics were composed, probably in the final quarter of the eighth century B.C.E., and that had roots in a still older Indo-European poetic tradition. The tradition behind the *Odyssey*, we know today, was one of oral poetry. In it a poet created a poem anew each time he said (or, rather, sang) it, for there was no established, written text: on each occasion, performance and composition were one and the same.[1]

The poems the poets sang in this oral poetic tradition were formulaic. That is, their language, meter, and style, as well as the kinds of events and even many of the specific events in the stories, were traditional and common to all poets who learned to work with the basic building blocks of the medium: fixed formulas consisting of repeated, metrically patterned words, phrases, half-lines, and lines, and typical scenes or "themes"—"recurrent elements of narration or description"—such as a feast, an assembly, or a ship beginning or ending a voyage, or, on a larger scale, a son's quest for his father or a hero's descent to the underworld or journey homeward.[2] The knowledge of these building blocks and the ability to use them artistically are attributed both by the singers of the epics and by poets and audiences within them to the inspiration of a Muse or Muses (e.g., *Il.* 1.1, 2.484–92; *Od.* 1.1–10, 8.63–64, 487–88, 22.347–48). These goddesses were the

---

[1] That the *Odyssey*, like the *Iliad*, is composed in a traditional, oral, formulaic style was the discovery of the American classical scholar Milman Parry. He demonstrated his discovery in a series of publications in French and English during the late 1920s and early 1930s. These are gathered together (the French pieces in English translation) in *The Making of Homeric Verse: The Collected Essays of Milman Parry*, edited and with an introduction by Adam Parry (Oxford, 1971).

[2] See A. B. Lord, "Composition by Theme in Homer and Southslavic Epos," *Transactions of the American Philological Association* 82 (1951), pp. 71–80 (the words quoted appear on p. 73); *The Singer of Tales* (Cambridge, Mass., 1960; reprint, New York, 1965), pp. 68–98.

daughters of Zeus and Mnemosyne (Memory); they endowed the poets with the memory of the formulaic and thematic building blocks that made it possible for them to compose and perform simultaneously in the traditional style. A poet in full command of the building blocks could manipulate them as he wished: a poor, unimaginative poet would produce dull, derivative songs; a poet like Homer would produce imaginative, innovative poetry. The fact that the Homeric epics are composed in traditional, formulaic language, meter, and style and according to strict narrative conventions in no way means that they are therefore unoriginal or inartistic—quite the opposite.

The study of composition by formula and theme is part of the study of the *Odyssey* as traditional poetry. If, however, the *Odyssey* is stylistically and thematically an end product of an oral poetic tradition, it is equally (together with the *Iliad*) the first work in Greek literature, that is, in writing. Evidence suggests that the Phoenician alphabet was introduced into Greece in the third quarter of the eighth century B.C.E. (though some scholars believe it came centuries earlier). It is reasonable to suppose, though not demonstrable, that the poem as we have it was written down, or perhaps dictated to a scribe or amanuensis, by a poet trained in the oral tradition who took advantage of the new linguistic medium to create something special. This would account both for the poem's traditional formulaic style and for its overall profundity and artistic excellence. It has even been suggested that the alphabet may have been introduced specifically to create the Homeric poems.[3] Although this seems unlikely, it does call attention to the significance of literacy for creating our *Odyssey*: through writing the text was fixed in a way that would have been impossible in oral composition. In an illiterate tradition, each singing, even by the same poet, yields a new and different poem produced from the basic building blocks in the poet's memory; within a few generations, to judge from the comparable evidence of Serbo-Croatian poetry, even a work as large as the *Odyssey* would become so drastically altered as to be no longer the same poem.[4] Undoubtedly the introduction of writing brought the oral tradition to an end. Although some of the earliest extant Greek elegiac and lyric poets, like the seventh-century Archilochos, may well have been trained as oral singers and some oral "recomposition in performance" may have continued after the introduction of writing, the enormous influence of Homer on later Greek (and Western) literature and civilization was the influence of a more or less fixed text into which lines might be interpolated or from which lines might be omitted by any given oral performer, but which, as an artistic whole, was unchanging.[5]

[3]H. T. Wade-Gery, *The Poet of the Iliad* (Cambridge, 1952), pp. 38–41; B. B. Powell, *Homer and the Origin of the Greek Alphabet* (Cambridge, 1991). Cf. G. P. Goold, "Homer and the Alphabet," *Transactions of the American Philological Association* 91 (1960), pp. 272–91.

[4]A. Parry, "Have We Homer's *Iliad?*" *Yale Classical Studies* 20 (1966), p. 189 = *Essays on the Iliad: Selected Modern Criticism*, ed. J. Wright (Bloomington and London, 1978), p. 8.

[5]G. Nagy, *Pindar's Homer: The Lyric Possession of an Epic Past* (Baltimore and London, 1990), p. 19, argues that "so long as the traditions of oral poetry are alive in a given society, a written record cannot by itself affect a composition or performance, and . . . it cannot stop the process

Although the diction and style of the *Odyssey*, along with its mythological and folkloric content, are traditional, the poem generates new and distinctive meanings by selection, adaptation, and transformation of this traditional material in accordance with its own distinctive ideas and values. Through parallels, juxtapositions, and contrasts of places, societies, individual characters, and their actions, a dramatic situation is created that invites readers to view Ithaca (with the restored Odysseus as king) as the locus of morally sound, human reality in the poem and Odysseus himself as the human hero par excellence.[6] For example, the story of Agamemnon's death at the hands of Aigisthos and Klutaimestra and Orestes' vengeance on the killers, to which the poem refers so often, makes Orestes a positive model for Telemachos, and Agamemnon and Klutaimnestra negative foils for Odysseus and Penelope.[7] Similarly, the representation of Sparta and its ruling family as wealthy, selfish, escapist, and trivial clarifies by contrast the moral health of rocky Ithaca and the household of Odysseus. Moreover, the representations of the Cyclopes as institutionally, technologically, and morally savage and the Phaeacians as supercivilized clarify by contrast the quintessentially human community of Ithaca, in which Odysseus is able to be fully himself as he cannot be in those societies.[8]

In this way, to put it simply, the *Odyssey* is about what it means to be human. On the other hand, the particular ways in which Odysseus is represented as heroic and human and Ithaca is represented as his home and the

---

of recomposition in performance." On the one hand, Nagy argues for an evolutionary model of "textual fixation" within oral traditions, even without the influence of writing; on the other hand, he suggests that writing a text does not necessarily freeze the process of "recomposition in performance" unless and until the written text becomes an alternative to performance and is considered an authoritative alternative. See especially pp. 52–81, 84, 404.

On orality and literacy generally, see W. Ong, *Orality and Literacy* (London and New York, 1982), who builds on the work of M. Parry, A. B. Lord, A. Parry, and especially E. A. Havelock, *A Preface to Plato* (Cambridge, Mass., and Oxford, 1963; reprint, New York, 1967).

[6] Cf. P. Vidal-Naquet, "Land and Sacrifice in the *Odyssey*: A Study of Religious and Mythical Meanings," in *The Black Hunter: Forms of Thought and Forms of Society in the Greek World*, tr. A. Szegedy-Maszak (Baltimore and London, 1986), pp. 15–38 [this volume, pp. 33–53] (originally published in 1970); H. Porter, "Introduction," in *Homer, The Odyssey*, tr. G. H. Palmer, ed. H. Porter (New York, 1962), pp. 4, 7–10.

[7] Cf. U. Hölscher, "Die Atridensage in der *Odyssee*," in *Festschrift für Richard Alewyn*, ed. H. Singer and B. von Wiese (Cologne/Graz, 1967), pp. 1–16. But S. D. Olson, "The Stories of Agamemnon in Homer's *Odyssey*," *Transactions of the American Philological Association* 120 (1990), pp. 57–71, argues suggestively that the tale of Agamemnon is not merely "a foil for the larger story of Odysseus and his family" (p. 57), and that "its contents" and purpose "vary in each retelling, depending on who is repeating the story, who is listening to it, and what information, presuppositions or intentions the various parties bring with them to the narrative" (p. 70).

[8] On contrasts between the Cyclopes and the Phaeacians, see Vidal-Naquet, "Land and Sacrifice," p. 27 [this vol., p. 50]; C. Segal, "The Phaeacians and the Symbolism of Odysseus' Return," *Arion* 1 (1962), p. 33; Porter, "Introduction," pp. 7–9; H. Clarke, *The Art of the Odyssey* (Englewood Cliffs, 1967), p. 54; N. Austin, *Archery at the Dark of the Moon: Poetic Problems in Homer's Odyssey* (Berkeley, Los Angeles, London, 1975), pp. 153–57; J. S. Clay, *The Wrath of Athena: Gods and Men in the Odyssey* (Princeton, 1983), pp. 128–32.

source, goal, and scene of his heroism, differ from the ways in which heroism and the human condition are represented in the *Iliad*. In recent years scholars have come to think of these differences as characteristic not only of the poems themselves but of distinct Iliadic and Odyssean traditions within the overall poetic tradition. Whether the *Odyssey* is consciously aware of its companion epic as we have it or only of an Iliadic tradition in which a particular kind of warrior heroism was represented, it certainly has in mind, and often defines itself against, the heroic mood and values characteristic of the *Iliad*.[9]

For this reason, perhaps, the *Odyssey* has often been thought to have been composed later than the *Iliad*, despite the likelihood that the Iliadic and Odyssean traditions evolved together within the overall poetic tradition. Moreover, though most ancient writers speak unquestioningly of Homer as the author of both poems, many modern readers feel they cannot be by the same poet owing to supposed differences in style as well as in their characteristic themes, values, and ideas. In particular, the *Odyssey* has seemed more self-consciously moralistic than the *Iliad*: from the first scene, in which Zeus refers to Aigisthos to support his assertion that human beings are responsible for their own sufferings (1.32–43), to Odysseus' justified vengeance on the Suitors and defeat of their families, the poem emphasizes the punishment of evildoers and the triumph of those who deserve and receive the gods' aid—a different situation from that in the *Iliad*, where characters are not represented or designated as good or evil, and the gods are divided in their loyalties to various human protégés for reasons that have little or nothing to do with morality.

Nowadays the arguments based on style have been refuted or judged unconvincing: there are no significant linguistic, metrical, or formulaic differences between the two epics and no reason to consider either work as dating from much later than 700 B.C.E. (though within both poems it is possible to take a diachronic view of the style and to be aware of linguistic developments up to this date). There are, however, many who still feel on aesthetic, intellectual, or spiritual grounds that the two epics cannot be from the same date, let alone by the same poet.

It is difficult not to be subjective on this topic, since we actually know nothing about the poems' relative chronology of composition. Some speculate that the *Odyssey*, a post-Trojan War poem of return, presupposes the *Iliad* or at least the mythology of the war as sung traditionally. Others would say that reflection on the story of the return of Agamemnon gave

[9] On the *Odyssey*'s consciousness of itself in relation to the *Iliad*, see G. Thalmann, *Conventions of Form and Thought in Early Greek Epic Poetry* (Baltimore and London, 1984), pp. 164, 167–70, 182–83. The *Iliad*, on the other hand, rarely alludes or refers to the Odyssean tradition, though a few occasions in the poem call the Odyssean Odysseus to mind—most notably the night-spying episode in book 10, when Odysseus and Diomedes, with Athene's help, treacherously kill the Trojan Dolon, then butcher the Thracian king Rhesos and his followers as they are sleeping and escape to the Greek ships with his horses and armor.

birth to the romance of Odysseus, and that Agamemnon's return logically presupposes the war from which he returned.[10] However we put it, there is a complementarity between the *Iliad* and the *Odyssey* that may lead one to conclude either that they developed together in the mind of the same poet or that whoever composed the second of them, whether the same or another poet, had the first of them in mind. It has been observed that, except for the general outcome, no episode in the Trojan War that is narrated or mentioned in the *Iliad* is narrated or mentioned in the *Odyssey*, and vice versa.[11] Since it is almost impossible to imagine that two poets composing in the same poetic tradition could have done this accidentally,[12] it follows, again, either that the same poet composed both epics or that whoever composed the second of them had the first constantly in mind. It is perfectly possible that the *Iliad* and *Odyssey* are complementary works of a single poet who took at different times a tragic and a romantic/comic view of reality, as Shakespeare did, for example, in *King Lear* and *The Tempest*. On the other hand, the question of authorship is relatively unimportant, and it seems more productive to think of the epics as final products of different subtraditions within the main poetic tradition, each with its distinctive subject matter, ideas, and heroic values. Both poems were fixed in writing toward the end of the eighth century B.C.E., and in this form both together became, as it were, the "bible" of the Greeks of historical times, exercising a decisive artistic and moral influence on their (and later Western) culture.

The overwhelming fact of life for the warrior heroes of the *Iliad* is their mortality, which stands in contrast to the immortality of the gods. This mortality prompts them to risk an early death in battle, striving for "imperishable glory" (*kleos aphthiton*) in the form of poetic remembrance as heroes of songs that will keep alive their names and achievements and so endow their ephemeral lives with significance that transcends death. The *Iliad* simultaneously idealizes this heroic way of life and invites its readers and listeners to consider it critically and view as tragic the contradictions inherent in it. The central hero of the *Iliad*, Achilles, moves toward disillusionment with warrior heroism to reach a new clarity about human existence in the context of his own death and of the eventual destruction of Troy. He does so in an environment consisting almost entirely of war, an environ-

---

[10] W. J. Woodhouse, *The Composition of Homer's Odyssey* (Oxford 1930; reprinted, Oxford, 1969), p. 247.

[11] D. B. Monro, ed., *Homer's Odyssey, Books XIII–XXIV* (Oxford, 1901), p. 325; cf. R. Lattimore, tr., *The Odyssey of Homer* (New York, 1965), pp. 19–20. There is one exception to this observation: the death and burial of Patroklos are narrated in the *Iliad* and referred to at *Od.* 24.77, 79.

[12] But this is the argument of D. Page, *The Homeric Odyssey* (Oxford, 1955), pp. 158–59, who, however, improbably conceives of the two poets as belonging to two completely different traditions. Against Page, see G. Nagy, *The Best of the Achaeans: Concepts of the Hero in Archaic Greek Poetry* (Baltimore and London, 1979), pp. 20–21.

ment that offers scope for various kinds and degrees of heroic achievement, but only at the cost of self-destruction and the destruction of others who share the same values.

By contrast, the central fact of life in the *Odyssey* is not mortality and the effort to transcend it by dying young in battle and achieving "imperishable glory." Rather, it is the need to survive in a postwar world, where options are more numerous and complex than in the *Iliad*. Unlike Achilles, Odysseus is a survivor; he does not die in the Trojan War but returns home to his family and kingdom. His distinctive heroism, for which he is designated "best" in the *Odyssey* as Achilles is designated "best" in the *Iliad*, is indicated by his survival and triumphant return.[13] Odysseus achieves his *nostos*, his "return home," not so much by physical prowess and warrior heroism (though these too are needed) as through mental toughness, which helps him endure the sufferings he undergoes and keeps him mindful of Penelope and Ithaca when he might be tempted to forget them for the easy life with Kalypso (1.56–57) or Nausikaa.

The *Odyssey* is filled with characters who do forget, who can't or won't concentrate mentally and so fail, both ethically and practically (in the *Odyssey*, there is no difference): the companions who ate the lotos flower and "wanted to remain with the lotos-eating men, / munching lotos, and to forget their return home" (9.96–97); the simple Elpenor who broke his neck when he fell off Kirke's roof, because he "forgot in his mind" (10.557) and "didn't think / to come back down, going to the tall ladder" (11.62–63); the men for whom Kirke "mixed into their food / drugs working evil effects, so they would forget entirely the land of their fathers" (10.235–36); the Ithacans, not one of whom, in Mentor's words, "remembers divine Odysseus" (2.233); the Suitors who frequently "remember the feast" (20.246) and their own pleasure but forget the norms of appropriate behavior and the possibility of Odysseus' return.[14]

Throughout the poem, improper eating, like that of the Suitors, is a mark of moral inadequacy, as one would expect in a poetic universe where every meal is, or involves, a sacrificial ritual.[15] The cannibalistic Polyphemos, the Companions who eat the cattle of the Sun, as well as the Suitors who devour the herds of Odysseus are all on the wrong side of the poem's moral dividing line: they are "violent, savage, and not just" rather than "friendly to strangers, with a mind that reverences the gods" (6.120–21 = 9.175–76 = 13.201–202). All are punished for appropriating another's property to satisfy their own appetites and for thinking they can get away without pay-

---

[13] Cf. Nagy, *The Best of the Achaeans*, pp. 26–41.

[14] Even Zeus, at the beginning of the poem, seems to have forgotten Odysseus while remembering Aigisthos, though he asks Athene, defensively and rhetorically, "How could I forget divine [*theioio*] Odysseus, / who is beyond mortals in intelligence and in giving sacrifices / to the immortal gods . . . ?" (1.65–67).

[15] Cf. Clarke, *Art of the Odyssey*, pp. 15–18; S. Saïd, "Les Crimes des prétendants, la maison d'Ulysse et les festins de l'*Odyssée*," *Etudes de littérature ancienne* (Paris, 1979), pp. 9–49.

ing for this appropriation. The Suitors, in particular, are repeatedly characterized as evildoers, who "devour the livelihood of another without payment" (1.160, 377; 2.142; 14.377, 417; 18.280) and who risk "perishing
themselves within the house without payment, / if ever Zeus grants that
there be acts of requital" (1.379–80 = 2.144–45). Their appetite for Penelope (and for the servant women with whom some of them sleep) is another
sign of their immoral lack of respect for another's property. It is a cardinal
theme of the poem that such immorality is punished, when, like Odysseus,
the offended party is tough enough, with the gods' help, to exact vengeance. Odysseus himself insists on his moral right to such vengeance when
he tells the Suitors:

> Dogs, you thought I wouldn't come anymore, returning homeward,
> from the community of the Trojans, because you pillaged my household
> and slept with my servant women by force,
> and, while I was alive, you wooed my wife,
> having feared neither the gods who hold the broad heaven
> nor the righteous blame of mortals afterward.
> Now for you, for all of you, the cables of destruction have been fastened tight.

(22.35–41)

In response to the plea of Eurymachos, Odysseus further insists that he
won't stop the slaughter "before the Suitors pay back all the transgression"
(22.64), just as he rejects the supplication of the seer Leiodes (22.312–19)
with the accusation that "you no doubt often prayed in the halls [of my
house] / that the goal of my sweet return home be far off / and that my wife
follow you and beget children" (22.322–24). "Transgression" (*huperbasiē*)
is the poem's general term for the Suitors' trespass against Odysseus and his
family (3.206, 13.193, 22.64). The word is used in the *Iliad* of the offense of
violating oaths made to Zeus (*Il.* 3.107), and it is noteworthy that Achilles
uses it (*Il.* 16.18) to describe the behavior of the Argives against himself,
for which "they are [deservedly] perishing / by the hollow ships" (*Il.* 16.17–
18). In each epic the hero is represented as taking vengeance on his enemies
"as if he were a god to punish." In the *Iliad* this vengeance is problematically self-defeating, in accordance with that poem's emphasis on the tragic
contradictions inherent in traditional, mortal heroism, but in the *Odyssey*
Odysseus overcomes his enemies completely and unambivalently, and there
is nothing at all self-defeating about his triumph. In the *Iliad* there are no
villains, so every death is tinged with tragedy. In the *Odyssey* the gods validate
the hero's right to kill 108 Suitors, all conceived as thoroughgoing villains, in
defense of his wife and property. This is made clear when Zeus and Athene
impose a truce between Odysseus and his supporters and the families of the
Suitors, after Laertes kills Eupeithes (24.526–48). Normally, as Odysseus observes to Telemachos, even if "someone kills a man in the community / who
does not have many helpers behind to avenge him, / he flees into exile, aban-

doning his kinsmen and native land; / but we have killed the bulwark of the city, who are best / of the young men in Ithaca . . ." (23.118–22). It is a programmatic feature of the *Odyssey*, and perhaps an innovation in the poetic tradition, that its special kind of hero is not bound by this convention. The poem in effect redefines justice in terms that privilege the individual over the community, since Odysseus' vengeance brings on neither exile nor death at the hands of his victims' families. One main function of the much-maligned twenty-fourth book is to insist on the correctness of this new kind of justice.[16]

Unlike the *Iliad*, the *Odyssey* is not confined to a setting of war and death: its hero journeys far and wide through the real world and lands of fantasy, unreality, and half-reality in his effort to reach home and family. En route, he several times explicitly contrasts himself to those heroes who died at Troy, and on other occasions the poem calls attention both to how he differs from Achilles and the other Iliadic heroes and to how the Trojan War is but a part of the experiences that make him who and what he is.

A clear sense of the major difference between Odysseus and Achilles, between heroism in the *Odyssey* and in the *Iliad*, emerges from a consideration of *Iliad* 9.410–16, where Achilles tells Odysseus:

> My mother, the silver-footed goddess Thetis, says that
> a twofold destiny carries me toward the final limit of death:
> I stay here and fight around the city of Troy,
> my return home is lost, but there will be imperishable glory;
> but if I go home to my dear native land,
> my noble glory is lost, but my lifetime will be
> long, and the final limit of death would not seize me quickly.

The contrast could not be more explicit. "Imperishable glory," what is said and sung about someone after he is dead, is what heroes conventionally fight for in the *Iliad* and the poetic tradition behind the *Iliad*. It is also, as Gregory Nagy has shown, the formulaic phrase by which the poets designated "their own medium, when it serves the function of glorifying the deeds of heroes"; as Achilles makes clear, such glory *cannot* be achieved by returning home alive, but only through fighting and dying; *kleos* and *nostos* are mutually exclusive.[17]

---

[16]Cf. Porter, "Introduction," pp. 13–16. Jenny Strauss Clay has suggested to me that perhaps it is not quite right to speak of "privileg[ing] the individual over the community": after all, the Suitors are not Ithaca, and they oppress the community as well as Odysseus' family. Nevertheless, the poem does insist on the right of an individual to kill a large collectivity of personal enemies without himself having to pay a penalty. It is noteworthy that when Aristotle (*Poetics* 17, 1455b16–23) summarizes the story (*logos*) of the *Odyssey*, he includes among its essential features—those "specific to the poem" (*to . . . idion*)—that "when [Odysseus] attacks, he destroys his enemies but he himself is saved (*esōthē*)."

[17]G. Nagy, *Comparative Studies in Greek and Indic Metrics* (Cambridge, Mass., 1974), p. 261. On the contrast between *kleos* poetry and *nostos* poetry, see Nagy, *Best of the Achaeans*, pp. 29, 34–41.

In the *Odyssey*, however, Odysseus' *kleos* is based on his having sacked Troy rather than having died in the effort, and his heroism is a product not only of his ability as a warrior, but of the ruse of the wooden horse and the "cunning intelligence" (*mētis*), "trickery" (*dolos*), and "deceit" (*apatē*) through which he survives to win his way home and reclaim his wife and kingdom.[18] Just as *kleos aphthiton* in the *Iliad* denotes both the "imperishable glory" attained by heroes through poetry and the genre of poetry that confers such glory by celebrating their deeds, so *nostos* in the *Odyssey* denotes both the return home that Odysseus strives for and achieves (1.5, 77; 1.87 = 5.31, etc.) and the genre of poetry that narrates and celebrates that achievement (1.326; cf. 9.37, 23.351). When Odysseus identifies himself to the Phaeacians at 9.19–20, he says,

> I am Odysseus the son of Laertes, who by all deceits
> am in the minds of all men, and my glory [*kleos*] reaches heaven.

Similarly, when Athene describes to Odysseus the fundamental similarity between herself and him (13.291–302), she too speaks of his characteristic "deceits" (*apataōn*) and "thievish words" (*muthōn te klopiōn*) before calling him "far the best of all men / for planning and words, while I among all the gods / have *kleos* by reason of cunning intelligence and profits" (13.297–99). Here, the phrase "far the best of all men" (*och' aristos hapantōn*) recalls "far the best of the Achaeans" (*och' aristos Achaiōn*), which is used of Achilles in the *Iliad* (1.244, 412; 16.274; cf. 2.761, 768–70) as the most powerful warrior hero; in effect this phrase redefines heroic excellence in terms characteristic of the *Odyssey* and its hero.

A similar redefinition occurs in Odysseus' description to the Phaeacians of his meeting with the shade (*psuchē*) of Achilles in the Land of the Dead.[19] Odysseus relates how, in effect, he told the shade what he thought it would want to hear, based, apparently, on his own memory of Achilles when he was alive:

> Than you, Achilles,
> no man was ever more blessed, earlier or later.
> For we honored you when you were alive equally to the gods,
> we Argives, and now in turn you have great power over the dead,
> being here.

(11.482–86)

---

[18] Cf. Nagy, *Best of the Achaeans*, p. 39: "Unlike Achilles [in the *Iliad*] who won *kleos* but lost *nostos* . . . , Odysseus is a double winner. He has won both *kleos* and *nostos*." On Odysseus' *kleos*, see C. Segal, "*Kleos* and Its Ironies in the *Odyssey*," *L'Antiquité classique* 52 (1983), pp. 22–47 [this volume, pp. 201–21]. Cf. K. Rüter, *Odysseeinterpretationen: Untersuchungen zum ersten Buch und zur Phaiakis*, ed. K. Matthiessen, *Hypomnemata* 19 (Göttingen, 1969), p. 254; A. T. Edwards, *Achilles in the Odyssey, Beiträge zur klassischen Philologie*, 171 (Königstein, 1985), pp. 71–93.

[19] Cf. Rüter, *Odysseeinterpretationen*, pp. 252–53; Edwards, *Achilles in the Odyssey*, pp. 43–69.

But Achilles is no longer interested in honor—his main concern through most of the *Iliad*—nor in the kind of power that was the source of his warrior *kleos*:

> Don't try to console me and cheer me up about death, glorious Odysseus.
> I would wish to serve another man even as a field hand,
> a man with no property of his own and not much livelihood,
> rather than to rule over all the dead corpses.

> (11.488–91)

Achilles can remember his warrior exploits, "when in wide Troy / [he] slew a heroic people defending the Argives" (11.499–500), and he even can rejoice in his son's outstanding prowess (11.540), but, as in his speech to Odyssseus in *Iliad* 9.308–429, he sees the futility of the death and glory such heroic greatness entails—heroic greatness that he would gladly exchange for the least heroic kind of life.

Odysseus' description of Achilles to the Phaeacians is completely consistent with the characterization of the son of Peleus in the *Iliad*, including Achilles' sense of how, for all his power, he is unable to do anything for his aged and dishonored father (*Il.* 24.538–42). At the same time, Odysseus' description is characteristically self-serving in its portrayal of Achilles as wishing he were alive like Odysseus rather than one of the "mindless corpses". (*nekroi/aphradees*, 11.475–76) whom it is Odysseus' great achievement to visit in Hades without first having to die (11.474–75). From the standpoint of the *Odyssey*, too, as well as of its hero, Achilles is inferior to Odysseus: after all, in book 24 Odysseus' new kind of heroism, in pointed contrast to the helplessness of the dead Achilles to do anything for Peleus, brings with it the ability to rescue *his* father Laertes from the weakness and suffering of old age and restore his youthful power.

The superiority of Odysseus to Achilles is driven home in book 24, in the poem's second scene in the Land of the Dead, just before Hermes appears with the shades of the Suitors slain by Odysseus, when the shade of Agamemnon describes to the shade of Achilles the latter's death and funeral at Troy (24.36–94). Actually, in this scene the poem suggests the superiority of Odysseus' ability to survive and return home, over both the royalty of Agamemnon, who was "dearest of warrior-hero men to Zeus . . . , / but . . . it was fated that [he] be slain by a most wretched death" (24.24 . . . 34), and the *kleos*-heroism of "godlike Achilles" (24.36, 93–94). Odysseus, as it were, has his cake and eats it too: Agamemnon's shade hails him as "blessed son of Laertes" (24.192), just as he had addressed Achilles' shade as "blessed son of Peleus" (24.36), but this parallelism only emphasizes the huge difference between the figure who "died at Troy, far from Argos" (24.37) and "lay dead great in [his] greatness" (24.40), surrounded by the Greeks and Trojans who died fighting over him, and Odysseus, whose enemies all flutter feebly down to Hades, while he lives to enjoy his successful return home and the glory of their death. This contrast is further heightened when the shade of Agamemnon reminds the shade of the dead suitor Amphimedon how they first met when he and Menelaos stayed at Amphimedon's house for a month, while they were trying to persuade "Odysseus sacker of cities" (24.119) to take part in the war against Troy. "Sacker of cities" (*ptoliporthos*) necessarily evokes the fall of Troy through Odysseus' ruse of the wooden horse (cf. 8.494–95), his greatest heroic achievement prior to his return home and one in which Achilles could not share, for all *his* heroism and the presence of gods at his funeral (24.46–56, 60–62).

Another of Odysseus' reported encounters in the Land of the Dead confirms this new standard of heroic excellence. When Odysseus meets the "image" (*eidōlon*) of the mighty Herakles—for Herakles himself now lives a life of festive ease "with the immortal gods" (11.601–3)—the image tells him:

> O wretch, you too are undergoing some evil doom,
> the very one that I suffered beneath the rays of the sun.
> I was the son of Zeus, son of Kronos, but I had
> endless suffering.

> (11.618–21)

The clear implication is that Herakles became a god by enduring and triumphing in a series of difficult struggles (*chalepous . . . aethlous*, 11.622), including a forced journey to Hades (11.623–26). He identifies his heroic career as a triumphant survivor with that of Odysseus, who, by analogy, can become through *his* struggles, and through celebration in heroic song, as "divine" as is possible for a mortal who is not the son of Zeus.

This passage can be compared with one in book 18 of the *Iliad*, after Thetis warns Achilles that he must die soon after taking vengeance on Hektor for the death of Patroklos. Achilles accepts this consequence in a passionate speech of self-reproach for his friend's and comrades' deaths (*Il.* 18.98–116) and acknowledges that even the greatest hero is subject to the limitations of mortality:

> For no, not even the strength of Herakles avoided death,
> who was closest to the lord Zeus, son of Kronos,
> but his portion mastered him, and the hard anger of Hera.

> (*Il.* 18.117–19)

The Iliadic Herakles represents the highest possible achievement of a traditional warrior-hero, including a previous sack of Troy (*Il.* 5.642, 14.251). Achilles' self-comparison to him sets a seal on his own decision to die, since Herakles in the *Iliad*, like all warrior-heroes, is in the end mortal. In accordance with the themes of this epic, the poem ignores and makes Achilles ignore the alternate tradition that Herakles achieved deification for his heroism.

But, as 11.601–3, 619–20 indicate, this is just the tradition followed in the *Odyssey*; Odysseus' attitude toward heroism is shown by his story of meeting with Herakles, just as Achilles' attitude is shown by his self-comparison to Herakles in *Iliad* 18. If we think in terms of poems rather than heroes, in the *Odyssey*, an epic whose generic conception of heroism involves survival and eventual triumph rather than early death, it would be as inappropriate for Herakles simply to die as a mortal hero as it would be in the *Iliad*, a poem in which mortality is the decisive human reality, for him to be deified and live the easy life of a god.[20]

The emphasis in the *Iliad* on mortal heroism—on the honor it wins for a warrior when he is alive and the imperishable glory in song that transcends his death—makes it a profound but, in a sense, a one-dimensional poem. Its action and its vision of human existence are almost claustrophobically restricted to a single way of life in a single setting: the war on the Trojan plain. Although the narrative moves back and forth between earth and Olympos, the gods and their world function primarily as foils to clarify and heighten by contrast both the limitations of human existence and its concomitant opportunities for meaningful heroism. It is not that the gods' supreme brilliance, power, and knowledge of destiny are in themselves trivial: rather, the gods, with their life of ease, their immunity from serious consequences of their actions, and their sublime frivolity seem ethically lightweight in comparison to humans. The divine condition in the poem, which is wholly anthropomorphic physically, psychologically, and sociologically, repeatedly brings a reader back to human existence with a heightened sense of its tragic conflicts, pain, and sorrow, and of the splendors of its heroic achievements.

This may be true also in the *Odyssey*, but, apart from Athene's care and constant assistance to Odysseus in Scheria and Ithaca, the Olympians have far less to do either with defining the human condition or with the poem's action than they do in the *Iliad*. Human existence in the *Odyssey* is rarely contrasted explicitly to that of the gods, except in Odysseus' conversation with Kalypso (5.206–220); rather, it is positioned, as it were, midway between that of the gods and that of the bestial Cyclopes. More important, every society and way of life encountered by Odysseus and Telemachos on their journeys has its place between these divine and bestial extremes and serves to clarify by contrast human life in Ithaca, which is much more the focus of the poem than human life generally.

[20] Clay, *Wrath of Athena*, pp. 90–96, argues that the *Odyssey* contrasts Odysseus to Herakles: "[T]he man of *mētis* ["cunning intelligence"] rivals, if indeed he does not surpass, the hero of force [*biē*]" (p. 95). Clay notes that Odysseus' adventure with the Cyclops also "recounts the triumph of *mētis* over *biē*" (p. 95); then she uses the song of Demodokos summarized at 8.73–82, which refers to the "quarrel of Odysseus and Achilles son of Peleus" (8.75), as the point of departure for a discussion of Achilles and Odysseus, and the *Iliad* and the *Odyssey*, as traditional heroes and epics of *biē* and *mētis*, respectively. For different formulations and conclusions on this question, see Nagy, *Best of the Achaeans*, pp. 21–25; W. Marg, "Das erste Lied des Demodokos," in *Navicula Chiloniensis: Festschrift für Felix Jacoby* (Leiden, 1956), pp. 16–29; Rüter, *Odysseeinterpretationen*, pp. 247–54.

Unlike the conflicts among the gods, which set in motion so much of the action of the *Iliad*, the hostility of Poseidon to Odysseus in defiance of the other gods (1.19–21), though motivated by the blinding of Polyphemos (1.68–75) and manifested in the storm that shatters Odysseus' raft (5.282–96, 365–81), seems (to a reader, though not to Odysseus) primarily symbolic: an expression, on the narrative plane, of the sea as an elemental barrier through which Odysseus must pass in order to restore himself to his home, family, and identity in Ithaca.[21]

On the other hand, Athene's care for Odysseus, though not essentially different from her support of Achilles, Diomedes, and Odysseus in the *Iliad*,[22] goes beyond anything in that poem in the frequency and variety of ways in which it is given. More important, it is morally motivated in accordance with the poem's emphasis on Odysseus as the just king (2.230–34, 4.689–93) and on his restoration as husband, father, and king as the renewal of social and political order.[23]

Just as the representation of the gods differs in the *Iliad* and *Odyssey* in accordance with the main themes of each poem, so, too, do the similes that constitute one of the poems' most distinctive stylistic features. The similes in the *Iliad*, as many scholars have pointed out, expand the universe of the poem and the range of experience it comprehends. Nevertheless, they always exist to clarify a specific action or event in the war or a mood or thought in the mind of a character in the story. They always return explicitly to the situation in the narrative from which they take off, and in this way they end up enhancing, not mitigating, the claustrophobic one-dimensionality of the poem and of the war in which its characters are, so to speak, trapped. Like many similes, but on a larger scale, the description of the shield of Achilles (*Il.* 18.478–608) constitutes an interval of calm in a

[21] Porter, "Introduction," p. 9, notes that Odysseus "was already lost at sea, hence the victim of the sea god's wrath, for years before he reached the country of the Cyclops." Cf. Porphyry, *The Cave of the Nymphs in the Odyssey*, 34–35, who cites Plato's description of the sea as "the material substrate" (*hē hulikē sustasis*) and, like many pagan and Christian allegorizers in late antiquity, sees Odysseus as a symbol of the soul journeying through the material realm of becoming to its final restoration in pure being.

[22] M. M. Willcock, "Some Aspects of the Gods in the *Iliad*," *Bulletin of the Institute of Classical Studies in London* 17 (1970), p. 6 = *Essays on the Iliad*, ed. Wright, p. 67, remarks that all these heroes are "winners" and that Athene's "function, . . . which in her case is parallel to sexual attraction for Aphrodite and killing for Ares," is "winning, success. . . . [The] favourites of Athene are the naturally successful, the natural winners."

[23] Porter, "Introduction," p. 9, argues that Athene's "partiality for Odysseus is never . . . motivated" as is Poseidon's enmity; "[s]he is his patronness simply because he is the human embodiment of those qualities of which she is the absolute expression." On the other hand, Clay, *The Wrath of Athena*, sees the similarity between Odysseus and Athene as giving rise to a relationship that is almost competitive. She argues that Athene's wrath, not Poseidon's, is responsible for the hero's wanderings, until this wrath is transformed and redirected against the Suitors' violations of political and social order. In Clay's view, unlike Porter's, Athene cares for Odysseus precisely because he is the just king and his restoration is the restoration of that order.

world of heroic passion and fury: it reveals how small a part of life war is, and, by its emphasis on the beauty of Hephaistos' artwork, provides a powerful contrast to the increasingly savage fighting narrated before and after it. Yet just as the similes come back in the end to the action of the poem from which they take off, so the description of the shield exists for Achilles to carry that shield into battle during his grim rampage in books 20–22, which culminates in the death and disfigurement of Hektor. The shield's detached, objective, cosmic beauty arises from and enhances Achilles' personal tragedy. In a sense the description of the shield, like the *Iliad* as a whole, can be viewed as a transformation of human existence into sublime art that, in the words of one poetic formula, is "a wonder to behold." This sense of beauty, however, does not efface the degree to which both shield and poem are grounded specifically in the destructive and self-destructive condition of Achilles', and all human, experience *within* the narrative.

The *Odyssey* contains far fewer similes than does the *Iliad*, and for the most part they function differently.[24] Because the poem itself is set in a wider world of many societies and physical settings, instead of being restricted only to the Trojan plain and city, the similes usually do not expand the poem's universe and range of experience, and so clarify the particular event or thought from which they originate. Rather, they tend to function dramatically and thematically, referring to ideas and characterizations that have been established in the narrative and action of the *Odyssey* itself. For example, when Odysseus' joy at catching sight of the land of the Phaeacians is compared to that of children at seeing their father released from a wasting illness (5.394–98), the simile seems dramatically appropriate because Odysseus himself has been established as a suffering father, particularly from his son's viewpoint, in the first four books of the poem. Similarly, the so-called "reverse simile," in which Penelope's gladness at seeing her husband is like the gladness of the survivors of a ship wrecked by Poseidon who have managed to swim to shore safely (23.233–40), has particular force because Odysseus himself, in books 5 and 12, has been represented as just such a survivor. This simile and others that reverse normal male and female sex roles and experiences, notably 8.523–31, are of special thematic importance in a poem that seems to value highly the ability to enter into others' viewpoints and that is concerned with analogies between the heroism of Odysseus and that of Penelope and with the powerful role of Penelope and of women generally.[25]

---

[24] Cf. C. Moulton, *Similes in the Iliad and Odyssey, Hypomnemata*, 49 (Göttingen, 1977), p. 117: "The *Odyssey* has only about one third as many similes as the *Iliad*, and many of them are much shorter; developed similes account for about three fifths of the total in the *Iliad*, for about one third of the total in the *Odyssey*." For statistics, see D.J.N. Lee, *The Similes of the Iliad and the Odyssey Compared* (Melbourne, 1964), p. 3, with List A, pp. 50–61.

[25] See H. P. Foley, "'Reverse Similes' and Sex Roles in the *Odyssey*," *Arethusa* 11 (1978), pp. 7–26 = *Women in the Ancient World: The Arethusa Papers*, ed. J. Peradotto and J. P. Sullivan (Albany, 1984), pp. 59–78.

Just as the *Odyssey* differs from the *Iliad* in its conception of heroism and of the kind of achievement that merits celebration in song, so the world it represents differs greatly in the varieties of individuals and societies that inhabit it and the physical settings in which they live. There is nothing at all claustrophobic about a poem that begins in the "real" world of Ithaca, Pylos, Crete, and Sparta; moves first, in Menelaos' narrative (4.351–582), to the remote and symbolically resonant Egypt;[26] then in book 5 to Kalypso's Ogygia; next to the Phaeacians in Scheria who seem, institutionally and symbolically, a halfway house between the surreality or unreality of the peoples and places Odysseus tells of in his first-person narrative of his adventures (books 9–12) and the reality of Ithaca, where the second half of the poem takes place and Odysseus reestablishes himself as husband, father, son, and ruler.[27]

This geographical variety is matched by a narrative complexity far removed from the straightforward scheme of the *Iliad*, in which the action proceeds from the beginning in a chronologically straight line and a single narrative voice.[28] The *Odyssey* begins with two simultaneous actions, Athene going to Ithaca to stir up Telemachos and Hermes going to Ogygia to instruct Kalypso to send away Odysseus. Books 2–4 narrate Telemachos' responses to Athene's suggestion—his summoning of the Ithacan assembly and his journey to Pylos and Sparta, where he hears Nestor's, Helen's, and Menelaos' stories of Odysseus at Troy, followed by Menelaos' tale of his seven-year return homeward from Troy, including his adventures in Egypt. Next book 5 relates Odysseus' voyage from Ogygia to Scheria and safety from the enmity of Poseidon. Books 6–12 take place among the Phaeacians, to whose rulers Odysseus addresses the long first-person account (books 9–12) of his adventures from the time he left Troy through his stay with Kalypso. Book 13 begins with Odysseus' return to Ithaca on a Phaeacian ship and encounter with Athene, who helps him plan his course of action against the Suitors. Then the poem's narrative proceeds to Odysseus' reunion with Telemachos at the shelter of the swineherd Eumaios, followed by his return in disguise to his palace, triumph over the Suitors, recognition by Penelope and Laertes, and successful defiance of the Suitors' families.

Such a narrative structure is exceptionally complex and makes the poem

[26]On Menelaos' story of his journey to Egypt as a version of Odysseus' narrative of his voyage to the Land of the Dead, see B. B. Powell, "Narrative Patterns in the Homeric Tale of Menelaus," *Transactions of the American Philological Association* 101 (1970), pp. 419–31. Cf. W. F. Hansen, *The Conference Sequence: Patterned Narration and Narrative Inconsistency in the Odyssey* (Berkeley and Los Angeles, 1972), pp. 8–19.

[27]On the Phaeacians, see Porter, "Introduction," pp. 5–10; Segal, "The Phaeacians," *passim*, and "Transition and Ritual in Odysseus' Return," *La Parola del Passato* 116 (1967), pp. 331–42; Rüter, *Odysseeinterpretationen*, pp. 228–46; Austin, *Poetic Problems*, pp. 153–62.

[28]Cf. L. M. Slatkin, "Composition by Theme and the *Mētis* of the *Odyssey*," this volume, p. 223.

more difficult to interpret than the *Iliad*. This difficulty is magnified by the many disguises in which Odysseus appears and by the many lies told by the good as well as the bad characters, to one another as often as to their enemies—for example, Athene / Mentor to Telemachos, Telemachos to Eumaios and Penelope, Odysseus to practically everybody. The most striking falsehoods are Odysseus' lying tales to Athene (13.253–86), Eumaios (14.191–359), the Suitors (17.414–44), Penelope (19.164–203, 220–48, 269–307, 336–42), and Laertes (24.239–79, 303–14) about his identity and provenance. These lying tales and the poem's overall atmosphere of deceit raise doubts about the veracity at any given point of Odysseus' first-person story to the Phaeacians. Even though the naive Alkinoos explicitly contrasts Odysseus' bardlike performance to the lies of a cunning deceiver (11.363–68), he and all the inexperienced, easily beguiled Phaeacians (with the possible exception of Arete) are easy game for Odysseus' sophisticated, cunning intelligence and mind bent on profit, his ability to tell them and others what they want to hear.

Odysseus' penchant for lying and the poem's general atmosphere of disguise and deceit help make the *Odyssey*, unlike the *Iliad*, a poem in which the characters offer narratives against which a reader or listener must be constantly on guard. The narrator usually indicates when a character is lying, often by making him or her claim to be telling—or to be about to tell—the (whole) truth.[29] Nevertheless, the problematic veracity of so much direct speech makes "truth" itself a subject of the poem, together with the poetic art that is supposed to present and represent it.[30]

The *Odyssey* is far more self-conscious about such poetic art than is the *Iliad*. In the latter poem Helen mentions that Zeus "put an evil doom" on herself and Paris, "so that even in time to come / we might be objects of song for human beings who live in the future" (*Il.* 6.357–58), and she rather complacently represents in woven art the battles fought over her by the Greeks and Trojans (*Il.* 3.125–28). Yet the only bardic performance represented in the *Iliad* occurs when Achilles sings to himself and Patroklos the "glorious deeds of men" (*Il.* 9.189), "delighting his mind with the clearsounding lyre" (*Il.* 9.186). It is noteworthy that at this point in the poem, Achilles is cut off by his wrath from the Greek army and from his heroic self. Normally a bard performs for a large audience in his social role as a *dēmioergos*, a "worker for the community" (*Od.* 17. 383–85), but Achilles' isolated singing is, as it were, a measure of his dislocation; similarly, the

---

[29] See T. Todorov, *The Poetics of Prose*, tr. R. Howard (Ithaca, N.Y., 1977), p. 60. Cf. J. Peradotto, *Man in the Middle Voice: Name and Narration in the Odyssey*, Martin Classical Lectures, N.S. 1 (Princeton, 1990), pp. 32–93, esp. pp. 82–93, for illuminating discussion of narrative ambivalence, open-endedness, and dialogism in the *Odyssey*.

[30] On the relationship between poetry and truth in the Homeric epics and early Greek literature generally, see M. Detienne, "La Mémoire du poète," in *Les Maîtres de vérité dans la Grèce archaïque* (Paris, 1967), pp. 9–27; L. H. Pratt, *Lying and Poetry from Homer to Pindar: Falsehood and Deception in Archaic Greek Poetics* (Ann Arbor, 1993), pp. 11–55.

subject matter of his song is a displacement of his frustrated desire to function as "the best of the Achaeans."

The *Odyssey*, on the other hand, not only depicts poets and poetry socially and positively in its representations of Phemios in Ithaca and Demodokos among the Phaeacians, but it repeatedly characterizes Odysseus himself as a poet when he is speaking the words and doing the deeds that bring about his successful *nostos*. When, at the end of book 8, Alkinoos asks him to identify himself and tell his story, the king's diction echoes that of the poem's implied narrator at the beginning of book 1 and virtually invites Odysseus to sing his own heroic epic.[31] Odysseus in effect accepts this invitation at 9.37, when he says, "Come now, I will tell to you my song-of-return-homeward filled-with-many-sorrows" (*ei d' age toi kai noston emon polukēde' enispō*). In this line "tell," *enispō*, is from the same verb as *ennepe*, the word used in the first line of the poem when the speaker calls on the Muse to "tell of the man of many turns . . . ."; "filled-with-many-sorrows," *polukēde'*, recalls the "many sea-sorrows that man suffered in his spirit, trying to save his life and the return home of his companions" (1.4–5); while *noston* is used not only of an actual "return home" but also, as I have suggested (above, p. 11), in the quasi-technical sense of the genre of poetry that narrates and celebrates such a return. Later in the poem Odysseus is explicitly compared to a singer—a bard—by Alkinoos (11.368) and Eumaios (17.518–21). The climax of this pattern in which he is associated with poetic art comes in the simile at 21.406–11, when he is about to string the bow with which he is to kill the Suitors. Here Odysseus is compared to a "man knowledgeable about the lyre and song" easily stretching a new string around the peg of a lyre. In taking vengeance on the Suitors and reclaiming his wife and kingdom, he is, in effect, not only the subject but the singer, in a specially charged communal setting, of a new heroic song.

According to Odysseus' narrative, when he and his men leave Troy, their first landing is at nearby Ismaros, land of the Kikones (9.39–61). The Ithacans' raid on this people, which includes sacking a city, killing its men, and plundering their wives and property, before having to flee from Kikonian retaliation, locates this episode on the same plane of heroic reality as the Trojan War itself. From that point on, however, when a storm blows Odysseus and his men off course as they round Cape Malea in the southeast corner of the Peloponnese and they are carried for nine days "by the accursedly destructive winds over the fishy sea" (*oloois anemoisi/ponton ep' ichthuoenta*, 9.82–83),[32] all the adventures narrated by Odysseus in books 9–12 take place in the realm of the imaginary and the fantastic.

[31] See Slatkin, "Composition by Theme," p. 233.

[32] The formulaic phrase "over the fishy sea" (*ponton ep' ichthuoenta*) is particularly effective here, as Odysseus begins to describe the adventures that took his men's lives and threatened his own. For a sense of difficulty and danger, a notion of "une étendue périlleuse ou accidentée," is "latent in Homeric collocations of *pontos* ["sea"] with the harmless-looking epithet *ichthuoeis*

It is no accident that most casual readers of the *Odyssey*, if asked years later what they remember of the poem, mention these adventures. Though they constitute only one-sixth of the entire work, they draw on story patterns and folk-motifs that are memorable in themselves and familiar from such tales as the adventures of Sinbad the Sailor. Each of these stories and folktales is carefully adapted to the distinctive themes, ethical concerns, and symbolic patterns of the *Odyssey* as a whole,[33] but that is not what makes them so memorable. Rather, they constitute a series of diverse, wide-ranging stories about the pleasures and dangers of human existence: stories that tend to represent what is "human" as male, and most of the "pleasures" and "dangers" as female—or what a male imagination fantasizes as such.

I say "male imagination" precisely because these stories are narrated in the first person by Odysseus and constitute *his*, not the poem's, versions of heroic experience. Many of them involve nonhuman, female figures who threaten the hero or his return homeward. These females, to hear Odysseus tell of them, are often monstrous, and their menace is literally or symbolically sexual—specific instances of the general danger of being swallowed, engulfed, concealed, or obliterated against which he constantly struggles. In this respect they are vividly imagined versions of the sea itself in which Odysseus is lost, through which he struggles to return home, and with which, according to Teiresias' prophecy (11.121–37), he must make his ultimate peace by bringing the knowledge of ships and the worship of the sea god Poseidon to inland agriculturalists among whom they are yet unknown. Odysseus represents his experiences with sea-dangers as encounters with the feminine and repeatedly tells of escaping these dangers when the threatening females eventually befriend him, after he survives or overcomes them.[34]

["fishy"]." Here I quote F. Householder and G. Nagy, "Greek," *Current Trends in Linguistics* 9 (1972), p. 768, who in turn quote E. Benveniste, *Problèmes de linguistique générale*, vol. 1 (Paris, 1966), pp. 297–98 [= *Problems in General Linguistics*, tr. M. E. Meek, Miami Linguistics Series, 8 (Coral Gables, 1971), p. 256]. For a recent discussion, see R. Sacks, *The Traditional Phrase in Homer: Two Studies in Form, Meaning and Interpretation*, Columbia Studies in the Classical Tradition, 14 (Leiden, 1987), pp. 45–62.

[33] On the adaptation and transformation of folktale into epic, see especially K. Reinhardt, "Die Abenteuer der *Odyssee*," in his *Von Werken und Formen* (Godesberg, 1948), pp. 52–162 = *Tradition und Geist: Gesammelte Essays zur Dichtung*, ed C. Becker (Göttingen, 1960), pp. 47–124 [this volume, pp. 63–132]; U. Hölscher, "The Transformation from Folk-Tale to Epic," in *Homer: Tradition and Innovation*, ed. B. Fenik (Leiden, 1978), pp. 51–67, and *Die Odyssee: Epos zwischen Märchen und Roman* (Munich, 1989), with the review by S. Murnaghan, *American Journal of Philology* 111 (1990), pp. 271–74. Still interesting is L. Radermacher, *Die Erzählungen der Odyssee*, Sitzungsberichte der Kais. Akademie der Wissenschaften in Wien, Phil.-Hist. Klasse, 178, vol. 1 (Vienna, 1915), though Radermacher does not specifically address the poem's programmatic transformation of traditional folktales into epic. On the adaptation of the folktale behind the story of Odysseus' encounter with Polyphemos to the distinctive themes of the *Odyssey*, see S. L. Schein, "Odysseus and Polyphemus in the *Odyssey*," *Greek, Roman and Byzantine Studies* 11 (1970), pp. 73–83; G. Dimock, *The Unity of the Odyssey* (Amherst, 1989), pp. 117–18.

[34] Cf. M. N. Nagler, "Dread Goddess Endowed with Speech," this volume, p. 147. The

The poem offers still another, complementary way of interpreting the adventures narrated by Odysseus. When he returns from the fantastic world of these adventures to something approaching reality in the land of the Phaeacians,[35] he does so in accordance with Kalypso's sailing directions, which include keeping the constellation Arktos, also known as the Wagon [our Big Dipper] on his left hand (5.276–77). In other words, he voyages from West to East or, in the poem's symbolic terms, from Death toward (re)Birth.[36] In effect, the characters Odysseus encounters in the never-never lands of his narrative threaten a literal death, as in the case of the Laistrugones and Skylla and Charybdis; constitute a symbolic death—a loss or forgetfulness of self—as in the case of the Lotos Eaters, Aiolos, Kirke, and Kalypso; or do both, as in the case of the Cyclops and the Sirens. The most obvious encounter with death is the hero's voyage to the Land of the Dead in book 11, which takes place at the very center of the poem and in the middle of his adventures.[37] But each of these adventures, as I have said, involves the danger or temptation of a literal or symbolic death that Odysseus survives in order to continue his journey homeward. Douglas Frame has shown that the second of two lines that occur at the end of several adventures (9.62–63, 565–66; 10.133–34),

> From there we sailed forward saddened at heart,
> yet glad [asmenoi] at emerging from death, though
> having lost dear comrades,

contains a Greek instance of a very old Indo-European poetic formula for a hero's return from death. Frame also argues that the verb neomai ("return home"), its nominal derivative nostos, and noos ("mind"), as well as asmenoi in the line just quoted, are etymologically cognate forms from the root nes-, which originally had to do with "returning to light and life."[38] If this is correct, the poem suggests linguistically as well as dramatically that Odysseus' characteristic mental strength and tenacity are intimately connected

---

notion of the sea as feminine may seem peculiar, since Poseidon clearly is a masculine god. But the sea has several features commonly ascribed to females in Greek thought, including the wandering irregularity of its waves and tides and its mere materiality. This is the medium in which Odysseus struggles to survive and return home, and so establishes part of his distinctive identity. (A certain femininity may also be inherent in the notion of a natural element violated, as it were, by a male cultural implement like a ship, just as in the notion of the earth violated by a plow that cuts into it in the course of cultivation.)

[35] On Scheria and the Phaeacians as positioned in between the unreality of the adventures and the reality of Ithaca, and constituting, in effect, a ritual barrier through which Odysseus must pass in the course of his return to home and selfhood, see Segal, "The Phaeacians" and "Transition and Ritual."

[36] See Porter, "Introduction," pp. 3–4.

[37] See Nagler, this volume, pp. 144–45. Cf. G. Germain, Genèse de l'Odyssée. Le Fantastique et le sacré (Paris, 1954), pp. 332–33; J .D. Niles, Patterning in the Wanderings of Odysseus," Ramus 7 (1978), pp. 46–60; G. Most, "The Structure and Function of Odysseus' Apologoi," Transactions of the American Philological Association 119 (1989), pp. 15–30.

[38] D. Frame, The Myth of Return in Early Greek Epic (New Haven and London, 1978), pp. 1–80.

with his distinctive heroic achievement of surviving death and returning home.

I have referred to some adventures as "symbolic deaths," by which I mean simply that in these instances Odysseus is temporarily unable to act or function like the hero who, by cunning intelligence and physical strength, successfully ends the Trojan War, then makes his way home to kill the Suitors and reclaim his wife and kingdom. In other words, a "symbolic death" for Odysseus is the inability to be himself.

This is true also of the hero of the *Iliad*: Achilles is symbolically dead when he is unable to function as Achilles—to fight and kill more brilliantly and effectively than anyone else. In that poem his return to action and to life as a hero is tragically counterpointed both by his continued dislocation from his own humanity, as reflected in the exceptional brutality of his warfare, his killing of Hektor, and his ruthless mistreatment of his corpse, and by his "actual" impending death, which his mother Thetis prophesies (Il. 18.95–96) and the poem repeatedly foreshadows. In the *Odyssey*, Odysseus' survival and "rebirth" in adventure after adventure and his characteristic resourcefulness and success are in no way tragic. Each episode constitutes a small version of the movement of the entire poem from Odysseus' physical dislocation and passivity on Kalypso's island to his right location and triumphant action on Ithaca.

Kalypso and her island offer a suggestive example of the way Odysseus' adventures in never-never land work, how each constitutes a coherent episode, thematically and ethically relevant to the entire poem. This is the only one of the adventures that is told both by the poem's narrator and, more briefly, by Odysseus in his first-person narratives to the Phaeacians (7.244–66, 12.447–50) and to Penelope (23.333–37). Kalypso is referred to emphatically in the opening of the poem (1.13–15, 49–57), and Odysseus' departure from Ogygia is the first adventure narrated after the Telemachy. These features make the episode especially prominent and give it a paradigmatic status in relation to the other adventures.

Kalypso, whose name means "the concealer," is also a good example of the poem's characteristic punning and etymological wordplay on the names and attributes of its characters—punning and wordplay that reflect these characters' essential natures and functions.[39] Kalypso "conceals" Odysseus

---

[39] Cf. Dimock, *Unity of the Odyssey, passim*. The most illuminating interpretive studies of this phenomenon have focused on the name of Odysseus—both the story of how he got this name, which is told at the point of his recognition by Eurykleia (19.392–466), and his exploitation of the name in his adventure with the Cyclops (9.250–566). See especially Peradotto, *Man in the Middle Voice*, pp. 93–170. Cf. G. Dimock, "The Name of Odysseus," *The Hudson Review* 9 (1956), pp. 52–70 = *Homer: A Collection of Critical Essays*, ed. G. Steiner and R. Fagles (Englewood Cliffs, 1962), pp. 106–21 = *Essays on the Odyssey: Selected Modern Criticism*, ed. C. H. Taylor (Bloomington, 1963), pp. 54–72 [my references are to the Taylor volume]; N. Austin, "Name Magic in the *Odyssey*," *California Studies in Classical Antiquity* 5 (1972), pp. 1–19; A. Bergren, "Odyssean Temporality: Many (Re)turns," in *Approaches to Homer*, ed. C.

on her island at the "navel of the sea" (1.50), which means, in effect, that as long as he is with her he is lost at sea and not himself—not able, as I have said, to function as Odysseus. All he "does," until the intervention of Hermes in book 5, is sit passively weeping, gazing out over the sea that should be the medium of his heroic achievement but now is merely a barrier to it, "longing to see even the smoke rising / from his native land" (1.58). He does, however, resist Kalypso's invitation to become her immortal consort, which would mean permanently "concealing" his mortality and return homeward and abandoning his distinctive heroic pattern of suffering, endurance, and ultimate triumph for the life of ease that characterizes the gods' existence. Despite temptation, Odysseus keeps his mind on "thoughtful Penelope," though "she is slighter than you [sc., Kalypso] in form and stature to look at; / for she is mortal, but you are immortal and unaging" (5.216–18); he keeps longing "to go homeward and to see the day of returning home" (5.220). In effect he chooses to be remembered in heroic song over the oblivion among mortals that would accompany an existence as Kalypso's husband.[40] This choice corresponds to Achilles' decision to die at Troy and achieve "imperishable glory" rather than to return home to a long life with no glory. Each hero chooses, in a different way, to be a hero and so chooses life over death.[41]

Odysseus' stay on Ogygia is not the only time in the poem he is "concealed" (or "Kalypsoed"). On two other occasions, when Odysseus' powers are at their weakest, he is said, in language echoing the name Kalypso, to be "concealed" (kaluptein) or "concealed over" (amphikaluptein) by sleep. The first is at the end of book 5, when, having struggled ashore on Scheria, he lies down beneath the intertwining branches of two olive trees and piles leaves over himself:

As when someone hides a fire brand in dark ashes—
someone with no neighbors nearby, at the farthest end of the cultivated
    fields—
preserving a seed of fire, so he might not have to get a light from somewhere
    else,

Rubino and C. Shelmerdine (Austin and London, 1983), pp. 38–73.

[40] Cf. J.-P. Vernant, "Le Refus d'Ulysse," in Le Temps de la réflexion 3 (1982), pp. 13–18, esp. pp. 16–17 [this volume, pp. 185–89, esp. pp. 187–88].

[41] H. Güntert, Kalypso: Bedeutungsgeschichtliche Untersuchungen auf dem Gebiet der indogermanischen Sprachen (Halle, 1919), argues that Ogygia is symbolically a Land of the Dead, Kalypso a goddess of the dead, and "concealment" the equivalent of death. Cf. W. S. Anderson, "Calypso and Elysium," Classical Journal 54 (1958), pp. 2–11 = Essays on the Odyssey, ed. Taylor, pp. 73–86; Vernant, "Le Refus," passim [this volume, pp. 185–89]; B. B. Powell, Composition by Theme in the Odyssey (Meisenheim am Glan, 1977), p. 5n.13, who refers to the interpretation of Kalypso and "concealment" by U. Hölscher, Untersuchungen zur Form der Odyssee, Hermes Einzelschriften, 6 (Berlin, 1939), p. 67; Porter, "Introduction," pp. 3–5, who terms Ogygia "an Eden-like Hell, or a hellish Eden" (p. 3). For a recent discussion of Kalypso with a summary of relevant scholarship, see G. Crane, Calypso: Backgrounds and Conventions of the Odyssey, Beiträge zur klassischen Philologie, 191 (Frankfurt am Main, 1988), pp. 15–29.

so Odysseus *concealed himself* with leaves. Then Athene
poured sleep over his eyes for him, to release him most quickly
from toilsome labor, *having concealed over* his dear eyelids.

(5.488–93)

The second instance is in book 10, when, in sight of Ithaca, Odysseus' men
open the bag of winds and a storm carries his ships out to sea. Odysseus
debates whether to jump overboard and perish or endure and remain
among the living—the only time in the poem he contemplates suicide:

> But I remained and endured, and *having concealed myself,*
> I lay as if dead [*keimēn*] in the ship.

(10.53–54)

In the *Iliad, kaluptein* is frequently used of the darkness of death "concealing" or covering over the eyes of a slain warrior.[42] The association of "concealment" and death is strong, too, in book 20 of the *Odyssey,* when Penelope, after wishing she were dead so she might go beneath the hated earth
and see Odysseus [whom she imagines dead, in the underworld], mentions
that "sleep makes one forget all things / good and bad, when it *conceals over*
the eyelids—except in my case a god also sends against me evil dreams"
(20.85–87). In other words, for her sleep is almost like the death she desires.

It is noteworthy that in the *Odyssey,* when Odysseus is sleeping but neither threatened by death nor at a low point in his ability to function as
himself, the words "concealed" and "concealed over" are not used. For example, even though he sleeps a sleep "most nearly like death" (13.80) when
he is transported by the Phaeacians from Scheria to Ithaca, this sleep is
called "deep, most pleasant" (13.80) and "brings forgetfulness of what he
had suffered" (13.92). It does not "conceal" him. Similarly, at the end of
book 19 and the beginning of book 20, when Odysseus sleeps in the porch
of his own palace, Athene throws a "sweet sleep over his eyelids" (19.603–
604), which, when it finally "takes hold of him" after he lies awake churn-
ing with thoughts of revenge against the Suitors, "relaxes his limbs" and
"releases cares from his spirit" (20.56–57). Here, too, the language of concealment and covering over does not occur. It is significant that in both
these cases, the sleep that "takes hold of" Odysseus is the prelude to his
renewed power and ability to be himself. Rather than symbolizing his weakness, it heralds his triumph. Given the (potentially) deadly associations of
Kalypso, *kaluptein,* and *amphikaluptein,* it is entirely appropriate that, at
these points in the narrative, Odysseus is not said to be "concealed."

---

[42] *Il.* 4.461, 503, 526; 6.11; 13.575; 14.519; 15.578; 16.316, 325; 20.393, 471; 21.181.
Cf. *Il.* 5.553, 16.502, and 22.361, where the "end" or "limit" (*telos*) of death "conceals" the
dead warrior(s) and 23.91, where *amphikaluptein* is used prospectively of the funeral mound
"concealing" the bones of Achilles and Patroklos.

Kalypso is but one of the females in the *Odyssey* who are represented as sexually threatening Odysseus and his return home. The power of these dangerous, nonhuman figures is sometimes signaled by the prototypically female activities of weaving (Kirke, Kalypso) and singing (Kirke, Kalypso, the Sirens). In other instances the threat to Odysseus is that of being swallowed, literally eaten alive (Skylla, Charybdis). Polyphemos, the Cyclops, though apparently a male figure, might well be included in this list of dangerous females: he seems to be symbolically "feminized" by the cave / womb in which he dwells, within which the hero is Nobody but from which he is, so to speak, reborn, conspicuously insisting on his identity as Odysseus.[43] Furthermore, when Odysseus overcomes the Cyclops, he does so by penetrating his eye with the pointed olive stake, a weapon analogous to the "phallic" means by which he defies or defeats other threatening female figures: the sword with which he confronts Kirke; the tall fig tree to which he "relentlessly" clings above the gulf of Charybdis until it regurgitates the mast and rudder of his smashed ship; the mast on which he is bound upright as he passes by the Sirens.

The Sirens apparently constitute a different kind of danger, because they neither invite Odysseus into a sexual relationship nor threaten to engulf or swallow him. Rather, they sing a song in a "honey-sweet voice" (*meligērun . . . op(a)*, 12.187) and claim that "when anyone has delighted in it, he will go on his way knowing more; / for we know all things, as many as, in broad Troy, / the Trojans and Argives toiled at by the will of the gods, / and we know as many things as happen on the earth that feeds many" (12.188–91). The song with which the Sirens tempt Odysseus suggests by its content and diction the kind of heroism associated with the *Iliad* and the Iliadic tradition.[44] If Odysseus were to give way to the temptation and relapse, as it were, into that poetic genre, he would be destroyed and his bones would join those of other men rotting on the Sirens' meadow. For no warrior heroism can resist the power of the Sirens' song. Only the heroism of *nostos* poetry, grounded in Odysseus' characteristic cunning intelligence and mental toughness, is sufficient to withstand the Sirens' temptation. It is noteworthy that while the diction and content of the Sirens' song are Iliadic, the dangerous pleasure it offers is characteristically Odyssean because it is fundamentally sexual. This is shown by *terpsamenos* ("has delighted in," 12.188), a participial form of the verb *terpō*, which is used frequently of sexual delight, and by the sexually connotative *thelgousin*, Kirke's word in 12.44 for the "enchanting" effect of the Sirens' singing. In addition, the "flowery meadow" (*leimōn' anthemoenta*, 12.159), in which the Sirens sit and sing and the bones of their victims rot (12. 44–46), also suggests a scene of sexual activity, given the erotic associations of meadows (and grass

---

[43] Cf. Dimock, "Name of Odysseus," pp. 58–59.

[44] See P. Pucci, "The Song of the Sirens," *Arethusa* 12 (1979), pp. 121–32 [this volume, pp. 191–99]. Cf. Segal, "*Kleos* and Its Ironies," pp. 38–43 [this volume, pp. 213–18].

and gardens) in Greek poetry.[45] Thus, through their song the Sirens menace Odysseus sexually, even though they do not explicitly invite him into a sexual relationship as Kirke and Kalypso do.

On the other hand, the human females whom the poem describes him as meeting—Nausikaa, Arete, and especially Penelope—are invariably helpful. It has been suggested that Penelope might be considered a positively charged version of the seductive and dangerous females.[46] When she weaves both plans and garments, she helps preserve Odysseus' home and kingdom. When he goes to bed with her in book 23, he is neither threatened with destruction nor deflected from his journey homeward. Rather, their sexual union marks the end of his wanderings, at least in this poem,[47] and his restoration to his full identity as husband and king.

But how should a listener or reader of the *Odyssey*, as opposed to its hero, understand Penelope's loyalty and resourcefulness? For the poem not only represents these qualities as existing for the sake of Odysseus and as an adjunct to his heroic identity; it also characterizes them and her in such a way as not only to call into question this representation but even to raise doubts about the possibility of any single, straightforward interpretation of the epic.

Considered in one way, Penelope, throughout the *Odyssey*, protects the *oikos* ("house" and "household") of Odysseus and Telemachos. Like Arete and Helen, she spends her time supervising servants and working wool, but *her* weaving is absolutely unique and so important that it is described at length three times (2.94–110, 19.138–56, 24.129–146). Undoing by night what she accomplishes during the day, she uses this typically female activity to deceive the Suitors, delay her marriage, and preserve the *oikos*.

In this salutary deception, Penelope shows the same cunning intelligence that is characteristic of Odysseus. The poem even shows hers to be superior to his, when, at 23.177–80, she tests the stranger who claims to be Odysseus by ordering Eurykleia to prepare his bed—the one, we hear, Odysseus himself had made—outside their bedroom. Odysseus rises to the bait: by suspecting that another man has entered their bedroom and cut the rooted olive trunk that formed one leg of the bed, he in effect acknowledges the

---

[45] The "soft meadows" (*leimōnes malakoi*) of Kalypso's Ogygia (5.72) have a similar connotation. Cf. A. Motte, *Prairies et jardins de la Grèce antique*, Mémoires de la classe de Lettres de l'Académie royale de Belgique, 2nd series, 66 (Brussels, 1973), pp. 50–56, cited by Vernant, "Le Refus," p. 15n.9 [this volume, p. 187n.9].

[46] Nagler, "Dread Goddess," this volume, pp. 160–61.

[47] In the epic sequel to the *Odyssey* entitled the *Telegony*, Odysseus' further adventures included journeys, wars, a second marriage to Kallidike, Queen of the Thesprotians, and death at the hands of Telegonos, his son by Kirke. In the *Odyssey* itself, Odysseus tells Penelope of the "immeasurable toil there will still be in the future, / toil abundant and difficult that it is necessary for me to finish completely" (23.249–50), according to Teiresias' prophecy (23.251, 267–84), and he says he will go raiding to replenish the herds destroyed by the Suitors (23.357).

power of Penelope over him—the possibility that she has been or could be unfaithful. By describing the construction of the bed, he provides her with the certain sign that he really is Odysseus and gives her the opportunity to assert clearly her actual faithfulness and her resourcefulness in preserving their marriage and household.

The mental similarity between Odysseus and Penelope, their shared *mētis*, is obvious both at 18.281–83, where he enjoys the way she trickily charms gifts from the Suitors, while "her own mind is eager for other things," and in the continuation of the recognition scene in book 23, when Penelope wishes to learn about the future trial imposed on Odysseus by Teiresias before going to bed with her husband, controlling her desires as so often in the poem he controls his (23.257–62). This mental likeness, or mutuality, is the poem's main example of the kind of harmony in marriage that Odysseus (opportunistically) wishes for Nausikaa at 6.181–85:

> May [the gods] provide a husband and a house and unity of mind
> that is good; for nothing is better and stronger than *this*,
> than when the two of them, man and wife, keep house,
> being of one mind in their thoughts; with many pains for their enemies
> and joy for their well-wishers, and they themselves are especially glorious.

The verb translated as "are . . . glorious"—*ekluon*, a form of *kluō* ("hear")—is linguistically cognate with *kleos*. It is characteristic of the *Odyssey* and its genre that having a harmonious marriage and an *oikos* can generate the kind of glory that in the *Iliad* and the Iliadic tradition comes only from heroic warfare. It is equally characteristic that a woman, Penelope, can win such *kleos* for her "excellence" (*aretē*, 24.197) in "remembering" (*memnēt'*, 24.195) her husband. As Agamemnon's shade says to that of Achilles at 24.194–98,

> How good was the mind of blameless Penelope,
> daughter of Ikarios; how well she remembered Odysseus,
> her wedded husband; therefore, for her the glory of her excellence
> will never perish, and for those living on the earth the immortals will make
> a song of grace for sensible Penelope.

As I've said, in the *Iliad* "imperishable glory" is attained by warriors when they have performed heroic deeds. Here in the *Odyssey*, the "excellence" (*aretē*) that leads to such glory is redefined so as to refer not to supremacy in battle but to the mental toughness and faithfulness illustrated by Penelope "remembering" Odysseus. This makes sense because elsewhere in the poem, "remembering" is the activity of mind that most distinguishes Odysseus from his companions, enables him to return home to Ithaca, his *oikos*, and his wife, and makes him the hero of the epic (see above, p. 8). For her "remembering," Penelope earns a "song of grace" in the future—a kind of reward that in the *Iliad* is limited to warriors and to Helen (*Il.* 6.358), who is the "cause" of warfare. In the *Odyssey* Helen, with her "drug" that "banishes grief and allays wrath, causing forgetfulness of all evils" (4.220–21), seems morally trivial in large part because she is more concerned with forgetting than with remembering; Penelope, by contrast, becomes a virtually equal, second hero of the poem, along with Odysseus.[48]

Penelope's "song of grace" is contrasted by Agamemnon's shade to the "song of hate" (24.200) he prophesies for Klutaimnestra and to the "harsh reputation" Klutaimnestra "will cause to attend on female women, even on one who does well" (24.201–2). In the world of the *Odyssey*, it seems, a woman who preserves or betrays her husband and *oikos* is as much the object of praise or blame as a man in the *Iliad* who acts heroically or like a coward; by the same token, a return homeward, which in the *Iliad* is incompatible with heroic glory, is in the *Odyssey* itself the source of such glory.

In the genre of traditional poetry represented by the *Odyssey*, the *oikos* is a suitable object of song; the poetic world is divided into those loyal to the *oikos* and those who would destroy it; the hero is permitted to kill in defense of his *oikos* and to escape the reprisals that usually would follow such killing. Furthermore, because women's place is in the *oikos*, their role and importance in the *Odyssey* is far greater than in the *Iliad*. This has even led some readers, notably Samuel Butler, to suppose that the poem was composed by a woman.[49] However unlikely this may seem, such a view reflects not only the prominence of women in the *Odyssey* but the sympathy with which they are portrayed. In particular the role of the wife, in the persons of Helen, Arete, and Penelope and in contrast to the poem's threatening, nonhuman females, is given special honor, and women's intelligence—especially Penelope's—is equated with men's.

All this seems clear and convincing. Nevertheless, I think it would be naive to equate Agamemnon's (and other male characters') interpretation of Penelope's virtue and of the proper relations between husbands and wives with the interpretation of the *Odyssey* itself or its implied author or readers. For Penelope's plans and behavior can be seen to have their own motivation, quite apart from her loyalty to Odysseus and his *oikos*.[50] For example, while the contest of the bow and the axes *results* in the murder of the Suitors and the restoration of Odysseus to the kingship, when Penelope

---

[48] For recent discussions of Penelope, see S. Murnaghan, "Penelope's *Agnoia*: Knowledge, Power, and Gender in the *Odyssey*," *Helios* N.S. 13 (1986), pp. 103–15, reworked and expanded in *Disguise and Recognition in the Odyssey* (Princeton, 1987), pp. 118–47; N. Felson-Rubin, "Penelope's Perspective: Character from Plot," in *Homer: Beyond Oral Poetry*, ed. J. M. Bremer, I.J.F. de Jong, and J. Kalff (Amsterdam, 1987), pp. 61–83, reworked and expanded in this volume, pp. 163–83, and in *Regarding Penelope: From Character to Poetics* (Princeton, 1994), pp. 15–43; J. J. Winkler, "Penelope's Cunning and Homer's," in *The Constraints of Desire* (New York and London, 1990), pp. 129–61; L. E. Doherty, "Joyce's Penelope and Homer's: Feminist Reconsiderations," *Classical and Modern Literature* 10 (1990), pp. 343–49; M. Arthur Katz, *Penelope's Renown* (Princeton, 1991).

[49] S. Butler, *The Authoress of the Odyssey* (1897; 3rd ed. Chicago, 1967).

[50] See Felson-Rubin, "Penelope's Perspective"; *Regarding Penelope*.

declares her intention to hold the contest (19.570–81), it must be understood that she does so in full preparation for her imminent marriage to one of her wooers. Similarly, when she solicits gifts from the Suitors at 18.274–80, we have only Odysseus' reported understanding that she is merely leading them on, "enchanting their feeling / with pleasing words, though her mind was eager for other things" (18.282–83). Why, however, should we accept Odysseus' reading of the situation, which obviously is self-serving? Similarly, why should we accept the statement by the shade of the Suitor Amphimedon to the shades of Agamemnon and Achilles that Penelope set up the contest at the bidding of Odysseus (24.167–69)? This directly contradicts what actually happens in book 19, where, as the poem makes explicitly clear, Penelope and Odysseus do *not* recognize one another, and she sets up the contest for her own reasons.[51] If we cannot trust Amphimedon's statement, why should we accept, and how are we to evaluate, the praise of Penelope by Agamemnon, to which that statement gives rise?

Finally, what are we to make of Penelope's implicit comparison of herself to Helen (23.218–24), immediately after she recognizes Odysseus by his knowledge of the construction of their bed and tells him of her continual fear during his absence that "some one of mortal men might come and deceive me / with words. For many men plan evil profits" (23.216–17)? Is it that she distrusts herself and therefore tests Odysseus, who clearly fits the description of the kind of man against whom she says she was on guard? Penelope asserts (23.218–24):

> Argive Helen, born from Zeus,
> would not have mingled in the bed of love with a foreigner,
> if she knew that the warlike sons of the Achaians
> were going to bring her back again homeward to her dear fatherland.
> Surely a god drove her to do an unseemly deed;
> earlier she had not put in her own heart the disastrous
> moral blindness, from which, to begin with, sorrow came to us also.

This is the most sympathetic thing anyone in the *Odyssey* says about Helen. Penelope refuses to join in the otherwise universal condemnation of her by the poem's male characters, a condemnation that usually is considered by readers to be that of the poem itself. Yet Penelope's independence of judgment should caution readers not to assume too readily that the poem, as opposed to certain of its characters, even makes such a straightforward, un-

---

[51] Nevertheless, in recent years, several scholars have argued that Penelope unconsciously or intuitively recognizes Odysseus in book 19. See, for example, P. W. Harsh, "Penelope and Odysseus in *Odyssey* XIX," *American Journal of Philology* 71 (1950), pp. 1–21; A. Amory, "The Reunion of Odysseus and Penelope," in *Essays on the Odyssey*, ed. Taylor, pp. 100–121; J. Russo, "Interview and Aftermath: Dream, Fantasy, and Intuition in *Odyssey* 19 and 20," *American Journal of Philology* 103 (1982), pp. 4–18. Cf. Winkler, "Penelope's Cunning," pp. 150–61, who describes Penelope as "only 99 percent certain" that the stranger "was really Odysseus" (p. 160).

complicated condemnation. In light of Penelope's comment, it might be more accurate to say that in the end the poem leaves the question of Helen's moral responsibility and even the moral status of adultery open and in doubt, however it may tempt a listener or reader to share in the majority judgment against her and her action.

The poem similarly tempts its audience to accept as its own the judgments of various male characters, including Odysseus, about Penelope. According to these judgments, her glory lies in loyalty to her husband and *oikos* and in the resourcefulness with which she expresses this loyalty. But the poem also shows a Penelope with a mind of her own, rather than one merely in harmony with her husband's. It would be simplistic to adopt the standard, patriarchal reading of Penelope, and of the role of women in the *Odyssey* generally, without recognizing how the poem partly undoes this reading.

There are other indications, too, that the *Odyssey* calls into question, critiques, or makes problematic its apparent meanings and values, including its valorization of Odysseus and constant representations of the Suitors as evildoers who merit punishment and of the Companions as weak and exclusively responsible for their destruction. For example, though Odysseus' crew lose their lives as a result of eating the cattle of the Sun, Odysseus himself makes this possible by falling asleep (which he blames on the Olympian gods, 12.338), and he seems more directly responsible for the deaths of those Companions who perish at the hands of the Laistrugones and the Cyclops. Elsewhere, nasty details about the hero emerge almost in passing, such as the fact that he poisons his arrows with a "manslaughtering drug"— something even the gods are felt to disapprove (1.260–64). Similarly, at the end of the poem, his utter ruthlessness toward his enemies, despite Athene's urging, leads to Zeus' direct intervention and Athene's warning to avoid his anger (24.528–44).

As for the Suitors, their reasonable argument in the Ithacan assembly in book 2, that Penelope, not themselves, is causing trouble by refusing to accept an orderly remarriage, and that she is deceiving them individually and as a group, is not entirely contradicted by Telemachos' response (2.130–37). Moreover, the arrogant, violent, and hypocritical speeches of Antinoos and Eurymachos are given prominence throughout the poem, while the morally better Suitors, such as Amphinomos, who "pleased Penelope most / with his words, for he was endowed with a noble mind" (16.397–98), are invisible or ineffective by comparison. Odysseus tries to warn Amphinomos, who seems to him, too, "well-mannered" (*epētēi*, 18.128) and "sensible" (*pepnumenos*, 18.125), but the poem conspicuously forces *all* the Suitors and *all* the Companions to their destruction. It insists on the deserved and analogously cleansing deaths of the two groups of men (12.417; 22.481–82, 493–94) and so veils over its suggestion that they might also be seen as victims of the arbitrarily valorized power and moral righteousness of Odysseus and his family. As in the case of Penelope, the *Odyssey* implies that its own main values and most frequently expressed viewpoints are neither unproblematic nor the only ones possible. Rather, they are to some extent open to criticism and negative evaluation, and the poem itself is correspondingly open-ended, interpretively ambivalent or indeterminate, and irreducible to a single, straightforward, one-dimensional reading.

This interpretive open-endedness of the *Odyssey* and, to use Bakhtin's term, its "unfinalizability" seem to me even more a function of the poem's genre than its redefinitions of heroism and narrative complexity.[52] The *Iliad*, although it too suggests a critique of the social system and values it appears to celebrate, is simpler and more straightforward in its action, its characterization, its narrative structure, and the clarity of the tragic contradictions in which its characters live and die. The *Odyssey*, on the other hand, like its cunning, shifty, adaptable hero, is harder to get a handle on. Its revisions of heroism and generic rivalry with the Iliadic norms are clear enough, yet it leaves in doubt how best to evaluate these revisions. More fundamentally, especially in the case of Penelope, the *Odyssey* is a kind of epic poetry that leaves itself open to re-vision and re-creation by audiences and readers, whom it challenges to achieve interpretive clarity in the face of formal, narrative, and ethical complexities and uncertainties.[53]

[52] Cf. G. S. Morson and C. Emerson, *Mikhail Bakhtin: Creation of a Prosaics* (Stanford, 1990), pp. 36–40, 281.

[53] On the poem's open-endedness and "indeterminacy," especially in regard to Penelope, see esp. Katz, *Penelope's Renown*, pp. 3–19, 155–95.

Land and Sacrifice in the *Odyssey*

A STUDY OF RELIGIOUS AND MYTHICAL MEANINGS

PIERRE VIDAL-NAQUET
(translated by A. Szegedy-Maszak)

THIS IS AN ESSAY about land. Perhaps paradoxically, I begin with some details taken not from Homer, but from Hesiod. Contrary to common opinion, both the *Theogony* and *Works and Days* can be used to elucidate not merely works composed after them but also those works that antedate them or are more or less contemporary with them—as is perhaps the case with the *Odyssey*.

I believe that the "myth of the races" and the myth of Pandora in the *Works and Days*, and the myth of Prometheus in that poem and in the *Theogony*, justify a definition that could be termed both anthropological and normative, both exclusive and inclusive. The exclusion is twofold. Hesiodic man is the man of the age of iron, which means in the first place that he is *not* the man of the age of gold, the mythical time when men "lived like gods," knowing neither old age nor true death: "They had all good things, and the grain-giving earth (*zeidōros aroura*) unforced bore them fruit abundantly and without stint. They pastured their lands (*erg' enemonto*) in ease and peace, with many good things" (*WD* 112–19).[1] The distinction between the age of gold and our own that I wish to study here—there are others—is that of work versus nonwork (agricultural work, of course).[2] As compared with the age of iron, the age of gold—the age of Cronos—is an absolute model; it is a condition the other ages can never hope to attain. The lot of the race of the age of gold during their lives is enjoyed by the race of heroes, or at least by some of them, after death: Zeus places them "apart from men" (*dich' anthrōpōn*) and apart from the gods, "under the rule of Cronos, at the ends of the earth." "And they dwell untouched by sorrow in the islands of the Blessed along the shore of the deep swirling Ocean, happy heroes for whom

---

[1] On the myth of the races, see J.-P. Vernant, "Hesiod's Myth of the Races: An Essay in Structural Analysis," in his *Myth and Thought among the Greeks* (Boston and London, 1993), pp. 3–32, and "Hesiod's Myth of the Races: A Reassessment," *Myth and Thought*, pp. 33–72.

[2] Strictly, the contrast is between the "race of iron" and all the earlier ones. Even the race of bronze, who "work with bronze" (*chalkoi d'eirgazonto*: 151), do not "work" in the strict sense; they perform a military rite (cf. Vernant, "Myth of the Races," p. 15). Only the "race of gold" is described explicitly as not working.

the grain-giving earth bears honey-sweet fruit flourishing thrice a year."[3] The age of gold in "time" is succeeded here by an age of gold in "space," in the islands of the Blessed, which are characterized also by the richness of the earth.

Elsewhere, in the myth of Pandora,[4] Hesiod summarizes in advance, as it were, the lesson of the myth of the races: "Before this the tribes of men lived on earth remote and free from ills and hard toil (*chalepoio ponoio*) and heavy sickness which bring the *Kēres* upon men: for in misery men grow old quickly" (*WD* 90–93).[5]

To have been excluded from the age of gold means that man is not a god.[6] But he is not an animal either; and the second exclusion bars him from *allēlophagia*, cannibalism: "For the son of Cronos has ordained this law for men, that fishes and beasts and winged birds should devour one another, for Right (*dikē*) is not in them" (*WD* 276–78). The practice of *dikē* is what enables man to escape from the animal state: man is the creature that does not eat its fellows.

The inclusions are closely related—simultaneously inverse and complementary—to the exclusions. The *Works and Days* itself is about the working of arable land and all that is implied by it: the planting of trees and the rearing of animals, especially for plowing. *Dikē* is a means of regaining— perhaps not the age of gold, for men are obliged to labor—but at least prosperity and fruitfulness in human beings, land, and flocks: "The earth gives them [i.e., those who practice *dikē*] a life of plenty, and on the mountains the oak bears acorns on high, and in the midst, bees. Their fleecy sheep are laden with wool; their women bear children resembling their fathers. They flourish continually with good things; and do not travel on ships, for the grain-giving earth bears them fruit" (*WD* 232–37).[7] This human work is linked in turn to the possession (thanks to Prometheus) of fire

---

[3] *Work and Days* 167–73, restoring 169 (in the rule of Cronos) to its position in the manuscripts [= 173a in F. Solmsen, ed., *Hesiod: Theogonia Opera et Dies, Scutum*, with *Fragmenta Selecta*, ed. R. Merkelbach and M. L. West (Oxford, 1970)].

[4] Vernant has demonstrated the close connection between this myth and that of the races: "Myth of the Races" (above, note 1), pp. 18–19; similarly, "The Myth of Prometheus in Hesiod," in *Myth and Society in Ancient Greece*, tr. J. Lloyd (Sussex and New Jersey, 1980), pp. 184–85.

[5] Line 93, which I have restored here, is a quotation from *Od.* 19.360.

[6] Commentators have perhaps been too quick to reject *WD* 108 as an interpolation (Lehrs, followed notably by Mazon[and Solmsen]). For the line introduces the myth of the races by connecting it with the myth of Pandora: "for gods and men have the same origin": *hōs homothen gegaasi theoi thnētoi t' anthrōpoi*.

[7] It is well known that these formulae appear frequently in the texts of oaths: see in particular the oath of the Amphictyons in Aeschines, *Against Ctesiphon* 111, and the oath of the people of Dreros in *Inscriptiones Creticae* 1.9 (Dreros) 1.85–89. And when *hybris* is triumphant, as at the end of the myth of the races, we are told that "the father will no longer resemble his sons, nor the sons their father" (*Works and Days* 182).

for cooking, that fire which had previously been concealed by Zeus (*WD* 47–50). In revenge for the theft of fire, at Zeus's command Hephaistos made Pandora, who is both earth and woman (*WD* 59–105).[8] The hints contained in *Works and Days* are filled out by the *Theogony*. The quarrel between gods and men at Mekone has two carefully paralleled episodes.[9] The first incident consists of the primordial sacrifice of an ox and its unequal division, the gods receiving the smoke and men the flesh, which results in the confiscation of fire by Zeus and its theft by Prometheus. Second, man is given the ambiguous gift of woman, to make up for the gods' acceptance of the state of affairs brought about by Prometheus. Arable land, cooking, sacrifice, and sexual and family life within the *oikos*—even, at one extreme, political life—form a complex, no element of which can be separated from the others. These are the terms that define man's estate, in between the age of gold and *allēlophagia*, cannibalism.[10]

The limits marked out here by Hesiod, with their characteristic features (which are also features of the crisis of this period) are repeatedly employed throughout subsequent Greek thought. From the end of the sixth century B.C. in particular, these patterns were taken up in the violent political disputes that divided the Greek world and led theorists to adopt contrasting "positive" or "negative" views of primitive man; the age of gold jostles against the theme of the misery of primeval man. One might be tempted—and some scholars have not resisted the temptation—to trace these disputes back to the time of Hesiod and to portray Hesiod himself as an opponent of progress.[11] It is not perceptibly more plausible to make him both a supporter of "chronological primitivism" (because he starts with an age of gold)

[8]Cf. Vernant, "Myth of the Races" (above, note 1), pp. 18–19; P. Pucci, *Hesiod and the Language of Poetry* (Baltimore and London, 1977), pp. 82–135; and especially N. Loraux, "Sur la race des femmes," *Arethusa* 11 (1978), pp. 44–52. Pandora is given to bring "unhappiness to bread-eating men" (*pēm' andrasin alphēstēisin*; *Works and Days* 82). It may be relevant that *alphēstēs*, "bread-eating," which is a Homeric adjective, is formed from the root *ed/*od, "to eat" and is a formation parallel (and in sense opposite) to *ōmēstēs*, "raw-eating"; cf. Chantraine, *La Formation des noms en grec ancien* (Paris, 1933), p. 315.

[9]The parallelism is emphasized by the repeated use of *epeita* in *Theogony* 536 and 562. The whole affair takes place in the same period of time: "It was in the time when the quarrel between gods and mortal men was being settled" (*hot' ekrinonto* . . . [535]). See Vernant, "Myth of Prometheus" (above, note 4) and in *The Cuisine of Sacrifice in Ancient Greece*, ed. M. Detienne and J.-P. Vernant, tr. P. Wissing (Chicago and London, 1989), pp. 46–58.

[10]Note that the Hesiodic accounts leave no space for a nomadic period in the history of man; man is either a cultivator or no man at all.

[11]A typical example is Havelock's book, *The Liberal Temper in Greek Politics* (London, 1957), the second chapter of which, "History as Regress" (36–51), analyzes the "myth of the races" side by side with the myths in Plato's *Politicus* and *Laws*. Needless to say, neither the idea of "progress" nor that of "regress" was thinkable in Hesiod's time, for there was no idea of "history" in our sense. This objection, however, does not apply to a very useful book by a follower of Havelock, T. Cole, whose *Democritus and the Sources of Greek Anthropology* (Ann Arbor, 1967) concentrates on a precise period and deals with genuine ideological disputes.

and an opponent of "cultural primitivism" (in that he contrasts civilization with cannibalism).[12] For these two positions are in fact one.

It is not my intention to discuss this post-Hesiodic literature here.[13] I note simply, for reasons that will shortly become clear, that Hesiod's age of gold, the age of Cronos, the "vegetarian" age before cooking and before sacrifice, which is described for us in so many texts,[14] is also the period of cannibalism and human sacrifice in at least part of the tradition. Some of the texts that make this association between opposites may seem very late,[15] but we should not forget that as early as the fourth century B.C. the Cynics developed a theory of a "natural" way of life that both condemned the eating of dead flesh and cooked food and championed raw food, cannibalism, and even incest, the opposite *par excellence* of culture.[16] And it would be wrong to see this as merely a view held by theorists: Euripides' *Bacchae* oscillates between the atmosphere of paradise described by the messenger early on in his speech and the orgy of flesh-eating which culminates in the quasi-incestuous murder of Pentheus by his mother (*Bacchae* 677–768, 1043–1147). Hesiod's Cronos is also a god who eats his own children (*Th.* 459–67).[17] From this perspective, it is Plato who is "theorizing" when in the *Politicus* he chooses to define the age of Cronos as the time when cannibalism was unknown—a choice that happens to be the same as that made by Hesiod in his version of the myth of the races.[18]

[12] A. O. Lovejoy and G. Boas, *Primitivism and Related Ideas in Antiquity* (Baltimore, 1935), p. 196.

[13] The book by Lovejoy and Boas is certainly the most useful collection of material for such a study. For the myth in the *Politicus*, see P. Vidal-Naquet, *The Black Hunter: Forms of Thought and Forms of Society in the Greek World*, tr. A. Szegedy-Maszak (Baltimore and London, 1986), pp. 292–94.

[14] One example (there are many others) is Empedocles, *Purifications* F 128 Diels-Kranz [H. Diels and W. Kranz, *Die Fragmente der Vorsokratiker*, 5th ed. (Berlin, 1934)]: In the reign of Kypris (Aphrodite), all sacrifices consisted of myrrh, incense and honey. Blood sacrifices, and indeed all eating of meat, were considered abominations. Plato's myth in the *Politicus* (272a–b) says much the same, and vegetarianism is implicit in what Hesiod says. For a general survey, see J. Haussleiter, *Der Vegetarismus in der Antike* (Berlin, 1935); also, more recently, M. Detienne, *Dionysos Slain* (Baltimore, 1979), pp. 56–62, and D. A. Dombrowski, *The Philosophy of Vegetarianism* (Amherst, Mass., 1984).

[15] For example, Euhemerus apud Lactantius, *Institutiones Divinae* 1.13.2: "Saturn and his wife and the other men of this time used to eat human flesh. Jupiter was the first to prohibit the practice" (Euhemerus as translated by Ennius); "ancients sacrificed to Cronos according to the mode used in Carthage while that city existed"; Sextus Empiricus, *Outlines of Pyrrhonism*, in *Pyrrhoneiōn Hypotyposeōn libri tres*, ed. H. Mutschmann, rev. I. Mau (Leipzig, 1958), p. 190. "Some people sacrificed a man to Cronos in the same way that the Scythians sacrificed strangers to Artemis." See Lovejoy and Boas, *Primitivism* (above, note 12), pp. 53–79.

[16] Cf. Diogenes Laertius, *Lives of the Philosophers* 6.34, 72–73; Dio Chrysostom 10.29–30; Julian, *Orationes* 6.191–93.

[17] On the subject of cannibalism and *allēlophagia* in Greek literature, see, in addition to the works already cited by Lovejoy and Boas and Haussleiter, A. J. Festugière, "A propos des arétalogies d'Isis," *Harvard Theological Review* 42 (1949), pp. 209–34.

[18] See *Politicus* 271d–e: *Out' agrion ēn ouden oute allēlōn edōdai, polemos te ouk enēn oude stasis to parapan:* "There were no wild tribes among them [the animals], nor cannibals; and war and

If we begin from the other end, we find agriculture intimately linked with cooking, as for example in the Hippocratic treatise *On Ancient Medicine* 3 (ed. Festugière), where it is shown that the cultivation of cereals, which replaced the eating of raw foods, is founded upon a form of food that has to be cooked. An association between agriculture, family life, and the origin of civilization similar to that implied by Hesiod also occurs in the Athenian myths about Cecrops, who, guided by Bouzyges ("Ox-team Man"),[19] invented agriculture, and also invented the monogamous patriarchal family.[20] The purpose of this essay is to see whether such associations already existed in Homer.

When Odysseus realizes that he is at last on Ithaca, his first action is to "kiss the grain-giving earth in a greeting to his native land" (*Od.* 13.354).[21] Now this is not merely the act of a man returning to his native land: it contains a fundamental point that deserves close analysis.

In talking about the *Odyssey*, we have to make further distinctions: not between the compositions of different bards detected by "analytic" critics in the light of criteria that differ with every scholar and produce results at once predictably divergent and fatally untestable, but between units that have a significance in the poem as we have it. To put it crudely, we cannot discuss Cyclops or Calypso in the same way that we discuss Nestor or Telemachus. In effect, as has often been recognized, the *Odyssey* contrasts a "real" world, essentially the world of Ithaca, but also Sparta and Pylos to which Telemachus goes, with a mythical world that is roughly conterminous with that of the stories in Alcinous's palace.[22] Similarly, Shakespeare's *Tempest* contrasts Naples and Milan on the one hand with Prospero's magic island on the other.[23] Odysseus enters this mythical world after his stay with the Cicones, a perfectly real Thracian people known to Herodotus (7.59, 108, 110), in

---

political strife were completely absent." The passage concerns animals, but the language employed is deliberately "human."

[19] See the vase described and illustrated by D. M. Robinson, "Bouzyges and the First Plough on the Krater of the Painter of Naples Hephaistos," *American Journal of Archaeology* 35 (1931), pp. 152–60; see also U. Kron, *Die zehn attischen Phylenheroen* (Berlin, 1976), pp. 95–96.

[20] Cf. the passages collected by S. Pembroke, "Women in Charge," *Journal of the Warburg and Courtauld Institutes* 30 (1967), pp. 26–27 and 29–32, and P. Vidal-Naquet, "Slavery and the Rule of Women in Tradition, Myth, and Utopia," in his *The Black Hunter* (Baltimore, 1986), pp. 205–23.

[21] The formula *kuse de zeidōron arouran* ("he kissed the grain-giving earth") occurs earlier, in the description of Odysseus's arrival on Scheria (5.463), but naturally the first part of the line is different. The connection turns out not to be accidental.

[22] Cf. C. Segal, "The Phaeacians and the Symbolism of Odysseus' Return," *Arion* 1 (1962), p. 17. The two separate worlds of the *Odyssey* are clearly delineated by G. Germain, *La Genèse de l'Odyssée: Le Fantastique et le sacré* (Paris, 1954), pp. 511–82.

[23] For the value of this distinction in *The Tempest*, cf. R. Marienstras, "Prospéro ou la Machiavélisme du bien," *Bulletin de la Faculté des lettres de Strasbourg* 42 (1965), 899–917.

whose territory he eats, fights, and plunders just as he might have done at Troy, and after a ten-day storm[24] that he encounters while rounding Cape Malea, the last "real" place on his travels before he gets back to Ithaca.[25]

Proof that this contrast is indeed relevant is supplied by the text itself. Telemachus's route never crosses that of Odysseus. There are two points of contact only between the two worlds. One is plainly magical: Menelaus tells Odysseus's son how he was informed by the magician Proteus, in Egypt, the land of wonders, that Odysseus was detained on Calypso's island (4.555–58; 17.138–44).[26] The other is the land of the Phaeacians, professional seamen who have been shown to occupy a strategic place at the junction of the two worlds.[27] I need hardly press the point. Odysseus's travels have nothing to do with geography, and there is more geographical truth in the "untrue" stories he tells Eumaeus and Penelope (14.191–359; 19.164–202)[28] than in all the stories in Alcinous's palace.[29] Crete, Egypt, and Epirus are real enough.

For Odysseus, leaving this fantasy world means leaving a world that is not the world of human beings, a world that is by turns superhuman and subhuman, a world in which he is offered divinity by Calypso but also threatened by Circe with reduction to the condition of an animal. And he must leave it to return to the world of normality. The *Odyssey* as a whole is

---

[24]To be exact, a nine-day storm; on the tenth day, they reach the Lotus-Eaters (9.82–84). "The number nine is used essentially to symbolize a period of time at the end of which, on the tenth day or year, a decisive event happens" G. Germain, *Homère et la mystique des nombres* [Paris, 1954], p. 13).

[25]"Der Sturm verschlägt den Helden ins Fabelland" (P. von der Mühll, "Odyssee," *Pauly-Wissowa*, Suppl. 7 [1940], c. 720).

[26]Menelaus has just come back, as Nestor puts it (3.318–20), from a region whence one wouldn't expect to return.

[27]Cf. Segal, "Phaeacians" (above, note 22). There is one other place from which communication is feasible but fails: Aeolus's floating island (10.3).

[28]The second account to Penelope (19.262–307) contains a serious difficulty: Odysseus introduces the Phaeacians where they are clearly out of place, since Penelope does not yet know anything of Odysseus's adventures or his identity. Of the "interpolations" discovered by nineteenth-century critics, lines 273–86 are one of the few passages that almost certainly deserve to be rejected. In his first account, Odysseus heads for Crete after rounding Cape Malea (19.187), which is perfectly reasonable and restores "geographical" truth precisely at the point at which it was abandoned. Elements of "truth" slipped in among the "lies"—and contrasted with the "lies" that constitute the "true" tales—are fundamental to the Homeric story. See T. Todorov, "Le Récit primitif," *Tel quel* 30 (1967), pp. 47–55 and L. Kahn, "Ulysse," in *Dictionnaire des mythologies*, vol. 2 (Paris, 1981), pp. 517–20.

[29]I hardly need add that I do not expect to discourage enthusiasts for Homeric "geography" and the "identification" of sites, although the sport has been aptly likened by J.-P. Darmon to the search for the rabbit hole through which Alice entered Wonderland. Of course this is not to deny that Homeric wonders, like all wonder, bear some relation to the realities of their time, which means essentially the western Mediterranean (and perhaps in an earlier period, the eastern Mediterranean, if one believes K. Meuli, *Odyssee und Argonautika* [Berlin, 1921]). After all, there is presumably more resemblance between the wonders seen by Alice and Victorian England, than between that Wonderland and Manchu China.

in one sense the story of Odysseus's return to normality, of his deliberate acceptance of the human condition.[30]

There is therefore no paradox in saying that, from the Lotus-Eaters to Calypso by way of the land of the Cyclopes and the Underworld, Odysseus meets with no creature that is strictly human. There is of course sometimes room for doubt: the Laestrygones, for example, have an agora, the mark of political life, but physically they are not as men are, but giants (10.114, 120). Circe causes us to wonder whether we are dealing with a woman or a goddess: but finally, just as with Calypso, the humanity is merely in the outward form, in the voice. She is in truth *deinē theos audēessa*, the "terrible goddess with a human voice" (10.136; 11.8; 12.150, 449; cf. 10.228). Twice Odysseus asks himself what "eaters of bread" he has landed among—that is, what men; however, in each case the point is that he is not among "bread-eaters," but among the Lotus-Eaters and the Laestrygones (9.89; 10.101).[31]

There follows from this a signal implication, that the "stories" rigorously exclude anything to do with working the land, or with arable land itself insofar as it is worked.[32] The Thrace of the Cicones is the last cultivated land Odysseus encounters: there he eats mutton and drinks wine, and there he obtains the wine he later offers the Cyclops (9.45 ff., 161–65, 197–211).[33] Euripides' Odysseus, when he comes to an unknown land, asks Silenus, "Where are the walls and the city towers?" The answer comes: "Stranger, this is no city. No man dwells here" (*Cyclops* 115–16).[34] Here fortifications are the symbol of the presence of civilized humanity, or indeed of humanity at all. But Homer's Odysseus looks for cultivated fields, for the sign of human labor.[35] When the Achaeans reach Circe's island, they search in vain for the *erga brotōn*, the "works of men," that is, for crops. But all they see is scrub and forest, where staghunts can be organized (10.147, 150, 157–63, 197, 251). In the land of the Laestrygones, the sight of smoke might be taken as evidence of domestic hearths and the presence of human beings (10.99),[36] but there is "no trace either of the work of oxen or of the work of

[30]"The movement of the *Odyssey* is essentially inwards, homewards, towards normality" (W. B. Stanford, *The Ulysses Theme* [Oxford, 1954], p. 50); see above all Segal, "Phaeacians" (above, note 22).

[31]Similarly, Polyphemus "did not resemble a man who eats bread" (9.190–91).

[32]This is a point overlooked by W. Richter, *Die Landwirtschaft im homerischen Zeitalter* (Göttingen, 1968).

[33]I cannot understand why Haussleiter thought that the Cicones were cannibals (*Vegetarismus*, 23). The text does not mention it.

[34]Cf. Y. Garlan, "Fortifications et histoire grecque," in *Problèmes de la guerre en Grèce ancienne*, ed. J.-P. Vernant (Paris and The Hague, 1968), p. 255.

[35]The use of the phrase *zeidōros aroura*, "grain-giving earth" (and life-giving as well), is not very satisfactory as a criterion, because Hesiod uses it of the golden age. For what it is worth, of nine occurrences in the *Odyssey*, only three refer to a precise place (Ithaca: 13.354; Phaeacia: 5.463; Egypt: 4.229). The rest have a more general referent, roughly "here below."

[36]There is also smoke coming from Circe's house (10.196–97), and when Odysseus ap-

men" (10.98). The Sirens live in a meadow, as do the gods elsewhere (12.159).[37] Although Calypso's island is wooded and even possesses a vine, this is never said to be cultivated (1.51, 5.63–74).

There is one specifically human tree present in the world of the "stories": the olive, the tree of whose wood Odysseus built his bed, the fixed point of his home (23.183–204). In fact, the olive is on occasion the means of Odysseus's escape from danger, in several different forms. It provides the stake with which he bores through the Cyclops' eye and the handle of the axe with which he builds his boat (9.319–20; 5.234–36).[38] And, although it is true that when he is with Aeolus, Circe, or Calypso, Odysseus has plenty to eat, and that the poet playfully draws attention to the vast difference between the gods' meals and those of men (5.196–99), we are never told where the food comes from or who produced it.

A second exclusion is entailed by the exclusion of cultivated land: that of the sacrificial meal, which we saw from Hesiod to be so intimately related to the first. One could almost, in a sense, extend to the entire world of the stories the remark Hermes jokingly makes to Calypso when he arrives on her island: "Who would choose to cross this waste of saltwater? There is not in these parts a single city of mortal men to offer rich hecatombs to the gods" (5.100–102). But only in a sense. For the sacrifice that Odysseus offers to the dead in accordance with Circe's instructions and with lambs she has provided is performed in a trench and is intended to provide blood for the feeding of the dead (10.516–40, 571–72; 11.26–47)—it is the opposite of a sacrificial meal, whose purpose is to feed the living. And the same is true of the victims Odysseus promises to offer the dead and Teiresias on his return: a barren cow and a black ram (10.521–25; 11.29–33).

In the land of the Cyclopes, Odysseus's companions offer sacrifice (9.231; *ethusamen*), as Polyphemus himself does not, but it is not a blood-sacrifice because they are living on cheese (9.232).[39] And the sacrifice they offer on the island just across from that of the Cyclopes—which is abnormal because the victims are the sheep that belong to Polyphemus, animals not reared by man—is rejected by Zeus (9.551–55); even when a human community does sacrifice in nonhuman territory, the sacrifice is improper.

We should now go back over Odysseus's journey and examine more or less in sequence the several types of nonhuman creatures he meets. I take it for granted that Scylla and the inhabitants of the Underworld are not human: Achilles has made the point so that we shall not forget (11.488–91). Sim-

---

proaches Ithaca after leaving the island of Aeolus, he can see men around a fire (*purpoleontas*; 10.30.).

[37] Cf. the Homeric *Hymn to Hermes* 72; Eur. *Hippolytus* 74. On the *leimōn* see A. Motte, *Prairies et jardins de la grèce antique* (Brussels, 1973) and L. Kahn and N. Loraux, "Mort," in *Dictionnaire des mythologies*, vol. 2 (Paris, 1981), pp. 117–24.

[38] Cf. Segal, "Phaeacians" (above, note 22), pp. 45, 62, 63.

[39] For the failed sacrifice of the Cattle of the Sun, see pp. 43–44 below.

ilarly, the Lotus-Eaters are not bread-eaters: they eat flowers, and the food they offer Odysseus's companions deprives them of an essential facet of their humanity, memory (9.84, 94–97). Except during the encounter with Scylla (12.227), Odysseus is constantly the man who remembers in the poem, the true man who stands out from his forgetful companions.

Much more difficult are the problems presented by the Cyclops episode. For here the mythical aspects with which I am concerned are conflated with a quasi-ethnographical description of pastoral peoples (nonhumanity may be just a different sort of humanity: savages)[40] and with an overt, realistic reference to colonization. If these men had been sailors, "they would have made their island a well-built place. The land is not bad; it would bear crops in each season. By the shores of the grey sea are soft, well-watered meadows, where vines would never wither, and there would be rich harvests every year, so rich is the soil under the surface" (9.130–35). This vision remains unfulfilled. The land of the Cyclopes is divided, it will be remembered, into two different areas. One is the "small island," which is utterly wild and where hunting is unknown. There Odysseus's companions find memorable sport (9.116–24, 131–35). The other is the land of the Cyclopean shepherds. Such a division implies a hierarchy: cultivators-hunters-shepherds, and it may be relevant to note that the same series recurs later in Aristotle (Pol. 1.8.1256a 30–40). But the Cyclopes are not merely barbarous herdsmen who lack political institutions and are ignorant of planting and plowing (9.108–15). Conditions on their land are very close to Hesiod's age of gold: "They do not plant or plow, but the earth provides them with all things: grain, vines, and wine from heavy clusters of grapes, which Zeus's rain swells for them" (9.109–11; cf. 123–24). Although they have sheep, they have no true draft animals: there are "no herds or plows" on the island (9.122). So it is, even if we may suspect that the vintages of the golden age lacked breeding (9.111, 357–59).

However, the real point is that the counterpart of the age of gold is cannibalism.[41] The details are so curious that it is impossible to believe that they are not intentional. Polyphemus brings in wood to make a fire for supper, but he does not use it: he is not an eater of bread, and even the

[40] The identification of the figures encountered by Odysseus with savage tribes is explicitly raised as a possibility in 1.198–99, where Athena, in the guise of Mentes, wonders whether he is the prisoner of men who are chalepoi, agrioi ("harsh," "brutish"), and when Odysseus himself asks what class of men the inhabitants of Cyclopia belong to: hybristai te kai agrioi or dikaioi ēe philoxenoi, "violent and brutish" or "righteous men who welcome strangers" (9.174–76). The same question recurs at 13.201–2, on Ithaca, before Odysseus recognizes that he is in fact at home, and earlier, when he lands on Phaeacia (6.120–21). See the excellent chapter on the Cyclopes in Kirk, Myth: Its Meaning and Functions in Ancient and Other Cultures (Berkeley, 1970), pp. 162–71, and also the semiological analysis by C. Calame, "Mythe grec et structures narratives, Le Mythe des Cyclopes dans l'Odyssée," Živa Antika 26 (1976), pp. 311–28.

[41] It is scarcely sufficient to say, as does Haussleiter, that "the cannibalism of the Cyclops Polyphemus seems on the whole to be an isolated case" (Vegetarismus, p. 23n. 2). The incident deserves more than a mere footnote.

humans he eats he does not cook as we might expect. He devours them raw, like a lion: "entrails, flesh, bones, marrow—he left nothing" (9.190–92, 234, 292–93).[42] Equally, he performs none of the actions characteristic of a sacrificial meal, for example the setting aside of the bones for the gods; and in any case the relations of these golden-age cannibals with the gods are fundamentally ambiguous. Homer stresses both that the Cyclopes trust in the gods (*pepoithotes athanatoisin*; 9.107)—which allows them not to plow or sow; and Odysseus will later have cause to rue the kinship of Polyphemus and Poseidon (1.68–73)—and that Polyphemus treats appeals in the name of Zeus Xenios [who protects strangers and guests] with total indifference: "The Cyclopes have no regard for Zeus who bears the aegis, nor for the blessed gods" (9.275–76). This detail bears a little further attention. The author of the *Iliad* seems to know of good Cyclopes, the *abioi* (without food), who milk mares and live on the milk, and are the "most just of men" (*Il.* 13.5–6). These men, now called *gabioi*, reappear as Scythians in Aeschylus's *Prometheus Unbound* (F 196 Nauck²).[43] They too are "the most just of men and the most generous to strangers. They possess neither the plow nor the hoe, which break the earth and score the plowland. Their furrows seed themselves [*autosporoi guai*] and give men food which never fails." Later, Homer's literary heirs elaborated the theme of the Cyclopes' way of life as part of the picture of the "noble savage,"[44] but the inheritance was not solely literary. When Ephorus (*FGrH* 70 F 42) contrasted two types of Scythians—actually referring to Homer's *abioi*—one of them cannibal, the other vegetarian ("they reject [all] living things"),[45] he was rationalizing and locating geographically a mythical opposition that is also an equivalent. The vegetarian is no less inhuman than the cannibal.[46]

The island of Aeolus offers us another type of the nonhuman that is no less classic. The details are worth lingering upon for a moment. It is a "floating island" with bronze walls. There is naturally no cultivated land, although there is a polis, in perpetual banquet, but the feast is not sacrificial, and the bull in whose hide the winds are imprisoned is not offered to the gods (*Od.* 10.3–19). Of course it is incest that is the oddest thing about

---

[42] These and other details have been well stressed by Page, who compares Homer's Cyclops with the Cyclopes in folklore: *The Homeric Odyssey* (Oxford, 1955), pp. 1–20.

[43] Quoted by Lovejoy and Boas, *Primitivism* (above, note 12), p. 315. On the *abioi, gabioi,* or *hippomologoi,* see also Nicolaus of Damascus, *Die Fragmente der griechischen Historiker,* ed. F. Jacoby (Leiden, 1923–), 90 F 104.

[44] The main texts are collected by Lovejoy and Boas, 304, 358, 411. The most curious of them is doubtless the speech Plutarch puts in the mouth of one of Odysseus's companions who was turned into a pig on Circe's island. Having tasted both human and animal existence, he praises the "life of the Cyclopes," comparing Polyphemus's rich earth with the thin soil of Ithaca (*Gryllus* 986f–87a).

[45] Note also the *androphagoi* (man-eaters) in Herodotus 4.18, who live on the edge of the desert and are themselves at the limits of the human.

[46] See p. 36 above. In the *Iliad,* when Achilles and Hecuba reach extremes of grief and anger, they fantasize about eating their enemies: 22. 347; 24.212–13.

Aeolus's island: there is no exchange of women. The six daughters of Aeolus and his wife are married to their brothers (10.6–7). This is a closed world, where one banquets by day and sleeps at night (10.10–12). It is not a human *oikos*.

The Laestrygones look in some ways like another version of the Cyclopes, although the metaphor here is not hunting but fishing—they harpoon the Greeks like tuna fish and then eat them (10.115–16, 121–24). On Circe's island, nature presents itself at first as a hunting-park and Odysseus kills an enormous stag (10.168: *deinoio pelōriou*; 10.171: *mega thērion*; cf. 180).[47] Nonhumanity is here revealed in two forms, that of divinity and that of bestiality. The latter is itself twofold: Circe's victims are changed into wild animals, lions, and wolves, which nevertheless behave like domestic dogs (10.212–19). Circe has a drug added to the bread[48] served to Odysseus's companions, which turns them into pigs, although they retain their memory (10.239–43). Odysseus escapes this fate by taking with him a plant, the famous *moly*, which itself perfectly symbolizes the theme of reversal: "Its root is black, its flower the color of milk" (10.304).[49] Whereas Odysseus's companions regain their shape, the men who had been turned into wild animals do not. The episode thus contains a clear hierarchy: men—domestic animals—wild animals. This last category has no connection with humanity and cannot be restored to it even by magical means.[50]

The Cimmerians, whose land borders on the country of the dead, are nonhuman, in spite of possessing a demos and a polis, in that they never behold the sun, just like the dead (11.14–19). The Sirens are a fiercer version of the Lotus-Eaters. To surrender to their seduction means never to return home (12.41–45), but, like the Lotus-Eaters, they can be foiled. These are the only two of Odysseus's passages that he endures without harm. But if the Cyclops is to humanity what the raw is to the cooked, the Sirens belong to the rotten: their victims' corpses rot uneaten in the meadow (12.45–46).[51]

The episode of the herds of the sun, heralded in advance at the beginning of the poem (1.8–9), merits closer attention. The cattle and sheep are immortal, that is, they do not share the condition of the animals humans use

[47] On Circe herself, see C. Segal, "Circean Temptations," *Transactions of the American Philological Association* 99 (1968), pp. 419–42.

[48] There is no reason to alter the *sitōi* of the manuscripts at line 235.

[49] In line 287 Hermes simply says to Odysseus that if he "carries this excellent remedy," *tode pharmakon esthlon echōn*, he will be safe. It is then not a charm to be used but a talismanic object.

[50] It is Hermes, the god closest to humankind, who gives Odysseus the *moly*, and it is to Hermes that Eumaeus sacrifices the pig (14.435).

[51] Cf. L. Kahn, "Ulysse, la Ruse et la Mort," *Critique* 393 (1980), pp. 116–34. For an analysis of the Sirens' song as a critical reading of the *Iliad* by the poet of the *Odyssey*, see P. Pucci, "The Song of the Sirens" [this volume, pp. 191–99]. The grisly depiction of the situation on their island is Circe's, but when Odysseus himself tells the story, the skeletons have disappeared and the meadow is covered with flowers (12.159).

for farm-work and sacrifice. Just as Calypso and Circe appear to be human, and just as the dead can pass as beings of flesh and blood at first sight, the herds of the sun appear domestic: they are protected only by the prohibition against sacrificing them. While Odysseus and his companions still have bread and wine, they respect the interdict (12.327–29), but with their supplies exhausted they must make a choice, between wild nature—to hunt and fish (the legitimate alternative, which Odysseus chooses: 12.330–32)—and the forbidden herds, which involves the sacrifice, the classification as "domestic," of animals that they have to capture, to bring in from the wild. This latter is the choice of Odysseus's companions (12.343–65). We should note how Homer emphasizes the sacrificers' lack of the essential requisites for proper sacrifice: the barleycorns (*oulai* or *oulochytai*) for sprinkling on the animal before its throat is cut are replaced by oak leaves (12.357–58),[52] the "natural" substituted for the "cultural"; the wine for the libations is similarly replaced by water (12.362–63).[53] The manner in which they perform the sacrifice itself also renders it an anti-sacrifice, and later, the flesh, both raw and cooked, begins to groan (12.395–96). But of course: these herds are immortal; the human share of the sacrifice is the meat of the dead animal, the remainder passing to the gods. The herds of the sun are utterly unsuitable for sacrifice, and the companions of Odysseus do not escape unpunished for their sacrilege.[54]

The last stage of the hero's travels in the land of myth—he is now quite alone—sees him on Calypso's island, the navel of the sea (1.50). Here he is offered the possibility of becoming immortal, by marrying the goddess (5.135–36; 23.335–36). Now the point of this, as I have said, is that on Calypso's island the normal means of communication between men and gods, sacrifice, is unknown. Calypso can indeed dream of a code-breaking

---

[52] See Eustathius's comment on 12. 359: *kai ta hexēs tēs pollachou dēlōtheisēs thutikēs diaskeuēs* "and throughout the following description of the sacrificial preparations"; and on 357. On the role of the *oulai-oulochytai* in Homeric sacrifice, see J. Rudhardt, *Notions fondamentales de la pensée religieuse et actes constitutifs du culte dans la Grèce classique* (Geneva, 1958), p. 254.

[53] The most curious feature of this episode is that normally water is used in Homeric sacrifice to prepare for the actual killing (it is contained in the *chernibes*, "bronze vessels"; cf. again Rudhardt, *Notions fondamentales*, p. 254.) Here, however, Homer does not mention water. Instead he concentrates on the libation of wine that follows the killing. This passage was noticed by S. Eitrem (*Opferritus und Voropfer der Griecher und Römer* [Kristiania, 1915], pp. 278–80), who believed that it presented evidence for a rite more ancient than blood sacrifice, as did the scattering of leaves attested in some funeral rituals: "They [Odysseus's companions] knew that in a previous period or in other places, the form had been used." Of course, when explained [!] in this way, the text loses all significance. Ziehen, by contrast, saw it as "an idea of the poet's, influenced by the situation" ("Opfer," *Pauly-Wissowa*, vol. 18.1 [1939], c. 582).

[54] In Herodotus, the legendary Ethiopians, who in the *Odyssey* feast with Poseidon, enjoy food that is the exact opposite of Odysseus's companions' sacrilegious feast. On a plain outside their city, the earth itself supplies them directly with the "Table of the Sun"—the boiled flesh of domestic animals (3.18). With their scented fountain of youth (3.23), the "long-lived Ethiopians" are scarcely mortal. Even their corpses do not smell unpleasant (3.24). In relation to the sun, they are guests, not utter strangers like Odysseus's companions.

union, but she herself recalls earlier attempts that ended disastrously: Eos (Dawn) and the hunter Orion and Demeter and the farmer Iasion (5.121–28). And although the ancient allegorists understood the island as a symbol of the body, of the matter from which man's soul must free itself,[55] Homer's text scarcely supports such a reading. When he quits Calypso, Odysseus is deliberately choosing the human way over all that is nonhuman.[56]

In contrast to this world whose features I have just sketched, Ithaca, Pylos, and Sparta belong undoubtedly to the "grain-giving earth."[57] Although Ithaca, the "island of goats," is unable to support horses like Sparta (4.605–6), it is nevertheless a grain-producing land, and a land where the vine grows: "It has grain and wine in quantity beyond telling, rain in all seasons and heavy dews, a good land for goats . . . a land good for cattle" (13.244–46).[58] As a famous, and archaizing, passage affirms, it is for the king that "the dark earth bears wheat and barley, and the trees are heavy with fruit; the flocks bear without fail; the friendly sea brings forth fish under his good rule, and the people thrive under him" (19.111–14).[59] Odysseus's wheat, barley, wine, and livestock are, no less than Penelope, the prize in his dispute with the Suitors. To return to Ithaca is thus to return to a land of grain. But Ithaca is not sufficiently land-locked: it is not here that Odysseus will one day meet death "far from the sea"; he will have to go beyond Ithaca, pressing on inland until someone mistakes an oar for a winnowing-shovel (11.127–28; 23.274–75).[60] There a threefold sacrifice to Poseidon will call a halt to his wanderings, and stability will prevail over movement.

Nor do I need to stress that Pylos and Sparta are corn-raising and stock-breeding countries (3.495; 4.41, 602–4, etc). But this fact does not make the three different places all of a kind. Pylos is the land of perpetual sacrifice, the model of a religious country: Nestor is sacrificing to Poseidon when Telemachus makes his appearance—all the ritual details are mentioned (3.5–9)—and a little later it is Athena's turn (3.380–84, 418–63).[61]

---

[55] Cf. F. Buffière, *Les Mythes d'Homère et la pensée grecque* (Paris, 1956), pp. 461ff.

[56] Cf. Segal, "Phaecians" (above, note 22).

[57] The same applies to other countries that receive simply a bare mention. One of them, Syros, from which Eumaeus comes, presents a particular problem. It certainly produces corn and wine (15.406), but there is no illness or hunger there, and death comes without pain (407–11). It lies "where the sun sets" (404) and cannot therefore be the Aegean island of the same name. (I am grateful to F. Hartog for bringing this point to my notice.) I cannot here discuss the problem of the mysterious "Taphians."

[58] For corn, see also 13.354; 20.106–10 (mills); for cows, 17.181. Odysseus also owns cows on Cephallenia (20.209–10).

[59] On this text, which suggests a conception of kingship very archaic even in Homer's day, see M. I. Finley, *The World of Odysseus* (New York, 1965), pp. 97–98.

[60] See W. F. Hansen, "Odysseus' Last Journey," *Quaderni Urbinati di cultura classica* 24 (1977), pp. 27–48.

[61] Note the details: barley and lustral water, 3.440–47; the ritual cry of women, 450–52; cf. also 15.222–23.

At Sparta things are a little different, and we find features belonging to the world of myth. Menelaus's palace is different from Odysseus's but like that of Alcinous; with its decoration of ivory and amber, it is a residence worthy of Zeus (compare 4.71–75 and 7.86–90). At Sparta, as on Scheria, there are objects made by Hephaistos (4.615–19; 15.113—19; 7.91–94). Sacrifice at Sparta is retrospective: Menelaus mentions a hecatomb he had to make during the journey when he learned that Odysseus was on Calypso's island, which thus connects with the world of myth (4.352–53, 472–74, 477–79, 581–83). Again, unlike Odysseus's, Menelaus's destiny is not death, but that other golden age, the Elysian Fields (4.561–69).[62] And there is another respect in which Pylos and Sparta contrast with Ithaca: they are orderly kingdoms, where the sovereign and his wife are present, where the treasure-house is not looted, and where the ordinary rules of social life are respected. When Telemachus arrives at Sparta, Menelaus is celebrating the marriage of his son (4.3–14). In contrast, on Ithaca society is in crisis: the three generations of the royal family are represented by an old man (whose exclusion from the throne becomes slightly mysterious when we compare him with Nestor), a woman, and an adolescent youth, who is portrayed as slightly backward (1.296–97).[63] A society upside down, a society in a crisis symbolized by the revolt of the *kouroi*, the young aristocrats, and waiting for the reestablishment of order.

Sacrifice here turns out to be both the sign of the crisis and the means of its resolution. Who makes sacrifice on Ithaca? If our sole criterion is the use of the words *hiereuō* and *spendō* and related terms, the answer is everyone—both the Suitors and Odysseus and his followers.[64] But if we examine the texts in which sacrifice is specifically addressed to the gods, we find that the Suitors do not sacrifice. More precisely, one of them does suggest a libation to the gods, but this is Amphinomus, the one suitor whom Odysseus attempts to exclude from the coming massacre.[65] Antinous suggests a sacrifice to Apollo according to the rules, with the thighs burnt, but he is unable to fulfill his promise.[66] In contrast, on Odysseus's side, sacrifice, either retrospective or immediate, is perpetual. Eumaeus's piety is stressed: "The swineherd did not forget the immortals; he had a good heart" (14.420–

[62] In contrast, Odysseus says, "I am not a god" (16.187).

[63] Cf. Finley's remarks, *World of Odysseus* (above, note 59), p. 76. Despite the nineteenth-century arguments recently revived by K. Hirvonen (*Matriarchal Survivals and Certain Trends in Homer's Female Characters* [Helsinki, 1968], pp. 135–62), there is nothing in the treatment of Penelope to justify a reference to matriarchy, or even "traces" of it. Penelope's "special position" is to be explained simply by the absence of Odysseus.

[64] See 2.56; 14.74; 16.454; 17.181; 17.600 [*hiera*]; 20.3; 20.250–53.

[65] See 18.414–28. Amphinomus is killed at 22.89–94; the hecatomb of 20.276–83 is anonymously offered, but clearly not by the suitors.

[66] Leiodes, the suitor's *thyoskoos*, is killed by Odysseus at 22.310–29, making it clear that the sacrifices performed in the past on the suitors' behalf have not been accepted. A *thyoskoos* is a seer; cf. J. Casabona, *Recherches sur le vocabulaire des sacrifices* (Aix-Gap, 1966), pp. 118–19.

21).[67] The comparison certainly suggests that we have to allow that *hiereuō* sometimes has a meaning that is not specifically religious.[68] More importantly, sacrifice is a double criterion in the *Odyssey*: of humanity, between humans and nonhumans; and of social and moral values, between human beings.

But there is in the human world of Ithaca at least one place directly connected with the world of the myths—the complex consisting of the harbor of Phorcys, named after Cyclops's own grandfather (1.71–72; 13.96–97),[69] and the cave sacred to the Nymphs, the divinities of nature and of water. This cave has two entrances, one for the gods and the other for mortals (13.109–12). Appropriately enough, just near it is a sacred olive tree, under which Athena speaks to Odysseus (13.122, 372), and it is here that the Phaeacians leave Odysseus and his treasures.

Charles Segal has observed that the Phaeacians are "between the two worlds": they are placed at the intersection of the world of the tales and the "real" world, and their main function in the poem is to transport Odysseus from the one to the other.[70] When Odysseus comes ashore in Phaeacia, naked, after completing, or almost completing, his return journey home "without the help of gods or mortal humans" (5.32),[71] he takes shelter under an olive tree. But this olive tree is remarkable: it is double, *ho men phyliēs, ho d'elaiēs*, both wild and grafted, oleaster and olive (5.477).[72] The very land of Scheria is double, comparable at once both with Ithaca, Pylos, and Sparta and with the lands of the stories. Phaeacia contains all the characteristic elements of a Greek settlement in the age of colonization, physically framed as it is by the "shadowy peaks" that can be seen from afar (5.279–80). It has arable land distributed by a founder (*edassat' arouras*; 6.10).[73] Its fields are beyond doubt the "works of humans": *agrous . . . kai*

[67] See also 2.423–33 (Telemachus); 4.761–67 (Penelope); 14.445–48 (Eumaeus); 18.151 (Odysseus); 19.198 (Odysseus's "false" story); 1.60–62; 4.762–64; 17.241–43 (Odysseus's past sacrifices); 19.397–98 (list of sacrifices offered by Autolycus, the grandfather of Odysseus). And we should remember the sacrifices promised by Odysseus as well.

[68] Casabona observes, "the idea of 'banquet' becomes predominant"—which is quite an understatement (*Sacrifices* [above, note 66], p. 23).

[69] Cf. Segal, "Phaeacians" (above, note 22), p. 48.

[70] Cf. Segal, "Phaeacians" (above, note 22), p. 17, and also p. 27: "The Phaeacians . . . while the instrument of Odysseus' return to the world of reality, are also the last afterglow of the fantasy realm he is leaving." I believe that the whole of Segal's case should be accepted, but without the "symbolist" and psychological language he sometimes employs. See also Segal's article "Transition and Ritual in Odysseus' Return," *La Parola del passato* 116 (1967), pp. 321–42; H. W. Clarke, *The Art of the Odyssey* (Englewood Cliffs, N.J., 1967), pp. 52–56.

[71] Nonetheless he was helped by Ino-Leucothea and the river god of Phaeacia (5.333–53, 445–53).

[72] The two trees share the same trunk. The ancient world unanimously understood *phyliē* as "wild olive" (see Richter, *Landwirtschaft*, p. 135). It is only in the modern world that a few critics have thought that a myrtle was intended (Pease, "Ölbaum," in *Pauly-Wissowa*, vol. 17.2 [1937], c. 2006).

[73] Much has been made of this line by historians of colonization; see D. Asheri, *Distribuziom di terre nell' antica Grecia. Memorie dell' Accademia delle scienze di Torino* (Turin, 1966), p. 5.

erg' anthrōpōn, "fields and human tillage" (6.259)—exactly what Odysseus has looked for in vain in all his travels. It has a fortified citadel distinct from the fields: *polis kai gaia* (6.177, 191; also 6.3: *dēmon te polin te*). The country has wine, oil, and corn in abundance: Alcinous has a flourishing vineyard of his own (6.77–79, 99, 215, 259, 293; cf. 7.122–26). In sum, the Phaeacians are human just like other humans, and they "know the cities and rich fields of all men" (8.560–61). When Odysseus lands in Phaeacia, he is returning to humanity. As he draws near to Nausicaa, he is likened to a lion that descends from the hills and kills livestock or deer, but when he leaves Phaeacia to return to Ithaca, he is likened to a tired plowman returning home (6.130–33; 13. 31–35).

However, at the same time Phaeacia is sharply contrasted with Ithaca. There are no seasons in Alcinous's magic garden (7.113–32).[74] The west wind blows there perpetually, and the vine bears blossom and unripe and ripened grapes simultaneously. In effect, it is no ordinary orchard, but a golden-age land in the heart of Phaeacia. By contrast, Laertes' garden is normal: "each vine had its own time to be harvested, and the clusters of grapes were of every color, as the seasons of Zeus caused them to change" 24.342–44).[75] On the one hand, the age of Cronos; on the other, the age

[74] It must be clear that we cannot excise this famous description from the *Odyssey* on the staggeringly inadequate grounds that the "solid but narrow precincts" of the Mycenaean cities could never have had "room within their walls for the four acres of this orchard, double vineyard and kitchen-garden" (V. Bérard, in *Introduction à l' Odyssée*, vol. 1 [Paris, 1924], p. 186). It is instructive to note that the passage's utopian and mythical character was clearly recognized in antiquity; for example, Iamboulos's Hellenistic Utopia quotes lines 7.120–21 (Diodorus Siculus 2.56). See A. Motte, *Prairies* (above, note 37), p. 121.

[75] Cf. Segal, "Phaeacians" (above, note 22), p. 47. Here there is a difficulty that I feel incapable of resolving. All the comparisons made in the present article tend, it seems to me, to support those who accept at least an overall "architect"—what Kirk calls a "monumental composer"—who gave the Homeric poems their present structure (Kirk, *The Songs of Homer* [Cambridge, 1962], pp. 159–270; to be supplemented by A. Parry, "Have We Homer's *Iliad?*" *Yale Classical Studies* 20 [1966], pp. 175–216). This is also my position. But it must be admitted that there are many anomalies, especially in the language, in book 24, and that it presents special problems (see Page, *Homeric Odyssey* [above, note 42], pp. 101–36—an extreme view— and Kirk, *Songs*, pp. 248–51). We also know that the Hellenistic critics Aristarchus of Samos and Aristophanes of Byzantium regarded the *Odyssey* as ending at line 296 of book 23. If, for the sake of argument, we accept these criticisms as valid, does it follow necessarily that the parallel drawn between book 7 and book 24 is nonsense? For those who practice structural analysis on the basis of linguistic criteria alone, the question has little meaning; and indeed it is difficult to see why they should not "structure" a complex composed of the *Iliad*, the *Mahabharata*, and *Paradise Lost*. . . . At this point the historian must make a graceful exit. But quite a different approach is possible. The work of Propp, and his immediate and later followers, suggests that, within a common cultural area, a complex of stories may occupy a variety of different structural positions (Propp, *Morphology of the Folklore* [Austin, TX, 1968]; Brémond, "Le Message narratif," *Communications* 4 [1964] and "Postérité américaine de Propp," *Communications* 11 [1968]; and the whole of *Communications* 8 [1966]). It seems clear to me that, in the *Odyssey*, the motif of the golden-age garden is parallel to that of the garden cultivated by humans, just as the motif of the hospitable girl is parallel to that of the girl who prepares visitors for death. I also believe that thematic analysis of the epic narrative of the kind

of Zeus.[76] The contrast can be developed. The dogs guarding Alcinous's house and the creations of Hephaistos in gold and silver are immortal and naturally possess eternal youth; but everyone remembers the story of the dog Argo, whose life is commensurate with the period of Odysseus's absence (7.91–94; 17.290–327).[77]

And what of sacrifices here? They are performed in Phaeacia much as they are at Pylos or on Ithaca. "We shall offer choice victims to the gods," declares Alcinous (7.191; cf. 7.180–81). Before Odysseus's departure an ox is sacrificed in the proper manner (13.24–27; cf. 50–56, libations to Zeus). And when the Phaeacians are threatened with destruction by Poseidon and Zeus combined, their fate turns on the result of the sacrifice that Alcinous decides to offer them: "and they prepared the bulls" (*hetoimassanto de taurous*; 13.184). This is the last act of the Phaeacians recounted in the *Odyssey*, and we never discover their fate—the only case of a fate left in the balance. Yet, even here, the Phaeacians are not like other humans. Alcinous can say; "When we sacrifice our magnificent hecatombs to the gods, they come and sit by us and eat with us" (7.201–3).[78] That sort of sharing has nothing in common with normal sacrifice, which, in contrast, separates men from the gods.[79] The Phaeacians are of course human: Alcinous and Odysseus remind each other of their mortality (7.196–98; 13.59–62), and the Phaeacians'

---

practiced by the followers of Milman Parry leads in the end in the same direction (e.g., A. B. Lord, *The Singer of Tales* [Cambridge, MA, 1960], esp. pp. 68–98), by showing that an ancient theme—and it is hard to imagine that the long-awaited meeting between Odysseus and Laertes could be anything but an ancient theme—may have acquired a fixed form only relatively late. These two approaches would benefit from mutual acquaintance. For these reasons, I do not believe that an *Odyssey* that is partially composite, historically speaking, cannot also be, from a structuralist point of view, homogeneous, although I admit that a strict proof has yet to be offered.

[76] More accurately, these are the equivalents to those states to which Hesiod and his successors gave the names "age of Cronos" and "age of Zeus"; for of course the land of the Cyclopes is also tended by Zeus (9.111, 358). Homer's Cronos is the father of Zeus and is imprisoned in Tartarus (*Il.* 8.478–81).

[77] Eumaeus too has dogs that are quite real and that bark: 14.21–22.

[78] That is, the Phaeacians have the same privileges as the legendary Ethiopians (1.23–26); see also 6.203–5: "We are very dear to the immortals; we live in seclusion in the midst of the swelling sea, at the edge of the world [*eschatoi*], and no mortals visit us"; see S. Eitrem, "Phaiaker," *Pauly-Wissowa*, vol. 19, c. 1523. The familiarity with the gods that is symbolized by shared feasts is correlated with isolation from mortals. When Athena takes part in the first sacrifice offered by Nestor and his sons (3.41–44), she does so in disguise [as Mentor], whereas Alcinous stresses the fact that among the Phaeacians the gods do not assume disguise: *ou ti katakryptousin* (7.205); they eat the sacrificial meal in common (7.203). Similarly, Poseidon is present at the Ethiopians' feast (*daiti parēmenos*; 1.26). It might seem as though Athena does the same in Nestor's palace (*ēlthe es . . . daita*, "she came to the feast; 3.420); but after she has revealed herself by turning into a bird (3.371–72), she takes her share as an invisible divinity (3.435–36). Nestor and Telemachus do not therefore enjoy the same privilege as do the Phaeacians.

[79] On the contrary, in a Hesiodic fragment (F1 in R. Merkelbach and M. L. West, *Fragmenta Hesiodea*, [Oxford, 1969]), sharing meals characterizes relations between mortals and gods prior to the establishment of sacrifice.

last appearance in the poem clearly shows them facing the precariousness of the human condition, but they are also *ankhitheoi*, "relatives of the gods"— nor merely a polite epithet, for Homer uses it twice only, and both times of them (5.35; 19.279). They were once neighbors of the Cyclopes and suffered from their attacks until Nausithoos set them "apart from men who eat bread" (*hekas andrōn alphēstaōn*; 6.4–8); indeed, in one sense they are the complete reverse of the Cyclopes.[80] All their human virtues, the practice of hospitality,[81] piety, the arts of feasting and gift-giving, are the inverse of Cyclopean barbarism. Moreover, the present disjuncture and previous proximity of the Phaeacians and the Cyclopes are signs of a more subtle relation: "We are intimates [of the gods]," says Alcinous, "like the Cyclopes and the savage tribes of the Giants" (*hōsper Kyklōpes te kai agria phyla Gigantōn*; 7.205–6)—those same Giants whom the Laestrygones are said to resemble (10.120). Proximity and kinship: surely an invitation to search in Phaeacia for both the pattern of the world of fantasy and its reverse.

After landing in Alcinous's country, Odysseus meets a girl washing clothes, who invites him to come and meet her father and mother (7.290– 307). He had met another girl, elsewhere, drawing water from a spring, who gave him a similar invitation, but she was the daughter of the king of the Laestrygones. Both in the cannibal and in the hospitable kingdom Odysseus meets the queen before he meets the king (10.105–15; 7.139– 54; cf. 7.53–55). And is Nausicaa a girl or a goddess? A cliché, of course; but we must realize that she is a girl who looks like a goddess, while Circe and Calypso were goddesses who looked like girls (6.16, 66–67, 102–9; 7.291; 8.457).[82] Alcinous, and very discreetly Nausicaa herself, entertain ideas of her marriage to Odysseus, parallel to the goddesses' more energetically prosecuted plans. The seductive Sirens sing like bards of the Trojan War (12.184–91), just like Demodocus at the court of Alcinous, who brings tears to Odysseus's eyes (8.499–531). The first represent the perilous, Demodocus the positive, aspect of poetry.[83]

---

[80] Cf. Segal, "Phaeacians" (above, note 22), p. 33. J. Strauss Clay, "Goat Island: *Od.* 9.116– 141," in *Classical Quarterly* 30(1980), 261–64, makes the ingenious suggestion that the island that is home to the Phaeacians is none other than the island of goats, near that of the Cyclopes; she develops this theme of similarity between the two peoples in *The Wrath of Athena* (Princeton, 1983), 125–32.

[81] The hospitality, though, is fairly ambiguous, for Athena, in disguise, warns Odysseus: "The people here do not welcome strangers or give a friendly reception to visitors from abroad" (7.23–33). Nothing in what follows justifies the warning, of course, but Nausicaa has just said that few mortals visit them (6.205); and Athena covers Odysseus with a mist "in case one of the proud Phaeacians should cross his path and demand to know his name" (7.14–17). Peeping through the motif of the Phaeacians' hospitality is the image of a Phaeacia comparable to the land of the Cyclopes.

[82] One sees here the problem that, in the Hesiodic poems, will belong to Pandora—the first woman at one and the same time resembles a young girl and looks like the goddesses; cf. N. Loraux, "Race des femmes" (above, note 8), pp. 45–49.

[83] Cf. M. Detienne, *Les Maîtres de vérité dans la Grèce archaïque* (Paris, 1967).

It will no doubt be objected that there is a limit to the number of utterly different situations a man like Odysseus can encounter. That is true, but there is one coincidence that is perhaps more than usually curious. Before meeting with his eventual carriers, the Phaeacians, Odysseus encounters another, who brought him to the neighborhood of Ithaca—Aeolus, master of the winds (10.21), who spends his time, like the Phaeacians, in feasting. In the course of both "returns" Odysseus falls asleep; disastrously after his sojourn with Aeolus, fortunately after Scheria (10.23–55; 13.78–92).[84] Now it will be recalled that Aeolus's family practice incest, and, if we are to accept the lines that introduce the genealogy of Alcinous and Arete, the same is true of the Phaeacian royal couple: "Arete [the well adapted] is the name she is called, and she comes of the same parents as in fact produced the king Alcinous" (7.54–55; tr. Lattimore, slightly altered). The rest of the text as we have it (55–56) corrects the inevitable impression by claiming that Arete is not Alcinous's sister but his niece; but in this case there is some justification for invoking the hypothesis of interpolation.[85]

All the same, the "mythical" aspect of Scheria is counterbalanced by what I have termed the "real" world. I have already shown this for land and sacrifice, but the point can be extended to its entire social organization. The social institutions of Pylos, of Sparta, and of Ithaca particularly, are to be found on Scheria,[86] and the details of palace organization are identical in Ithaca and Alcinous's court: is it an "accident" that there are fifty servants in Alcinous's house, and the same number in Odysseus's (22.421–22; 7.103), and the same with everything else?[87] But these categories do not produce identical societies. For example, although there is at least one "angry young

[84] On the theme of sleep in the *Odyssey*, see C. Segal, "Transition and Ritual" (above, note 70), pp. 324–29.

[85] A scholiast notes that "Hesiod" regarded Alcinous and Arete as brother and sister (cf. scholion on *Od.* 7.54 [I, p. 325 Dindorf] = Hesiod F222 Merkelbach-West [above, n.79]); cf. also Eustathius on 7.64 [p. 1567]. This leaves two possible solutions: to agree with what the scholiast says, *touto machetai tois hexēs*, "this conflicts with what follows," and then—as has been done since the time of Kirchoff, *Die Composition der Odyssee* (Berlin, 1869), pp. 54–56— regard as interpolated lines 56–68 and 146 (where Arete is called the daughter of Rhexenor), or to accept that the poet gave the royal couple the appearance of incest, which was later corrected, so as to draw a parallel between Aeolus and Alcinous (see Germain, *Genèse* [above, note 22], p. 293).

[86] Most obviously, of course, the king and queen: the same formulas are used to describe the royal couples' retirement for the night at Pylos and Sparta, and on Scheria; 3.402–3; 4.304–5; 7.346–47.

[87] For example, there is a housekeeper on Scheria (7.166, 175; 8.449), as on Ithaca (17.94) and at Pylos (3.392); a nurse (7.7–12) as on Ithaca (19.353–56, 482–83); and a bard (8.262 ff.) also as on Ithaca (22.330–31). The Phaeacian episode and the scenes on Ithaca have often been compared: note, for example, the arguments, so curiously similar despite the time lapse of sixty-five years and the difference in the explanations offered (a mass of "interpolation" against oral composition) of Eitrem, *Die Phaiakenepisode in der Odyssee*, Videnskapsselskapets Skrifter: Hist.-Filos. Kl. no. 2:1 (Kristiania, 1904) and M. Lang, "Homer and Oral Technique," *Hesperia* 38 (1969), pp. 159–68.

man" on Scheria, Euryalus, who insults Odysseus, he is compelled to apologize (8.131–415, esp. 396–415). One could hardly find a swineherd, a cowman, or a goatherd in Phaeacia, and there would be no chance of finding on Ithaca those professional sailors who steer infallibly without the aid of pilots (7.318–28; 8.555–63, 566; 16.227–31; cf. 16.322–27). Ithaca is an island whose men once went in ships, but it is in no sense a country of sailors, for all that Odysseus has acquired the necessary skill. Once back in harbor, he puts the equipment of his ship to purely static use—as when the ship's cable is used to hang the faithless servant girls (22.465–73).

Yet Phaeacia is at once an ideal and an impossible society: Homer, at the height of the Dark Age crisis of monarchy, pictures a king who can restore peace, who rules over twelve obedient vassals (8.390–91), over docile sons, over a wife whose role, despite claims to the contrary, is limited to intercession,[88] and over old men whose sole function is to give advice (7.155–66), and who are neither discarded like Laertes nor embittered like Aegyptius.[89] In this sense Alcinous's palace constitutes an ideal *oikos*, and yet it is impossible, as I have stressed. The Phaeacians are ignorant of physical struggle (8.246) and of political struggle as well: the stormy *agora* (political assembly) of Ithaca (2.6–336) should be compared with the agora in Phaeacia (8.24–49). On Ithaca, even a youth as inexperienced as Telemachus earns the label *hypsagorēs*, "assembly loudmouth" (1.385, 2.85); and there can be little doubt that we have here a direct glimpse of historical reality. Both Pylos and Menelaus's Sparta, it may be argued, escape the crisis of monarchy, but both are orderly states, and the historical reality of crisis makes its appearance only when the logic of the story demands it. The crisis is on Ithaca, not necessarily everywhere in the human world.[90]

But in that case, what is the difference between Phaeacia and Pylos or Sparta? The answer lies unhesitatingly in the land-based character of the latter. And this is the paradox: at the very moment when a few Greek cities were embarking on the maritime adventure of colonization in the west, the poet of the *Odyssey* describes a city of sailors as something wildly utopian. In a sense, what Odysseus would like to restore on Ithaca is a system comparable to that existing among the Phaeacians, but he cannot succeed. He can never reproduce the perpetual feasting of the people of Scheria, with or without the gods' participation; in Book 24 he must seek a reconciliation with the families of the slaughtered suitors. The Phaeacians have cast him back into the human world; their departure causes the images of antihumanity that he encountered at every stage of his travels to vanish. Scheria may be the first utopia in Greek literature,[91] but we have not yet reached the

---

[88] As will be seen by reading 7.146 ff. free of the kind of preconceptions about matriarchy such as found in Lang, "Oral Technique" (above, note 87), pp. 159–68.

[89] Compare Echeneus's speech with that of old Aegyptius, 2.25–34.

[90] A point made to me by M. I. Finley.

[91] Cf. M. I. Finley, *World of Odysseus* (above, note 59), pp. 100–102, 156.

point at which political utopias are to be distinguished from images of the golden age.[92] For the age of gold remains present in Phaeacia, and it is that element that distinguishes this ideal society from another representation of the perfect city—that portrayed both in peace and war by Hephaistos on the Shield of Achilles in Book 18 of the *Iliad*. Every scene here, from the ambush to the lawsuit, is taken from the "real" world: the golden age must disappear; Odysseus's journey must culminate in his return to Ithaca.[93]

[92] M. I. Finley, "Utopianism Ancient and Modern," *The Critical Spirit: Essays in Honor of Herbert Marcuse* (Boston, 1967), pp. 178–92. I fully accept the general tenor of Finley's remarks here, but it should be remembered that by the time of the later Hellenistic period, utopias used a complex mixture of archaic and millenarian myths and political images (cf. L. Gernet, "The City of the Future and the Land of the Dead," in *The Anthropology of Ancient Greece*, tr. J. Hamilton and B. Nagy [Baltimore and London, 1981]). The situation was different in the fifth century B.C.; a utopia like that of Hippodamus of Miletus (Aristotle, *Politics* 2.1267b30 ff.) cannot be explained by appeal to mythical thinking.

[93] This study has given rise to several amplifications, notably H. Foley, "'Reverse Similes' and Sex Roles in the *Odyssey*," *Arethusa* 11 (1978), pp. 7–26, and S. Saïd, "Les Crimes des prétendants, la maison d'Ulysse, et les festins de l'*Odyssée*," in *Etudes de littérature ancienne* (Paris, 1979), pp. 9–49.

Death with Two Faces

JEAN-PIERRE VERNANT
(translated by Janet Lloyd)

As PORTRAYED IN EPIC, where it occupies a central position, Greek death appears disconcerting. It has two contrary faces. The first face is a glorious one: death shines out as the ideal to which the true hero devotes his existence. With its second face, death embodies the unsayable, the unbearable; it manifests itself as a terrifying horror.

The purpose of the following discussion is to bring out the meaning of this double aspect more clearly and to indicate the necessary complementarity of the two opposed images in archaic Greek thought.

•

I.1

As we have shown elsewhere, there is a parallelism or continuity between Greek funeral rituals and epic verse. Both are directed to the same end, but the epic goes a step further than the funeral ritual. The funeral rites aim to procure for the person who has lost his life access to a new state of social existence, to transform the absence of the lost person into a more or less stable positive social status, that of "one of the dead." Epic goes further: through glorifying praise, indefinitely repeated, it ensures for a small minority of the chosen—who thus stand out from the ordinary mass of the deceased, defined as the crowd of "nameless ones"—the permanence of their name, their fame, and the exploits they have accomplished. In this way it completes and crowns the process that the funeral rites have already set in motion: the transformation of an individual who has ceased to be into a figure whose presence, as one of the dead, is forever a part of the existence of the group.

I.2

In comparison with other civilizations, the strategy of the Greeks with regard to death comprises two characteristic and intimately connected features. One concerns certain aspects of the personality in death, the other the various forms of social commemoration.

In his status as one of the dead, the hero is not envisaged as the representative of a family line, as a link in a continuous chain of generations, nor—for those at the summit of the social hierarchy—as the holder of a royal office or a religious priesthood. In the verses that celebrate his glory, and on the stele that marks his tomb, he is commemorated as an individual defined in personal terms by his valiant deeds; in death, he is still identified with the career that was his in life and that, in his prime, at the peak of his vitality, found its fulfillment in the "fine death" of the warrior.

For the Greeks, to exist "as an individual" meant to make oneself, and to remain, "memorable": the "individual" has escaped from anonymity, from oblivion, from being wiped out—and so from death—by means of death itself, a death that *by* allowing him access to glorification in song has made him even more present to the community, in his status as a dead hero, than the living are to one another. It is epic verse, as oral poetry, that is chiefly instrumental in maintaining his continuous presence within the group. By celebrating the exploits of the heroes of years gone by, it performs, throughout the Greek world, the function of a collective memory.

I.3

First through commemoration in song, repeated for all to hear, and second through the funerary memorial set up for all to see, a relationship is established between a dead individual and a community of living people. This is not simply a family community, nor is it limited to the boundaries of a particular social group. In wresting the hero from oblivion, commemoration by the same token strips him of his purely private characteristics; it establishes him within the public domain, it makes him into one of the elements that form the common culture of the Greeks. In and through the epic poem, the heroes represent "the men of years gone by"; for the group as a whole, they constitute its "past." They thus form the roots of the cultural tradition that binds together the entire Greek people and in which they recognize themselves and each other, because it is only through the exploits of these departed figures that their own social existence acquires meaning, value, and continuity.

I.4

The individuality of the dead man is not connected with his psychological characteristics or with the personal aspect of him as a unique and irreplaceable being. Through his exploits, his brief life, and his heroic destiny, the dead man embodies certain "values": beauty, youth, virility, and courage. But the rigorous nature of the course of his life, his rejection of all compromise, the radical nature of his commitment, and the extreme compulsion that makes him choose death in order to win glory make him a model of "excellence" for the living and lend that excellence a luster, power, and lasting quality that no ordinary life can have. Through the exemplary nature of the figure of the hero, as he is described in epic and depicted on the stele, the vital "worldly" values of strength, beauty, youth, and ardor in combat acquire a consistency, stability, and permanence that enable them to elude the inexorable decline that is the stamp of all human things. By wresting the names of its heroes from oblivion, the social memory is really attempting to root a whole system of values in the absolute, in order to preserve it from precariousness, instability, and destruction: in short, to shelter it from time and from death.

In the relationship that is established, through the various forms of collective commemoration, between the individual with his heroic biography and the public, the Greek experience of death is transposed onto an aesthetic and ethical plane (with a "metaphysical" dimension). Just as they elaborated in mathematics the concept of space as an idea, one could also say of the Greeks that they constructed the concept of death as an idea or, to be more precise, that they undertook to socialize and civilize death—that is to say, to neutralize it—by turning it into an "ideal type" of life.

•

II.1

However, epic did not simply give the face of death the dazzling glory of the ultimate degree of existence, the brilliance of life—a life that in order to fulfill and sublimate itself must first be lost, that in order to assert its worth in perpetuity must disappear from the visible world and be transmuted into glory in commemorative poetry. In a number of ways, epic also denied the very idealization that its song had the function of establishing in its verses.

When the epic text is content to counterpose the fine death of the young warrior who has fallen as a hero in the heat of battle, in the flower of his youth, and the dreadful death of an old man slaughtered defenselessly like a beast, or when, in contrast with the wonderful corpse of the hero stretched out on the field of battle where "all is beauty," it describes a body abused and unrecognizable, disfigured, mutilated, cut into pieces, a piece of carrion left for the wild animals or rotting in the open, then the denial does not really pose any problem: two contrary forms of death lend each other confirmation and reinforcement by their mutual exclusiveness. But there are some cases where the denial, as if operating from within, calls into question the very thing that epic is celebrating in the fine death, namely the glorious destiny of the hero. At times it presents death in general and the fear that it inspires in every human being in a picture so horrible and terrifying in its realism that the price to be paid for "commemoration" seems a very high one and the ideal of "imperishable glory" is in danger of appearing a very poor bargain.

II.2

Let us begin with the most general aspect of the problem. If death did not appear in epic as the ultimate horror, if it did not assume the monstrous mask of Gorgo so as to embody all that is beyond humanity, the unsayable, the unthinkable, all that is radically other, then there would be no heroic ideal. There would be no merit in the hero confronting death, choosing it and making it his own. There can be no heroes if there are no monsters to fight and overcome. Establishing an ideal concept of death does not mean ignoring or denying its dreadful reality. On the contrary, the ideal can only be constructed to the extent that the "real" is clearly defined as being opposed to it. (The construction of an abstract and perfect mathematical space presupposes, as its condition, the depreciation of perceptible space.) Far from underestimating the reality of death, its "idealizing" takes this reality as its point of departure, depends on it, just as it is, and aims to pass beyond it by reversing the perspective and inverting the terms of the problem. How is it that life is destroyed and sinks into death? That is the common question. To this question epic adds another: How is it that certain of the dead remain forever present in the life of the living? The first question presents death as the irremediable human evil; the second presents the heroic death as the condition for glorious survival in the memory of other men. Both questions, however, concern only the living. Whether it be dreadful or glorious, real or ideal, death is the exclusive concern of those who are alive. It is the impossibility of conceiving death from the point of view of the dead that constitutes its horror, its radical strangeness, its complete otherness and that at the same time makes it possible for the living to bypass it by instituting within their social existence a constant commemoration of certain types of death. From the point of view of its function as a collective memory, epic is not composed for the dead; when it speaks of them or of death it is always addressed to the living. About death as such or about the dead among the dead, there is nothing to say. They exist on the other side of a threshold that nobody can cross without disappearing, that no word can reach without losing all meaning: in a world of night where the indiscernible reigns, a world both of silence and indistinguishable sound.

II.3

In book II of the *Odyssey*, Odysseus, having passed through the land of the Cimmerians, enveloped in night, crosses the waters of the River Ocean, the frontier of the world, and lands on the shores of Hades. Here the living hero meets the shade of the dead Achilles. This encounter brings together on the one hand the champion of endurance whose ideal, in the teeth of winds and tides, is to return safe sound to his home and, on the other, the "best of the Achaeans," the model of the heroic warrior whose memory the entire *Iliad* is devoted to exalting because he chose a brief life and through his fine death managed to achieve imperishable glory. What words do they exchange? No doubt at all is involved where Odysseus, the living man, is concerned. Having learned from the trials and endless misfortunes that he has endured, one after another, in this life, Odysseus salutes Achilles as "the happiest" of beings, the one who was honored as a god by everyone on earth and who continues, in Hades where he towers high above the others, to know nothing of misery, the common lot of all mortals. But Achilles' reply seems, at a stroke, to demolish the entire edifice the *Iliad* constructs to justify, celebrate and exalt the fine death of the hero. What Achilles says to Odysseus is, "Don't come and sing the praises of death to me in order to console me; I would rather live as the least of the servants of a poor peasant than reign as master over the innumerable masses of the dead."

Even allowing for the extent to which the *Odyssey* might stand in polemical contrast to the *Iliad* and for the way in which the characters of Odysseus and Achilles in the two works stand in opposition to one another, the fact remains that this episode truly appears to introduce within epic writing itself the most radical denial of that heroic death which the bard's poem presents as a survival in imperishable glory. But is there really any contradiction here? There would be if this glorious survival was localized in the kingdom of the dead for the Greeks, if the reward for a heroic death was entering Paradise rather than continuing to live on in the memory of living human beings. In the land of shadows, the shade of Achilles has no ear for the song of praise celebrating his exploits, no recollection to evoke and preserve the memory of himself. Achilles can only recover his senses, mind, and consciousness—his identity—during the brief moment when, having drunk the blood of the victim sacrificed by Odysseus to call up the dead, he reestablishes a kind of fleeting contact with the world of the living. Before being lost, dissolving once more into the indistinct crowd of the dead, he has just enough time, having for a moment become once again Achilles, to rejoice at the news that, among the living, his son is of the same heroic cast as his father.

The glorious survival for which Achilles gave his life and chose death is the thing that haunts the memory of Odysseus and his companions, who are convinced that there is no destiny happier than his; it haunts Neoptolemus, so anxious to equal his father; it haunts all the living—Homer's audience—who can only conceptualize their own existence, their own identity, by reference to the heroic example. But in Hades there can be no glorious survival; Hades is the land of Oblivion. How can the dead remember? Why should they? Recollection can only take place within time. The dead do not live within time, not in the fleeting time of perishable living creatures nor in the constant time of the eternal gods. For the dead, with their empty heads, without energy and swathed in shadows, there is nothing to recollect.

II.4

The episode of the *Nekuia*, one moment of which we have described here, ends with Odysseus' precipitous departure for his ships. All of a sudden the hero was seized with "green fear" at the idea that Persephone could send up to him from the depths of Hades "the Gorgon head of the terrifying monster" (II. 633–35). This head, a glimpse of which changes a person to stone, marks the limit between the dead and the living; it stands guard over the threshold, forbidding entrance to those who still belong to this world of light, this world of clear, articulated speech and recollection where every being, with its own form (its *eidos*), remains itself at least as long as it has not tipped the balance over into the other kingdom, the place of darkness, oblivion, confusion, that no words can describe.

This dreadful terror that the mask of Gorgo inspires is one that Odysseus has already experienced right at the beginning of the *Nekuia*, and he expressed it then in exactly the same terms: "green fear clutches me" (II. 43). What then overwhelmed him with alarm was not the mask of Gorgo but the monstrous otherness that can be glimpsed through it. What Odysseus was afraid to see—on the other side of the threshold, so to speak—was the dead gathering together in their own land, the swarming, indistinct mass of them, the innumerable crowd of shades who are no longer anybody and whose huge, confused, inaudible clamor has no longer anything human about it.

To call forth the dead, as Odysseus undertakes to do to question the shade of Tiresias, is to introduce order and number into their formless magma, to distinguish individuals by compelling them to fall into line, one behind the other, each one stepping forward in turn, on his own, to speak in his own name and remember.

Odysseus, the hero faithful to life, by executing a ritual of evocation that for a brief moment reintroduces the illustrious dead into the universe of the living, accomplishes the same task as the bard: when the poet, inspired by Memory, begins his song of recollection, he admits that he is incapable of telling the names and exploits of the entire obscure crowd of warriors who fell beneath the walls of Troy. From among this anonymous faceless mass, he selects and concentrates on the exemplary figures of a small number of the chosen. In the same way Odysseus, wielding his sword, wards off the immense crowd of insubstantial shades from the blood of the victim and only allows it to be drunk by those whom he recognizes because their names, saved from oblivion, have survived in epic tradition.

The episode of the *Nekuia* does not contradict the ideal of the heroic death, the fine death. It strengthens and completes it. The terrifying world of death is a world of confusion, chaos, unintelligibility, where nothing and nobody can exist anymore. The only values that exist are the values of life, the only reality that of the living. If Achilles chooses to die young, it is not that he values death above life. On the contrary, he cannot accept sinking, like just anybody, into the obscurity of oblivion, merging into the indistinct mass of "nameless ones." He wants to continue forever in the world of the living, to survive in their midst, within them, and remain there as himself, distinct from any other, through the indestructible memory of his name and his renown.

The Greek ideal concept of death is this heroic attempt to push away as far as possible, beyond that uncrossable threshold, the horror of chaos, the horror of what has no form and no meaning, and to affirm in the face of and despite everything, the social permanence of this human individuality that must, by its very nature, be destroyed and disappear.

The Adventures in the *Odyssey*

KARL REINHARDT
(translated by Harriet I. Flower)

Origins

When stories about wonders become clever, and when cultures begin to be reflected in fairy tales, possibilities develop for a particular kind of interplay with, as it were, an exchange of roles between, older and newer stories. In this process the more recent elements do not replace the older ones but rather absorb them into their own world. There they function as a balance and contrast and as an element of transcendence, which is an essential part of any art form. I suppose it is possible to see such an interplay with fairy tales and novellas in nearly all collections of stories from times of rich cultural growth, but especially in those cases where the storytellers feel that irony is an essential element in their tales.

Let us consider as an example the story of Aladdin and his magic lamp, a story taken from and contemporary with the *1,001 Nights*. How crude the miracles in this story are. How crude is the way in which the terrifying, omnipotent spirits are conjured up, slaves of anyone who owns the lamp and the ring. How primitive and almost clumsy is the magic that grants a series of ever more impossible wishes, until the owner of the lamp himself succumbs to its enchantment. How full this story is of primitive belief in magic, the presence of spirits and joy in fantasy and the unreal. If it were simply a question of these elements in the story, one would have to think of this story as having originated in very ancient layers of composition.

Yet how different and unconnected to this is the story about the life of the tailor's son. Born in humble circumstances, he starts out as a naive boy, a foolish lout, but he is matured by his circumstances and by the world that he enters, and his behavior becomes increasingly refined. How different in spirit is the contrast between him as the true lover and his aristocratic rival, the Vizier's son, whose ardor is already dampened at the second night spent in shame. How different in spirit is the poor, unassuming mother, hopelessly waiting outside the door and scheming on behalf of her good-for-nothing son, who is in love. How different in spirit are the descriptions of the splendor, the jewels, the costumes, the banquets and palaces, not to

This article is an expanded form of the original Leipzig inaugural lecture given in 1942.

mention the speeches, ceremonies, customs and manners. How much more cultured is this picture of the Orient, probably reflecting nothing earlier than the seventeenth century. And yet this dichotomy does not tear the whole story apart, but rather, for the first time, makes it a real unity, because these revelations of the supernatural world bring to light the true character of the world of the humans, and the contradictions and limitations of their society.

The story tells of how a ruler allows himself to be impressed by wealth that is beyond his dreams. "'My son,' replied the sultan, as he embraced him again, "you would be quite wrong if you wanted to doubt, even for a moment, the sincerity of the promise which I have given you."' How ironic this is after all that has happened before. And how love for a princess transforms a ne'er-do-well into a young man of the noblest principles overnight. The genie is now summoned for very different purposes than for sweets! How the psychological elements are clothed in marvels! This is the story of the rise of a lucky man, in which the outer miracle that happens to him causes an inner miracle to take place inside him. So the lamp conjures up for its owner all the accomplishments suited to the rank that he receives through it. What dual significance the magic takes on! As soon as one tries to grasp the psychological elements, they blend into the fairy-tale elements. And yet something is sketched here by means of a fairy tale, which could just as well be told in the plot of a novel by Balzac.

But, you will ask, what has this to do with the *Odyssey*? The material has no connection at all. Yet as an example of the possibilities that exist, when fairy tales become wise, and when the wonders of fairy tales are combined with patterns of human behavior, the story of the magic lamp can show us the goal we are aiming at with the *Odyssey*. How is the contrast *here* between the world of the wonderful adventures and the world of the heroes of the *Iliad*, that contrast between the stuff of fairy tales and great epic with its very different conventions, mastered, bridged, and made into a poem?

With this question we are advancing, if not into the holy of holies, at least into the inner sanctum of the *Odyssey*. It is no accident that we would hardly pose ourselves this question in the case of the *Iliad*. For in the *Iliad* the raw material is already heroic. In the *Odyssey* we cannot even assume that these adventures were already in a heroic, "Homeric" form before they entered the epic through this poet. But for the philologist there is an additional consideration: in dealing with this question he can breathe freely again.

Philological criticism had almost become a kind of game of dominoes. Whole epics and eventually the whole *Odyssey* were composed of complete epics, like lots of little building blocks, which could be identified by their joins. People played this game against each other and were happy when it worked out evenly, without leaving any remainders. The game went on until it was discovered that the joins, by which the blocks were being differentiated, were not breaks or gaps but overlapping joints, carefully shaped to fit each other. That is to say, these are signs of very intimate connections. Now what? One might have thought that if we have finished playing with little building blocks, then the *Odyssey* is simply the *Odyssey*. In the future the philologist may still have plenty to explain to me about it, but from now on let him leave me in peace with his theories about origins! Not so the heart of the philologist that thinks, "Isn't the way really open now for theories about origins?" Everything that is a creation and has its own existence and effects, has its own origins. The question in each case is what constitutes its origin. It is necessary to develop an idea and type of origin that is suitable for each creation.

To make use of another example, in the case of Goethe's *Faust*, even if all the old versions of Faust were lost to us, as well as Goethe's rough drafts, we would still be differentiating the various "origins" of this poem. For example, the scene "In Auerbach's Cellar" has its origin in folk jesting, in the spirit and character of the old versions of Faust, while a scene like "In the Woods and Caves" has its origins in the "Storm and Stress" movement. The spirit of Shakespeare shines through the Frau Marthe scenes. The same influences would soon also be recognized in the composition of the whole. This can be the case without introducing foreign, contrary elements into the poetry. Rather, the unity of the poem can only be understood in its diversity. Its form can only be described by its content. Likewise, in the case of the *Odyssey*, the question about its origins can really be posed after the bankruptcy of all kinds of hypotheses about origins. Origins would surely no longer be presumed to consist of the manufacture of whole epics consisting of other whole epics, immediately before which there lay, like a chaos, an endless sea of "motifs" allowing for comparisons. Rather, instead of this an origin would be seen as something that should be gleaned from the poetry itself. The origins of the *Odyssey* would therefore not necessarily have to be the same as the origins of *Faust*. Nevertheless, here also we will soon have three elements to distinguish: the element of folklore and fairy tale, the element of contemporary spirit belonging to the beginning of a new age, and an illustrious model, the *Iliad*.

The poet of the *Odyssey* found his great teacher in the poet of the *Iliad*. From him he learned to cross over the threshold before which the older epics about the *Thebaid* and the Argonauts, as well as the later ones of the Epic Cycle, stood still. That is to say, he learned to manage actions taking place in different locations at the same time, to tie together his threads from different directions, and to tell his story in a meandering and torturous way, instead of in a linear order. In other words, to express it in a literary-historical way, he learned to create a story with many strands rather than only one. From the *Iliad* poet he learned to interweave the path of his hero meaningfully with the lives of a certain number of others, to retell the endings of certain previous stories, to delay his story from moving to its conclusion, and to interrupt the main flow of the epic with all kinds of digressions. In this way he transformed the story of a returning husband into a poem about a father, mother, and son; about masters and servants; about the old and the young; and about the fates of a great number of additional characters also. This poet learned to include didactic material side by side with warnings. He came not only to describe personal relationships but to place these in their social context. At the same time, he sees himself as the educator of his whole people, much more so than the poet of the *Iliad*, who is still paying homage to the courts of princes. In brief, in his poem about a return home or *nostos*, his poetry embraces everything that represents his world. This world is in many respects more contemporary than that of the *Iliad*, but it does include both the heroism of the *Iliad* and very ancient fairy-tale elements. Only a plan to portray a complete world picture enabled these two themes of revenge on the one hand and adventure on the other, which were quite separate in the raw material of the *Odyssey*, if not to become one, at least to blend into each other. The adventures, transformed into epic situations by the hero's narration of them, could become an episode in Odysseus' return.

The problem of the *Odyssey*, that is to say the question of the coherence and unity of its diverse elements, will be addressed in terms of its oldest component, the adventures. This is an investigation into the possibility of an inquiry about its origins, not in the traditional sense, but in the new way that we are trying to develop.[1]

OLD AND NEW ADVENTURES

When faced with the many different adventures that the *Odyssey* brings together, we must first distinguish between the old, fairy-tale adventures and the newly composed ones added later, which belong to a more recent and already historical world. The second group notably includes the lies Odysseus tells about himself in Ithaka. The more deceptive these inventions are, the more circumstantially and historically credible, the more "realistic" they seem to us. In the *Iliad* such differences hardly exist, but rather the action takes place in a much more unified way in the great age of legend, when "heroes" still lived on the earth. How different is the kind of age pictured, for example, in the fourteenth book of the Odyssey (199ff.). It tells of attacks on foreign coasts, the capture of slaves, privateering, greed for gain and deception, piracy, and the mercenary spirit of the Phoenicians who dominate the seas. And against what is almost too historical a background,

---

[1] For this is not an inquiry into the history of motifis, but is confined to the work itself. All such questions, e.g., whether the Phaiakes might once have been people who ferried the dead, are left out of consideration. The history of motifs is used only for clarification and characterization. The opposite point of view can be found in the comprehensive treatment of Ludwig Radermacher in *Die Erzählungen der Odyssee* (*Sitzungsberichte der Akademie der Wissenschaften in Wien* 178 [1915]). Important points are also made by Karl Meuli, *Odyssee und Argonautika* (Berlin, 1921).

contrasting with it, we have the life story, the rise and fall of a man driven by a daemon, who is ready to sell himself again, body and soul, to this creature as soon as he has escaped from it. We see shipwrecks, escape from slavery, etc., and as an end to all this, the pathetic figure of the homeless beggar, who has grown old and points to himself as a warning example. The hero of this story is not a hero, whether in the old sense or in any kind of new one. By birth he is a royal bastard and an audacious fellow (Eumaios is the opposite, a bondsman, but born a king). The luckier he is, the more restless he becomes. And as far as his heroism is concerned, he shows it in very dubious circumstances, dubious not only by comparison with the *Iliad*, because he appeals for mercy to the generosity of the Egyptian king after the failure of the raid.

Do these two series of adventures have anything at all in common? This question was posed, and their styles were seen to be so different that they were adduced as evidence for two separate poets.[2] And yet the new adventure, which seems so realistic to us, grows out of the fairy-tale adventures, taking them as its origin, just as a picture is created through metamorphosis from another one.

Naturally this second series of adventures is not realistic in the nineteenth-century sense of the word. Ancient epic is not realistic in its aims, either in contrast to a romantic episode, or as a spontaneous development of style. It is foreign to epic to portray a slice of "life" simply because it is life. Although these two series seem at first to be very different, there is no lack of common elements between them.

Even the verses are sometimes the same. In both places we find the same description of the journey (14.256 = 11.10, etc.). The storm at sea from the fairy-tale adventure repeats itself in its entirety, apart from a few changes, in the adventure in the real world (14.301f. = 12.403f; 14.259f. is taken with small changes from the adventure with the Cyclops 9. 193f.; 9.43 partly contaminated by 14.259). The difference is that the storm is only a storm now, while in the fairy-tale adventure it was a punishment for sin and a link in the chain of events that led from Skylla to Charybdis. In this way certain realistic, poetical devices, which were already present in the fairy-tale adventure, emerge and combine into a new unity that is no longer fantastic. The "dear" or "godlike" companions become nearly as disobedient to their leader, forgetting his warnings, as the companions of Odysseus in the fairy-tale adventure, when they slaughter the cattle of the sun; but in this case, the warning comes only as a result of human foresight. The course of this new adventure has a certain fairy-tale element: that is, the better the start of the story, the more unpleasant is the surprise later. In this case,

---

[2] U. v. Wilamowitz-Moellendorff, *Die Heimkehr des Odysseus* (Berlin, 1927), p. 18: "Vivid pictures from the violent and changeable lives of the sons of Greek lords and of pirates. . . . Anyone who reflects upon the character of 13 and 14 will tell himself that 13 and 14 are not by the same poet."

however, it is not masses of onrushing giants, as in the adventure of the Laistrygones, but experienced troops and Egyptians who attack to destroy the fleet and crew.

But, above all, the fairy-tale hero and the real adventurer have this in common, that they both see the meaning of their changeable fates in terms of the rule of Zeus. As in the fairy-tale adventure, a causal chain of events gradually takes shape, which points more and more to Zeus rather than to Poseidon. Similarly, the beginnings of a type of autobiographical self-analysis are closely tied to a belief in Zeus, as in the lyric genre that was soon to emerge. Personal elements do not emerge separately from religious ones. But how ironic is the appeal to the king of heaven in the mouth of the adventurer in the *Odyssey*, when compared with the fairy-tale hero:

> But how I wish I had died and met my destiny
> there in Egypt, for there was still more sorrow awaiting me.
> At once I put the well-wrought helm from my head, the great shield
> off my shoulders, and from my hand I let the spear drop,
> and went out into the way of the king and up to his chariot,
> and kissed his knees and clasped them; he rescued me and took pity.

Or

> But Zeus himself, though I had pain in my heart, then put
> into my hands the giant mast of the ship.

Or

> and Zeus who delights in thunder flung down
> a foul panic among my companions

> (14.274–79, 310–11, 268–69)

In the flux of life, Zeus is the constant, here as in later time in Solon's great elegy of self-examination "To Himself," which naturally treats this theme in a much more profound way. But how different the same reference to the rule of Zeus already sounds in the *Odyssey*, where the same verses are addressed to Antinoos before the Suitors (17.437f.) and the allusion becomes a test of the humanity of the ambitious young noblemen. The tone here is as serious and ominous as it was ironical before. The difference in tone, of which the same verses are capable, is almost greater in the *Odyssey* than in the *Iliad*.

Poetical traits, which were already realistic in the fairy-tale adventures, have become purely human stories in the "real" adventures. Conversely, one of the newer adventures has also intruded among the traditional tales of the world of fairy tale, namely the fight with the Thracian Kikonians (9.39ff.). The story is like the invented adventure in Egypt: attack, division of spoils, disobedience of the companions, who refuse to be persuaded to flee (9.43 ~ 14.259), then on the next day a pitched battle in which the Achaians are defeated. But this, the very first adventure that Odysseus tells to Alkinoos, rightfully stands on the boundary between the real and the fairy-tale worlds of the epic. Only after the Kikonians do they travel to the Lotus Eaters, into the world of distant wonders. At the same time, the wine with which Odysseus will deceive the Cyclops becomes the guest-present of the priest whom Odysseus spared in the land of the Kikonians. The interweaving of the Kikonian adventure with the story of Polyphemos has a moral. But simultaneously the Kikonian adventure functions as a dire prelude, a warning of what is to come because of the disobedience of the companions. And so the realistic story, which frees itself from the fantastic, in turn mirrors itself in the fairy-tale world. Adventures in the real and fairy-tale world do not mean different poets, but variations in one and the same spirit.

THE NUMBER OF SHIPS

In the case of the fairy-tale wanderings, there exists an external but sure way to differentiate between what is newly composed and the old traditions, that is to say, observing the *number* of ships. According to the original tradition, Odysseus sailed with only one ship, like the Argonauts, not with a whole fleet as he does now in our *Odyssey*. Only the transformation of the old sailors' yarns into the style of the *Iliad*, resulted in Odysseus' travels to this completely different world of distant wonders as a hero of the *Iliad* and leader of an army. But for this he needed a fleet. He sets out, as we learn incidentally (9, 159), with twelve ships, the same small contingent as he is given in the Catalogue of Ships in the *Iliad*. Accordingly, the number of "companions" is increased to five hundred. This occasioned, at the same time, an advantage, namely that the excessively regular series of adventures is divided into two halves, each with a different outcome, one with the fleet and one without. The results were variation, interruptions, and additional disasters. At the same time, of course, the disadvantage was that the poet had to accept a certain number of contradictions between his poetry and the logic of the original stories.[3]

Let us examine the story of the Sirens. We can only imagine that when Odysseus plugs the ears of his comrades with wax and orders them to tie him to the mast, he is the commander of one ship. Otherwise what would happen to the rest of them? The same thing is true in the episode of Skylla and Charybdis. Being able to steer a course between the two of them is enough of a marvel for one ship. What would happen to this story if Odysseus were to steer through the grasping arms of the monster with twelve ships at once? Therefore both adventures do not happen until the second

---

[3] These contradictions are noted by D. Mülder (*Philologus* 65, 1906), p. 241; Eduard Schwartz, *Die Odyssee* (Munich, 1924), p. 41. P. Von der Mühll, "*Odyssee*," in Pauly-Wissowa, Suppl. 7 (1940), c. 721 (in P. von der Mühll, *Ausgewählte Klein Schriften*, ed. B. Wyss, *Schweizerische Beiträge zur Altertumswissenschaft*, 12 (Basel, 1976) pp. 59–60) and "Die Dichter der *Odyssee*," *Jahrbuch des Vereins Schweizer Gymnasiallehrer* 68 (1940), pp. 92–93 (=*Ausgewählte Kleine Schriften*, pp. 135–36). The conclusions reached here naturally go further.

half, after the loss of the fleet. In the case of the Underworld, it is self-evident that Odysseus was not allowed to travel this far with a fleet. Something so remote does not reveal itself to a crowd. In the case of the adventure with Circe, too many would be cast under her spell if the crew of a whole fleet were to fall into the trap of the enchantress: 250 pigs . . .

On the other hand no one would object if the cattle of the sun on Thrinakia were slaughtered by more, instead of just by the crew of one ship. And yet this adventure has its place between the Sirens and Skylla and Charybdis. Therefore, the grouping of these stories is not dictated only by the logic of the number of ships. Moreover, the poet sometimes ignores the logic of the numbers to such an extent that it is surprising that critics of Homer have not picked up on this a long time ago.

The *Aiolos* adventure is in the middle of those that Odysseus must survive with his fleet. And yet the fleet is no less impossible here than it would be in the adventure with the Sirens. Let us think about this. Finally Odysseus is sure of reaching his destination. He has tied up and captured all the evil winds in a sack, which he has hidden carefully in the lowest part of the ship's hold. He is sitting by the rudder himself, holding the sail, and never takes a rest. Already home is in sight—then sleep overcomes him. Then comes a discussion among his companions—their curiosity and their greed. So they open the sack. Punishment follows immediately on their folly. Forced back to Aiolos, Odysseus must see how the Lord of the Winds, who was so well-disposed shortly before, now shudders and turns away from him. But the very action of holding a conference, becoming outraged, and opening the bag of winds, is all only possible for the crew of one ship. Odysseus' worry, care, and caution is exercised only toward one ship. That they perished as a result of their own folly (10.27) can be said only about the crew of one ship. The men on the other eleven ships play not even the smallest role in all that happens either internally or externally. Let the audience forget the fleet just for this adventure! However clear the demands of this story, the poet has tolerated the presence of an accompanying fleet. Why has he put up with what seems so out of place to anyone examining the story carefully later? We search in vain for an answer in the story itself. Why did he not move this story into the second half?

And now for the third example, let us take the Cyclops. This also leaves no room for a fleet. If Odysseus chooses the twelve bravest men from his crew, then the crew of even one ship would be too many for the present danger of blinding the Cyclops and then of the daring escape. Equally the stones thrown by the blinded Cyclops at those trying to escape should not threaten more than one ship. And yet this adventure is the third in the series. But in this case the same poet who showed so little concern for the number of ships in the Aiolos story has had the foresight to remove the fleet from this story. He invented the island of the goats, lying in front of the coast of the Cyclopes, so that the fleet could lie at anchor there while Odysseus' ship proceeded to the adventure. More will be said later about the "realistic" elements introduced into the adventure here. It is enough to note here that the rule about the number of ships is only confirmed by the exception, the story of Polyphemos.[4]

The question now is, from what adventures can the fleet not be removed? In fact the only ones remaining in this category are in the first place the Kikonians—it has already become clear that the poet of the *Odyssey* invented this story—and second the Laistrygones. Yet the latter adventure seems, from the way it is told, to be there for no other purpose than to explain the destruction of the fleet, with the exception of Odysseus' ship. But if one looks for fairy-tale elements here, then one discovers another story quite evidently invented later. In itself this adventure is one of the ogre stories, like the adventure of the Cyclops, except that this time Odysseus keeps himself out of the danger. The trap into which the three scouts fall is all the more terrifying. A king's daughter who is drawing water at a famous spring shows them the way—to the castle of the man-eating king. One man is eaten and the other two escape, but not, as expected, to report disaster. We do not find out what happens to them.[5]

Now the other part of the invention takes over, for the fleet has also already fallen into a trap by entering the narrow, rocky harbor in order to land. Now it is destroyed by the stones thrown by the giants. Only Odysseus has moored his ship outside the narrow inlet. Disaster strikes the heedless sailors here not purely as a result of the terrors of a fairy-tale wonder, but only when these are combined with the natural character of the coastline. The story of the man-eaters could probably have been told in a different way, without the destruction of the fleet. But the landscape here, a sinister landscape high in the extreme north, is described in such a way that the coast combined with the man-eating only makes sense in the place where it has been put in the *Odyssey*. Everything else, apart from Charybdis, can be switched around, but this cannot. From now on Odysseus is a different man from the one he was, the leader of only one ship.

If the only adventures from which the fleet cannot be removed are the Laistrygones and Kikonians, then the order is evidently not dependent on the number of ships. Whether an adventure tells of one or more ships depends on another order, according to which the numbers are adjusted. But, in the last analysis, what kind of a criterion of differentiation do we have to decide the arrangement of the stories?

It used to be thought that the ordering principle was geography, half

---

[4] Cf. also how in the Telemachy the fleet of Menelaos is eliminated because it would not have fitted in with the Proteus adventure, 3.298.

[5] There must have been much more here originally. The story of the giantess who invites a guest and of the giant who comes home in the evening and turns out to be a man-eater, is a widespread motif in ogre stories. See Leo Frobenius, *Das Zeitalter des Sonnengottes* (Berlin, 1904), pp. 376f. and p. 388. But here this motif remains undeveloped. The contrast between grotesque and gruesome content and elevated epic form is characteristic of the poet. Out of different elements he has created a unity, which makes sense only in this context.

mythical but also half based on actual experience. Originally this was the hypothesis of Krates of Mallos, the leader of the Pergamene grammarians. He had already divided the wanderings to the different oceans into those of the far west and those of the far east and, where this principle is concerned, he has not lacked followers down to the present day. Yet here one must not ask what is the geography of the poet and what belongs to his tradition. Even without this differentiation the result is vague enough. One part of the adventures seems to take place in the far west and from there to Crete, another group in the northeast of the Aegean, and the Black Sea. Yet this happens without the two groups being really separate from each other, nor is it clear how the hero travels from west to east and again from east to west.[6]

If one avoids hypotheses, one conclusion is sure. The adventures are arranged in such a way by the poet that a fate is fashioned, a fate with three interweaving strands: first for the companions in the fleet, then for the single ship that is saved, and in the end only for Odysseus on his own. If we leave aside the last, brief and precipitous finale, the result is a double cycle of events. Twice we start off with relatively harmless adventures with a mild outcome, and twice things take a rapid turn to destruction. The first cycle comprises the Lotus Eaters, Polyphemos, Aiolos, and the Laistrygones. The second cycle includes Circe (the only adventure with a completely happy ending, apart from the Phaiakes), the Underworld, the Sirens, Skylla, the cattle of the sun, the storm at sea, and Charybdis. Each time Odysseus and his men bring the disaster on themselves. Although Poseidon is angry with Odysseus, our knowledge of ruin caused by sin directs our attention not to him but to Zeus. So on a higher level of causal connections, the authority of Zeus overshadows the wrath of Poseidon. Even the storm at sea in the first-person narrative is sent not by Poseidon but by Zeus.

In the ancient folk tradition before the *Odyssey*, the adventures were unconnected and the differentiation between a single ship and the whole fleet was missing. (One exception is the cattle of the sun, about which more later.) This lack of connection is generally characteristic of folk traditions. Similarly the old folktale collections about Eulenspiegel and Dr. Faust consist of a series of stories following on one another without a plan, only very loosely fitted into their biographical framework. An inner shape following the pattern of a life, fate, or climax, etc. is usually missing. The adventures of Sinbad also allow themselves to be interchanged. If this unity, which is composed of a meaningful order interweaving fate, fault, and the will of the gods and which holds the *Odyssey* together, is not out of place even in its world of fairy tale, how could the poet of these fairy-tale adventures not be

---

[6]W. Kranz, "Die Irrfahrten des Odysseus," *Hermes* 50 (1915), pp. 93f., manages to distinguish two distinct poems about wanderings by two different poets on the basis of geographical premises. There hardly seem to be any analyses that dispense with geographical considerations.

the same man who wove into the life story of his hero so much biographical material, so much that attests to the same order in the real world?

THE FIRST-PERSON NARRATIVE

Another external device to see through the poetry to the tradition behind it, apart from the number of the ships, is available in the differences resulting from the transformation of the fairy-tale adventures into a first-person narrative. This transformation from the jesting and the dreadful wonders to the personal experience of a hero of the *Iliad* can still be spotted thanks to the transparence of the poetry. The purpose of this inquiry is not to break up the poem into either motifs or individual epics, but to understand the finished product as something growing from raw material, something that has been thought out. Meanwhile, let us leave the general question of the age and origins of the first-person narrative as a self-contained one.[7] Odysseus first becomes the narrator of his own adventures at the stage of our *Odyssey* and obviously, even in our poem, not by any means of all of them. The material that could be expanded and adapted to create an epic of the new style, fitted in with the conventions of epic. Material that resisted change was transformed into the first-person narrative. The first-person narrative is the means by which the old fairy-tale elements were absorbed into new epic, remote and at the same time true to life, distant fairy tales and yet personal experience. All this is quite obvious. Yet conclusions have hardly been drawn from it.

There are adventures that can easily be imagined without the first-person narrative. Others are so rooted in first-person narrative that the whole adventure would have to be taken apart to remove it. In other words the development from third-person to first-person narrative reaches different depths in different adventures. In some cases, although not in all, this also means a change of ethos and style.

An example of what still seems to be wholly fairy-tale in tone is the encounter with Skylla (12.201ff.). But anyone who thinks that to reconstitute the old fairy story it is enough to change the narrative from first person to

---

[7] Sinbad stories in the first-person narrative are already extant from the year 2000 in Egypt. See A. Wiedemann, *Altägyptische Sagen und Märchen* (Leipzig 1906), pp. 25f; L. Radermacher (above, note 1), p. 38. But in this case the adventurer is not a famous hero and the adventures are not intended to keep showing him in his own characteristic light. This new purpose doubtless required strict selection from among the abundance of the available wonder stories. The clashing rocks, for example, were no longer needed. The particular character of the hero could probably only be rendered in simple narrative and not in the first person. Self-characterization, in which the impression made by the adventures is transferred more and more to the narrator figure who survives them, is a very developed form. Many events, such as the end of the Sirens or the Phaiakes, could not be told at all in the first-person narrative. The parallel fairy tales, such as the numerous ones about Circe, demonstrate this same principle very clearly.

third, has completely missed noticing how a deeply ironic contrast gives the old fairy story its new tension in the *Odyssey*. The clash between the heroism of the *Iliad* and that of fairy tale is nowhere else represented with such a fantastic sense of horror. The terrors of fairy tale overcome even the worst horrors of the world of heroes with the same paralyzing force, just as here, after so many other adventures, the force of the fairy tale finally pulls all elements of epic, which are in its way, along with it. The encounter with Skylla turns into a triumph of the fairy-tale world over the reality of the *Odyssey*. The warning of Circe as she sees into the future is in vain (12.116ff.):

> Hardy man, your mind is full forever of fighting
> and battle work. Will you not give way even to the immortals?
> . . . .
> . . . . and there is no fighting against her,
> nor any force of defense. It is best to run away from her.

Odysseus gets into this adventure in a different way than anticipated. He probably warned his helmsman about the Rovers, following Circe's advice—it is part of the overriding care he feels for his crew that he does not tell him about Skylla—and yet the hero of the *Iliad* is not able to accept losses without a fight (12.226ff.):

> I let go from my mind the difficult instruction that Circe
> had given me, for she told me not to be armed for combat;
> but I put on my glorious armor and, taking up two long
> spears in my hands, I stood bestriding the vessel's foredeck
> at the prow, for I expected Skylla of the rocks to appear first
> from that direction, she who brought pain to my companions.

Meanwhile Charybdis is threatening opposite him from below, with such a terrible din, steam, and whirlpool, that he is not aware of Skylla grasping from above (12.244ff.):

> We in fear of destruction kept our eyes on Charybdis,
> but meanwhile Skylla out of the hollow vessel snatched six
> of my companions, the best of them for strength and hands' work.

Skylla and Charybdis probably originated as a twin adventure in their old fairy-tale context. Like the Rovers in the *Argonautica*, they lie opposite each other in a narrow strait, like double jaws.[8] But the hero of the *Odyssey* does not fall into the whirlpool of Charybdis as he comes from Skylla, but rather because he is paralyzed by the terror under and beside him, he forgets the terror over him. The result, instead of the effect of double jaws, is rather that of an incommensurability between the fairy-tale world and the heroism

---

[8] Regarding the common motif of the "clashing rocks," cf. L. Frobenius, *Das Zeitalter des Sonnengottes*, p. 405.

of the *Iliad*, for which the prophecies of Circe have already prepared the way. If Odysseus did not behave like a hero, and as the protector of his men, then this incommensurability would not become clear. Nowhere do we come across heroism that is so misplaced. The first-person form of the narrative is connected here with irony—even a little self-irony—that puts the old fairy-tale adventure in a new light. The hero becomes a victim of the contrast between two worlds. There are horrors that can only be suffered. At the same time it is clear why the Skylla adventure had to become separate and independent from the Charybdis adventure, for Charybdis has no part in the contrast intended here.

The transformation of the adventure of the Sirens seems to be less extensive. And yet even in such a short, unelaborated episode as this one there is a blending of the world of the *Iliad* and the fairy tales. Naturally this does not lead to their separation in an ironical contrast as in the Skylla adventure; rather, the purpose is to make the marvel of temptation even more tempting for the hero of the *Iliad*. The Sirens entice Odysseus with the prize of epic heroism, as if they had been waiting for no other purpose on their distant, fairy-tale cliff (12.184ff.):

> Come this way, honored Odysseus, great glory of the Achaians,
> . . . for we know everything that the Argives and Trojans
> did and suffered in wide Troy through the gods' despite.

The chord they must have struck in Odysseus' heart here is revealed, although in a very different setting, in the adventure with the Phaiakes, when the hero no longer holds back his tears at the fame of his deeds. But the man whose identity is not guessed there, sees himself recognized and celebrated here as soon as he approaches. The magical song becomes a heroic epic. The Sirens know the overwhelming effect of fame from the mouth of a poet. One is almost tempted to ask whether the companions would have been as irresistibly attracted as Odysseus, if they had no wax in their ears. Is there not a play on double meanings here with hearing and deafness? Yet if one tries to imagine the same story as epic narrative instead of in the first person, then one feels that the charm also is immediately gone.

> So they sang, in sweet utterance, and the heart within me
> desired to listen.

(12.192–93)

If one replaces "within me" with "within him" here, then the invention does not hold. The introduction of the heroism of the *Iliad* into this story cannot be separated from the first-person narrative.

But the end of the adventure, as it was once told, has also changed. At one time it ended with the death of the Sirens, just as the adventure in Scheria concluded with the end of the Phaiakes. On a red-figure vase from the end of the sixth century in the possession of the British Museum (just as already on a vase sherd about one hundred years older from Naucratis), the Sirens, portrayed as monster birds with human heads, throw themselves into the sea from their high nest on the cliff, as Odysseus passes them by.[9] The same story is reported in the parallel tradition, which goes back to Timaeus, the historian of the West, that is to say, it goes back to the fourth century. They did this "in desperation at their defeat," or because it had been prophesied to them as their fate, that they would live as long as no mortal withstood their song. Try to imagine this ending in the first-person narrative: "As soon as we had passed beyond them and out of earshot, I already saw how they threw themselves into the sea." One can see that the transformation could not accommodate this. In the experiences of Odysseus, there is no more room for the fate of the Sirens.

The landscape has also changed in the *Odyssey*. In the version of the vase-painters, the Sirens do not sing on an inviting "meadow," but on a high cliff, and the tradition preserved by Timaeus agrees with this. The vase-painters evidently also imagined a narrow strait, like the one between Skylla and Charybdis. Their song becomes even more inescapable, if it is not only a question of sailing past it, but through it and under it.

The source for Timaeus and the vase-painters is the folk tradition. The idea that Odysseus outwits the Sirens is lost in our *Odyssey*, if only because Odysseus is following the advice of Circe, instead of coming up with a way of breaking their spell on the spur of the moment from his own fund of tricks. Originally cunning was matched by cunning. But the song of the Sirens was also cunning. Cunning and magic went hand in hand. This is also the case with the song of Circe.

Naturally the Sirens do not suspect that the rowers have wax in their ears. Otherwise they would have spared themselves the trouble. And they probably have even less understanding of the meaning of the man who is tied to the mast. They only see that their magic no longer works. They do not suspect the powerful effect it is actually having. In that picture on the vase, one Siren, Himeropa, is still making an effort, bewildered and beating her wings, while her sister has already given up and is throwing herself into the sea with a look of despair. In the new context of the *Odyssey*, the victory of the man of many schemes, his successful outwitting of the Sirens and his breaking of their spell, which no one has ever been able to withstand yet, becomes his suffering and escape. Do the Sirens remain the same as they were? We are not supposed to ask this. The significance of the adventure of the Sirens comes from its position in the *Odyssey* as a whole.

[9] Illustrations and evidence can be found in H. W. Roscher's *Lexikon der griechischen und römischen Mythologie*, s.v. "Seirenen," by G. Weicker. Other material is in E. Bethe, "Die griechische Dichtung," in O. Walzel's *Handbuch der Literaturwissenschaft* (Wildbad-Potsdam, 1924), p. 39. Illustrations there are after the *Journal of Hellenic Studies* 13. For the significance of the Sirens as wonderful and alluring demons of death, cf. also E. Buschor, *Die Musen des Jenseits* (Munich, 1944), p. 7. The Sirens' Promontory opposite Capri and the Sirenum Petrae east of it at Positano show that they were thought to have been there probably since Timaeus.

LANDSCAPE

We speak of *Odyssey* landscapes, not of *Iliad* landscapes, and there is a good reason for this. Landscape is something native to this poet. However, his landscapes do not play a role like those in the novels of more modern times, as a mirror or background to the lives and moods of the characters. They are a part of the same sequence as the fairy-tale wonders, although with the difference that they do not need heightened or magic elements to be a wonder. Homeric landscapes have the same relationship to magic lands as a sea storm in Homer has to the fairy-tale adventure of the Charybdis. They come into being, shedding traditional forms, just as biography springs from fairy-tale adventures. Like the human being or spirit, the landscape is also an element that is latent in mythology, as if asleep, and that one morning wakes up to its own potential.

The fact that the cave of Polyphemos simultaneously conjures up such a picture of the south in our imagination, that it almost seems to have a bucolic or Theocritean connection, is not least the result of the small island of the goats, which is situated right in front of it. The island serves as its foreground and foil. It frames the adventure with the ogres, which takes place behind it, in such a way that little needs to be added in order to locate it completely in a landscape. The idyll comes before the adventure. And yet it was necessity that forced the poet to place this island in front of the coast. Through this island he frees himself for this adventure of the fleet which he invented as an addition. He makes himself a virtue of necessity. Nowhere else in the *Odyssey* is landscape described in such detail for its own sake. Nothing happens except that they hunt a few goats. Otherwise there is just the landing and the sight of untouched land, and wild, flourishing nature. They look over at the coast nearby, where they see smoke rising up. From there adventure tempts them.

Many aspects of the landing, the utter darkness of the night, their inability to see the coast, and the calm of the wind in the natural harbor suggest the beginning of disaster. Is it not like the Laistrygones? But no, morning comes and, behold, a marvel! It is not so very far from here to Claude Lorrain, although we should not forget the Augustans as a stage in between. Just as they are somewhat influenced by Italian agriculture, so here this picture is affected by the spirit of early Greek colonization.

Is it a coincidence that the purest landscapes, like this one and the one at the beginning of the Circe adventure, are in the story that is retold by Odysseus? In the direct narrative, in the case of Kalypso and the Phaiakes, there is no lack of an audience; the guide, the slayer of Argos, stood and marveled (5.75). But the godlike sufferer Odysseus stood still and marveled (7.133). In the indirect narrative, this is left out. As a result the whole episode becomes all the more of an experience. The first-person narrative first creates the opportunity for the marvels of the landscape to emerge completely from myth. Let us test this theory:

There is a wooded island that spreads, away from the harbor,
neither close in to the land of the Cyclopes nor far out
from it; forested; wild goats beyond number breed there,
for there is no coming and going of human kind to disturb them,
nor are they visited by hunters, who in the forest
suffer hardships as they haunt the peaks of the mountains,
neither again is it held by herded flocks, nor farmers,
but all its days, never plowed up and never planted,
it goes without people and supports the bleating wild goats.
For the Cyclopes have no ships with cheeks of vermilion,
nor have they builders of ships among them, who could have made them
strong-benched vessels, and these if made could have run them sailing
to all the various cities of men, in the way that people
cross the sea by means of ships and visit each other,
and they could have made this island a strong settlement for them.
For it is not a bad place at all, it could bear all crops
in season, and there are meadow lands near the shores of the gray sea,
well watered and soft; there could be grapes grown there endlessly,
and there is smooth land for plowing, men could reap a full harvest
always in season, since there is very rich subsoil. Also
there is an easy harbor, with no need for a hawser
nor anchor stones to be thrown ashore nor cables to make fast;
one could just run ashore and wait for the time when the sailors'
desire stirred them to go and the right winds were blowing.
Also at the head of the harbor there runs bright water,
spring beneath rock, and there are black poplars growing around it.
There we sailed ashore, and there was some god guiding
us in through the gloom of the night, nothing showed to look at,
for there was a deep mist around the ships, nor was there any moon
showing in the sky, but she was under the clouds and hidden.
There was none of us there whose eyes had spied out the island,
and we never saw any long waves rolling in and breaking
on the shore, but the first thing was when we beached the well-benched
   vessels.
Then after we had beached the ships, we took all the sails down,
and we ourselves stepped out onto the break of the sea beach,
and there we fell asleep and waited for the divine Dawn.
But when the young Dawn showed again with her rosy fingers,
we made a tour about the island, admiring everything
there, and the nymphs, daughters of Zeus of the aegis, started
the hill-roving goats our way for my companions to feast on.

(9.116–55)

Odysseus is almost as excited as if he wanted to become a colonist. But
like praise of his home, praise of the wilderness also depends on the person

speaking. Without the first-person narrative there is no landscape. Although the homeland Ithaka is additionally endowed with a few details of landscape, here the olive tree, there the cave of the nymphs, these are only identification points and as such they have less significance in themselves. There are also landscape elements rendered as part of the description of the journey, but again only in the case of Odysseus, only around him, as his experience. How often Telemachus comes and goes on the same roads in Ithaka, which only really become part of a journey when Odysseus travels on them. It is the same in the case of the weather. Only personal experience, only the first-person narrative lends the fairy-tale landscape an awareness of its splendor and magic.

POLYPHEMOS

The cave of Polyphemos is the only place among the fairy-tale adventures where Odysseus comes not as a sufferer, but willingly and knowingly. In no other case does he feel himself so attracted by danger. In Circe's realm he also sees smoke rising in the distance. But at that point adventure no longer tempts him. He sends out his companions to follow the rising smoke on Circe's island because he has lost his bearings, and he no longer knows in which direction between sunrise and sunset his home lies. By contrast nothing forces him to push onward from the goat island, which offers him everything that he needs, to the coast of the Cyclopes opposite. Indeed he has a premonition of what lies before him. He chooses his men accordingly and he takes along with him the magic wine against all eventualities. He is attacked by the Laistrygones because he innocently tries to find out what kind of people inhabit their land. Nothing like that happens here. He knows that the Cyclopes live over there. The meeting with this giant in the *Odyssey* does not happen in the same way as in the satyr play by Euripides. There Odysseus lands in order to fetch water and provisions, and then, to his dismay, he finds himself facing the monster. The invention of the dramatist shows, if there is still need for it, how easily the epic poet could have found a different motive for the adventure, if he had wanted to.

The feeling of wonder at the unusual elements, at the careful dairy farming of this ruthless monster, at the love for his animals felt by the man-eater, at the arrangement of the cave and of the world in which he lives and moves, at his transformation from being defeated to cursing demonically— all these qualities rightly make this adventure stand out from the rest. But they should not entice us to see a separate poem in this. This adventure is the freshest because it is the first. The Kikonians, who precede it, serve only as a preparation for this, and the Lotus Eaters show that now they are traveling into a fairy-tale land. Here Odysseus sets out to meet danger, in a world of wonders that is just opening up before him, with an undampened zeal that will naturally fade soon enough. What a different person he is inside in the Circe adventure, which starts in a similar way. Odysseus survives all the subsequent adventures, which are summarized in Circe's prophecy, merely as suffering imposed as part of the manifold demands of his fate. The Odysseus who finally reaches Scheria and in the end his home, begins to wail before he knows where he is. One may ask whether this is the same hero and whether the creation of the same poet, as the man who meets Polyphemos with such daring. The answer to this question is yes, because his many adventures have changed him. The answer to this question would only be no if the Polyphemos story were not the first in a long chain, if the adventures did not lead to a climax in their order and significance, just as they do in our *Odyssey*. In fact, according to everything that can be gathered about the plan of our *Odyssey*, these stories were put together in this series for the first time here. The Polyphemos adventure can only serve as a warning example because it is the first one, exemplifying the complete fearlessness and inexperience of the start of the journey.

But if Odysseus is transformed from someone who delights in adventure to someone who survives it and finally to a man who fears adventure, we in turn notice a parallel development in the life of the adventurer, who has no part in fairy tale anymore, and whom Odysseus pretends to be for Eumaios. In addition, this life-story could not start with such pleasure in dangers and adventure if it did not end with such weariness. But the question as to whether it is still the same becomes unnecessary because of the logic of the story. In his youth he was so daring:

> Ares and Athene endowed me with courage, that power
> that breaks men in battle. Whenever I detailed the best fighters
> to go into ambush, planning evil things for the enemy,
> the proud heart in me had no image of death before it, . . .
> but now I wish I had died and met my destiny
> there in Egypt, for there was still more sorrow awaiting me.

$$(14.216–19 . . . , 274–75)$$

The one who was once so eager for booty ends up as booty himself, tied up to be sold as a slave (14.337f):

> but their hearts were taken with a bad counsel
> concerning me, so I still should have the pain of affliction.

And when he escapes once more, his life is a matter of simply surviving:

> . . . So now life is still my portion.

$$(14.359)$$

Since one would hardly be inclined to see the one as the model for the other, we must recognize the same poet in both sequences.

But the urge that impels Odysseus to wait for the giant—which makes the start of this adventure different from the others—is surely strange. He wishes to "test" and "find out" what kind of people the Cyclopes are,

> whether they are savage and violent, and without justice
> or hospitable to strangers and with minds that are godly.

(9.175–76)

Where else does he feel this urge? As far as I know, only in Ithaka, when he dresses up as a beggar and tests nobles and people, servants and maids. He designs his plan as one who is testing (16.304f.) and takes action as Athene advises him (13.303ff.). Yet who gives him this task in relation to the Cyclops? In fact, the testing has another significance here: it leads to an ironic clash between the two worlds, the one from which Odysseus is coming and the one he is now entering. He is testing as a hero of the *Iliad*, who is accustomed to receive the highest honors and the richest guest-presents everywhere because of his rank and fame. The reply to this is the eating of his companions. And it almost seems to us that this completely alien behavior, however horrible it is, does challenge the standards of heroism for the moment. For what other reason is there that Odysseus does not put himself in this position as a hero of the *Iliad* at any other time? How he flatters in attesting his loyalty! How pathetic!

> We claim we are of the following of the son of Atreus,
> Agamemnon, whose fame now is the greatest thing under heaven,
> such a city was that he sacked and destroyed so many
> people; but now we come to you and are suppliants.

(9.263ff.)

The collapse of his self-image seems to be of almost the same kind as what occurs when the hero of the *Iliad* faces the grasping tentacles of Skylla with his weapons and armor. The play on the contradictions between the two worlds is the same. It need hardly be said that here also this game coincides with the transformation of the objectivity of fairy tale into the subjectivity of a first-person narrative.

For the story is no longer told in a naive way.[10] The irony results from the fact that Odysseus sets out into this world as the one with the upper hand, the one who is confident in himself and puts others to the test. And yet this world hardly withstands his testing. The heroic, knightly world of the warriors of the *Iliad* is also a civilized one. When Odysseus appears before the giant as the representative of this world, a more sophisticated tension is added to the basic one. Once told merely as outwitting a trick, the adventure now becomes a battle between civilization teamed up with intelligence,

---

[10] For the fairy-tale motifs in the Polyphemos adventure, cf. Friedrich v. d. Leyen, *Das Märchen* (Leipzig, 1925³), 104f. (Heidelberg, 1958⁴, p. 127). Wilhelm Grimm, *Die Sage von Polyphem, Abhandlung der königlichen Akademie der Wissenschaften* (Berlin, 1857), *Kleine Schriften IV*, pp. 428f. Meuli, *Odyssee und Argonautika* (Berlin, 1921), pp. 66f.

and barbarity allied with raw strength. What will be the outcome? The initial result is that Odysseus falls into a terrible trap.

The play between the contrasting elements of two worlds is mixed up with Odysseus outwitting the trick of the Cyclops—something unthinkable without the first-person narrative. The same play of tensions results in the disappointment of the blinded Cyclops that his conqueror, who had long been foretold to him, should turn out to be such a wretch: "I always thought that he would be someone like myself." The biggest change in the meaning of the whole adventure is brought about by the contrast between the two worlds. Through this Odysseus takes on the role of testing and in the end he boasts that he is the victor through the favor and care of the same Zeus, the protector of strangers, in whose name he undertook this adventure. In his triumph he calls out to his enemy from his ship, when he is barely out of reach, that he has suffered a just punishment (9.478f.):

> Hard one, who dared to eat your own guests in your own house,
> so Zeus and the rest of the gods have punished you.

And then, after surviving the danger, in the midst of his companions, he ceremonially sacrifices the ram that carried him out of the cave as a thank-offering to Zeus "the dark-clouded son of Kronos, lord over all." And Zeus?

> But he was not moved by my offerings,
> but still was pondering on a way how all my strong-benched
> ships should be destroyed and all my eager companions.

(9.553–55)

The foreshadowing takes place in the style of the great heroic epic. A model for this deception is in the *Iliad*. The kings and people, Danaans and Dardanians, are in a similar situation of error in *Iliad* 3.298ff. at the most solemn sacrifice and prayer.

> "Zeus, exalted and mightiest, and you other immortals,
> let those, whichever side they may be, who do wrong to the oaths sworn
> first, let their brains be spilled on the ground as this wine is spilled now,
> theirs and their sons', and let their wives be the spoil of others."
> They spoke, but none of this would the son of Kronos accomplish.

The fruitless prayer of Hecabe (*Il.* 6.305ff.) is the same:

> She spoke in prayer, but Pallas Athene turned her head from her.

(*Il.* 6.311)

The sacrifice of the Trojans is the same also at *Iliad* 8.550f. And yet there is a difference. When Zeus makes himself deaf to entreaties in the *Iliad*, the reason is not that there was some fault in the prayers, and the humans are deceived because of their simple, honest trust in the gods. The refusal of the gods to listen borders on betrayal. Just as the *Iliad* is full of this, so the *Odyssey* intentionally avoids it.[11] Zeus himself rules this out in the council of the gods in the first book. Not even the Suitors, feeling that they have been betrayed, turn to the gods. The only exception, this sacrifice of the ram by Odysseus, should be assessed very differently, according to all the indications. Naturally, Odysseus is not in the wrong here in the sense of "sin," as his companions later sin on Thrinakia, and yet he is in the wrong in his triumph and in his enjoyment of the victory (how different it is when he forbids Eurycleia to triumph in victory after his completed revenge) and in his delusion that he is carrying out a task without being instructed to by a god. Yet his delusion, as human delusion, is quite different from that of a hero in the *Iliad*. When Odysseus errs, the irony of his mistake is subjectively conditioned. He only errs as far as he himself is concerned. When people pray and make a mistake in the *Iliad*, then their mistake is objective, and the irony of its rests on the inscrutability and contrary nature of the gods.

Despite all of its own brilliance, the Polyphemos story does play a part in the picture of a life as a whole. It has more than just the outward function of providing a motive for the wrath of Poseidon. It leads to the stage where humans and their values, both blameless in themselves, begin to become questionable to each other. As surely as Odysseus represents humanity, and as surely as the man-eater despises all that is right, there is a human element mixed into the judgment, which does not pass the test of the gods: namely hybris, although in its most subtle form, hybris as moral awareness. Not that this would be made clear. Self-representation, in the objectivity of the available means, is a wonder of foreshadowing narrative both subjectively and objectively. At first a fairy tale, as exciting as fairy tales are, the Polyphemos story ends almost like a novel or biography. At first glance it seems the brightest of all the adventures, but in fact it is the darkest of all. It casts its shadow over the rest of the sequence.[12]

THE WRATH OF POSEIDON

The story of Polyphemos ends with two opposing scenes, which parallel each other in the style of great epic. On the one hand is the curse of the vanquished, on the other the thank-offering of the victor. Here is Poseidon who listens, there Zeus who is planning destruction. In this way days of

---

[11] *Od.* 12.371ff. should not be cited here, because Odysseus is the only one who is saved from destruction, and he is not guilty of the sacrilege of his companions.

[12] The newest analysis that I am aware of is by Friedrich Focke, *Die Odyssee* (Stuttgart-Berlin, 1943). He differentiates between the Cyclops adventure and the Aiolos adventure, including the "adventure poem" (books 10–12). He attributes the latter to the poet of the *Odyssey* and the former to a particular, older poem (p. 185). In his book the connections referred to here remain without explanation.

battle in the *Iliad* end with the opposing expectations of the Trojans and Achaians. But how much further the consequences reach here, how much more inscrutable are the reasons! The person who is now vanquished becomes the victor one day, and the victor the victim, but without a scene between the gods, as in the *Iliad*, which explains the position of both gods.

The sacrifice and the curse both point in the same way to what is to come. The sacrifice foreshadows the loss of the ship and the crew, the curse something more distant, which the blinded Cyclops asks for. What Poseidon grants him is the same in its result as what Zeus is planning, that is, to spoil the victor's victory. But how is it that Zeus has the same thing in mind as Poseidon? Of course, the reasons that both have are not the same. Poseidon, naturally, thinks, as it were, in a more primitive way; he is angry and outraged for the sake of his son. Zeus turns away from the sacrifice because the fulfillment of judgment in his name does not fit in with this intention. He is angry for the sake of Odysseus. This makes their unanimity and their preordained harmony even more curious.

People used to think that there were two moral codes here, two layers of belief superimposed on each other, that is to say, an older one according to which a god takes revenge and a more recent one in which a god, now Zeus instead of Poseidon, punishes a transgression. The former was seen in the curse of Polyphemos, and the latter in the adventure on Thrinakia. But people did not stop at this; rather, in contrasting two sequences of causation, they separated out two poets: an older one who would have written about the wrath of Poseidon and a more recent one who dealt with the intervention of Zeus.[13] But is the curse of Polyphemos imaginable without the thanksgiving and victory sacrifice of Odysseus? Can one picture one god listening to a prayer without the other one's denial? Does it make sense for a second, more recent poet to add the vital connection that made one part relate to the other? Is it possible that each poet was trying to write his own imitation of the *Iliad*—or something like the *Iliad*—and that their model was only equaled by a combination of these different poems?

If we ask how the plans of these two gods actually *work*, then we find out that, in relation to the importance accorded to the wrath of Poseidon, the number of places in which he is mentioned is very small. Zeus is mentioned much more often. The first place is in the council of the gods in the first book, which imitates the *Iliad* in motif and style. Poseidon is not present at the assembly because he is taking part in the sacrifices of the Ethiopians. For the same reasons Zeus and all the other gods are not on Olympus in the first book of the *Iliad*. Here, as in the *Iliad*, this gives space for a digression, although here it is a much more extensive one, namely on both Kalypso and the voyage of Telemachus.

---

[13] Cf. the remarks of Rudolf Pfeiffer (which are correct in many respects) in *Deutsche Literaturzeitung* 49 (1928), c. 2362 [reprinted in Pfeiffer, *Ausgewählte Schriften* (Munich, 1960), p. 15]. Focke, in *Die Odyssee*, pp. 247f., did not convince me.

The council of the gods ends with a surprise. If one is moving from the general to the particular, from the example to its application, then Athene's impatience finally anticipates the others asking, "If this is so, then why is this the fate of Odysseus?" Zeus' reply is: "If Poseidon were not angry about the blinding of his son, then help would have come to Odysseus a long time before. So let us all think about how he is to return home. Poseidon cannot maintain his wrath alone against everyone." And already Athene is ready: "Let us send Hermes to Kalypso! Meanwhile I . . . ," and she is already putting on her sandals. Without a "Telemachy" the busy goddess would be idle,, she would have to wait, until—well, until when? She would have to wait until Poseidon had retreated after the storm at sea, and for a very modest role at that! She smooths out the sea in his wake—in all this takes six lines. She takes the initiative. With this she begins her move against Poseidon, although at a great distance still. Her sphere of influence is Ithaka.

Then comes the second surprise: after the first day we imagine that meanwhile something is happening on Olympus—only to hear suddenly, in the fifth book, that still nothing has been done. We find out that even the decisions of the gods can be delayed. Athene presents her case again, pointing to the deterioration of the situation: on the one hand the indolence of the people in Ithaka, on the other Odysseus with Kalypso and, on top of all this, his son now in extreme danger! And Zeus? He answers with the same, slightly bemused question as on the first day: "O, what a word, my child . . . ? Did you not yourself want all this? You must take care of Telemachus now, for you are able." And as if everything were in the best hands, he now takes the necessary steps for the first time. (Meanwhile concern for Telemachus is delayed here in the same way that concern for Odysseus was after the first council of the gods.)

It is the misunderstanding of a philologist to assume that here the poet had tried to carry on two different actions happening at the same time and had lost control of his material. The second council is not simply a repetition. In it Athene becomes the one who makes her own decisions, and as a result, she becomes Poseidon's opponent. Only her actions lead to a situation where Zeus *must* help immediately, if matters are not to end in disaster. Only in the second council do we reach that "almost" point, the danger of a situation that has not been thought out, so typical of quarrels between the gods in the *Iliad*. The first one could be wide-reaching and leisurely but the second takes place under pressure from the new situation. The repeated lines (5.8ff. = 2.230ff.; 5.14ff. = 4.557ff.) are like recommitments. Only now one thing leads to another and everything is more urgent. Athene: "Odysseus does not even have a ship to sail in!" Zeus in answer: "Let him sail on a raft!" (The same lines are made to refer to each other, 5.14f. and 4.557f.; there the impossibility of returning home, here the solution to the puzzle). Now, for the first time, the control of the highest ruler of the heavens is set a task. If his order is something of a prophecy—he foresees the repetition—that is not a reason to object to it: his orders do come to pass.

But what would come of all this without the wrath of Poseidon? The invention of his anger carries the whole action up to the level of Olympus.

In the storm at sea in the fifth book, Poseidon is the opponent of Athene in the style of the *Iliad*. And yet there is a difference here also. When one goes, the other comes, and so Athene's eagerness, which has just been demonstrated, reveals her restraint. The more she dares to do on Ithaka, the less in his domain. This move and countermove, this opposition to each other and yet yielding and giving in to each other, with Zeus over all, allowing and directing, is part of the schema of the poem and of the world, as the poet sees it.

The next and last time Poseidon intervenes, he turns the ship of the Phaiakes to stone (13.125ff.). Here again there is a scene with the gods of the type in the *Iliad* (*Il.* 20.13f., 8.445, 15.185, 4.37). The prophecy of Alkinoos (13,175), which does not involve a scene with the gods, has no knowledge of the wrath or its cause. What this means will be discussed later.

In the actual fairy-tale adventures, Poseidon nowhere appears as the enemy, with one exception: Teiresias points to him in the Nekyia. But as soon as the wrath is mentioned, the punishment decreed by Zeus follows immediately again. Teiresias' prophecy and the curse of Polyphemos are interdependent both in language and content. We are told twice (1.20 and 6.330) that Poseidon's wrath does not relent. But where do the adventures show this? When Odysseus is held captive by Kalypso for seven years, then that is Kalypso's fault and not Poseidon's. The "daemon" (7.248) leads him to her. Circe and Kalypso account for over eight years. Is Poseidon's wrath supposed to have rested all this time? Moreover, Odysseus has been blown off course long before Polyphemos curses him. If there is no need for Poseidon's wrath to reach the Lotus Eaters and the Cyclopes, then it is not needed for the adventures of the Sirens and Charybdis. If the council of the gods were not to take place until *after* the adventures rather than where the poet wants it, then the wrath of the god would lack every reason. But surely we should not make calculations.

Yet even without calculating, we can see that Poseidon's wrath is not mentioned for so long because the adventures have their own magic. Not only Thrinakia, but all the others clash with Poseidon's wrath in the same way. What would happen to Aiolos if we think of the angry Poseidon? But also the Sirens, Skylla and Charybdis, even the Underworld, would all be stripped of their own magic qualities by the wrath of Poseidon. When seen as a fate dependent on Zeus, all this can be understood as a unity or sequence, just as, for example, the eye of Sinbad the sailor is always directed to Allah in all his crises. But the wrath and character of Poseidon surely does not do this.

The conclusion to be drawn is that Poseidon's wrath is there for the sake of the action of the gods. It is a given element in the style of great epic and prescribed by the genre of the *nostos*. Just as the fleet of the Achaians is buffeted by the anger of Athene (5.108), and just as Locrian Ajax is destroyed by the rage of Poseidon (4.502), so Odysseus is threatened with the same fate. Poseidon's wrath is a link, not a story that can be told in itself, neither as the end of an adventure nor without any reference to Zeus. The storm at sea makes it into great poetry. And the storm in its turn is required by the poetic genre of the *nostos*. But above all, the wrathful god is the opponent of the helping goddess. Consequently, the whole is articulated into two parts, each of which is subject to its own god.

But a poem is not simply a composition. One can hardly maintain that the end of the Cyclops adventure is on a more primitive level of belief than the adventure on Thrinakia. The fact that Poseidon brings about something, which fits in with the will of Zeus, takes on an even greater significance because it is against all the rules of the game for gods in the *Iliad*. Here the will of both gods *coincides* until their last scene, at 13.125ff. They take each other into consideration, although Zeus naturally does this in a different way than Poseidon. In Poseidon's wrath there is a negative element. He simply wants his rights as a god. He is not concerned with anything else that happens. But even his negative side is subject to the great positive element, which is Zeus. Zeus allows him to have his way, although his wrath affects the whole.

If the world experience of the *Iliad* is the result of a battle in which Zeus remains victorious despite all setbacks, then the fates of the *Odyssey* are decided by a game of opposing and yielding, which leaves Zeus as the one on top, the one to whose will all the other gods submit. The mystery of this coincidence of will, with which we started, in which Zeus and Poseidon both aim for the same goal while each is thinking something different, points to a theological background of the poetry.

AIOLOS AND THE LAISTRYGONES

In the adventure of the Laistrygones, we miss the storytelling element, finding it undeveloped, dark, and crude. This is actually quite understandable, as long as we do not take it as the conclusion to the Aiolos story that comes before it. In order to do this, we must first differentiate between tradition and fresh composition, between old and new, in the Aiolos story.

What elevates the Aiolos story so far above everything more primitive is surely not the misfortune of letting the winds out of their prison, but rather the contrast between Odysseus' first and his second reception, that is to say, his failure to repeat his initial experience. It is remarkable how the epic poet, who portrayed the Cyclops' cave so vividly, in this case denies himself any elaboration of the fantasy elements, such as the palace, the cave of the winds, etc., that the floating island and its king had to offer for his imagination. He does this in order to bring out, with even greater force, the single contrast on which he has made everything depend. If he wanted to indulge in the fairy-tale elements, then the drama and the new meaning of the story, which was his own addition to the fairy-tale adventures, would be lost.

The more this story is lacking in vivid elements when compared with the Polyphemos story, the more it surpasses the latter in terms of economy. Because of the two acts, into which the whole story is divided, this fairy tale reaches a climax, of the kind usually thought to be originally suited to a novella. A comparison can be made with the two-part novellas in Herodotus, such as the one about Croesus or Pythios (7.27, 38). More and more we see that the aim of the story is to make clear that the worst of it is not the storm caused by the winds rushing out of the sack, nor the uselessness of all his efforts—although Odysseus would very much like to throw himself into the sea because of this (the usual Sinbad-motif)—rather, the worst of it is what this all means: that as Odysseus is hated and cursed by the gods, so Aiolos in his castle must increasingly become the perfect example of the man whom the gods love: "beloved by the immortal gods" (10.2). For this reason and for this reason alone, the poet attends us at the beginning with things that are quite different from what we expect.

What we are expecting can be seen in Virgil. In the *Aeneid* (1.50ff.) the castle is described and in the hill under the castle, the cave of the monsters, the dungeon of the winds, and how Aiolos rules them with a strong hand, letting them in and out. But none of this is here. At the beginning we do not even find out that Aiolos is the King of the Winds. We hear about this for the first time when he gives his guest-present. What different issues come into the foreground instead! While the winds in the *Iliad* are in very high spirits as a group and eager for feminine beauty as they meet for feasting on their home ground (Il. 23.200f.), here the Lord of the Winds becomes the embodiment of domestic harmony. The poet of the *Odyssey* never tires of praising the happiness of marriage, but nowhere in his poetry does it appear with such fairy-tale qualities as here. The man whom the gods love gave his six daughters in marriage to his own six sons. So their days are one long feast, accompanied by unceasing song and music on stringed instruments, and their nights are all nights of love. They are more intense versions of the Phaiakes. (Reports of marriages between siblings in distant dynasties may have contributed, but that is not what is meant). And the man whom the gods love becomes the guest-friend of the wanderer and keeps him lovingly according to the rules of the most select guest-friendship, as we have learned to understand it in the Telemachy. He keeps him no longer and no shorter than is suitable, and when he is sending him on his way, he does this in accordance with tradition, not without a guest-present. In this case, to distinguish it from all the other times, the guest-present is the most precious thing that Aiolos has to give—the sack, in which the winds are trapped. Here, for the first time, we hear about his sovereignty: "For the son of Kronos had set him in charge over the winds." Does the old fairy-tale element not appear as a surprise in this transformed version? Is what used to be the main point not delayed to the end, for the sake of the new meaning?

The concern of the king is so far-reaching that he ties up his gift himself in the hollow of the ship with a silver string, with the same care that Alkinoos shows when he himself takes care of stowing his guest-present in the ship's hold (13.20). The second departure is all the more terrible, since the first one was so very kind.

For the sake of this repetition, the poet has accepted that the winds rushing out of the sack do not unleash a huge storm, as we expect. Nor do they scatter the twelve ships, as in Virgil, but rather these quickly land back where they started, so that they put ashore and eat their meal. For the second time Odysseus sets out, only this time he takes two companions with him and sits meekly on the floor by the entrance, while the same carefree feasting is going on inside. And then comes the answer, in direct speech, that unexpected ending, which is probably much more the model for Schiller's *Ring des Polykrates* than Herodotus, but how much more unprecedented as a gesture! (10.64ff.):

> "What brings you back, Odysseus? What evil spirit has vexed you?
> We sent you properly on your way, so you could come back
> to your own country and house and whatever else is dear to you."
> So they spoke, and I though sorry at heart answered:
> "My wretched companions brought me to ruin, helped by the pitiless
> sleep. Then make it right, dear friends; for you have the power."
> So I spoke to them, plying them with words of endearment,
> but they were all silent; only the father found words and answered:
> "O least of living creatures, out of this island! Hurry!
> I have no right to see on his way, none to give passage
> to any man whom the blessed gods hate with such bitterness.
> Out. This arrival means you are hateful to the immortals."

An enemy of the gods is a man for whom mercy turns into disaster. It is part of the nature of a curse that it is pronounced without warning. Nowhere else are Odysseus' eyes opened in this way. What he did not know, when he sacrificed the ram to Zeus Xenios after surviving the Cyclops adventure, he now knows: that the prayer of the blinded Cyclops was heard rather than his own.[14] This new ending, to which the whole adventure is now tailored, points both to the past and the future. The Aiolos story is not there for its own sake; one cannot stop after it. The tension it leaves behind points to what follows, the adventure of the Laistrygones. This story in turn, which is the more spooky as it is unelaborated and without any epic detail, takes our breath away with the breakneck speed of its unfolding. It

---

[14] *Contra* Focke, *Die Odyssee*, p. 187: "The gruff dismissal of the returning voyagers lacks a poetically satisfying explanation."

answers the question that the Aiolos story left open. There is no word of explanation about Odysseus' carefulness. Anything additional would impede the speed that keeps going until the end, that ending that forms the great caesura in the rhythm of adventures (10.131f.):

> Gladly *my* ship, and only mine, fled out from the overhanging
> cliffs to the open water, but the others were all destroyed there.

In the translations the antithesis and the final character of the second line generally do not emerge. They were composed by the same poet, who invented a fleet to go with the one ship, the same man who diverted the ending of the Aiolos story into a curse. The result is that he has added a surprise of a different kind to the surprises in the fairy tales: the surprise created by a fate carried out in accordance with the will of the gods.

In the first series of adventures, Odysseus obviously cannot be completely absolved of some part in the destruction of the fleet. Clearly he does not have a share of the guilt in a literal sense, but in that difficult and obscure sense, which can be surmised from the adventure of the Cyclops. In the second series he becomes all the more innocent.

CIRCE AND KALYPSO

Philologists do not have a very high opinion of the Circe adventure. Their opinion is that although the legend is old and good, the poet of this story is a latecomer, someone who worked on and imitated the material of others, a poet who owes whole sections down to the last letter to the inventor of Kalypso, a poet who should be valued all the more disproportionately higher. Eduard Schwartz, following Wilamowitz, feels: "To an even greater extent than heroic greatness, human greatness has been lost. The relationship with Kalypso is of such purity, such as is only revealed to poets of originality, who discover the depths of human hearts: the Circe adventure is not far removed from a Milesian tale."[15]

In making a charge of base sensuality, they clearly overlook the rhythm of the story. They overlook how little, in comparison with fairy tales, pleasure in love is picked out as the goal of the adventure. The story almost passes over it. First it stops, and it only comes to its climax and changes its situation after they enjoy the pleasures of love. Odysseus, wonderfully washed and dressed by elfin hands, is sitting opposite Circe and is gloomy and silent, after the preparation of all the fantastic, good things—all this is used in the service of creating a feeling of tension. The spell is not broken until Odysseus' comrades are changed back.

One cannot aim at two effects at the same time in the same story, or the

[15] Eduard Schwartz, *Die Odyssee*, p. 270. U. v. Wilamowitz-Moellendorff, *Homerische Untersuchungen* (Berlin, 1884), pp. 115f. P. Von der Mühll, "*Odyssee*."

story will not be effective. To demand that the magic of Circe would have to be described with the same enchantment as the grotto of Kalypso or with the same charming bucolic surroundings as the cave of Polyphemos, in order to have been composed by the same poet, is to set a goal that was not the aim in this case. Before one provides that the creator of Kalypso and Polyphemos would not have been the kind of poet to want what was intended here, one will not be able to deny him the Circe adventure for such reasons of taste.

For now another element is added to those already considered: namely, the changing relationship between the hero and his companions. That Odysseus cares for his men and feels responsible as a leader for his followers, is another element that does not fit in at all with the old fairy-tale material. In fact, it is something so characteristic of the poet of the *Odyssey,* that this is also not the least criterion by which he is differentiated from the poet of the *Iliad.* In the *Iliad* the men serve no purpose other than to be led, to create the feelings of the crowd and to comprise the waves of battle in attack or flight. Yet the cares of the great heroes are not fixed on them. In the *Odyssey* Odysseus' concern for saving his companions is immediately stressed at the beginning. With each adventure it becomes clearer that they are causing their own destruction through their own fault. For this very reason Odysseus' concern for his men has to grow all the more. This necessitates that the relationship between leader and companions become tense and that in the end a rival leader should put himself forward.

So then again, for the sake of these elements, it is no coincidence that the Circe adventure stands in the middle between the Cyclops adventure and Thrinakia. In the Cyclops adventure Odysseus is still more audacious than concerned, and that is why one could never place it at the end. In the adventure on Thrinakia, Eurylochos becomes mutinous. What breaks out as a result, is prepared for in the Circe adventure. There protest, which eventually leads the crew to destruction, is once again calmed in a friendly say. So this looks, as it were, in both directions. Nowhere else does Odysseus face danger for the others as here. This time the fairy-tale adventure becomes epic because the magic test becomes simultaneously a test of the loyalty between leader and companions. And nowhere else is he rewarded with such heartfelt thanks. The magic fairy tale becomes a tale of the happiest reunion. The heartfelt groans can sound all the stronger this time—"more sentimental" in the reproof of the critics—since soon enough they turn into the opposite, in the sacrilege offered to the cattle of the sun; and Eurylochos, who is humbled one more time, will triumph.

But now what jumping for joy there is! May we detect irony in this?

> And as, in the country, the calves, around the cows returning
> from pasture back to the dung of the farmyard, well filled with grazing,
> come gamboling together to meet them, and the pens no longer
> can hold them in, but lowing incessantly they come running

around their mothers, so these men, once their eyes saw me,
came streaming around me, in tears, and the spirit in them made
   them
feel as if they were back in their own country, the very
city of rugged Ithaka, where they were born and raised up.

(10.410–17)

But this means that these men, who are now leaping with joy, will not see Ithaka again. The contrast, which is already being adumbrated here, is the mutiny and the breaking of the oath on Thrinakia:

> and Eurylochos put an evil counsel before his companions
> "Listen to what I say, my companions, though you are suffering . . ."

(12.339–40)

As a foreshadowing of Thrinakia, this also points back to Polyphemos at the same time. The more Eurylochos refers to the adventure of the Cyclops in his opposition—people have wanted to discard the lines that are indispensible[16]—the more the adventure with Circe must, as it unfolds, become the mirror of the Cyclops adventure. It is for this reason that it begins in the same way; one can see smoke rising and that is enough to cause a general outcry. But there the adventure was very different. After the most terrible losses, after the survivors have barely escaped, Odysseus the daredevil risks all at the end and does not rest until he has drawn the curse of Polyphemos down on himself. Here, after the most terrible beginning, we have a fairy-tale-like happy ending, and not only for Odysseus! Those who are turned back into men become much more handsome than they ever were! The good life enjoyed by all, freshly bathed and dressed, is described with all the conventional epic detail. Yet how the conventional, when contrasted with the pigs' food, does now become unconventional and significant! Heroic elevation at the end of its most terrible opposite. For this contrast we can grasp why the poet used only the pigs instead of the various transforma-

---

[16]*Od.* 10.435–37 is often rejected as spurious. "Cut out by Kirchhoff; the Cyclops did not shut Odysseus and his companions in his cave so that they could be his watchmen." (E. Schwartz, *Die Odyssee*, p. 318). Yet for the man-eater, consuming the companions is no different than casting the spell is for the sorceress. These lines are necessary to explain why Odysseus can be calmed only with difficulty. A hero only reacts in this way when he has been insulted. See *Il.* 1.190 for a model. Odysseus would not snap the head off someone who was merely fearful and warning him. Focke, *Die Odyssee*, p. 254, agrees with Schwartz in also distinguishing two adventure cycles by two different poets. But these references back to the Polyphemos story in the Circe adventure do not rely only on these verses, as has been demonstrated. *Od.* 10.437, in the accusation "for it was by this man's (Odysseus') recklessness that these two perished (in the cave of the Cyclops)," presupposes the opposite: 1.7, "they were destroyed by their own wild recklessness." Therefore the proem, Circe, and Thrinakia are very closely connected. On the other hand, the justification becomes meaningless without at least the appearance of the opposite. Yet how should this impression be created if not in the Polyphemos story? If one makes a serious effort to cut out the Polyphemos story, then one will soon notice that as a result the Circe and Thrinakia adventures also lose their context.

tions into wolves, lions, etc., that the fairy tale offered. The rest of them, a favorite theme in vase painting, are referred to at the beginning and in Eurylochos' speech, yet they are not employed in the story. The pigsty becomes the direct opposite of the description of the heroic banquet.

So that the house of Circe should not lack landscape around it, the stag hunt provides the idyllic element here to balance the island of the goats. Yet the prologue is a heroic idyll in this case, unlike the one before the Cyclops adventure. The stag, on the way to his watering place, falls like a hero in the *Iliad*.[17] At the same time the hunt also reveals Odysseus' concern.

But what is the relationship between the Circe story and the Kalypso episode? Is Kalypso really the original and Circe the copy? Wilamowitz once set himself the task of making the comparison, line by line, to show how the imitator fails, and others up to the most recent time have followed him in this. But here it is a question not only of comparing line by line, but also the different styles and stages.

Circe, the mistress of Aiaia, sister of the treacherous Aietes, reminds us of the magic land in the East, of which Aietes is king, the land to which the Argonauts sailed, later known as Colchis on the east coast of the Black Sea. But the mythical atmosphere suggested by such a genealogy and region is disproportionately stronger, according to the will of the poet, than the geographical connection between the two magic lands, which is still only shadowy. This does not mean that Aiaia is to be equated with Colchis in "Homeric geography" or that it lies in the Northeast; rather it tells us that Odysseus is stepping onto ground where magic and trickery are hereditary.

Sorceresses instead of witches, women like Circe and her niece Medea, are only possible as figures in a world no longer magic. The innumerable parallels with the voyage of Jason or Odysseus in the myths and fairy tales, which are more distant in time, show that magic places of all kinds are all the more intensified and multiplied to an overwhelming extent. Where everything works magic and every step is a spell, there can be no special gods in this field like Hermes or Hekate among the Olympians, nor can there be sorceresses like Medea or Circe. Both have, in turn, differentiated themselves as sorceresses, the one in a terrifying way, the other, Circe, to bring happiness, just as Hekate and Hermes are differentiated as gods. If Medea, as demonically in love and ruining both others and herself, can become a tragic figure, then Circe by contrast becomes a dangerous enchantress, but one who brings luck to a real hero. The Circe adventure is the only one where magic is overcome by a contrary spell. According to its layering this is a very old story, one of those many magic tests, by which the fairy-tale hero must prove himself.[18]

---

[17] *Od.* 10.163 = *Il.* 16.469. U. v. Wilamowitz-Moellendorff, *Homerische Untersuchungen*, p. 121.

[18] For the fairy-tale parallels, cf. the fairy tale by Grimm about Jorinde and Joringel, and the comments by J. Bolte and G. Polivka, *Anmerkungen zu den Kinder- und Hausmärchen der Brüder Grimm* (vol. 2, Leipzig, 1915), p. 69. See also E. Bethe, *Die Gedichte Homers, Wissen-*

Compared with Circe Kalypso already shows a very well-developed psychology. The fairy tale does not demand this. And yet, if we deny it a psychological element, that does not mean that it misleads us by being unpsychological or psychologically faulty. It only means that one should not measure it in terms of psychology. If Circe becomes charming in an instant after having been a monster, then something psychological is being hinted at, which great epic would hardly accommodate if it were told directly. Equally it would be easy to transcribe the motif of fairy-tale magic into a tone of psychological development, of which no romantic novelist need be ashamed. Why else would Circe be described as so beautiful, so tempting, so seductive, so inviting, triumphing so contemptuously over all the other men, if it were not her foreordained fate to have to do this, until she meets the man whom she recognizes as her master? He is the fortunate and brave man, who does not fall under her spell, like the stupid ones, nor does he run away from her like Eurylochos the coward. Drawing a sword in the style of epic is surely more suitable than swallowing an antidote in the style of fairy tales? The meeting with the god of luck, Hermes, expresses nothing other than that Odysseus is that man. The favor of the gods is only bestowed on people ready to receive it. And now that this finally happens to her, it really is the unconscious goal of all her schemes, which took malicious pleasure in the ruin of others. A miracle happens to her and she is transformed, as if freed from a spell. She immediately invites Odysseus to her bed and becomes a godlike and very loyal mistress.

There is no clash here with the rule of what is psychologically possible, but other things do take the place of psychology. Yet this other element is not only a fairy-tale one; later, novelistic elements are blended in. It is an integral part of this development that a prophecy is fulfilled, that her conquerer was foretold to her, so that instead of putting Odysseus under a spell, she is released from one herself and recognizes her fate in recognizing him. She is released by meeting her match. Stories of this type, which end with the fulfillment of a prophecy, like those known to us from Herodotus, must have been current (cf. the end of the Cyclops and Phaiakian adventures, 9.507 and 13.172!). Yet the fairy-tale elements are shown to be related to the novelistic ones inasmuch as the antidote, which breaks the spell, is already virtually part of the transition and points, by analogy, to a spiritual quality. In the power of the magic, we recognize another, the power of the spirit (10.329):

There is a mind in you no magic will work on.

Is she making a mistake because she does not recognize the power of *moly* and attributes the gift of the god of magic to Odysseus' "spirit," his *noos*?

So it is only the ending that is not touched by this irridescence, this more-than-fairy-tale quality of the story. The poet certainly knows how to delight in the contrast between the two Circes, the hostile one and the loving one!

Yet Odysseus represented as the stranger and inquirer testing hospitality of the most varying kinds, does not belong to the ancient fairy-tale tradition; rather he is the invention of our *Odyssey*. When Circe also fulfils her own destiny, which is expressed in the prophecy of which she experiences the fulfillment, fairy tale is turned into poetry. Now that they recognize each other, they are allowed to love each other and Odysseus is allowed to spend a year with her. Indeed he does not resist her magic for so long that we almost begin to fear that he could forget himself and Ithaka. So this adventure ends with a long, drawn-out pause. This is different from the others, which have a sudden climax at the end. The one who usually warns the others, must this time be reminded of himself by the others—which is also an adventure! The Kalypso adventure stands in stark opposition. Circe remains his companion through her advice. The Circe adventure stretches and forms something like a frame around the other stories, like happy forgetfulness before the gloomy revelations of the Underworld. The ordering of the stories creates all these interrelationships. Everything loses its references if one changes this sequence as the philologists have been doing up to most recent times.

Now let us compare Kalypso to Circe. If Circe is the sister of "malicious" Aietes, that is her attribute as a sorceress. Yet Kalypso is also the daughter of a malicious god, "malignant" Atlas (1.52). But how does she show what she has inherited from her father? As is demonstrated at the end, her malice consists only in the mistaken fear of the hero. Circe's malice fills her story. There is no story at all that can be told about Kalypso. What Odysseus has to watch out for with her is described by the same word as what Circe threatens him with: *enchantment* (1.57 ~ 10.213, 291, 318). Yet the tools of "enchantment," for Circe a magic potion and a wand, are for Kalypso only words and the charms of her beauty. The spiritual replaces magic.

> And ever with soft and flattering words she works to
> charm him to forget Ithaka; and yet Odysseus,
> straining to get sight of the very smoke uprising
> from his own country, longs to die.

> (1.56–59)

In the case of Circe, her surroundings and the way in which she appears, as one first stands before the gate, then hears her voice, in fact everything around her, relates to her "magic." She sings, tempts, invites, entertains. The characteristic element for her story is the participation she provokes, a participation aimed only at the result of the event. By contrast, at Kalypso's it is the inner situation that demands all participation, no longer needing any outer miracles. The surprise happens in the sphere of the heart, rather than of deeds and wonders. And yet what an assimilation! What insistence on formal elements even in the complete transition from fairy tale almost to the novel! Kalypso also sings like Circe. Both sing with beautiful voices as they go up and down at the loom. The same line is in both places. Circe's song cannot be cut from her story in that it is a necessary part of the adventure. How lyrically the threefold repetition is dwelt on, first in the fate of the companions, then in the story of Eurylochos running away, and at last confirmed in the experience of Odysseus. Yet we ask, For whom does Kalypso sing? Does she also sing so that a surprised stranger may want to come in, so that he will call to her and she can open the door and invite him in? Odysseus is sitting far away by the sea. Is she singing for Hermes, whom she is not expecting? Or is she singing for herself? She must be. Does what is pretence and malice for Circe become the truth for Kalypso?

The song of Circe cannot be separated from her magic. In the case of Circe also, of course, some of that other magic is added to the old fairy-tale magic, the magic of beauty and figure. She is no longer a witch as in the fairy-tale parallels. But whom is Kalypso singing for? Her song is part of another unity, i.e., the magic of landscape, rocky caves, sweet smells coming from her stove, springs, poplars, and cypresses, birds on the branches. Her song becomes an accompaniment. Instead of a magic fairy tale, we have the magic of an idyll here. This is indeed an enchanting place, before which even a god like Hermes stands still for a while—a picture complete in itself and yet not without connections.

As the god is amazed, Odysseus sits alone by the sea and groans and weeps. One picture contrasts with the other. This is the relationship between immortality, with which the nymph tempts, and the longing for his home, the same as the relationship between love for Kalypso and love for Penelope. For Penelope is present too, although far away, and her presence creates a unity out of everything and introduces a third person where they were only two. A different *Odyssey* would begin with Kalypso without a word about Penelope before her. Would something not be missing in Kalypso's cave if this was the construction? Would it not stop being what it has to be, a complement?

But there are more elements like this in the transformed whole. The god who helps Odysseus escape the spell of both sorceresses is Hermes on both occasions. In the first case he comes as the god of magic, who brings luck on the strength of his own attributes; in the Kalypso adventure he is the stylized messenger of the gods from epic. This may be coincidence. But what adaptation causes Odysseus, in both cases after breaking the spell—i.e., in Kalypso's cave, after she has promised to let him go—to ask for an oath from the goddess.

> to swear me a great oath
> that there is no other evil hurt you devised against me.

$$(5.178–79 = 10.343–44)$$

And both are equally willing to do him this favor (again in the same lines). And yet the "evil hurt" that Odysseus is guarding against, is of a very different nature in each case. The first time he fears the loss of his manly strength—there is reason enough for such a fear if one shares the bed of Circe—the second time he fears something that cannot be described, something threatening in a dark future.[19] Yet when he asks for this oath from Circe, he proves to be foresighted and clever, a master of the situation, the hero of the adventure; but in the other case, when making the same demand, he makes a mistake. But because of this mistake, because he remains the old Odysseus and takes precautions as if Kalypso were a Circe, she loves him all the more. Disdaining the love of a nymph could easily be dangerous. One only has to think of Daphnis. But in this case the sad Kalypso, weeping at being disdained and denied, raging at her fate as she quotes mythical examples, becomes full of loving concern and smiles. The transformation is quieter but for this reason almost more surprising.

Odysseus' care, his demand for an oath from the goddess, is a crucial moment in this new turn (5.180ff):

> So he spoke, and Kalypso, shining among divinities,
> smiled and stroked him with her hand and spoke to him and named him:
> You are so naughty, and you will have your own way in all things.
> See how you have spoken to me and reason with me.

But what can this be except a new variation of the epic scene in which Odysseus is needlessly fearful? This is, more particularly, a different version of his meeting with Athene, when after not recognizing his home, he does not recognize and lies to the goddess who protects him (13.253–86):

> So he spoke. The goddess, gray-eyed Athene, smiled on him,
> and stroked him with her hand, and took on the shape of a woman
> both beautiful and tall, and well versed in glorious handiworks,
> and spoke aloud to him and addressed him in winged words, saying:
> "It would be a sharp one, and a stealthy one, who would ever get past you
> in any contriving; even if it were a god against you.
> You wretch, so devious, never weary of tricks . . ."

(13.288–93)

Which is earlier and which later here? Odysseus as the one who is groundlessly afraid or as the man who is cautious with a reason? There is no

---

[19] U. v. Wilamowitz, *Homerische Untersuchungen*, pp. 119f., tries to prove the independence of the lines around 10.300 or 10.344 (Circe) from the lines at 5.179 (Kalypso), by judging the connection in book 10 to be insufficient. But this only succeeds at the price of an impossible construction. In 5.179 he claims *allo* is in apposition to *pēma kakon moi autōi*. This is supposedly the original construction. In the tenth book *pēma* was changed to an object and *allo* to an attribute. One should just try to read the line in meter in the original form restored by Wilamowitz! Although such appositions floating in the middle of a sentence are at best possible in Aeschylus, they are certainly not so in epic. Also there are no parallels for this. *Allo* does not mean "something different from what you are saying, namely an evil for *me*," but "another new evil." In the tenth book the first evil is what she did to his *companions*. The new evil he fears is what she will do to *him*, to his body, if he does not protect himself. For a similar usage, cf. *Il.* 24.551, 16.262, *Od.* 4.698.

possibility of a doubt. Odysseus can only fear needlessly after the gods want his return, after the council of the gods with which the *Odyssey* begins. In its irony this is part of the poet's plan. The other is a part of the old fairy-tale tradition. The latter cannot be older than the former.

Now let us go back to the question we were asking at the beginning: if, as has turned out, the Kalypso episode as poetry depends on the Circe adventure, and on the form found in our *Odyssey*, is this not an extra reason why it should be by a different poet? I do not want to go through a refutation of this point by point here. At best this would lead to an *Odyssey* that would be like ours but could not be allowed to be the same. Enough of this.

The question here is not what is the original and what an imitation; rather, it is how is the difference qualified as a difference of layers, which the epic uses, as it combines older and newer material, traditions and what is created out of the spirit of the times? Sometimes the epic creates situations from stories, on the model of the *Iliad*, and then digs back again into the traditions of fairy tale. One often becomes the echo of the other. The Kalypso episode is related to the Circe adventure in the same way that Hektor's farewell to Andromache, as an epic situation, is related in material and legend to Hektor's death and the fall of Troy. Or, to keep to the *Odyssey*, in the way the story of Penelope's trick with her weaving is related to her appearance before the deluded suitors, in the epic situation of the eighteenth book. If one wants to look further, then the Gyges fairy tale can also be compared in a similar way to the Herodotean novella. Poetry of this kind forms a transition. In the adventure on Scheria, the fairy-tale element keeps itself hidden under the guise of epic, notwithstanding its contradictions, while here the fairy-tale and the epic elements separate into two figures: Kalypso and, next to her, Circe.[20]

---

[20] It remains to deal with one objection—also stemming from Wilamowitz. The oath itself is sworn solemnly enough by Kalypso in direct speech:

> Earth be my witness in this, and the wide heaven about us,
> and the dripping water of the Styx, which oath is the biggest
> and most formidable oath among the blessed immortals,
> that this is no other painful trial I am planning against you.

(5.184ff.)

Of Circe Odysseus merely says, "She at once swore me the oath, as I asked her." So is the first not, after all, the model for the second? Yet this oath in these words is only possible if what she swears really does come to pass fully afterward. In the Kalypso adventure the oath is followed by the building of the raft and the whole farewell, so rich in associations. But as a storyteller one cannot have Circe swear an oath of the gods in four lines when nothing happens afterward except, "I mounted the surpassingly beautiful bed of Circe." A preparation must not outweigh what is being prepared for. That this would be the case here is a result in turn of the fitting and molding of the Circe adventure to accommodate the unity of Fate represented by all the adventures together. The objection is overruled by the economy of epic. The oaths in *Iliad* 3.276ff. need not have been sworn so solemnly if a truce and the start of new battles with all their ramifications did not depend on them. [For the relationship between the Gyges fairy tale and Herodotean novella, see K. Reinhardt, *Vermächtnis der Antike* (Göttingen, 1960), pp. 139ff.]

The Kalypso adventure ends with the building of the raft. Without the raft there is no Kalypso. Whoever invented Kalypso did his best to thwart any previous hope that could humanly be conceived, that Odysseus would ever come home again. In the fairy-tale tradition, the shipwrecked sailor came to the hospitable Phaiakes. Now he has landed on the furthest island, which is even out of the way for the gods, and in addition he has met a nymph who is in love with him! No more hopeless situation could be imagined. Everyone who longs for something can picture the way the poet of the Telemachy—we assume he is the same person—is concerned in his own sphere to add a hopelessness in Ithaka equal to the one felt out there. These situations are calculated toward unhoped-for solutions. In the fairy-tale traditions it is the helpful spirits who show the fairy-tale heroes a way out. In the world of epic, the spirits also take on another form.

Telemachus is helped by Athene herself, if not through a magic potion, through what is called a miracle in the real world. Yet the nymph does not help Odysseus with a fairy-tale marvel either, no veil or shoes with wings, but she helps him, under orders from Zeus, to make himself a raft with an axe, hatchet, wood, and advice. What a new spirit in an ancient form! The magic help turns into the advice "help yourself!" Odysseus is probably also a master craftsman as inventor of the wooden horse. Here the man, who is rich in designs, enters into a new area, which is dear to the heart of the poet of the *Odyssey:* the spirit of craftsmanship. Why is it that the nymph, in this case, advises him and not Athene? Why does the nymph suddenly have all these tools in her cave of love and bring them to her lover with the diligence of a helpful little elf? This surprising turn of events belongs to the concessions, without which the plan of the *Odyssey* could never have been carried out. But how charming that this is not glossed over but rather explained away, as if to create wonder! How aimless longing turns into beneficial help and how different from Circe!

Naturally Odysseus does not suspect that Zeus has issued the order for building the raft. The surprising part of this reversal, for both father and son, is wrought by the second council of the gods on Olympus, so often undervalued for its ease and superiority. Why then does Hermes not mention the raft in his instructions to Kalypso? Why does Kalypso anticipate him (5.140f.)? Perhaps because otherwise the invention would lose some of its charm. If one thinks about the instructions to build a raft—it is better after all the way it is written.

THRINAKIA

Why must the adventures that come after Circe be prophesied by her? Why does the poet dispense with the surprises that the stories offer? If they are unannounced, they bear witness to the ever new presence of mind of the hero in situations that are constantly more difficult. They were, after all, devised simply for this effect. The stories about Sinbad are no different. It may be said that we now reach a different excitement instead of the initial one, an excitement aimed at how, exactly, prophecies are actually fulfilled. What has been foretold, when it happens, is something different from the unexpected. Prophecy turns the dangers into a fate that has been imposed. The hero who must survive them becomes less inventive, but in return he becomes more of a "sufferer." How this is connected to the plan of the whole *Odyssey* has already been partially revealed to us. Yet one thing still needs to be added here.

Among these adventures there is one to which prophecy has not been added later, one that could not be told at all without prophecy and warn-ing. This one has evidently pulled the other stories along with it as well. Prophecy opens up two possibilities, the "either-or" of foretelling, which has nothing to do otherwise with the nature of the danger, such as, for example, the clashing rocks, the Rovers, about which it is foretold, "Either you must go through them or past Skylla and Charybdis." In one case this either-or cannot be separated from the whole meaning of the adventure, because it becomes a test, a *peira* sent by the gods, a question of passing or failing a test, but in a much more moral rather than a fairy-tale sense. For this very reason the story of the sacrilege done to the cattle of the sun is essentially different from all the others. Precisely because of it the poet de-cided on the constrictions of this format.

He places a unique and particular stress on this adventure. Not only the prologue points to this (1.8) but also the nineteenth book (275), when the explanation for the shipwreck points back to this by mentioning only this one adventure instead of the rest. Although it is positioned like a fairy-tale adventure among other fairy-tale adventures, as if framed by Skylla and Charybdis, yet in its nature it is something different, no Sinbad story. Ac-cording to its inner format, it is something legendary, that is to say, some-thing religious. It is a warning, a first step into misfortune, which they do not sail past. First we have the promise backed up by an oath, then the test, the temptation through hunger, through the constant adverse winds, the complaining, the triumph of evil, the evil premonitions at the sacrifice . . .

All this is much more reminiscent of cult-legends than of any fairy-tale element. Such legends tell about the punishment of some kind of sacrilege against the god's possessions, the temple's goods, sacred groves, hearths, or the like.[21] According to an old temple legend, Zeus puts Tantalos to the test, because he is keeping something he has stolen from the temple, the dog from Zeus' sanctuary on Crete. As a warning he asks him about it through Hermes (scholion on Pindar, *Olympian* 1.91). The punishment of Erysichthon, when he fells Demeter's sacred grove in order to build himself

---

[21] Radermacher also categorizes the Thrinakia adventure as a legend from the point of view of a general comparison of motifs. We are concerned with the Greek, literary elements.

a banqueting hall, is also introduced by a warning. The goddess, in the disguise of the priestess, warns him, as is narrated by Callimachus in the style of a legend. The poet of the *Odyssey,* as if it were a question of the same kind of thing, warns Aigisthos, who surely would not have deserved on his own account that Zeus should bother about him and send Hermes to enlighten him (1.35ff). Similarly, the following elements are clearly all part of a religious form. A person announces the sacrilege to the god who has been injured, the anger of the god follows and his threat not to carry out his function in the future, if he is not given his due, and then Zeus' guarantee of his rights. Just as here the Heliad Lampetion reports to Helios what has happened, so the raven reports the faithlessness of Koronis to Apollo in Hesiod's *Catalogue of Women* (scholion on Pindar, *Pythian* 3.48). Similarly Helios tells Hephaistos about Aphrodite's adultery in *Odyssey* 8.270. In all three cases the same formula is repeated. Helios' threat not to shine on the earth anymore is equivalent to Demeter's refusal in the Homeric hymn to let sown corn grow. In both cases it is Zeus who affords reparation to the insulted divinity.

If Odysseus the narrator knows about such things but has to rely on information from Kalypso to make this knowledge believable, then the boundaries of style are being crossed, because Odysseus not only knows about something he has not found out for himself; he knows something that is quite beyond human experience. Yet this is indispensable to the meaning of the adventure, but only this particular adventure, an adventure different from all the others.

Sleep overcomes the hero. Outwardly considered, this is the same as the Aiolos adventure. Here he goes across the island to pray, there he is not alert at the helm. So the sleep seems "unmotivated." It overcomes him like a seeming release as he prays, a refreshing sleep. This is part of the plan, laid down in the prophecy; the companions must be responsible for themselves in order to be tested. If they pass the test, they will see their home again; if not, they will perish.

Just as necessary as the warning here, is also the punishment, specifically a punishment brought about by Zeus. This can only be a storm with lightning. But a storm that is neither miraculous nor a Sinbad adventure, but purely and simply a storm is not part of the tradition or fairy tale, but rather a poetic invention. The part played by the poet seems much greater in this adventure than in any other one. Despite the borrowings from the *Iliad* (12.385, 16.742), the storm is composed nicely enough. But it has only enough weight as poetic invention to counterbalance what has come before, that is to say, as a moral and poetic sequel.

What is left over if one looks beyond the threads that tie this adventure to the whole? What if the mutiny, the spokesman Eurylochos, the sacrilege of the sacrifice, etc.—what if all this is not there on its own account but is all required by the plan of the *Odyssey*? All that is left is the name three-Promontory Island, which is a puzzle, and the delay and hunger caused by contrary winds (although this happened in Aulis before they set out and again on Pharos). And in the end there are the cattle sacred to Helios. But cattle, which are sacred to Helios, existed for cult also at Tainaron (according to the *Homeric Hymn to Apollo* 411–13), at Gortyn on Crete (Servius on Virgil's *Eclogues* 6.60), and equally at Apollonia in Epirus, as attested by legend. Herodotus 9.93 tells how carefully they were cared for and how the herdsman once paid a penalty for failing in his duty. The same can be found in legend. On Chalkidike Heracles killed the giant Alkyoneus, who possessed the "cattle of Helios" and had probably stolen them (scholion to Pindar, *Isthmian* 4.47).[22]

The adventure on Thrinakia may have developed from such a kernel of saga; or else the widely spread legend about the stars, according to which the children of the sun were killed, may lie behind it. Whatever it may be, as was noted before, the actual origin here lies in a formal element, in the influence of legend.

The dependence on religious forms in a part of the poem which stands out so clearly from the rest is characteristic of the poet of the *Odyssey*. The poet of the *Iliad* composes in a different way. But if the adventure on Thrinakia cannot be told at all without a warning, where should we get the person who is to warn? This question is all the more complicated because the connection with the Circe adventure or with Teiresias is obviously secondary, that is to say, is no earlier than the work of this poet. There is no answer to this question. The religious element only shows itself more clearly in connection with the whole. If the companions on Thrinakia are warned, if even Aigisthos is warned, that is all the more reason for introducing the final revenge on the Suitors with a warning, if it is to be a judgment! For this reason the poet of the *Odyssey* has interwoven the life of the seer Theoklymenos with the Telemachy, and with this a part of the seer's world enters into the poetry. The religious coloring, which the deed of vengeance takes on, can be seen in the miracle of the double face, and when the meal turns into blood and laughter becomes wailing (20.350). This is in the same spirit as the signs at the sacrifice on Thrinakia (12.394), when the meat begins to bellow and the skin to creep. This spirit is not at home in fairy tales or the heroism of the *Iliad;* it is a new addition.

CHARYBDIS

If the very different story of the cattle of the sun stands between Skylla and Charybdis in the middle of the fairy-tale double adventure, as if framed by these two, and if this arrangement were the work of this poet, then one question can no longer be avoided. What did this section look like as a double adventure, before the Thrinakia adventure was introduced in be-

[22] Cf. Kranz, "Die lrrfahrten des Odysseus," pp. 93f.

tween? Odysseus first sails past the jaws of Charybdis to Thrinakia only to be brought back again by the storm. Now after his ship has been wrecked, saved by the mast and keel, he must still survive this most terrible of all adventures, Charybdis. This version, with its climax and with epic retardation introduced, cannot have been handed down, but rather it is composed according to a poetic plan. And so do we see ourselves in the end once more facing one of those tasks that we were trying to avoid, the task of making a reconstruction? This is not the reconstruction of a poem but of a tradition.

If Odysseus went from Skylla to Charybdis as if from the frying pan into the fire, how did the story go on? In that case he was not caught in the whirlpool riding on his plank but with his whole ship still intact. Then Skylla was only the beginning. In the fairy tale the sea's jaws swallowed something that was worth swallowing, not just a measly plank but a whole ship at once. Only Odysseus, who was high on the deck and not swimming and half under water, caught hold of the overhanging fig tree. He hung there until Charybdis stopped sucking in and started to spit out. Instead of the ship, only bodies and wrecked fragments reappeared. Then he let himself fall on the mast and so, shipwrecked, he reached not the island of Kalypso, as in the *Odyssey*, but the Phaiakes, those spirits of the sea who save from all perils at sea.

This sequence has left a trace in the extant poem. We are not told how Odysseus drifted to the island of Kalypso, what happened there, and how she "saved" him. The more fruitful the epic situation of Odysseus missing and presumed dead by the world, hidden for seven years already by his "savior," the less it needs the narrative of a special journey to explain it. Kalypso is pure circumstance. A narrative in the same style of how Odysseus got to her could only have produced a doublet of his landing in the land of the Phaiakes.

On the other hand it is noticeable that in the advice of Circe the fig tree, which hangs over Charybdis, is mentioned, but there is no word of explanation about what purpose it should serve. The adventure demanded presence of mind on the part of the hero. So the fig tree was there for no other reason than for the hero to hold onto it. The whirlpool of Charybdis could not be there for any other reason than to swallow the ship and crew. From this it follows that the same poet, who made Circe into an advisor by transferring to her the role of someone who helps in need, separated Charybdis from Skylla and introduced the Thrinakia adventure between the two. It is evident that those two told together would follow each other in the logic of the fairy tale. But it is also clear why the poet made these changes. For if the story were told in its original version, then the companions would not perish "as a result of their own sin." Then Odysseus would not try to "save" them right up to the last minute, by word and deed, as their hero and advisor. So as a fairy-tale hero he was not the same man who ruled "mild like a father" when he was at home. Originally then there was no action in the sphere of the gods to parallel human destruction, but rather their ruin was a meaningless horror.

What this poet has added is retardation and variety, a mixture of fairy-tale and moral elements, dark foreshadowing of the future, thunder in the air and sudden lightning strikes. In a word, epic was introduced into his fairy-tale plot only by that restructuring. But who would care to reconstruct an older poem out of it now?

NEKYIA

The more the world of the dead refers to and connects the past and future of Odysseus, his ways and means to get home and at the same time, in a wider sense, his final goal beyond any home, it becomes the most other-worldly of all adventures and at the same time the most immediate. As a complete picture of fate both near and distant, surpassing all the other adventures in its scope, its style and content have much more in common with the great heroic epic than with fairy-tale tradition. There were and still are philologists who see in it a freely invented intermezzo, added by a more recent poet. On the other hand the Underworld appears as the goal of the magic journeys, as in mythical fairy tales from all places, not least because of the shamans at work behind the scenes here.[23] Be that as it may, the difficulty remains, which cannot be properly understood, as to what task Odysseus is supposed to accomplish among the dead. What the *Odyssey* tells us here about questioning Teiresias and burying Elpenor is not traditional but newly composed, not a story in itself but links between other stories.

Adventures and fairy tales about labors are generally distinct forms with little in common. It would be easy to invent an Underworld adventure for Odysseus in the style of his meeting with the Lotus Eaters or Sirens. For example: he drifted into ever more distant seas, until he reached the gates of the Underworld. Curiosity tempted him to enter and then he was almost caught by the dead. Persephone sent the head of the Gorgon up against him. He barely escaped. One of his companions, who looked back, was frozen where he stood. But that would be arbitrary. In any case, in the *Odyssey* the Underworld is the only one of all the adventures that turned into a kind of labor. Although he does not have to bring up the hound of hell, no other way leads home except through the dead. To visit the dead means to survive the impossible. It is no wonder that the hero loses his courage. Circe takes over the role of the helpful spirit here. Initially we must be satisfied with the conclusion that the poem is based here on the abstract and spiritualized *form* of a fairy story, but not the *content* of one.

The journey to the other world has some elements of a magic journey. Odysseus in his depressed state asks who will show him the way if he must travel to the dead. The sorceress answers that he should entrust himself to

---

[23] Cf. K. Meuli, "Scythica," *Hermes* 70 (1935), p. 168.

the North wind. Who steers? Is it she herself? Is this his predestined fate? What power leads him back to her again, like one risen from the dead? Even more mysterious is the instruction to question Teiresias. In the *Odyssey* there is hardly another figure who has less to do with Odysseus, and yet the whole of the rest of his fate is said to depend on him. How does the blind seer come to take on such significance? What connects the Theban with the man from Ithaka? Is this person from a completely different sequence of legends not being inserted into this one in a highly arbitrary manner? And is it not a contradiction in itself that Odysseus should have asked Teiresias about his way home but Teiresias revealed something quite different to him: that is to say, the consequences of his adventures on Thrinakia, the loss of his companions, his victory over the Suitors, and the end of his life? One element squeezes out the other one. The purpose of the journey for Odysseus disappears behind the purpose of the poet. Our view of the whole created by the connections glides superficially, without stopping long, over the interwoven motifs, which seem to surface only to disappear again immediately.

THE NEKYIA AND PROTEUS ADVENTURE

If one is looking for parallels, then the nearest one in the *Odyssey* is the Proteus adventure. Proteus prophesying in the Telemachy is related to Teiresias prophesying in the Nekyia, as the journeys of Menelaos parallel those of Odysseus. Proteus is not as serious as Teresias, just as the fate of Menelaos is not as burdensome as that of Odysseus. Yet both Proteus and Teiresias are questioned because they are the only source of information about the way home. Both are asked the same question in the same way, both prophesy beyond to the death of the questioner, both foretell a very happy ending, and both therefore make an effective exit. The question about the way leads into the distance, the same turn of fate in both cases, the same form of first-person narrative. If it were firmly established that the Telemachy was the work of a more recent poet, then the Proteus adventure would have to be modeled on the journey to the Underworld. The question as to their relationship becomes a question about the number of poets.

In the Proteus adventure people saw the attempt of the more recent poet to rival the adventures of the older one. Can this view be maintained? The starting point for a comparison in such cases is usually to ask in which places and in which contexts repeated lines clearly keep their original meaning.

The question is posed in the same words by Circe and Eidothea (4.389f. = 10.539f.):

> *He* could tell you the way to go, the stages of your journey,
> and tell you how to make your way home on the sea where the fishes
> swarm.

In the *Telemachy* these lines stand like a refrain in a narrative that moves forward evenly in stanzas, as it were. On the island of Pharos, a day's journey from the mouth of the Nile, Menelaos is detained by adverse winds. The daughter of the old man of the sea becomes his helper. First he asks *her* whether *she* knows what is holding him back,

> which one of the immortals hampers me here and keeps me from my journey;
> and tell me how to make my way home on the sea where the fish swarm.

(4.380–81)

She refers him to the old man:

> If somehow you could lie in ambush and catch hold of him,
> *he* could tell you the way to go, the stages of your journey,
> and tell you how to make your way home on the sea where the fishes
> swarm.

(4.388–90)

According to epic custom the same question is repeated to Proteus under duress, and he answers that Menelaos must turn round and go back to the mouth of the Nile first, to offer a hecatomb to the gods; only then will he be able to get out into the open sea.

Here the wanderer is, in fact, shown the way. The motif hardly mentioned in the Nekyia and then given up again, leads on here from daughter to father, as he alone knows the way. And yet what is Proteus like, as a figure of prophecy, compared with the shadowy seer of quite different powers! In the fourth book he is the character who overshadows everything else.[24] Teiresias in the Nekyia is like a makeshift resource by comparison. He prophesies and leaves, as the mass of meetings jostle on past him. Proteus remains in the character of the prophet throughout the adventure. He is the center holding together the outermost elements. Through him, the daemon of the sea, the fate of the other men traveling home is revealed: the storm in which Locrian Ajax is wrecked; the disastrous voyage of Agamemnon, who barely manages to land; and also the darkness around Odysseus. He himself, Proteus, saw him with Kalypso! Through him, for the first time, the return

---

[24]That the information about the journey must be obtained forcibly by overpowering a daemon is one of the more common themes that repeat themselves in fairy tales about labors. In order to find out the way in his search for the apples of the Hesperides, Heracles wrestles with the old man of the sea Nereus, who keeps changing his shape. Perseus discovers his way from the Graiae, whom he tricks. Phineas prophesies the way to the Golden Fleece for the Argonauts. Cf. Meuli, *Odyssee und Argonautika*, p. 102. For the motif of the neglected hecatomb, cf. *Il.* 7.450. Consider from the point of view of the history of form, the increasing popularity of the adventures of the old man of the sea since the seventh century; cf. Ernst Buschor, *Meermänner, Sitzungsberichte der Bayerischen Akademie der Wissenschaften*, Phil.-hist. Abteilung, 1941, vol. 2, part 1. The questioning of spirits in the Babylonian epic of Gilgamesh has a different meaning.

of Odysseus is revealed as a fate connected to that of others, with a place in the whole pattern.[25] What a climax such a surprise is for the Telemachy that began so gently and socially!

Although Egypt is not part of that distant world through which Odysseus is wandering and cannot be compared with it, yet suddenly the sea, the smell of salt, seal hunting, and the world of wonders combine into the magic of an adventure-filled, distant land! This is not one of those wrestling matches that Peleus had to endure with Thetis or Heracles with Nereus or Triton with his fish's body. Instead, the center of this adventure is the meeting with the daemon in the realistically described surroundings of his element. This fight is not in the naive style of the old mythical fairy tales; rather the adventurous element in the world of wonders, the element of grace in the monstrous, is relished as a contrast, and through this the narrative gains its charm. This beach scene serves as a complement to the pastoral episode in the cave of the Cyclops.

Early in the morning, after preparing himself with prayer, Menelaos takes his three best men to the beach with him, where Eidothea is already waiting for them with four fresh seal skins. Quickly she digs four trenches in the sand in which to hide the hunters. For the hunt can only succeed if it relies on the seal-like habits of the old man. At noon he appears on the beach, rallies his seals, and last of all himself lies down in the middle of his females and goes to sleep, like a shepherd in the middle of his flock. He counts the disguised men as the first seals. As far as knowledge of the animal world goes, one could quote whole pages out of Brehm's *Tierleben* for comparison.[26]

---

[25] For the perspective of the arrangement of the *nostoi* around the *nostos* of Odysseus, cf. Friedrich Klingner, *Über die vier ersten Bücher der Odyssee Sitzuhgsberichte der Sachsischen Akademie der Wissenschaften,* Phil.-hist. Klasse, vol. 96, 1944, p. 51.

[26] "All the seals are sociable to a high degree. The more remote the region, the more numerous their herds and families. The less man has contact with them, the more comfortable and even genial these creatures, which are extremely shy in more settled regions, tend to become. The lifestyle of the seals is nocturnal. They like to spend the day on land sleeping and sunning themselves. They object strongly to any disturbance of their comfortable situation. Many species hardly let themselves be chased away. With pleasure they stretch and roll over on their resting places. They offer first their backs, then their sides and soon their bellies to the friendly rays of the sun. Every seal group is a family. The male always couples with several females, and many of these sultans of the sea possess a harem of thirty to forty slaves. After every harem is full, the males roam complacently back and forth contemplating their family. . . . We decided to watch these animals, and for this purpose dug a hole in the sand. Our boat had hardly sailed some five hundred paces off when the whole group of seals appeared in the water nearby, listening with curiosity and apparent satisfaction to us imitating their sounds. They raised their bodies half out of the water, and in this remarkable position came closer and closer to the island's shore. When we then imitated the higher, weaker sounds usually emitted by the males, the much larger females were the first to crawl out of the water and soon approached our dugout, following the seductive sounds, although they could certainly see our heads sticking out. *Brehms Tierleben: Allgemeine kunde des Tierreichs,*[4] ed. O. zur Strassen, vol. 11 [Leipzig and Vienna, 1914], pp. 580–88 . . . 595, 605.

Yet we find quite original touches amid the fairy-tale elements. The helper in need, betrayer of her own father, unlike Medea or Ariadne or the numerous others, saves her hero from the tortures of a stench rather than from dangers! Do this long lying in the heat and the realistic elements of the hunt come as a new adventure before the old? How charming Eidothea is as a helper when compared with Leukothea! Instead of helping with a veil or another spell, she uses ambrosia. This fits in with the changed character of both the adventure and the hero. Kalypso keeps this back from Odysseus because he scorns immortality. But Eidothea at any rate puts a few drops under the nose of her chosen one.

In comparison with this, the questioning of Teiresias remains very undeveloped, weak, and shadowy. The motifs are the same but they are not firmly rooted in their context in the same way. If one is the model for the other here, then the Nekyia is modeled on the Telemachy, not vice versa.[27]

THE NEKYIA AND THE CIRCE ADVENTURE

And yet the Nekyia is the more significant episode when compared with the Proteus adventure. If it seems to pale in comparison with other poems about the Underworld, in comparison with Virgil and Dante, then we are not noticing what makes it different and how it stands out. Certainly its significance does not lie in the grandiose or fantastic. There is more of this in the few lines of the *Iliad* 20.61ff., when Hades jumps up from his throne and is afraid that his kingdom is about to be split open, than in the whole Nekyia. This poet is not concerned with primeval forces or elements, nor with mythical powers and their conflicts. Instead he describes some landscape even in front of the Underworld and he places a sacred grove there

---

[27] In the Proteus adventure and the journey to the underworld, we find a second group of identical lines, in which Menelaus despairs at the news of Agamemnon's death in the same way as does Odysseus when he learns he has to go to the dead: 4.538–41 and 10.496–99. Both sit and weep, their hearts no longer wish to live, but when each has wept and rolled around on the ground sufficiently . . . The only difference is that this takes place in the one case "on the shore," in the other "on the couch," that is, Circe's. The dependence of the tenth book on the fourth has been noted by A. Kirchhoff, *Die homerische Odyssee*[2], (Berlin, 1879), p. 223; the reverse by von der Mühll, "*Odyssee*," Pauly-Wissowa, and Focke, *Die Odyssee*, p. 201. Kirchhoff is probably right. At the height of his pain, the Homeric man "rolls" on the ground, in filth (*Il* 24.165); "to sit on the shore" signifies to think no longer of journeys (*Il.* 24.403). Odysseus' companions, when they hear they must go to the underworld, "sit down and tear their hair with lamentation" (*Od.* 10.567). The continuity in the fourth book is also more comprehensive and convincing. Proteus prophesies in the manner of a seer what awaits them at 4.494, which causes an outburst of excessive grief. The prophet must wait until he can point to a quick voyage home. The curve of the emotion is like that in 10.568. In the other case it is the questioner, Odysseus himself, who after his despair passes pulls himself together for new questions. The antitheses between the first and second person are more precise in the fourth book (my <heart> failed . . . but he . . ."). The conclusion is that whoever leaves the Nekyia as it is, as the work of the "first poet," cannot ascribe the Telemachy to a "second poet."

(10.509). Yet he also avoids the ghostly elements of folklore, the hound of hell, the gate of Hades, and such things. At the end even Gorgo is only a fear, without ever actually appearing. Heracles' journey to Hades, which is assumed to have been well-known and is even quoted, would have been quite different. So the emphasis falls all the more on the human encounters, and the surprises in question and answer. As the longest of all the adventures, the Nekyia is, at the same time, the most spiritual, as life measures itself against death and death against life. They cannot grasp each other, either physically or spiritually, but that only makes them all the more strongly drawn to one another. A tone that is new in relation not only to the fear of Hades but also to all the other adventures prevails over primitive beliefs about death. This new tone is sustained and arresting like the tone of an elegy. The hero falls under a completely new spell here. The Nekyia is the most distant of all the adventures not only in an outward sense but, at the same time, as the ultimate opportunity for human experience. For this very reason it is surrounded by all the others, and it overshadows the wonders of fairy tale. The fact that Odysseus sets out and returns home, a man for whom hope was given up but who was saved, shows that he has crossed not only the boundaries of the real world of epic, but also those of fairy tale.

There has been no shortage of attempts to separate this second journey from the Circe adventure on the grounds that it is an "interpolation." Yet these efforts merely reveal how close the connection between the two is. The same poet who designed the Circe adventure in this way must have had the Nekyia follow it. Without the latter, the former would not serve as contrast. The adventure ends abruptly with a dichotomy between external and internal elements, which is strange enough. After a year of delaying, Odysseus, on what is to be his last night of love with her, asks the goddess to send him on his way, because he has been admonished by his companions.

After they have enjoyed their pleasure, she reveals to him that he can leave if he wishes to but that he should know that he will not reach home unless he travels by way of the dead. At this Odysseus groans and moans. His despair is expressed in the same words as those used by Menelaos when Proteus reveals Agamemnon's death. These words are more in their original setting there than here, but here the contrast of life and death, horror and pleasure, forgetting and being reminded is much more "adventurous." He goes from the nights of love with the goddess into the ghostliness of the shadows and very different embraces. The road to the Underworld leads from Circe not because of some mythical geography but because in the rhythm of adventure, pleasure and death, forgetting and remembering, losing oneself with the goddess and finding oneself with the dead, all require each other as contrasts, and must follow on one another with such abrupt transitions. The change is so disconcerting that we do not ask why for long. "Who will show me the way there?" "Leave that to the winds!" The connection with the whole goes beyond the motivation for the individual parts.

How rough is the awakening of his companions, so innocent in their moralizing! On the day before, they were still urging Odysseus to think of his home, as he hesitated, but how desperate they are the next morning once they have what they wanted! How upset the same men are who were still so victorious the day before! Yet what would happen to all this if instead of the above Circe's answer were, "Go if you want, but you should know that first you must go to—the Sirens!" Philologists before whose criticisms the Underworld adventure did not stand up, have not hesitated to invent this in order to restore the original here.[28]

TEIRESIAS

Teiresias, however, remains a shadow compared with Proteus. And yet he was chosen as a character according to the very different content of his prophecy. Although the question is posed in the same words, here the issue is not the journey back home in the outward sense of the Proteus prophecy. The answer no longer corresponds to the question. The way to be shown has become an inner way—no longer the way over the seas but through the cliffs and dangers of one man's fate. Teiresias steps into the life of Odysseus as a figure from the Oedipus cycle or the *Thebaid,* as the prophet of tragic relationships, as one who warns of the wrath of the gods. Proteus was the right person to prophesy about the winds and the journey. How does this concern the blind seer? He knows about guilt and atonement, curse and blessing. He uncovers the wrath of Poseidon, as he once revealed the wrath of the gods toward Oedipus. He is the one appointed to predict a dark, looming future, a disastrous fate a man tends to fall into, the more he would like to escape it. If one takes away the prediction of impending doom from his prophecy, one also takes away, at the same time, its relation to the prophet.

Teiresias' speech is one of the most criticized parts of the whole *Odyssey,* a fact that does have some significance. As this part seemed to be crumbling, scholars demolished it only to erect more imposing hypotheses on its ruins. Their claim is that the main section, the prophecy of a death "far from the sea," is taken from another epic, the *Thesprotis,* by the second (or third) poet

---

[28] U. v. Wilamowitz-Moellendorff, *Homerische Untersuchungen*, p. 144: "The instructions for the journey to Hades have taken the place of the instructions for the adventures of the twelfth book. After 10.489 came the transitional thought, "'Certainly you must sail tomorrow, but that will lead you into new dangers,'" 12.38–142. Again in *Die Heimkehr des Odysseus*, p. 79, he says, "If Odysseus summons up the soul of Teiresias because he is to undertake more journeys after returning home, then the whole Nekyia has been inserted into the apologue by someone who wanted to tack on the *Thesprotis*." Similarly Erich Bethe, *Homer* II (Leipzig and Berlin, 1922), pp. 136f.: "He (the man revising the poem) fitted the Nekyia carefully into the poem at its beginning and end. He did this by using Circe's advice 10.490 and the return to her 12.1 as well as the Elpenor episode." Erwin Rohde, *Kleine Schriften II* (Tübingen and Leipzig, 1901), p. 268, also does not doubt this interpolation.

who reworked the *Odyssey,* and that it only makes sense coming from this source. This epic supposedly told the story of Odysseus' wanderings over-land to Thesprotia, during which this prophecy was fulfilled. Odysseus had not summoned the ghost of the Theban seer from the Underworld at the end of the world but at his own home, before he set out on his new wan-derings. He is said to have told this story himself, although not for the Phaiakes but for Penelope when he was once again taking leave of her.[29]

This is surely one of the most ingenious attempts to deduce the source from a poem itself. Let us examine what we have here.

The seer begins in an ironical tone: 'If the return home, which you seek, seems sweet as honey to you, a god will make it terrible for you!' In the next sentence the equivalent comes in the expression "I think," which does not express a doubt but certainty. "I think Poseidon will not, after all, for-get his anger about the blinding of his son." Here Odysseus does not hear something, for the first time, that he could not know; rather he learns of something that he should have guessed. Seers are in the habit of calling on their knowledge of the past in order to give proof of their knowledge of the future. Something like this ought to follow now: "rather, you will have enough to suffer." Instead the conclusion is drawn into the new beginning. "Despite all the sufferings you will undergo, you would still reach home— *if* greed does not seduce you to violate the cattle of the sun." This warning against transgression is the goal of the opening remarks, "Take care, or else. . . ." This element of "either/or," the decision on which everything else

---

[29] E. Schwartz, *Die Odyssee*, p. 134f.; Von der Mühll, *"Odyssee"* ([=*Ausgewählte kleine Schriften*, pp. 64–66), and "Die Dichter der *Odyssee*," p. 92. (=*Ausgewählte kleine Schriften*, p. 135). The so-called *Thesprotis* was supposed to have contained an account of how Odysseus, after coming home, set out on foot to perform the sacrifice to Poseidon required of him. On his way he won the heart of the queen of the Thesprotians and, as her husband, made war on the Thracian king (which, among other things, is listed as part of the *Telegony* in Proclus' *Chrestomathia* and Apollodorus' epitomy). Apart from all these things, a story that is not attested anywhere, before he set out again Odysseus conjured up the shade of Teiresias from the Underworld somewhere and obtained this oracle. With this information he directly bade forewell to Pene-lope and in the end he passed away, fulfilling the oracle by dying a blessed death as king of the Thesprotians. Instead of having to wander, Odysseus would ask, "Shall I go on wandering?" Meeting Teiresias would no longer be an adventure when removed from his whole marvelous context. But this means he would have nothing more to do with the character of Odysseus. To address the questions raised by Schwartz, people balk at insects in the *Odyssey* only to accept elephants in reconstructed epics. Among the explanations for this, we hear the following: oracles of this kind were usually attributed to founders. But does Odysseus become a founder in the *Telegony*? According to Proclus and Apollodorus, he wins the love of a queen along the way, after whose death he returns home and fulfills the oracle at home after his return. A trace of the original is said to be the first person plural of the possessive pronoun at 11.33, as if the first person plural did not serve to describe everything connected with home. "Our sheep" is supposed to be addressed to Penelope. "To you" in 11.134 stands as a contrast to the destruc-tion of the Suitors, which is left out at 23.281. The Eurytanes of Epirus have an oracle about Odysseus: Lykophron 799 with the scholia. Similarly Odysseus appears in countless local leg-ends as the founder of altars, etc. But there also I see no connection with Teiresias' prophecy, since it is Teiresias who prophesies and not Odysseus.

depends, is stressed with every technique and all the power of parallel sentence construction. When repeated in the instructions of Circe (12.137), the warning is less extensive but the characteristics of the magic island are more stressed. Such shades of meaning are part of the style of epic.

The future that has been promised, has conditions attached to it and more of these are added. "Yet if you do reach home, it will be late, without companions, and on a strange ship." People felt that this prophecy was impossible. As if there were not enough prophecies and oracles that are so conditional! For comparison one can cite Calchas' prophecy at the beginning of Aeschylus' *Agamemnon,* Darius' prophecy in Aeschylus' *Persae,* Teiresias' prophecy in Sophocles' *Antigone,* oracles such as those in *Trachiniae,* etc. The warning seems even more urgent, the more inevitably the prophecy will be fulfilled. There is no inconsistency between prophecy and warning. What follows is all a part of this. The "misfortune" Odysseus will find at home is contrasted with the "honey sweet return" he is promising himself.

The more the future is fixed, the more prophetic the speech becomes. And yet part of it overlaps word for word with the curse of Polyphemos (11.114f. = 9.534f.). Are the two lines about the late return and the misfortune at home taken from there? Have they been inserted clumsily, as has been claimed? One can just as easily claim the opposite. One thing is sure: they are dependent on each other. The words for "returning home" instead of "coming," for "arriving" instead of "finding" are more precise in the eleventh book than in the ninth. A prophecy may have limitations, but hardly a curse. The curse of Polyphemos also uses this prophetic format. That the blinded Cyclops believes he can hurt his mortal enemy most of all through the death of all his companions is less evident than when Odysseus hears these very words from the mouth of the seer, instead of the "honey sweet homecoming" he had been hoping for. Finally, the end of the prayer in book 9 asks that the trouble with the Suitors should also befall Odysseus because of Poseidon. This is not mentioned except in the curse of Polyphemos and is unthinkable.

Therefore Teiresias' speech is not a thoughtless repetition, but rather the curse of Polyphemos and the speech of Teiresias refer to each other. Just as the Nekyia holds together the different strands, layers, and locations of the *Odyssey* in a unity, so an additional connection is made, by Teiresias' prophecy, between the Cyclops, Thrinakia, and the killing of the Suitors. A thread is spun that runs through to the end and even beyond the end of the poem. Blindness, misunderstanding, revelation through a seer, warning, atonement and promise—the connection between all these integrated moments is not to be found only in Teiresias' speech. The arrangement of the adventures points to this.

The speech of the seer is above all *religious* both in the form and content. It is as religious in forms as only the adventure on Thrinakia. Guilt and atonement point to each other. Why would the seer start with the wrath of the god, if he did not know a way to appease the divinity? Proteus was simply a teller of fortunes, his words were unambiguous. The speech of Teiresias ends in the style of an oracle. Mystery, or *griphos*, is of the essence for an oracle. His advice is that after the murder of the Suitors Odysseus should shoulder an oar and journey inland until someone asks him what kind of a "winnowing-fan" he is carrying. There he should plant the oar in the ground and sacrifice a ram, a bull, and a boar to Poseidon. After coming home he should offer a hecatomb to every Olympian god and then he would die a gentle death at a great old age, far from the sea, in the middle of his happy people.

"Winnowing-fan" instead of winnowing shovel is a rare word, artifically sinister, a paraphrase, which is popular in the language of oracles. An example is Aristotle, Frag. 561 (in V. Rose, *Aristotelis Fragmenta,* 3rd ed. [Leipzig, 1886]) (Plutarch, *Quaestiones Graecae* 15). The Opuntian Kabyes is instructed by the Delphic oracle to found a colony where he is bitten by a wooden dog. He travels into the country of the Ozolian Locrians and there he steps on a rosehip bush, called "dogrose" in Greek. As he is resting for a few days as a result of his injury, he understands the oracle and recognizes the "dogrose" as the "wooden dog." Similarly the "winnowing-fan" is wordplay for a "winnowing shovel." When asked about his "winnowing shovel," Odysseus is supposed to remember that mysterious "winnowing fan" and recognize the fulfilment of the prophecy.[30]

A prophecy of death, especially for a hero who returns to this world as the only one living through so many brushes with death, is hardly to be missed, if only for its biographical significance in a poem so concerned with any biographical detail. Such a prophecy is not lacking in the wanderings of Menelaos. If the death of the hero himself were missing in the great parade of the dead in the Nekyia, then the connecting element would be missing in the fates of all the others—Agamemon, Ajax, and Achilleus. An added factor is that, since the *Iliad,* the prediction of death counts as one of the means of incorporating the whole life of a hero in a few days, by using references to

---

[30] Anatole France wrote a charming and learned little piece about the winnowing shovel in *Le Génie latin.* Some of the meaning of the puzzle seems to have been revealed to English sailors. I found the following in Irene Seligo's *Zwischen Traum und Tat* (Frankfurt, 1938), p. 208:

The story goes that once an English sailor became thoroughly sick at heart with the dangers and insecurities of his profession. When he returned to his home port, he shouldered an oar and traveled inland in search of people who did not know about the wild sea. He went from place to place with his burden and did not stay anywhere long, until he came to a village where the people asked him what kind of a strange instrument he was carrying. There he settled. This parable can be found in various old sea stories where shipwrecked sailors tell it to their comrades to comfort them. Harrassed and disheartened sailors swear to each other that they will follow his example once they return to English soil. There is as little evidence about whether anyone ever did this as there is about the eventual fate of the traveler with the oar.

Here at least it is recognized that this "parable" points to the future and becomes impossible when narrated as a fulfillment of something.

the past and future. Achilleus' death is also prophesied. The latter's is as close as Odysseus' is far removed, the one tragic and heartrending, the other among a blessed people. One is in a foreign country, the other is at home— not in the sea, not a seaman's death. The words "apart from" do not indicate where but how he will die, not a geographical reference, not "in the land of the Thesprotians." The blessed people are not the Thesprotians, who are complete foreigners, but the freed people of Ithaka, who have their fatherly king again. (O the philologists who invent poetry!) Models do not reveal themselves only in imitations and borrowings but also in the tendency toward variation and reversal. What a change this is when compared with the *Iliad!* A "gentle," natural death, a death in harmony with the gods, is highly praised here.

A teller of fairy tales could have ended with the reunion of husband and wife, "and so they lived happily ever after." The epic poet thinks through to the end. Odysseus will have to go on another journey, as he is no Menelaos and his reward is still far distant. And yet what a reversal, how characteristic of this poet that the most prominent prophet of doom known to legend foresees such a peaceful death at the end of all the troubles he has predicted. What would be the meaning of this whole prophecy without this turn of events? What would be the point of the character of the seer? Would it be worth summoning up a Teiresias if one could not anticipate what misfortune was threatening or if there were nothing to lose and no dangers to avoid? Yet where would Odysseus be in this situation at the beginning of the reconstructed *Thesprotis?* Would he have just returned home happily? Would he have just successfully punished the Suitors? Is it not a circular argument to try to reconstruct a *Thesprotis* from this prophecy as the source for that same prophecy, whose original form would then be reconstructed in turn from the *Thesprotis?* Is there not a misunderstanding about what an origin actually is in the opinion that the source is a text, and the resulting material is also a text, and that the latter has been derived in an inadequate way from the former?

ELPENOR

Elpenor is a name that speaks, a name of the kind the poet likes, and it points to hopes that have been dashed. "Elpis" is not consoling like the hope of a Christian. The youngest member of the crew, no hero, "not terribly powerful in fighting nor sound in his thoughts," he becomes the only victim of the Circe adventure that ends so well. After the farewell supper he wakes from his drunkenness and falls from the upper story of the house, breaking his neck. He did not need a journey into distant wonders to end like this. But with what consideration the insignificant man, who was no more than a companion, is chosen to mediate between the living and the dead! The reunion with him comes before those with the famous heroes.

Surely, as a result, the house of death becomes a region where, despite all the horrors, loyalty and the memory of loved ones are recalled and awakened with ever new voices. After Elpenor the mother comes as a climax. People have objected that the ghostly and vampirelike elements are so absorbed into the soul that even a mother needs to drink the blood before expressing her love. Virgil naturally would have none of this and borrowed only noble elements. But for Aeneas the Underworld is no longer an adventure. The contrast between heroic content and the fear of ghosts is equivalent to the difference between heroic and fairy-tale elements. Without this there would be no paradox in an existence that no longer exists.

Does Patroklos not also appear in the same way to Achilleus in the twenty-third book of the *Iliad,* as an unburied "comrade," who has gone ahead in death and is pleading not to be forgotten? His soul has not yet entered Hades and warns that his corpse should be burned so that he can cross over. He wants a grave as a testimony to what his life was. Although Patroklos appears in a dream, a dream is reality. The soul disappears into the earth like smoke, when the hand of a friend stretches out for it. What the soul *tells* about its wanderings by the river of the Underworld becomes part of the adventure in the *Odyssey*. There can be no doubt that as the hero and his companion are united in conversation, in amazement and revelation, plea and promise, the interconnections are too numerous to be accidental. Other elements from the same model are repeated in Odysseus' words to his dead mother (*Il.* 23.97f. ~ *Od.* 11.211f.). As Achilleus tries to take the hand of Patroklos, so Odysseus does the same with Agamemnon, but in vain. The same beginning line that introduces the appearance of Patroklos becomes the formula of introduction in the Nekyia.

And yet what a complete change! In the *Iliad* the call of the dead man is met by willingness to die in the one being called. A hero calls on another hero; the other world steps into this one with a challenge. The amazing thing for the one who is summoned is the survival of his dead friend in this weakened state, which will soon also be his. The dead man penetrates his soul as he stands at his sleeping head and the living man takes him in, just as his ashes will soon rest side by side with those of his friend. Of all epic foreshadowing this is surely the greatest. In the *Odyssey,* in which tragedy is not the most important element, its place is taken by the fulfillment of duty in this world toward a nameless comrade. Instead of heroic closeness even in death, we see here a loving sense of duty. Fame is not diminished in value by this. But it does not relieve him "whose fame reached up into the heavens" of his duty toward the man who has no part in this glory. The ideal of Odysseus for the poet of the *Odyssey* has some elements of instruction for a lord. The didactic element, which becomes the theme of the Telemachy, does appear in the adventures, even if only as an accompaniment. Elpenor represents those who are nameless.

Achilleus and Patroklos share the same spirit. Elpenor and Odysseus are opposites. However one tries to characterize the two relationships with one expression, there is an element in them which defies any resolution. Wila-mowitz, who has a tendency to look for local legends, surmised that this was the remembrance of a grave. But the Elpenor episode does not look like a local legend.[31]

ANTIKLEIA

The meeting with his mother, separated from the reunions that are waiting at home and advanced to Hades, is emphasized for its special significance. This meeting goes beyond anything that could have been represented in a relationship between the living. In word and gesture, in question and an-swer, in the epic, developed formula of three attempts and three failures, in misunderstanding and instructing, and last of all, in the way the dead woman points to the living one, who will take the place of the mother, this episode becomes a kind of separate poem. It has its own beginning, sus-pense, and climax as it climbs, as if in steps, from wife to son to father, until it reaches that wonderful point of stress, "for your sake," and then ends. At home there would be no room left for the mother between Eurykleia and Penelope. A whole intimacy of tone is needed on both sides, on the side of the dead as well as the living, so that her death from longing for her son does not remain a mere story. Who would have had her die in this way, if not this poet? What other significance can the twice-repeated "thrice" have here, if one compares this with its use in the battle scenes of the *Iliad* (cf. *Il.* 5.436; 16.702, 784)? The wish of the living man to satisfy himself with weeping for the dead woman, is taken word for word from the *Iliad* (*Il.* 23.97f.) but becomes a part of a new, more powerful unity quite different in tone. What a repetition of once heroic elements of style in an intimate context! And yet if one takes the Nekyia from the *Odyssey*, then one also takes away the mother. And this concerns this very poet, who portrays nothing better than reunions. Through this poet the reunion with the mother becomes a poem in itself, similar to an elegy, with the result that it could become, even more than the Elpenor episode, a model for classical German literature—for Goethe's *Euphrosyne*.

People have criticized the fact that Odysseus could question his mother so innocently, as if Teiresias had not just prophesied the upcoming battle with the Suitors to him. But that is to undervalue this as a poem. The battle with the Suitors does not belong with the whole. And the whole in turn is not connected in tone with Teiresias nor with Elpenor. But instead of a linear progression, the poet chooses here, as he often does, to interweave his threads.

[31] Mention should be made of the explanation of Marie Luise Kaschnitz in *Griechische Mythen* (Hamburg, 1947).

THE REST OF THE MEETINGS

It is part of the character of the encounters in the Nekyia that they must be comprehensive if they are to be meaningful. This completeness is already anticipated in the plan of the *Odyssey*. This turns out to be a meeting with the whole world of Greek heroes, and even beyond it, with all of humanity that has gone before. Even if they are only glimpsed, this impression is still indelible. A concept of humanity seems to take shape only in the face of death. In any case this is the first poem about humanity, not only because of the numbers mentioned but also because of their behavior and their pathos. Yet humanity and the world of heroes need contrasts and divisions to appear whole. They come and go as if arranged in a procession, men and women, heroes of Troy and heroes from earlier times. The sequence begins with the youngest who lacks deeds or fame, to end with the most powerful hero of earlier times, Heracles. Divided into two parts by a division in the middle before the main section, it twice lapses into increasingly lengthy catalogue form. Interrupting at the moment of greatest tension was probably already a technique of the rhapsodes. In the procession of heroines, we see at the same time a whole series of the fates of their sons, both glorious and wretched. Odysseus sees wonders related in legend as vividly in the world of shadows as the shadows preserve what was once alive.

As the groups follow each other, horror turns to participation, and participation into an eagerness to see, until new horror overwhelms this curiosity to see. A basic ingredient of adventure is attraction and temptation. So Odysseus here sees things from an ever more distant past until he nearly pays the penalty for his enjoyment. The paradoxical nature of the shadows, which still go their ghostly way in the empty shapes of their previous lives, as if they were still living, is revealed in fruitless attempts to embrace and is heightened in the ghostly "as-if" of the wonders from earlier times. There is Minos, with a dense crowd jostling around him, recognizable by his golden scepter, giving judgments among the dead. Here is Orion, who, with his club, is chasing the game in the meadows of asphodel, that in previous times he used to chase over the desolate mountain peaks. The third figure is Heracles surrounded by a crowd that scatters like frightened birds, as he bends his bow and aims. These three represent the whole previous age. Whether the other inserted group of three "penitents," Tityos, Tantalos, and Sisyphos, belongs to the original design in the same way is a question open to debate. But the meetings could not end with the heroes of Troy. Without the wonders of a previous age, there would be no climax toward the end.[32]

---

[32] This means also disagreeing about, e.g., the portions rejected by Wilamowitz, *Homerische Untersuchungen*, pp. 199ff. He cuts out lines 566–631 as an "Orphic interpolation." So the flight from the dead follows immediately on the meeting with Ajax: "Then I would still have spoken to him, but such hordes crowded around me that I was afraid." This is not possible. In the first place the encounter with Ajax cannot have such significance that Odysseus almost does

The most significant encounters are those with which the teller of tales starts anew, those with the heroes of Troy—Agamemnon, Achilleus, and Ajax. The limitation to these three is a testimony to the art of contrast and connection. This technique alone allows tension to be created in a new poem of the same genre by the repetition of figures that have been completely finished with previously. What will the heroes of the *Iliad* say as they speak on behalf of the dead as though living and present to all?

All three have in common that they have not got over their deaths. Their pain at having had to end their lives in this way marks them more than do their gaping wounds. None of them accepts his fate as something sent from the gods the way Odysseus does. As the ghostly elements of the dead bodies disappear and at the same time become internalized in the Hades picture of epic, a strange confusion is evident in the dead men, half touching but half shocking, which makes them cling to the limitations that were imposed on them in life. Even in death none of them looks beyond himself. The dead Agamemnon feels a ghostly but deep-rooted mistrust of all women, and so each one remains confined to his experiences. Odysseus meets each one as a friend, who is surprised when he shares their experience and who was not anticipating such things. Their answers become adventures.

All three, who stand for the many, act in their contrasting and similar attitudes as symbols of a general condition, like shorthand, typical cases of violent death in general. The fate of Agamemnon contrasts not only with that of Odysseus, and Clytemnestra not only with Penelope; it also stands as most unworthy when compared with the worthiest fate. When measured by epic standards, Achilleus' death is the most glorious of all the fates of the heroes. The hero's praise with which Odysseus greets him is the more high-flown, just as his mourning was all the greater for the death of the commander of the army (11.483ff):

> No man before has been more blessed than you, nor ever
> will be. Before, when you were alive, we Argives honored you
> as we did the gods, and now in this place you have great authority
> over the dead. Do not grieve, even in death, Achilleus.

The answer is all the more unexpected (11.488–91):

> O shining Odysseus, never try to console me for dying.
> I would rather follow the plow as thrall to another
> man, one with no land allotted him and not much to live on,
> than be a king over all the perished dead.

---

not return because of it. Second, this lacks any element of temptation, although only temptation causes this danger. Not heeding his mother's warning almost costs Odysseus his life. Third, "men earlier still" in line 630 assumes that it is not only the heroes of Troy who have been mentioned in what went before. Like Wilamowitz, Schwartz, *Die Odyssee*, p. 319. For line 612 = Hesiod *Theogony* 228, cf. Focke, *Die Odyssee*, pp. 229f. Inez Sellschopp, *Stilistiche Untersuchungen zu Hesiod*, Ph.D. dissertation (Hamburg, 1934), p. 52, with references to parallel passages, *Il.* 24.548 and 7.237.

People have felt that the poet who could have written this had lost touch, in a strange way, with the sense of greatness found in the heroism of the *Iliad*. And yet the answer seems all the more like Achilleus for being unexpected. What would the dead Achilleus be like if not the reverse of the living one? The futility of death, which is more evident to him than to anyone else, reverses all standards. Even among the dead he remains the one who is greatly dissatisfied, a victim of the forces that struggle against each other inside him, resisting his fate as he fulfils it. The element common to all the shadows, from the lowest to the highest level, from the thirst for sacrificial blood to the tense question about what is to come, namely the longing for life, finds its most powerful expression in him. And how he strides off across the meadow of asphodel with great strides, the same man who was just cursing his hero's lot, once he has learned of the heroic achievements of his son!

In contrast to him and apart from all the others stands the third man who cannot forgive his enemy, the destroyer of his honor, even in death, and who cannot be moved to answer even by the most heartfelt and wooing words. He is the only one who is silent and untouched by the eagerness of the others. He is Ajax who killed himself. His turning away is all the more disappointing after Odysseus' generous speech. Where in the *Iliad* was the difference between them so fully described in word and gesture? An additional aim was probably also to justify the man of many ruses, who probably appeared in a less favorable light in other poems. Scholars have criticized that as the procession of the dead proceeds further, their enjoyment of the blood is gradually forgotten. And yet how would Ajax be represented in this way, if the poet kept closely to this? Should the suicide drink the blood with the same desire for life that the others manifest? Or should he deny himself this pleasure and thus fail to recognize his enemy? Whatever expedient one could think of, the whole meeting would become impossible. And yet without Ajax there could be no Achilleus. The heroes of the *Iliad*, the centerpiece of the whole Underworld, would be omitted.

But what is it that holds everything together? There seems to be a consensus about the form of the Nekyia: it is not a journey to Hades like those of Orpheus or Heracles. It is a spirit-raising situated at the end of the inhabited world, that is to say, a calling up of the dead, yet without keeping too closely to this format. From a conjuration things gradually advance to an invasion of the dead, as the scene seems to shift imperceptibly.[33] In fact initially Odysseus is not *in* the Underworld, but at its entrance, and it is the dead who come to his sacrificial pit, rather than he mingling with the dead. But at the end he sees more and more of the scenes that are actually taking place in the Underworld. And for this reason the poet does not adhere strictly to that characteristic quality of the dead, that they must first drink of the sacrificial blood in order to become fully aware of him. As

---

[33] Cf. Eduard Norden, *Vergils Aeneis, Buch 6*[3] (Berlin, 1927), p. 354, on lines 236f.

things progress more and more, the crowd of faces swamps the introductory motif. But is this really a spirit-raising, as has been assumed?

At a conjuration the dead person whom one needs is forced to come up, mostly in a time of great need or danger, by magic, called by sacrifices and prayers like the soul of Agamemnon in Aeschylus' *Oresteia* or the soul of Darius in the *Persae* or the ghost of Samuel by the witch of Endor in the *First Book of Samuel*. It is always specific dead people who are called, not indiscriminate hordes. This is also true of that description of such an event in Maximus of Tyre 8.2, which seems to be closest to the Homeric one. He reports that by the lake of Avernus there is a cave where a visitor may, after sacrifice, prayer, and libation, call up any one of his friends or ancestors whom he wants. Then a shadowy image (*eidōlon*) appears, which is hard to see but is fully able to speak. It speaks with him and then goes away again. It is characteristic of the summoning of the dead that the dead person who is desired will answer when called by name, but as a rule only unwillingly, irritated at having been disturbed. The ghost usually does not feel well up here and immediately wants to go down there again, in cases when the gods of the Underworld do not order him down. "Why did you call me?" asks the ghost of Samuel, just as Darius does.[34]

Instead Odysseus has to *fend off* the hordes of ghosts swarming up. His sacrifice causes the whole Underworld to move at once. There is no need for any incantation or call and not even Teiresias is forced up; rather he is simply ahead of the general mass, thanks to his special spiritual powers, and appears as one of the first among the hordes who begin to collect. He shares his desire for sacrificial blood with the others. Moreover, the rites are not those of a conjuration. The sacrificial pit is dug for the dead collectively, the blood flows for all of them. The libation of honey, wine, and water is for all, and equally the prayer and promise of a sacrifice after his return home. Teiresias is promised a black sheep as a special offering, not as a means to attract him but as thanks for the information. Then the souls come up from "Erebos" and "gather." With prayers to the couple who rule the Underworld, the sheep, whose blood has been spilled, are skinned and burned. In long lines the ghostly army marches past, sent and recalled again by Persephone.

Their thirst for blood signifies their desire for life. Where else were dead people, who had been called up, so thirsty for life? Here they are not forced, but they crowd around; they are not resistant, rather they are eager. By drinking the blood, they sense their condition, realize that they were once alive and are able to speak again. They seek contact with the living, to have a share in the world above again, even if only in words. A dull, almost rapturous urge awakes in them, both in heroes and unknowns, in men and

---

[34] Other examples: the spirit-raising in Heliodorus, *Aethiopica*, 6.15; Silius Italicus, *Punica* 13.400f.; Seneca, *Oedipus* (the conjuration of the dead Laius). Aeschylus has replaced the homeric Nekyia with a regular spirit-raising in *Psychopompoi*. He also love conjurations for the impressive choruses they could give rise to.

women—only the suicide remains apart. They stretch out their hands and would like to embrace. But where else do souls that have been summoned to the world above and entranced do this? The closest analogy is not so much the oracles of the dead or their conjuration, as the well-known, great All Souls festivals, such as the Attic and Ionic ones of the Anthesteria. Then the spirits of the ancestors go about as people offer sacrifice, make libations and meals for them. Then the Underworld opens up: *mundus patet*.[35]

A release similar to these festivals of the dead seems to have been in the poet's mind as a precedent that enabled the hero to talk to so many spirits. And yet is something obvious not missing in the notion of a spirit-raising? In fact, a conjuration would seem to be what was required if the aim was simply to question Teiresias. Yet what a strange relationship between the purpose Odysseus was aiming at and the results that followed instead. How amazing that the whole world of the dead suddenly opens its gates so that that one man could be questioned! Perhaps this contradiction, and much more with it, can be explained primarily by the fact that the beliefs about the dead of that world and time, to which the great festivals of the dead belong, are so very different from the Homeric ones. The forefathers went around and were invited. They frightened, punished, and rewarded, as they were sent up by Persephone. They came not to talk about their heroic fates, but for quite different purposes! They were sent up to create new links between the Underworld and the world above, between the past and the present, as well as to cleanse and rejuvenate life above. But this age-old element, which keeps renewing itself in new forms, as can be seen in the *Demes* by the comic poet Eupolis, is anything but Homeric.

Although Virgil makes a bid to surpass his model with his descriptions of the surroundings, this model remains superior to its Roman imitation in the richness of its connections. Obviously for Aeneas the Underworld was no longer an adventure the way it was for Odysseus. But would the whole sequence of adventures not lose some meaning without the Nekyia? Only the Nekyia gives the wanderings a goal, an outward and a return journey. The meeting with the dead has the same significance for Odysseus as the Golden Fleece had for the Argonauts. The Underworld and his homeland, in their reference to each other, are the limits between which his journey-ings take place. But its significance is not exhausted by this connection. The relationships are stronger than the episodes motivated by them.

SCHERIA

Odysseus' experiences among the Phaiakes present two worlds on a single stage, the world of fairy-tale wonders and the enhanced world of contempo-rary history. The Phaiakes find themselves settled, according to the plan of

---

[35] For the original meaning of ghost and mask festivals, cf. Karl Meuli, *Schweizermasken* (Zurich, 1942).

the *Odyssey,* on the boundary where the world of distant lands meets the world of home, where the narrow confines of the fairy-tale adventures expand into the wide canvas of great epic with its many characters. Consequently their existence has a splendid aspect, an element of the most contemporary spirit of the *Odyssey* amid the fairy-tale magic.

The Phaiakes have also not escaped dissection by critics. They felt it was too much for Odysseus to spend three days as the guest of Alkinoos. Rather, since he was asked his name at the first opportunity, in the evening in the hall when he was crying at the bard's song, he had to reveal his identity and tell about the adventures he had experienced. Therefore, he would be sent home the next day with a guest-present. This would spare us the curious incognito in which the hero hides himself, with the same gesture, for two days. Alkinoos' promise, which he gives right at the beginning, would be kept: "Tomorrow I will send you home." And this would deprive us of the comedy of Ares' love adventure, which [the critics thought] would be all the better.[36]

This is all very well, except that this tidying up eliminates the element that gives everything its meaning, namely the epic situation of the unknown hero as a guest: this time not the guest of Eumaios, not disguised as a beggar, rather—and now we come to what really happens between a guest and his host.

It is easy to see that a complete elimination of the second day would in turn leave its own disadvantages. A Homeric day has its own cycle of increasing tension, climax, and end. From the beginning, since the meeting with Nausikaa, this day had one goal: acceptance and entering into a guest relationship. If it were also filled up with the recognition, its preparation, and the story that follows, the day would become too full of too many different things. Although different elements can be found in one day, they must contrast and happen in two different places or some such thing. But here the goal, instead of the acceptance, would be something different, that is, the recognition. But the recognition is the aim of the second day, just as the reception is of the first. The first, as well as the second time, the goal is reached in the evening. The sun goes down as Odysseus prays to the goddess at the sanctuary of Athene where Nausikaa leaves him on the way to the city (6.321). After reaching the palace, he meets the king and the elders at a convenient moment, after they have just finished their meal and, according to their custom, are making their last libation to Hermes before going to bed (7.138). Then suddenly, by a miracle, the stranger is among

---

[36]"Tomorrow": 7.318 describes the new day about to start, cf. *Il.* 8.535; 9.357, 429; 18.269; *Od.* 1.272. Is it imaginable that Alkinoos would say, "I will fix your return home for the day after tomorrow?" "Why not tomorrow?" everyone would ask. Then Alkinoos would have to say in explanation, "I foresee that you will not tell us your name before then." This line is only conclusive if one assumes that it has been left over by mistake from a previous plan. But since it cannot be any different from what we have, a dissection of the poem based on this line would rely on a circular argument.

them. There is a long silence and then the plea. The one who makes the decisions among the men in the room, Queen Arete, whose knees Odysseus immediately takes hold of as he was told to, says not a word. But she is powerful! As a "suppliant," he is under her protection from now on (cf. 11.338). She would only have to speak, if he were to be torn from her, but it does not come to that. Odysseus, while being served a late supper, uses his hunger as an excuse for not saying more about himself. This is the first delay in his giving of information about himself. And now a new, solemn libation is made to Zeus, the one who assures the rights of strangers. Since the arrival of the stranger, they are all taking part in a sacred rite (cf. *Il.* 24.480ff., 570; *Od.* 14.283, etc.). The question as to where he got his clothes would be improper here and can wait until the king and queen are alone with their guest. Before going to sleep, the end of the day looks back to the beginning, with the charming, half-true story about the clothes and the daughter. That is why Arete's question about his name and origins remains unanswered. If we try to make room for the disclosure of his identity, the whole thing would be unbalanced.

And yet we are left with that contradiction, the solemn promise of a journey home on the next day, which is not kept. But let us see what happens on the next day.

Odysseus has become the guest of the king, yet the king represents the collective will of the town's aristocracy, with whom Odysseus must enter into the same relationship of obligation. The nobles are called to an assembly in the marketplace, where the newcomer is introduced to them by the king. He is granted a safe conduct, and a ship and crew are made ready. The king invites the leading nobles to receive his guest in his house. During the meal, while the singer is singing one of the famous songs of Troy, the quarrel between Odysseus and Achilleus, the king sees his guest hiding the tears he is shedding. He interrupts and invites them to watch the games.

Everyone goes to the marketplace. Nine organizers take up their duties. Nothing would prevent Odysseus from reaching home on the same day, especially as the departure was planned for the evening anyway. In the same way, Telemachos leaves for Pylos at bedtime (2.357) and from Pylos to Ithaka (15.296). During the games the guest is insulted by Euryalos. Odysseus takes up the discus and almost gives himself away by word and deed. Alkinoos allows a lively part to follow the serious one: the dance by a group to the song of Ares and Aphrodite sung by the bard, and a display of juggling skill in a ball game. The hero of the *Iliad* is amazed. Delighted, the king suggests an exchange of guest-presents. Twelve members of the ruling council are responsible for these. Each one gives a robe and a pound of gold. Euryalos, who insulted him, gives him his sword. The sun goes down and the presents are all there (8.417). Nothing is stopping Odysseus from still setting out on the same evening. The king and queen's present is added to the others last. The chest that the queen has chosen is closed. Odysseus is bathed and dressed. Then he meets Nausikaa and there is a wonderful, short farewell between the two. Already the meal is beginning and the singer is summoned. Nothing is stopping Odysseus from leaving the same night. The presents, the meeting, the sinking sun, the whole atmosphere, everything points to the moment of farewell. Then we reach the point that was unavoidable and yet unforeseen, the point of recognition. Delayed for so long, it still reverses everything.

The recognition is so powerful, and on both sides, from the side of the questioner and the side of the person answering. So much energy that has been held back is released at once, that its waves extend as far as the last of the adventures told. Who is Odysseus? The answer to this question only comes in what he tells. The stream is held up at one point, yet at such a point where a halt is impossible and a stemming of the tide only leads to its sweeping away in a stronger current. When everyone is ready to hear about the heroism of the *Iliad* from the voices of the dead, Odysseus interrupts with a catalogue of famous women of earlier times, women, nothing but women and there is no end of them. It is night and time to sleep. He asks to be allowed to sleep, whether on the ship, which is lying ready for him, or here; it should be their and the gods' concern to escort him (11.330ff.). Even now his departure would be possible, but then the queen holds him back. He is *her* guest too, and she feels that he has not received enough presents yet. Her word carries weight and the guest is asked to be patient until morning. And Odysseus says, "By all means, for this prize." What has happened? He who was urging departure, and could hardly wait to leave, has caused himself this delay. Starting with "Yes, I am Odysseus," he ends by cheating himself of the fulfillment of his desires. Everyone feels that it is impossible for him to end with this catalogue of women. Also it is not his loss.

The points that have been stressed up to now are only relevant to one side of what is happening, only the guest/host relationship of the real world. And even on this level, there are some underlying impossibilities. How can the king introduce and commend his guest to the assembled people without saying his name or knowing who he is?

> Here is this stranger, I do not know who he is, come wandering
> suppliant here to my house from the eastern or western people.

> (8.28f.)

It never occurs to his guest to help him over his embarrassment. The king is taking something on himself here. For *this* right of guests only applies among equals. Ordinary travelers, although received with the utmost friendliness, have no part in this. It is a matter for equals to recognize one another. Receiving someone was often subject to considerations, because of the consequences it could have. On the other hand, it is a testimony to a noble nature if one does not ask too much, "Who are you?" "How did you come to this position?" In Herodotus the Lydian king Croesus does not hesitate to complete the rite of expiation for hapless Adrastus, before asking him the necessary questions. But what is this compared with Alkinoos? His discretion borders on the fantastic. Is this still the real world? And yet people believe they can sense a psychological element here. His discretion becomes all the greater, the more his amazement grows. He has not been in doubt for a moment since the first long silence. He has even thought of a god . . . and surprisingly soon of a future son-in-law. Instead Euryalos raises the possibility of a doubt. His insinuation is, "You do not know anything about games and are one of those traders." This is equivalent to saying, "You are not a nobleman; you have slunk in among us." And yet the stranger becomes all the more mysterious to the king's friend. This question finally erupts after he has held it back for as long as possible. Surely it must be associated with a turmoil of conflicting feelings and a mixture of head-shaking, irrelevant assumptions, and expectations. What a misunderstanding in front of everyone! Such tears are not for mourning lost friends, but tears of shock created by the poet!

At any rate, this Alkinoos can be understood. But what is the solution to the puzzle in the case of Odysseus? He is silent about his reasons, according to the will of the poet, and seems just as stubborn to us as to the king's friend. What should one infer? Is it sorrow that gnaws at him or longing for his home? Does he suspect that after all he has suffered he is not himself anymore? Is he suffering from alienation? Would they believe him? Is it pride or modesty? Or is it fear that if they knew who he was, they would keep him even longer? (Perhaps it is in the same way that Telemachos, through a similar fear, avoids his guest-friend Nestor at 15.200.) Whatever it is, he does not want to say. No motive for his silence is reflected in the narrative. At home his false identity has a purpose, namely cunning and disguise. But here? People have pointed to it as the difficulties experienced by a "reworker." And yet only through the ground bass of his silence does the way lead to his melodious revelation of himself. Only the hour takes him out of himself. But the hour belongs to the poet. Odysseus's own innermost wish is for what this trick does for him, just as with his discovery by the nurse, Eurykleia. And yet how much more glorious is the victory when he does not have to face a new battle but wins through to be himself! The unmotivated part lies above the motivated part according to the layers.

For now an additional element is added to all the others. One of those two possibilities must be the case; if not one, then the other. Suppose the *Odyssey* were not an epic, and Odysseus did not appear as a hero of the *Iliad* among the people of fairy tale, a famous man among happy people, a man who has been tested in the midst of carefree people? In this way his being incognito is a symbol—an example of a life of such pleasure meets an example of such patience. A stranger, yet wondered at and revealed, he steps through the ball game, the dance, and everything. He is a guest in quite a different sense from the rules of hospitality in early Greece.

Their mutual reserve, as an epic device, supports and frames the portrait of an idyll. Yet this time it is not a rustic scene, like Odysseus visiting Eumaios, but the picture of a town and its people. The poet of the *Odyssey* seems even more characterized than the poet of the *Iliad* by the richness of his inventive powers in dealing with similar scenes. When Odysseus, who has just been the unknown guest of the Phaiakes, returns to his house as an unknown beggar, then both these stories are hurrying on equally toward a recognition, which keeps being postponed. Here as there we have the same repetitions—twice the tears and twice the thrown footstool—the same devices for increasing tension, and in both places the same comments by the critics. For again the story seems to go somewhat further than it would seem to have originally. Why must he in both places nearly give himself away—by throwing the discus as with the washing of his feet? However, the difference is that his recognition does not become dangerous among the Phaiakes. It is the same game but with the opposite meaning. In Ithaka his removal of his mask leads, in the end, to a terrible bloodbath and judgment; here it results in revelation and in amazement at him.

Above all the scene here contains an element that this poet knows how to handle like no one else, the element of mutual discovery. Finding each other comes as confirmation of a suspicion. In this way husband and wife find each other, Telemachos and Menelaos, Odysseus and Eumaios, and also Odysseus and Alkinoos. An integral part of this process is that one shows himself a match for the other, that he loves him without knowing who he is, that he has a deeper knowledge than he is conscious of. If the journey leads from the fairy-tale king to the swineherd, if the former's kingdom creates the tension in the first story, then it is a logical part of this first story that Odysseus should *shun* Alkinoos. One does not have to be an Alkinoos to admire the famous hero. The reason why he, in his turn, does not immediately ask his guest for his name, can be found in convention. And yet what delicacy, consideration, shyness, and misgivings are added to custom here!

The *Iliad* is not like this. There people do touch each other deeply, violently, but then there is suddenly something between them that is dividing them. If one thinks this through, then one soon discovers a far-reaching difference. The constantly recurring contrast and alternation between extravagance and moderation in the *Iliad* is foreign to the whole *Odyssey*. However one chooses to formulate the play and replay of the same antithesis, this is a contrast between daemonic and human elements, between necessity in terms of oneself and becoming aware of the other person, between horror and vulnerability, harshness and gentleness. Even in the case of outwardly very similar meetings, such as Hektor and Andromache compared with Odysseus and Penelope, the same difference can be observed. The amazement felt when Odysseus suddenly kneels before Arete, is modeled on the last book of the *Iliad* as Priam kneels before Achilleus so suddenly. And yet what a different contrast exists there!

In the *Odyssey* the powers are missing both in actions and people, which sometimes rush them on beyond their plans or intentions. In this aspect

Achilleus, Patroklos, Hektor, Agamemnon, Helen, and even Paris are related. In the *Odyssey* there is not one of the characters, not even one of the suitors, who could be compared with this. Even as an avenger Odysseus does not let himself be carried away. He carries out even his most terrible deeds on instruction from Athene. Meleager suffers much more from himself and is driven much more by himself, like the young Phoinix in comparison to Theoklymenos, although the latter also has to go into exile because of a murder and becomes the follower of a foreign lord like Phoinix! In the *Iliad* an element of the extreme is par for the course, not only among the heroes but also in the events. As a result the impression made is often cruel. But cruelty only results from a basic gentleness. In turn, as we have said, the poet of the *Odyssey* writes in ever new tones about people finding each other. But part of finding the other person is also the danger of missing them, or losing them, either outwardly or inwardly. As an epic device we find that they are separated and then they almost fail to recognize each other when they meet again. We meet their doubts and their testing of each other. In addition we find the opposite: their loss of hope that they will ever find each other again, their alienation and hardening toward each other. This is the really inhuman element for the poet of the *Odyssey*. His richest tone sequences lie on this scale. This is the basic ingredient in his poetry which stays the same even when presented in the most varying forms, from the dog Argos to the game with the tokens of recognition. Is this a part of the age or of the material? Or rather is this more dependent on the poet in question?

A fruitful situation results in more than the original motif; it creates diversity and becomes a vehicle for new possibilities. In the end it allows something to be expressed in an indirect way, which if said directly would go beyond the genre. (In *Hamlet* we find something similar done in a different way). It is especially clear that the action is internalized here. It is no longer a question simply of deeds and actions but of tests, temptations, trials of the soul, and feelings such as friendship, love, loyalty, tenderness, doubt, and premonition. Odysseus' disguising of himself has as its basic reason the danger he is in. But actually this does not exhaust its meaning. Otherwise why would the game with the stranger in beggar's guise be maintained so long and drawn out until a whole world of high and low, of nobles and peasants, of right and wrong has been shown at three levels in society: lords, servants, and wanderers? The unknown avenger becomes the one who "tests," who "makes trial," a secret judge. His disguise becomes the touchstone that distinguishes true from false: true nobility in the form of a servant and false nobility in the sons of lords. What a view of the world from below! What a change in the format of ancient epic! What power this disguise has! For this reason the disguise sometimes seems thin and sometimes more convincing. Sometimes Odysseus *seems* to be a beggar only under the spell of Athene, and then he must drain to the last drop the bitterness of a man who is now old and homeless.

And, moreover, the disguise reflects the whole inner world of the love of husband and wife. Love does not show itself directly. How could he show his love without giving himself away? And a part of his disguise is also the lies that he spreads about himself. What started out as only the magic of a goddess, becomes the invention of a life story. Does he tell lies simply for revenge? Then why would he lie "like the poet," so that Eumaios listens to him as if under a spell? Why does he tell of a fate, which carries a kernel of truth in it, as a foil to his own fate, the story of a wanderer who must end in this way because he cannot give up the life of adventure? Ultimately he lies so that the born adventurer and his fate should not be missing next to that of the seer, singer, beggar, king, shepherd, etc. in the society pictured in the *Odyssey*.

With the repetition of this universal, primary form, the Phaiakes share in the real world of the poet. And yet, taking into account all these relationships, what would become of the story if it did not contradict itself? How would the story grow wings, as it were, if the real world did not alternate again and again for a moment with the world of fairy-tale wonders just as in Aladdin and his magic lamp? What were the Phaiakes once?

Of the many magic people into whose power the hero falls, giants, ogres, monsters, vampires, and the kings of fable, the latter are the only ones who help him to a good end, whose function and magic is of the opposite kind to all the others. Like elves of the distant seas, as they have been called, they bring shipwrecked sailors to their homes overnight in their magic ships as they are sleeping. From time immemorial they have been saviors, just as Asklepios the son of Apollo was once the healer of all the sick. But that was once upon a time. Just as Zeus with his lightning bolt made an end to this healing craft to ensure the god of death his tribute, so the Lord of the Seas, in order to maintain his power, ends this all-too-humane custom of safe conduct home. With his trident he heaps a mountain range over the city and people of the benefactors. This "movement of mountains," well-known as a motif, buries the ancient loveliness. As the Phaiakes come under the spell of the *Odyssey* legends, the hero from Ithaka becomes the last person whom they escort home.

The poet of this poem first separated this from the fairy-tale adventures and raised it above their level. If it were told to us as the last in a series of adventures, its fairy-tale elements would probably be preserved for us in a much purer form, and it would consequently lack "Homeric" content. Yet the more it has become a higher art form, the more the magic element is, as it were, pushed from the middle to the edges and seeks cover, hiding itself, only to appear again suddenly in a way that is all the more surprising. For the contradictions between the two distant worlds, which cause dilemmas, count in this new whole simply as one more part of its manifold magic. One may want to ask the poet hesitatingly, "Are these still the Phaiakes?" His answer would be, "Yes, they are."

Ships as swift as wings and thoughts (7.36), quicker than hawks and falcons (13.86), which know by themselves where they should sail, must be magic ships comparable to the artificial, magic horse in the famous Indian story in *1,001 Nights*. These ships glide along so gently and lightly that a wonderful sleep comes over their guest so that when he wakes up at home, he does not know what has happened. One should not ask why the sea is never stormy when the Phaiakes are sailing. "Calmed winds" (7.319) belong to their magic, like the secret nature of their nightly journey. The "grey ones" are invisible, not men but spirits.

And yet this magic power is mentioned only from time to time, virtually only by Alkinoos, as if talking about it directly were contrary to the spirit of the epic. We hear only once that the ships are in fact alive and all-knowing, that they row themselves in a mist that makes them invisible, and that they know all the coasts and can reach any destination without needing a steersman or rudder. We learn this only in that most exciting moment, when Alkinoos can no longer restrain himself after so many tests of his patience and asks his guest his name. How the fairy-tale magic is integrated into that long-awaited moment that was always meeting new delays! The tension of this moment is directed to quite different things.

> Tell me your land, your neighborhood and your city,
> so that our ships, straining with their own purpose, can carry you
> there, for there are no steersman among the Phaiakes, neither
> are there any steering oars for them, such as other ships have,
> but the ships themselves understand men's thoughts and purposes,
> and they know all the cities of men and all their fertile
> fields, and with greatest speed they cross the gulf of the salt sea,
> huddled under a mist and cloud, nor is there ever
> any fear that they may suffer damage or come to destruction.
> Yet this I have heard once on a time from my father, Nausithoos
> who said it and told me how Poseidon would yet be angry
> with us, because we are convoy without hurt to all men.
> He said that one day, as a well-made ship of our Phaiakian
> men came back from a convoy on the misty face of the water,
> he would stun it, and pile a great mountain over our city, to hide it.
> So the old man spoke, and the god might either bring it
> to pass, or it be left undone, as the god's heart pleases.
> So now come tell me this.

(8.555–72)

The kernel of the fairy tale is the excuse given as an explanation for this question that finally breaks out with such force. Direct epic narrative only touches on this subject once. And yet it makes the old miracle in turn serve a new one immediately. What was once magic for its own sake, now becomes the prize of this one man, the sufferer, inspired by nothing else but to boast of his uniqueness, and to reward his troubles.

... while the ship, as in a field four stallions drawing
a chariot all break together at the stroke of the whiplash,
and lifting high their feet lightly beat out their path, so
the stern of the ship would lift and the creaming wave behind her
boiled amain in the thunderous crash of the sea. She ran on
very steady and never wavering; even the falcon,
that hawk that flies lightest of winged creatures, could not have paced her,
so lightly did she run on her way and cut through the sea's waves.
She carried a man with a mind like the gods for counsel, one whose
spirit up to this time had endured much, suffering many
pains: the wars of men, hard crossing of the big waters;
but now he slept still, oblivious of all he had suffered."

(13.81–92)

The poet's transcendence makes sense of and explains the contradictions. Where the poet of the *Iliad* succeeds in composing what he wishes in an always new way with the most natural necessity, the poet of the *Odyssey* succeeds, by combining one element over the other in layers, through the contradiction between the old fairy tales and the new spirit. He does this by giving the former new life and giving the latter its footing in tradition. There is a clear contradiction here in that the Phaiakes bring every ship-wrecked person, whoever he is, to his home, and yet Odysseus is the only one for whom the gift of returning home is seen as such a high honor and reward. Among these hospitable people, strangers are not welcome after all, and Odysseus has to beg, almost like Priam in Achilleus' tent, for what was granted so gladly to everyone else. This points to the same phenomenon of the contradiction between fairy tale and epic. For it is only thanks to this contradiction that the higher consequence develops, which makes the Phai-akian adventure into that great turning point, giving it its place and posi-tion in epic. To create this turning point, we must have Odysseus in a position of vulnerability—the fearful moment, the pause, as Odysseus kneels before Arete, the slowly dawning premonition of the Phaiakes that this stranger is more than others, more than they themselves, the granting of his request and the delay of his journey, the repeatedly postponed discov-ery of who he really is.

A word should still be said about the end. Previously the ending had come with the mountains being moved. There is no need to quote refer-ences for this widespread motif. In the *Odyssey* we find instead of this story an epic scene as the angry Poseidon turns to Zeus—a scene involving the gods, modeled on the *Iliad* (*Od.* 13.145 after *Il.* 4.37, etc.). Does this not connect with the Polyphemos story? Yet here also the connection is not required for the sake of the fairy tale. If the Lord of the Seas one day puts an end to the magic of the Phaiakes, which he himself has tolerated for so long, then this does not happen because Odysseus has blinded his son but because this habit of saving people is getting out of hand. Therefore, the explanation of the mountains covering them does not point to Odysseus either in the conversation of the gods (13.151) or in the oracle of Alkinoos (13.174). Epic can be recognized in the transcending and unifying motifs, while fairy tale is visible in the contradicting ones.

The model of the *Iliad* is hardly more evident anywhere than in that scene between the gods. And yet, if Poseidon complains to Zeus in the role he plays in the *Iliad*, as an Olympian afraid for his image, then here again the imitation of the *Iliad* has been transcribed by the poet into his own tone. What a different object for their quarrel! In the *Iliad* the gods fight over the fates of kings and peoples. Here Poseidon declares himself agreed with the success of the other gods' wishes. Let Odysseus reach home if this is what Zeus has promised him. But it is contrary to the honor of the Olympian for him to come home with such presents, so honored with richer treasures than if he had come directly from Ilium. A new element here is that the concern of the slighted god is all the greater. The less he cares about the issue itself, the more he cares about the principle. That is to say that he takes exception to what this poet first made the result of this adventure, the splendor of the reversal of fortune! He is angry because Odysseus, who was just recently so naked and unknown, is now suddenly so famous and rewarded. And Zeus knows his Poseidon well. He tells him that it is right and he should do as he plans to the Phaiakes. But if he is going to destroy the ship as it is returning home, why not rather turn it to stone so that all humans may wonder at it? Poseidon would not be Poseidon if this were not evident to him. He hits the ship with the palm of his hand and plants it as a cliff in the sea. Then he goes, or rather he is already gone! The ship turned to stone becomes an invitation on the part of the Olympian gods. Poseidon takes no part in Odysseus' sufferings at home, however much his son begged him to. He becomes angry but he does not hate. His disappearance from the scene of the action is the same as after the storm at sea. His moods change in a dignified way.

And what becomes of the Phaiakes? While people are amazed—this again is modeled after the *Iliad* (*Od.* 13.145 after *Il.* 4.37)—Alkinoos sees his father's prophecy being fulfilled and warns them to cease from escorting travelers. He has twelve steers sacrified to Poseidon. Since the otherwise usual formula "but he was not moved by the offerings" is left out, the fate of the Phaiakes remains hanging in the balance. On the one hand we have Odysseus returned home happily, on the other the Phaiakes fearfully offering sacrifices. The transition from one sphere to the other is marked by the contrast of the two situations, like sustained pauses. An epic does not end with one conclusion like a narrative but with a wide sweep of opposing scenes. The poet of the *Odyssey* seems to owe this way of leaving things hanging in the balance to the poet of the *Iliad*.

Does what has been said here exhaust the theme of adventures in the *Odyssey*? Is what is waiting for the hero at home not just as much of an adventure? A new exile is waiting for him, if not in distant lands then in the depths of misery. He will misrepresent himself in quite a different way among people than among fiends and monsters. His transformation into a beggar—almost like an Ovidian metamorphosis—the magic, the magic wand, the hocus-pocus of Athene who does not seem like a witch—is all this not a reminiscence of Circe? One more time the fairy-tale element steps into the "realism" of great epic. This too would probably not be possible in the *Iliad*. But here also it represents and frames a transcendent theme—the theme of finding each other as a miracle. By way of a magic wand, the revenge story is linked to the adventures. Yet this leads to further questions, beyond those posed here. Here the purpose, within a limited sphere, was simply to bring the question of origins, which had gone astray, back to a negotiable path, without building castles in the air. All methods, however much they change, depend on what they yield on each occasion they are applied.

Penelope and the Suitors

UVO HÖLSCHER
(translated by Simon Richter)

THE STORY of the homecoming of Odysseus is preceded by a long "pre-story" that covers many years. It tells us of the wanderings and adventures of Odysseus that are depicted retrospectively in the *Odyssey* when he retells his story to the Phaeacians. But the prestory also includes the cunning of Penelope. We learn in a similar way, that is, retrospectively, though more casually, how the queen was pressured by her Suitors to marry again and in the moment of her need hit on the excuse that she first would have to weave a shroud for her old father-in-law, Laertes; how every night she undid the weaving she had done that day and thus was able to keep the Suitors at bay for three years. The Suitors in this story appear as complete dolts who would never have seen through her trick had it not been for the treachery of one of her maids. This story also tells how Penelope, once her deceit is uncovered, submits to the new marriage, not for appearances' sake, but in seriousness, and how Odysseus appears at the last moment, kills the Suitors, and resumes possession of wife, house, and kingship.

But why does Penelope cease waiting and resisting when her deceit is uncovered? There is an answer to this question. It can be found in a speech of Penelope, where she tells retrospectively of a time very early in the prestory. Here are Penelope's own words:

> . . . when the Argives took ship
> for Ilion, and with them went my husband, Odysseus.
>
> . . . .
>
> he took me by the right hand at the wrist, and then said to me:
> "Dear wife, since I do not think the strong-greaved Achaians
> will all come safely home from Troy without hurt, seeing
> that people say the Trojans are men who can fight in battle,
> they are throwers of the spear, and shooters of arrows,
> and riders with fast-footed horses, who with the greatest
> speed settle the great and hateful issue of common battle,
> I do not know if the god will spare me, or if I must be lost
> there in Troy; here let everything be in your charge.
> You must take thought for my father and mother, here in our palace,
> as you do now, or even more, since I shall be absent.

But when you see our son grown up and bearded, then you may
marry whatever man you please, forsaking your household."
So he spoke then; and now all this is being accomplished.
And there will come that night when a hateful marriage is given
to wretched me.

(18.252–53 . . . 58–73)

Penelope says this in a speech to the Suitors. This speech and its dramatic
context are one of the most puzzling and controversial scenes in the entire
Odyssey. If one takes her at her word, one understands why she now suddenly submits to the pressure of her Suitors: her son, Telemachos, is an
adult; the time has come that Odysseus himself had set to mark the end of
her waiting and the celebration of a new marriage. Indeed, without instructions of this kind, the original Odysseus folktale could hardly have been
told. For the faithfulness of Penelope to remain believable, she has to have
an exterior reason to give up her waiting, despite her faithfulness. The epic
could much more easily do without this, since it has recourse to altogether
different possibilities of depicting situations and states of mind, such that it
can represent contradictory elements. But the terms chosen by Odysseus to
describe this time, "when you see our son grown up and bearded," seem to
me to bear the stamp of the folktale.

These would be idle considerations if those interpreters were right who
see the parting speech of Odysseus, here recited by Penelope, as nothing
but a cunning invention of the moment, with which she merely feigns her
decision to remarry. "Whoever takes it seriously, steps into the same trap as
the Suitors," said Wilamowitz. "Or would a hero, departing for war, talk
about the fact that war is fatally dangerous? He would rather say, 'wipe
your tears, not every bullet hits home.'"

In order to understand how one can take Penelope's speech seriously, we
must consider the whole scene. Odysseus, disguised as a beggar, is already
in the house, when unexpectedly Penelope has the idea of going down to
the Suitors and leaving her chambers to which she usually withdraws to
escape the wild carryings-on in the men's hall. We do not know exactly why
she does this:

She laughed in an idle way and spoke to her nurse.

(18.163)

She suddenly has the desire, she explains, to show herself to the Suitors,
even though she despises them; and she ought perhaps also to say a word to
her son, who is sitting down there among them . . . (18.164–68). She does,
it is true, resist Eurynome's suggestion that she make herself look attractive—the days of holding court are past since Odysseus left—but in spite of
this, while she is asleep, Athene makes her look so much more seductive
that her appearance in the hall provokes the most lascivious wishes among

the Suitors. At first, admittedly, she directs her speech only to Telemachos, and it is not until one of the Suitors pays her an effusive compliment that she replies with the story, already cited, of Odysseus' departure and the news that the day of her remarriage is at hand. Nevertheless, she does not fail to express her horror at the thought and concludes by reproaching them for their parasitic ways and for not bringing food and gifts to the house, in accordance with polite custom. The result is that the excited Suitors do produce the most expensive clothes, with gold clasps, chains, necklaces, and earrings with magnificent gems, and she once again withdraws to her chamber with the gifts she has garnered.

This scene has alienated interpreters since antiquity. It seemed unworthy of the majestic, "circumspect" Penelope: *Regina prope ad meretricias artes descendit* [the queen descends nearly to the arts of a courtesan] was the often-cited judgment of scholarship. Different deletions have been attempted as means of solving the problem. Karl Reinhardt, who understood the genesis of the *Odyssey* not as an addition of parts, but rather as a structural transformation of the Odysseus folktale into the genre of grand epic, was the first to leave the scene untouched. He sees in it a remainder of the cunning Penelope, such as she is in the story of the loom, who is otherwise absent from the epic. According to Reinhardt's reading the entire scene would be an invention of the poet of the *Odyssey*, a means of transposing the old story of the cunning of Penelope into an actual epic situation. Penelope's deceitful tale about the departure of Odysseus thus takes the place of the loom motif.

The scene, however, does not amount to so unambiguous a representation of Penelope's cunning as Reinhardt's theory would lead one to expect. Nothing indicates that she is deliberately planning to deceive the Suitors. There is no doubt that the Suitors are deceived, but what is the nature of the deception? The three verses that follow her speech seem to answer that question:

> She spoke, and much-enduring great Odysseus was happy
> because she beguiled gifts out of them, and enchanted their spirits
> with blandishing words, while her own mind had other intentions.

> (18.281–83)

What are the "other intentions" that she has in mind? That she is in fact not thinking about remarriage at all? It is true that this same expression elsewhere designates the contrast between external appearances and internal meaning: "For she holds out hope to all, and makes promises to each man, / sending us messages, but *her mind has other intentions*" (2.91–92, cf. 13. 380–81). But even there the word does not mean "to be up to something else," but "to long passionately for something else." She longs for postponement, she longs for Odysseus' return. The same is true here, where her speech to the Suitors actually announces her "internal" meaning; it is just that now she sees no more hope of postponement.

The happiness of Odysseus, therefore, cannot be connected with her not being in earnest in her decision to remarry. Indeed, how could he know that? After all, she *is* in earnest. Just a few hours later she will tell him, the still unrecognized beggar, about her decision to marry and her intention to hold on the following day the contest that will determine her final choice (19.570–81). The announcement of her remarriage could disturb him? Why doesn't it, neither here nor there? Not because he suspects she is lying, but because he is there and will intercept her! Why does no doubt assail him with regard to the faithfulness of his wife? Because she has powerfully expressed her aversion to the new marriage! The "other intentions" she has in mind are not a secret plan, they are the feelings in her heart. What, then, is the basis of Odysseus' happiness? "Because she beguiled gifts out of them," says the text, and that indeed is the simple point of the episode.

But the episode has another meaning besides that. It marks the first encounter between Penelope and Odysseus, and an unforeseen one at that. Penelope had earlier that afternoon tried to arrange a meeting with the beggar, but Odysseus had rejected her formal welcome and postponed it to the evening, when the Suitors would have departed. This unplanned encounter is inserted between the encounter that failed to occur and the one still to come; it is, in other words, an encounter that is only partially a personal encounter. For even though not a single word is exchanged between them, and even though Penelope does not suspect that Odysseus is disguised in the form of the beggar, every one of Penelope's words is somehow meant for Odysseus. Here, where Odysseus sees her again for the first time, she should appear to her husband in all her glory—that is the will of Athene. At the same time, she must appear as the faithful one; as far as she is concerned, everything she does must seem to be unintentional. That is the source of the enigmatic quality in her behavior, which cannot be eliminated by any textual analysis in the usual sense. The scene shows as clearly as possible, right from the beginning, that its objective purpose is different from its subjective one. Both purposes, moreover, have a double aspect. The objective purpose coincides with the intentions of the goddess, who wants to excite the Suitors and so to increase Penelope's stature in the eyes of her husband and son. Thus the objective purpose of the scene is to elicit gifts from the Suitors and to allow the subtle encounter with Odysseus. The subjective purpose coincides with Penelope's rather tentative one. She wishes to reveal herself for once to the Suitors and perhaps also to give a few words of warning to her son. The poet is not only aware of the ambiguity, he intends it. He has done everything to remove from Penelope the conscious intention of exciting the Suitors: the goddess takes care of her *toilette*, and her speech to Eurymachos is as earnestly admonitory as the one she makes shortly before to Telemachos. Penelope's character in no way deviates from her usual manner; the slyness and coquetry that one might be inclined to expect, given the result of the episode, are not represented in the least: she is as majestic and restrained as ever. In short, she is not the cunning Penelope of the folktale, but the sensible, mourning Penelope of the epic. Finally, had the poet not explained why Odysseus was happy, we would not have noticed that the story results in a cunning triumph, the gifts, for which the introduction to the scene had prepared us.

Thus the ambiguity of the scene is somewhat more complicated than the mere interplay of cunning and appearance. The cunning takes place on the objective, factual level of the scene; it is the whole point of the story in its simplest form. An epic situation, however, has been inscribed into the simple story, the significance of which transcends the original tale of cunning. When Penelope appears before Odysseus, the queen before the beggar, for the first time in twenty years, she is not in mourning but shines in god-given glory and the majesty of a noble woman. What was once cunning is now superiority; the oppressors become the servants of queenly qualities. The gathering of gifts is also transformed: they are demanded as her due, what is owed "to a noble woman and daughter of a rich man" (18.276), and they are presented in knightly submission. Nor does anything hint that Penelope is pleased, as one might expect if she had carried out a successful deception. Such pleasure would contradict the character of Penelope. The cunning is thus transferred into a new interplay of consciousness and unconsciousness, an interplay for which the beautifying of Penelope as she sleeps, an invention of the epic poet, provides the necessary condition: Penelope does not want to deceive—but the Suitors are deceived. This deeper sort of ambiguity is a result of the transformation of folktale into epic.

An implication of what we have said is that this particular story of cunning is not necessarily original to the *Odyssey*. Antinoos talks about one cunning trick among many when he tells the story of the loom in book 2. It would be fair to count the gathering of gifts as another of these tricks. Nor is there anything to prevent one from supposing that in the folktale the cunning Penelope had adorned herself, intending to seduce the Suitors. It was the epic poem that had to free her of this aspect, in order not to contradict her epic character, and that accomplished this with a device that shows the artfulness of epic invention. The folktale formulation, "She held out hope to all," is translated into epic language and becomes a testimony of faithfulness and a sovereign statement against the abuse of hospitality. Imagine what would be missing, if this Penelope scene were edited out. All the other scenes where she appears—when Phemios sings in book 1, the report of Telemachos' journey in book 1, the return of Telemachos in book 16, and after the mistreatment of the beggar in book 17—all show her as mourning, as threatened, defensive, even scolding. Take away this scene and you have taken away the Penelope for whose sake Odysseus rejected Kalypso's offer of immortality, the Penelope whose royalty is praised by the beggar. In a word, the majestic Penelope would be missing.

Now there is also no longer any reason to doubt the truth of what Penelope says about Odysseus' departure and his instructions to her. There is a reference to Telemachos' coming of age in the prologue of the Penelope scene, in the speech of Eurynome: "For now your son is come of age, and you know you always / prayed the immortals, beyond all else, to see him bearded" (18.175–76). It should not be disturbing that a mother wishes for her son's maturity, even though that day also means the termination of hope for Odysseus' return. That is how Eurynome understands the day, as the time when her mistress' period of waiting and mourning finally comes to an end. Penelope herself in her conversation with Odysseus leaves no doubt that the recent maturing of her son is the decisive reason for her giving up on her husband's return: "He is a grown man now, most able / to care for the house" (19.160–61); "but now that he is grown a tall man and come to maturity's measure" (19.532). Much earlier, Athene had spoken to Telemachos about his coming of age:

> You should not go on
> clinging to your childhood. You are no longer of an age to do that.
> . . . .
> So you too, dear friend, since I can see you are big and splendid, be bold
> also.

> (1.296–97 . . . 301–2)

> At once he went over, a godlike man, to sit with the Suitors.

> (1.324)

> All of them bit their lips in amazement
> at Telemachos . . .
> and Antinoos answered,
> . . . .
> "I hope the son of Kronos never makes you our king in seagirt
> Ithaka. Though to be sure that is your right by inheritance."
> Then the thoughtful Telemachos said to him in answer:
> . . . .
> "I would be willing to take that right if Zeus would give it.
> Do you think it would be the worst thing that could happen to anyone?
> . . . .
> But I will be the absolute lord over my own household
> and my servants."

> (1.381–82 . . . 383 . . . 386–88 . . . 390–91 . . . 397–98)

The visit to Nestor is also set in similar terms:

> Telemachos, here is no more need at all of modesty.

> (3.14)

I have no experience in close discourse.

(3.23)

So you too, dear friend, . . .
be brave.

(3.199–200)

Dear friend, I have no thought that you will turn out mean and cowardly.

(3.375)

Finally, Penelope speaks once more in the scene with the Suitors:

> Telemachos, your mind and thoughts are no longer steadfast.
> When you were a child still, you had better thoughts in mind. Now,
> when you are big, and come to the measure of maturity, and one
> who saw you, some outsider, viewing your size and beauty,
> would say you were the son born of a prosperous man;
> your thoughts are no longer righteous, nor your perception.

(18.215–20)

And Telemachos answers:

> My mother, . . . I myself
> notice all these things in my heart and know of them, better
> and worse alike, but before now I was only an infant.

(18.227–29)

These are merely the words that refer directly to Telemachos' coming of age. They do not include all those situations that announce his newly achieved manhood loud and clear: Telemachos taking a stand against his mother, gruffly addressing the Suitors, calling the Ithakan assembly, undertaking a journey without the knowledge of his mother, the respect shown him by Nestor at his reception, his decisiveness in taking leave from Menelaos. Given all this, it is difficult to understand how anyone could have argued that a changing, growing Telemachos is represented in the *Odyssey*. The one change is change enough: as a child he had long submitted to everything; now for the first time he stands up for himself. One should never have seen in this single change a development in the sense of a *Bildungsroman*. All the scenes in the Telemachy in which the character of Telemachos is revealed are in fact no more than multiple representations of that single, critical moment of the passage from boyhood to manhood. The entire *Telemachy* is nothing other than the transformation of the folktale formulation, "when our son has grown a beard," into various epic situations. This is, as the moment of crisis, at the same time the basic situation of the whole epic—a situation, however, that is only really explained in the *Telemachy* and not in the books that treat Odysseus directly.

It has often been asserted that Telemachos, as an epic figure, is a more recent invention. But the figure of an only child, on whom the preservation of the family and the kingdom depend—preserved in the epic in a mythological frame—seems to me definitely to derive from folktale:

> For so it is that the son of Kronos made ours a single
> line. Arkeisios had only a single son, Laertes,
> and Laertes had only one son, Odysseus; Odysseus in turn
> left only one son, myself, in the halls, and got no profit of me.

(16.117–20)

It has more justly been pointed out that the story of the *Telemachy*, the journey in search of his father, is of more recent origin when compared with Odysseus' travels and *nostos* [return homeward] and is not based on any traditional mythological material. Indeed, all the events, in whole and in part, will have been the invention of their poet. Yet it is undeniable that the basic situation reflects a moment that was indispensable to the folktale. To remove the *Telemachy* from the epic is to remove a piece of its traditional story.

Dread Goddess Revisited

MICHAEL N. NAGLER

RECENT WORK on women in antiquity has led to useful reconsiderations of the *Odyssey*, where women and goddesses play complex and determining roles. Following that line of approach, I return here to a fragment of the *Gilgamesh* epic which seems to relate the littoral and otherwise liminal figure of Siduri in that poem to Circe and Calypso, and follow the trail opened by this connection to Odysseus's reunion with Penelope which is negotiated over the nature of their marriage bed at the heart of Homer's *Odyssey*. Along the way, various dimensions of a relationship between Penelope and these sea goddesses turn up which furnish soundings of the Odyssean conception of womankind, though space will not allow us to explore these echoes at great length.

Until the publication of the brief fragment in question from the Akkadian *Gilgamesh*, we knew Siduri only as a temptress who tries unsuccessfully to divert Gilgamesh from his quest for immortality by recommending a bourgeois, Menelaus-like existence with family consolations. The new fragment reveals an almost antithetical side to the goddess, yet one quite complementary and virtually predictable in the logic of myth. The fragment records part of a reply Gilgamesh makes to her:[1]

> Alewife, you sit on the (sea's) shore,
> And you see its depth (lit. heart) all (of its XX?)
> Show me the path (XXXX)
> If it is possible (I will cross the sea).

Homerists—particularly Franz Dirlmeier—were not slow to catch a Homeric resonance in this fleeting whisper of mythic language from the ancient Near East. Like Siduri, Calypso is the daughter of Atlas, who "knows all the depths of the sea" (*Od.* 1.52f.), and Circe guides the hero over the sea to Teiresias, who has the same expertise (10.539f., cf. 12.25–27). There can be little doubt that Siduri or a goddess of her type, tempting and/or helping, whose every word is *nēmertes*, "unerring" (cf. 4.349, *Theogony* 235), who if she does not know the ways of the deep herself "knows a man who knows them," is a prototype of Circe and Calypso, as well as Eidothea (cf. 4.384–86), Leukothea, the Sirens, and perhaps others in the *Odyssey*,

[1] Published by A. R. Millard, "Gilgamesh X: A New Fragment," *IRAQ* 26 (1964), 99–105.

depending on how strictly we define the type. There is a sea goddess named Nemertes in Hesiod's catalogue of the daughters of truth-possessing Nereus, and it is she who "has (access to) the mind of (their) immortal father" (*Theogony* 262, cf. 233).[2] Since Odysseus describes his entire life of adventurous experience as *porous halos exereeinōn*, approximately, "investigating ways (to get) through the sea" (12.259), there can be little doubt that his relationship with the sea-wise goddess is of central importance for his success or failure at whatever his quest represents.

Thus far we are indebted to Dirlmeier for drawing attention to the Akkadian parallel, and we can follow the main lines of his interpretation, which arises from the suggestive noun-epithet phrase used of Circe and Calypso, *deinē theos audēessa*, or "potent speaking goddess," which has puzzled commentators since antiquity: Aristotle, Dirlmeier points out, was thrown by the phrase and changed it to a *lectio facilior*;[3] Dirlmeier's explanation of the phrase seems less than convincing: since these are Mesopotamian goddesses, the poet reassures us that they can speak *Greek*. A more plausible surface meaning can be recovered from the poet's description of Ino, daughter of Cadmus;

> Leukothea, who first was an articulate mortal (*brotos audēessa*)
> but now enjoys divine status in the briny deep.

(5.334f.)

Ino used to be part of the mortal speech community, then became "white goddess" in the sea.[4] Right after his encounter with her, Odysseus will awaken in complete perplexity as to his location in the mortal-divine universe. Is the *thēlus aütē*, "female cry," which awakened him that of the wood nymphs (6.122), or is he finally in the neighborhood of "*anthrōpōn . . . audēentōn*," "people he can speak to" (125; cf. *Theogony* 142b). In other words, "speaking" is normally an attribute of humans; the phrase *theos audēessa* means (or at least meant, since at the oral epic stage we seem to be dealing with a typical dead metaphor embedded in a cult epithet) a divinity who had taken on, or in Ino's case perhaps retained, the ability to speak to humans. This is in line with the scholia also (cf. Scholia TQEP on *Od.* 5.334); the phrase reflects, as it were vestigially, the common poetic and

---

[2] On *nēmertea* as "prophetic," cf. Susan Scheinberg, "The Bee Maidens of the Homeric *Hymn to Hermes*," *Harvard Studies in Classical Philology* 83 (1979), 6.

[3] "Die schreckliche Kalypso," in *Lebende Antike: Festschrift für Rudolph Sühnel*, ed. H. Meller and H.-J. Zimmerman (Berlin, 1967). H. Güntert had briefly discussed the phrase in his *Kalypso* (Halle, 1919), 157.

[4] For the white goddess of folklore, closely related to our goddess, see the classic study of Adalbert Kuhn, "Die Sagen von der weise Frau," *Zeitschrift für deutsche Mythologie und Sittenkunde* 3 (1855), 368–99. Further evidence for our interpretation comes from Crates' substitute for line 142 of the *Theogony*, stating that the Cyclopes were originally divine but were turned into *thnētoi audēentes*. Although not a very early witness, Crates seems here to be following good mythic logic (i.e., inversion).

mythological code in which "voice" is a sign of ontological class or status.[5] The distinction between divine and human is, as I say, only a surface meaning that hints at the importance of the liminal figure through whom the two ontological orders can communicate; indeed Dirlmeier's observations about the mythical background of the goddesses are perceptive and invite further investigation.

Three out of the four times in Homer, the phrase is applied to Circe, in identical hexameters:

> Circe of the beautiful hair, dread goddess endowed with speech

$$(10.136 = 11.8 = 12.150)$$

The fourth describes Calypso, whose metrically different name has been given in the preceding line:

> Dwells (Calypso) of the beautiful hair, etc.

$$(12.449, cf. 7.245f. and 254f.).$$

All four usages mark the important structural articulations of the Apologue narrative: when Odysseus reaches Circe's island, when he leaves it again (he has trouble making a clean break in several adventures, cf. 9.473f.), and when he reaches his description of Calypso's island at the end of his recitation. The last occurrence is both a beginning and an end, since the hero pointedly refers back to the beginning and refuses, in an emphatic *praeteritio*, to recite the story again (12.440–53) Not too surprisingly, the actual beginning of the Apologue contains phrases that are unquestionably recalled by these four usages despite certain substitutions:

> Where dwells the daughter of Atlas, guileful Calypso
> Of the beautiful hair, *a dread goddess;* nor does anyone, etc.

$$(7.245f.)^6$$

> The gods brought (me) to the Isle of Ogygia, where dwells
> Calypso of the beautiful hair, *a dread goddess,* who taking
> me . . .

$$(7.254f.)$$

Our formulaic phrase thus invokes a potent mythological theme at the boundaries between episodes of substantially similar thematic value. These episodes and the language that marks them in this way are deployed in a concentric configuration around the thematic center of the Apologue, the *Nekuia,* or more accurately, *nekuomanteia,* the "divination of the prophetic

---

[5] See M. Nagler, *Spontaneity and Tradition* (Berkeley and Los Angeles, 1974), 140, with note. On *thēlus aütē,* see ibid. 25 note, and Deborah Boedeker, *Descent from Heaven: Images of Dew in Greek Poetry and Religion* (Chico, California, 1984), esp. 67.

[6] The end of this hexameter involves an extraordinary wordplay: *oude tis autēi misgetai,* "*outis* ['No Man,' Odysseus' false(?) name at 9.366ff.] sleeps with her."

dead."[7] The four *verbatim* occurrences of the phrase, along with the very similar language in books 7 and 9, both punctuate the narrative episodes and as it were embed them in a structure that gives the Nekuia climactic emphasis:[8]

NEKUIA

11.8*	11.640
Circe	Circe

(9.31f. and) 10.135f.*	12.150*
Calypso	Calypso

9.29f.	12.448f.*
Apologue	Apologue

7.241, 7.244ff.*	12.452, 453

*Explicit reference to "dread goddess, etc."

It is interesting to compare this structural scheme with the analysis of Gabriel Germain in *Genèse de L'Odyssée*:[9]

NEKUIA

Circe	Sirens
Laestrygonians	Scylla and Charybdis
Aeolus	Thrinacia
Cyclops	Calypso
Lotophagoi	Phaeacians

[7] See Cedric Whitman, *Homer and the Heroic Tradition* (Cambridge, Mass., 1958, 1965), 288, and for *nekuomanteia* Douglas Frame, *The Myth of Return in Early Greek Epic* (New Haven, 1978), as well as my "Entretiens avec Tirésias," *Classical World* 74 (1980): 103–5. This general question of formulas used to demarcate structurally similar junctures in oral narration is discussed in *Spontaneity and Tradition*, 200f.

[8] By contrast with the proem and the message of Teiresias, which make Thrinakia the central adventure (1.7–9, 11.105–17), Athena and Odysseus himself select the adventure with Calypso/Circe, as was seen by Wilhelm Mattes in *Odysseus bei den Phäaken* (Würzburg, 1958), 95. See esp. 1.14ff. and 50–55, with their echoes of the marking phraseology. The twin usages at 7.245f. and 254f. demarcate a false beginning to the recitation, which is part of a pattern of deferment. As is well known, Odysseus is loath to "tell his story," that is, to reveal his identity to the Scherians, and he defers it several times; see Bernard Fenik, *Studies in the Odyssey* (Wiesbaden, 1974), 41–43, etc.

[9] Paris, 1954, p. 333—in the context, incidentally, of many similarities to *Gilgamesh*. See too John Niles, "Patterning in the Wanderings of Odysseus," *Ramus* 7 (1978), 46–60.

Both these analytical schemes are valid. The first, which is modified from Whitman, treats the adventures in the order narrated by the poet while Germain treats them as they must be reconstructed from the fictional "history" recounted by Odysseus.[10] The main point here is that by either analysis the mantic revelations of the Nekuia have been placed at the thematic center of the Apologue and thus the center of the *Odyssey*. They are also, in either analysis, bracketed by "dread goddesses endowed with speech": Circe-Sirens in the fictional history, Calypso-Circe Circe-Calypso in the performance. The exact nature of the *nekuomanteia* is thus central to understanding both these figures and the epic.

The full story of Calypso and Circe and the Shadowy Prophetic Figure who lurks behind them has a very complex symbolic heritage.[11] We may regard it as fundamentally a consultation myth, in which a protagonist penetrates after many trials and often with the help of a female figure (Circe and Calypso) to a deeply guarded area of the mythic geography where he confronts or interviews a potent figure who alone can reveal something to him of a life-and-death significance. Just as Utnapishtim alone has escaped the common lot of death and he alone can provide the answer to Gilgamesh's agonized quest for immortality, so has Teiresias alone been granted the privilege to "remain conscious in the underworld" (10.493–95) and only he can show Odysseus "the ways of his return" (10.539f.). Speech at this level is not mere information, but power.[12] Had the story not been so rationalized by the time it reached the Homeric stage, we would undoubtedly have found Teiresias identified in some way with that calm center and motive power of the phenomenal world, beyond all dualities, the *axis mundi*.

Now, the axial figure *par excellence* in Greek mythology is Atlas, whose symbols, or office, are the "great columns" that hold aloft the heavens at the farthest boundaries of the world, who knows the depths of the sea—and who is the father of Calypso (1.51–53). Her "Oceanic," or primordial, island is itself an omphalos, a common axis symbol in Greek and Mesopotamian (including Sumerian) sources which later *allēgorēsis* was quick to restore.[13] What Homer has partly rationalized as Odysseus' seducers in a pair

---

[10] See further Norman Austin, "Odysseus *Polytropos*: Man of Many Minds," *Arche* 6 (1981), 40–52, and Meir Steinberg, "Ordering the Unordered: Time, Space, and Deceptive Coherence," *Yale French Studies* 61 (1981), 60–88.

[11] A provocative study of this myth is in Walter Burkert, "Das Proömium des Parmenides und die Katabase des Pythagoras," *Phronesis* 14 (1969): 1–30. Cf. also M. Nagler, "Entretiens" (n. 7, above) and R. J. Clark, *Catabasis: Vergil and the Wisdom Tradition* (Amsterdam, 1979), for the Near Eastern inheritance. Aspects of the Old Man of the Sea are treated by Marcel Detienne, *Les Maîtres de vérité dans la Grèce archaïque* (Paris, 1967), Chap. 3. Of particular interest is the Mesopotamian institution of the watery truth-ordeal (ibid., 34f.); this may lie behind the regular identification of Odysseus from the prologue onward as "he who suffered trials on the sea," especially since the institution validated kingship. Agathe Thornton, *People and Themes in Homer's Odyssey* (London, 1970), 22–37, gives the shamanic interpretation.

[12] See Scheinberg (n. 2, above), p. 10 and her references.

[13] Eustathius explicitly reports that the *omphalos thalassēs* was the *axis mundi* (1390. 7; cf.

of erotic interludes is not only the folkloric figure of the powerfully dangerous-or-helpful female, but the goddess who dwells close to the axis of the phenomenal world, associated if not identified with the source of life and knowledge.[14]

This background shows through both their behavior and their epithets in the epic. *Deinē*, "potent," suits them uncommonly well because such goddesses are powerful for good or for ill—depending on one's relationship to them. On the destructive side they can turn a man into an animal—the "Venusberg" motif of loss of identity through eroticism—or otherwise seduce him from his destiny with promises of a fool's immortality. From this point of view, there is nothing particularly Mesopotamian about Calypso and Circe, who may well be hypostases of the rapacious Indo-European Dawn Goddess, whose wont it was to snatch men off to a highly dubious immortality.[15] That puts them in Aphrodite's camp and would put Odysseus

---

F. Buffière, *Les Mythes d'Homère et la pensée grecque* [Paris, 1956], 580 who discusses further the Odyssean *kiones*, "columns," in the same connection [1389.63]). Perhaps the fir tree on Calypso's island is "heaven-reaching" (*ouranomēkēs*, 5.239) in more than a figurative sense. Cf. Tièche, "Atlas als Personifikation der Weltachse," *Museum Helveticom* 2 (1945), 64–83. "Atlas" in this function can be man or mountain; see Herodotus 4.181–85, Pausanias 1.33.5f., Euripides *fragment*, 594Nauck, and especially Vergil, *Aeneid* 1.238–58. (I owe the last-mentioned example to an unpublished study by Julie Hemker.) Hesiod locates Atlas at the "boundaries of the world," which in mythic logic are the same *locus* as its dead center (cf. *Od.* 11.13); note for our purposes that he situates Atlas "before the clear-singing (*liguphōnōn*) daughters of Hesperus" (*Theogony* 518). Hermes, who mediates between Odysseus and the singing Circe, is Atlas' grandson (Euripides *Ion* 1–4); for his relationship with mantic goddesses, see Scheinberg (n. 2, above).

Siduri lives at Mt. Mashu, which seems to mean "twins" (Alexander Heidel, *The Gilgamesh Epic* [Chicago, 1963], 65; Güntert, *Kalypso*, 240) and may thus be connected with the important abolition or, respectively, the emergence of the dualities of creation at the axial point; cf. also G. Germain, *Genèse de l'Odyssée*, 354ff. Further particulars in the useful and provocative study of E.A.S. Butterworth, *The Tree at the Navel of the Earth* (Berlin, 1970), esp. 29f.

[14] See Denys Page, *Folktales in Homer's Odyssey* (Cambridge, Mass., 1973), 8f. Passing over the considerable literature on the ambivalent character of Calypso and the others, I would point out the "benign" usage of *mēdomai* by Calypso at 5.189, just when Odysseus' suspicions are aroused. The *mēdea* of an immortal are usually baneful. Styx, the still center of Tartarus, makes perjurors *anaudoi* (*Theogony* 797); this is the converse of the dread goddess's ability to utter *nēmertea*, because perjury violates truth utterance at the deepest level. (The former item was communicated to me by Laura Slatkin; the latter, by Patricia Bulman). Note Maximus of Tyre's suggestive phrase, *phthengtikon te kai mantikon*, of the *nekuomanteion* that is an important landmark in Odyssean legend; cf. Gregory Crane, *Calypso: Backgrounds and Conventions of the Odyssey* (Frankfurt am Main, 1988), 94.

[15] See Gregory Nagy, "Phaethon, Sappho's Phaon, and the White Rock of Leukas," *Harvard Studies in Classical Philology* 77 (1973), 137–77; Deborah D. Boedeker, *Aphrodite's Entry into Greek Epic* (Leiden, 1974), esp. 39f., 71f., and 76f. (Nagy's White Rock, incidentally, is a faded omphalos or axis symbol; see *Od.* 10.515). Calypso instantly mentions Eos, as it were the paradigm under which she stands, when Hermes tells her that she must release Odysseus (5.121); then she launches into a catalogue of ruined lovers reminiscent of Ishtar's. An Indo-European inheritance overlain by the characteristics of a Near Eastern analogue (see Boedeker, 6; Page, *Folktales*, 49–70) is particularly characteristic of Aphrodite figures. One of the slight

in that of Cleitus (15.250f.), Orion, Tithonus, and others except that he overcomes the goddesses and turns their awesome power to his good; what could have been their ravishing storm winds become the "favoring breezes" that convey him back to his home, the real world.[16]

The Sirens, whom he does not visit and who do not furnish a conducting wind (12.168f.), represent the most destructive, or rather the purely destructive, aspect of this figure within the symbolic structure of the adventures. They whose voice itself is death to the obligations of this world sing "heroic glory" (12.189f.); that is, they seduce men (back) to the warrior world of the *Iliad*.

Siduri's tempting aspect corresponds to the adjective *doloessa* "deceitful," which alternates with *audēessa* in the description of Circe and—with less apparent justification, as Dirlmeier points out—of Calypso (7.245 and 9.32; see also *Atlantos thugatēr oloophronos*, 1.52, with the likely variant *oloophrōn* applying "baleful" to the goddess herself). We now have a complete picture on both sides: it must have been through withstanding Siduri's temptations, as he had done with Ishtar herself, that Gilgamesh won the former's guidance to cross the sea for his fateful confrontation with Utnapishtim. The same pattern of control turning a dangerous power to good emerges in a more rationalized vein when Odysseus comes to desire to leave Calypso and Circe (10.483–89). It is represented on the material level, as is much of Homeric symbolism, when Hermes (a grandson of Atlas; see n. 13) gives him a plant that allows him to have relations with Circe without "turning into an animal." Once he is being faithful to Penelope in his fashion, both these goddesses become guiding forces (see esp. 12.25–27). More generally, as Odysseus progressively disentangles himself from the erotic aspect of womankind symbolized by Circe and Calypso, "Athena" becomes by progressive stages more available and present to him.[17] She represents not only the protective aspect but both the domains in which Odysseus

---

differences between Circe and Calypso in the *Odyssey* is that the former is a daughter of Helios and seems slightly closer to Indo-European traditions of Eos and Usas, though her name may reflect some reminiscence of Sumerian Kir-gi-lu or Kurgi (see also Page, 60). The latter is a daughter of Atlas, who seems to be modeled on the Hittite Upellure and seems closer to the sea and earth than to the sun; but, to Odysseus, they were identical in function (9.31), and in other contexts the goddesses could be even less distinguishable. According to Pausinias 5.19.7, for example, the Eleans visualized the house-dwelling Circe in Calypso's cave.

[16] See Nagy, "Phaethon"; there is a dead calm in the underworld (11.640, no pun intended) and at the island of the Sirens, who represent the "dread goddess" archtype in her purely negative aspect (12.168f.), while both Calypso (5.268) and Circe send favoring breezes, the latter just at the time when other repeated language marks her special structural function, 11.6ff. amd 12.8ff. On the calm of the Sirens, which I believe is rationalized at the beginning of Ovid, *Amores* I.5, cf. Kurt Latte, *Kleine Schriften* (Munich, 1968), 106. On the ravishing winds, cf. Nagy, "Phaethon."

[17] See 7.14ff. and 13.311ff.; Odysseus' complaint in the latter passage should recall to our minds the wise words of Zeus in the opening scene of the epic, that mortals blame the gods for their own follies (1.32–34). This issue is ably discussed by Jenny Strauss Clay, *The Wrath of Athena* (Princeton, 1983), chaps. 1 and 4.

must alternately function, war and the *oikos*. We shall return to these points; the *deinotēs* of the exotic goddesses at any rate is eros itself. The poet's conception of which is on one level not very different from, say, Plato's: as encountered by the majority of humankind (see below), it can be a powerfully deceptive force; when mastered, the same force orients and empowers.

Underneath the surface, therefore, the traditional phrase *theos audēessa* invokes the lifesaving ability of this goddess to report verities of the mantic world and thus induce or at least indicate the hero's return to life and light.[18] On this level the "marked" meaning of *audēeis*, "uttering" or even "endowed with (prophetic) speech" (see *Il.* 19.407; Liddell and Scott, *A Greek-English Lexicon*, at *audēeis*), is surely operative, though in many contexts we feel it may not be consciously registered by the singer or his audience. The juxtaposition within the same formula of *theos* and *audēessa* is very effective. The wisdom and energy of the divine world are normally inaccessible to the human mind—in Homer's words, the gods "speak another language" than our own.[19] In this set of expressions, as in a related set describing sexual contact between the worlds (*thea brotōi eunētheisa*), the tradition has formulated a "given essential idea" of great power in briefest compass. Ino, whose translation from one realm to the other Homer describes in similar phraseology and who remained between mortal and immortal status (Aristotle, *Rhetoric*, Book 2.23.1400b5), was considered mantic in cult practice (Pausanias 3.24.4), just as Calypso was consulted as a prophetess connected not only with water but also with access to the death realm (Güntert, *Kalypso*, 13). When in the *Iliad* Hera makes the divine animal, Xanthos, "voiced" (*audēenta*, 19.407), it is to make known to Achilles the certain fate of his own death if he continues, while in the *Odyssey* the final conflict of the poem is resolved by the epiphany of Athena by her voice (*phōnēi, theas opos phōnēsasēs*, 24.530, 535; cf. 548), which magically confounds the attacking relatives of the slain suitors. But it is Ovid, whose imagination is more

---

[18] The one boundary in Whitman's diagram not marked by "dread goddess endowed by speech" phraseology, namely Odysseus' safe return to Aiaia, is marked by an explicit mythological reference to that island as a "home of Eos" (12.3f.), bringer of light. This "light of salvation" (Homeric *phaos*) was triumphantly foreshadowed in the imagery of 10.541, just after Circe predicts that Teiresias will show Odysseus his return: "So she spoke, and forthwith came Eos of the golden throne." On the connection with singing and (effective) prophecy, see Page, *Folktales*, 58 and 63; on effective prophecy itself, Uvo Hölscher, "The Transformation from Folk-Tale to Epic," in *Homer: Tradition and Innovation* (Leiden, 1978), 57.

[19] Calvert Watkins, "Language of Gods and Language of Men: Remarks on some Indo-European Metalinguistic Traditions," in Jaan Puhvel, ed., *Myth and Law among the Indo-Europeans* (Berkeley and Los Angeles, 1970), 1–17. Edward Bornemann, *Odyssee-Interpretationen* (Frankfurt am Main, 1953), 69, considers in fact that *Göttin (nach Menschenart) sprechend* is the literal meaning of the present formula, as does G. R. Palmer in *Homer: The Odyssey*, tr. G. H. Palmer, ed. H. Porter (New York, 1962), 132, who translates "human of speech"; see the interesting parallels at Hesiod, *Theogony* 584 and *Works and Days* 79f. and Apollonius of Rhodes, *Argonautica* 4.1322, in a passage clearly modeled on the Ino episode, with *chthoniai theai audēessai* "chthonian (and hence prophetic) goddesses endowed, etc."

sensitive to myth than those of many poets who still "believed" the old stories, who best expresses this capacity. The Sirens (*Metamorphoses* 5.552–63) were followers of Proserpina (as was Calypso; *Hymn to Ceres* 422), before they were partly sea-changed to a lower condition in the manner of Leukothea (note that one of them was called Leukosa; Lycophron 712ff.). Yet they retain their maiden voices lest their *canor . . . tantaque dos oris linguae deperderet usum* (561f.). Four centuries later still, St. Augustine will refer to the "prophetic" voice of his own mother in terms that are neither pagan nor mythological yet seem a continuation, in some sense, of the same idea: *et cuius erant nisi tua verba illa per matrem meam, fidelem tuam, quae cantasti in aures meas? (Confessions* 2.3).

To recapitulate the characteristics of this goddess as she appears in Homer: we may assume that like so many figures in Greek mythology she is associated with the *axis mundi*, either directly or in association with a male personification (typically her "father"); she is powerfully, one might say archetypically, seductive, but her power turns to good when she is resisted or overcome. Her helpful power is to prophesy to the hero or facilitate for him further stages of his symbolic journey "home," his "eternal return."

The poets had at their disposal other features than this basic set. While both the goddess's oceanic connection and her extreme liminal situation at the edge of the phenomenal world are parts of the *topos* of the *axis mundi*, weaving, as we shall try to show, became (partly, it seems through linguistic associations within Greek) as potent a symbol of her creative power. So did singing. Although singing was more closely connected with seduction and prophecy, it had been metaphorically associated with weaving from Indo-European times (see n. 26).

Not only Eidothea but Ino/Leukothea and on a still more rationalized level Nausicaa and in general all girls who meet a hero at a well and guide him to their fathers' palaces gain meaning from participation in this mythic archetype; they are, to various degrees, faded hypostases of the same goddess.[20] In fact, it is necessary also to say a few words about Thetis in the *Iliad* to fill in our picture of the role of this goddess in the *Odyssey* story.

When Thetis visits Hephaestus in book 18 of the *Iliad* (394–405), the poet makes an immediate association with the Oceanid Eurynome, along with whom Thetis "accepted the lame god to her bosom" and saved him for some nine years when Hera wanted to "hide" him.[21] Eurynome is a sister of

---

[20] Fenik, *Studies*, 31–35 discusses the daughter at the well from a somewhat different perspective. In Laconia Ino was worshiped as a prophetic goddess of terrestrial water sources (Pausanias 3.23.8 and 26.2), and she is connected on the other hand with the Latin dawn goddess, *Mater Matuta*; see G. Dumézil, *Mythe et épopée*, vol. 3 (Paris, 1973), 305–30. As Cicero says, Ino, Circe, and others *ex eodem fonte fluxerunt (de Natura deorum* 3.58) My colleague Robert Alter points out to me that virtually all betrothals in the Old Testament take place at wells.

[21] For connations of *krupsai* (397) and Calypso's name, see Güntert, *Kalypso, passim*. Ino, too, nurses a god in her cave, namely Dionysus (Pausanias 3.24.4).

Calypso, i.e., "Hider" (*Theogony* 358f.). Thetis' role in this salvation story may be more ad hoc than that of the Oceanid; nonetheless it is worth noting that she can be implicated in the same relationship to a god as that which Calypso and then Ino/Leukothea have with Odysseus.

Many scholars have felt that the various mentions in the *Iliad* of Thetis' prophecies to Achilles about his destiny (cf. 18.9–11, 95f.), though never developed, hint at an important traditional undercurrent in the narrative, and I have drawn attention to the connections Homer very adroitly makes at key moments between Thetis and Eos and, in another way, Thetis and Ino (*Spontaneity and Tradition*, 46 and 142). These three connections now seem intimately related. Achilles' piercing cry when he learns of the death of Patroclus is magically heard by his mother Thetis where she sits in the depths of the sea by the side of her old father Nereus, and she cries out in turn to all her sister Nereids (18.35–39ff.). In this scene we have three important elements of "dread goddess" mythology: the sea, the old man within it, and vocal contact (cf. Odysseus' lament at *Od.* 5.299–312 and the rerun of Achilles' own death, *Od.* 24.47–62). A "Hesiodic" catalogue of the Nereids follows as Thetis' sisters assemble from every cranny of the sea (including Nēmertēs and Apseudēs, 46). Thetis appears to Achilles by the seashore and touches, here and throughout book 18, on his destiny (9–11, 95f., 115–21, 464f.). She promises to bring Achilles a suit of divine armor, which is functionally parallel to the veil of Ino, that divine Mae West that protects Odysseus from death in the sea, though the armor is obviously connected, like Odysseus' scar, with Achilles' warrior identity.[22]

Finally, not only does Thetis link her next apparition to Achilles with that of the dawn (136; cf. the suggestive language of 135 and 190) but she finds occasion to bring into the story her unhappy liaison with the hero's mortal father, which is so much like that of goddess Ishtar and her lovers, like that of Aphrodite and Anchises, of India's Urvasi and Pururavasa, and particularly of Eos and Tithonus (54ff., 85ff., and esp. 432ff.). There can be no doubt that Thetis is a "dread goddess endowed with speech,"[23] connected equally with the (Indo-European?) dawn goddess and the (Near Eastern?) sea goddess. The identity is as patent as could be expected in epic mythology.

---

[22] On appearance "from the sea" (e.g., *ex halos* as in *Od.* 24.47) as a signal of an immortal destiny, see "Entretiens," 94f. and Gregory Nagy, "*Sēma* and *Noēsis*: Some Illustrations," *Arethusa* 16 (1983), 45. The Neoplatonic interpretation runs differently but is not without interest: "sea" = "flux of phenomenal change," cf. F. Buffière, *Mythes d'Homère*, 414f. Berkley Peabody, *The Winged Word* (Albany, 1975), 229, shows how deeply the armor-identity is embedded in the compositional process throughout book 18.

[23] Note the phrase *aphthongous gamous* ("speechless marriage") that Peleus uses of his marriage to Thetis in Sophocles, *Troilos* (A.C. Pearson, *The Fragments of Sophocles*, Vol. 2 [Cambridge, 1917; reprinted Amsterdam, 1963], p. 255), Fragment 615. This has been variously explained (cf. Pearson *ad. loc.*); Güntert (*Kalypso*, p. 132) connects it with the silence of the death realm, which may be correct.

The only differences between Homer's two versions of the mythology— and they are probably important at a level we shall not have time to explore—are 1) that where Odysseus characteristically goes to the sea, it is the sea personified as Thetis herself that comes to Achilles; 2) since Thetis is the immortal mother, there can be no question of temptation or an erotic liaison; 3) that Achilles' salvation can only be realized as "heroic" immortalization, i.e., after death, not as homecoming *and* immortalization as with Odysseus; and finally 4) that in the *Iliad* the oceanic venue of the *Odyssey* narratives splits into the sea (with father Nereus) and Olympus (with father Zeus). This polarization betrays the axial function of the *topos*, its communication and potential mediation between opposite poles in the mythic universe.

The epiphanies of Thetis to Achilles in books 18 and 19 occur at an even more important structural juncture than do the *Odyssey* passages we have so far discussed, namely, at the moment when the "wrath of Achilles" against Agamemnon and the actions set in motion by the hero's first appeal through Thetis to Zeus have run their course and ended not by resolution but by transferral to Hector and a new cycle of divine intercession and mortal action. Thetis draws attention to the parallelism right away (8.73ff.).[24] Thus even for Achilles, whose domestic life is suppressed in strongest contrast to that of Odysseus, a goddess, or the divine feminine principle, presides over his destiny, and his encounters with her mark the stages of its unfolding. Even more clearly than with Odysseus, her prophetic utterances predict his destiny and seem to be enabling conditions of its fulfillment.

It is the more interesting to note these facts because Achilles represents an ideological antipode to Odysseus precisely in regard to their relationship to the feminine and the contrasting tendencies of the social order those relationships imply. Achilles' case rests here; to go further with the hero's creative relations with the feminine, we must return to Odysseus.

As I have argued elsewhere, the exotica or adventures described by both the poet and Odysseus in the central portion of the poem hold a kind of ontological mirror up to the situation of Ithaca, a mirror in which we find the main features of the relatively "real" society reflected in a complex system of inversions and parallels.[25] In this symbolic structure Odysseus' crew in the adventure world answer to the Suitors at home, both standing for the hero's community. In both groups all or most of the men succumb to the sexual allure of a female figure through whom they come swiftly to grief; this figure is in the first instance Circe, and in the second Penelope.

[24] For further details cf. Peabody, *Winged Words*; Nagler, *Spontaneity and Tradition*, chap. 5, and "Toward a Semantics of Ancient Conflict: *Eris* in the *Iliad*," *Classical World* 82 (1988), 81–90.

[25] "Odysseus: The Proem and the Problem," *Classical Antiquity* 9 (1990), 335–56, and cf. Helene Foley, "'Reverse Similes' and Sex Roles in the *Odyssey*," *Arethusa* 11 (1978), 7–26, reprinted in J. Peradotto and J. P. Sullivan, *Women in the Ancient World* (Albany, 1984), 59–78.

Quite apart from the suppressed tradition that parallels Penelope, mother of Telemachus, with Circe as mother of Telegonus, we have good reason, then, to consider Penelope in relationship to the dread goddess of the *outre-mer*; indeed the symbolic framework of the epic virtually compels us to do so. What does the association mean?

In the *Iliad* a well-known line of Agamemnon's succinctly, not to say brusquely, describes the role of women in the home:

> *histon epoichomenēn kai emon lechos antioōsan.*
> plying the loom, and coming to my bed.

> (*Il.* 1.31; cf. 6.456)

This line adds male chauvinism to Agamemnon's unprepossessing characteristics and could be said to encapsulate the heroic conception of woman at its worst. But it is also possible to use these symbols of woman's role without negative value. Here it is specifically the wrenching of Chryseis out of her community (and the family-destroying action of the *Iliad* in general) that reduces Chryseis to the status of chattel and transfers all her value out of the home community, making it, as Homer would say, a blow to them and a gain for their enemies. This is not the perspective of the *Odyssey*, where once captured, aliens like Eumaios and Eurycleia are happily patriated, and domesticity is fully restored and valued.

One aspect of that domesticity is the great nurturing or economic value of the household weaving (2.117; 2.98 = 19.143 = 24.133) that complements the "import" economy of Odysseus, now and to come (23.356–8), and like it has a magical or life-force background in the exotica. In the *Odyssey, histon epoichomenē*, "plying the loom," describes both Calypso (5.62) and Circe (10.221f., 226f., 254f.), whose name may have been connected in Homer's mind with *kerkis*, "shuttle." Their weaving is closely connected with their singing as an expression of their daemonic identity and power—as their beds obviously are. Precisely when Polites, Odysseus' "most prudent and closest man" (*kēdistos . . . kednotatos te*, 10.225) is about to fall into the trap of the weaving daemon, singing at her loom, he wonders whether she is "woman or god" (228)—and four references to vocal contact swiftly follow.

However, the most interesting loom *and* the most interesting bed in the *Odyssey* belong to Penelope. It is her guileful weaving that keeps the Suitors at bay long enough for Odysseus to return (2.93–95; 24.128–30); it is her deceptive trick about the unique marriage bed that precipitates their climactic mutual recognition ("mutual" for reasons that will shortly appear). Her weaving, like Helen's, has been connected with the Indo-European conception of poetic creativity; but mediated through that of the dread goddesses by the epic, it would seem traceable to an even more primordial conception: the weaving of the *Weltmantel* by the mother of creation itself at the axis of being.[26] Needless to say, the primordial weaving of creation provides powerful valorization of the economic significance of woman's weaving in the *oikos*.

It is therefore a plausible, if not in fact compelling, suggestion that the living tree-bedpost whose secret precipitates the revelation of Odysseus' identity and their reunion may be meant to resonate with the primordial axis over which Penelope's alter-images in the exotic world, the dread goddesses, preside.[27] In the oral style, Homer alerts us four times in forty lines that a "great *sēma*" (sign) has been built into the tree (23.188, 202, 206, 225), and Odysseus says suggestively that the bedpost is "like a column" (*ēüte kiōn*, 191).

Furthermore the poem creates a set of objects that mediate between the *axis* and the bed, the archetypal symbol and the individuated, concrete object, and in so doing furnish a smooth and exactly calibrated symbolic modulation from the exotic world to the center of the *oikos*. That modulation involves several semantic axes. For example, in the tradition generally (though we can never be certain what was common to the tradition and what unique or unusual to any set of performances), the woman of the household is suggestively associated with a "pillar of the well-built roof" (cf. 8.458, for Nausicaa). In the *Odyssey* four scenes connect Penelope in particular with this pillar in an insistently repeated form, each time linking that pillar with a synergistic set of images whose meaning we will consider shortly.

Employing this traditional association dynamically, Homer constructs a series of axis symbols, beginning with the moving mast of Odysseus' ship (called *histos*, the same word as "loom [beam]") and the tall pine mast he builds for the raft on which he leaves Ogygia, through the wild pear tree growing in the circular wall of Eumaeus' steading, to Odysseus's first sighting of his own palace walls, and then through the traditional iconography

---

[26] The Greek *Weltmantel* is best known through Pherecydes (*fragment* B2 Diels/Kranz). If correct, this pedigree would certainly explain why "Women's weaving . . . exercised power over (Homer's) imagination" (Whitman, *Heroic Tradition*, 117), and I would regard this dimension as mythic grounding for the socioeconomic significance of her weaving that has been stressed by modern scholars. For the connection with singing (i.e., poetry), see Page, *Folktales*, 62f., and Ann Bergren, "Helen's Web: Time and Tableau in the *Iliad*," *Helios* n.s. 7 (1979–80), 19–34. See also Boedeker, *Aphrodite's Entry*, 73. Note juxtaposed singing and weaving of Calypso, with sense of impending danger slightly muted at 5.62. Cf. J. M. Snyder, "The Web of Song: Weaving Imagery in Homer and the Lyric Poets," *Classical Journal* 76 (1980–81), 193–96.

[27] First put forward by Jan de Vries, *Altgermanische Religionsgeschichte*, vol. 2 (Berlin, 1957), 385; cf. Günter Dietz, "Das Bett des Odysseus," *Symbolon* 7 (1971), 9–32. Note that in contrast to some marriage rituals (which the reunion of Odysseus and Penelope of course suggestively follow) in which the groom had to prove his competence by building a kind of honeymoon cabana around a sanctified tree, Homer has moved the tree into the *oikos*, itself, at the cost of some surface verisimilitude; cf. Dietz, p. 12; R. Eisler, *Weltmantel und Himmelszelt*, vol. 2 (Munich, 1910), 596–99.

of the woman of the home leaning against its pillar, to come to rest finally at the marvelously crafted bed.[28]

The series begins and ends (omitting the olive stake in Polyphemus' cave, in narrated time) with objects that Odysseus crafted himself and that represent an obvious inversion, since the first, the pine tree mast, enables him to get away from Calypso, and the last, the bedpost, to return to Penelope; the virtue of the former is mobility, of the latter stability, for through it the center of the *oikos* is grounded in living nature: "In greatest agitation Odysseus insists that he personally had anchored to the earth that chamber in which he would hide his secret self, and describes at length the solid construction of that anchor."[29]

In a series that moves in a general way from nature to culture, from the half-wild olive bush on Scheria in the world of the Adventures to the climactic, shaped olive tree-bed in the heart of the *oikos* of Ithaca, it is the more remarkable that this last is the only object Odysseus shapes yet leaves alive. Odysseus is establishing his typological identity as *tektōn*, or "builder," in the tradition of his father (24.206f.), who hews life-support systems out of nature. But he does not kill nature in the process. Scholars have recently come to appreciate the "ecological" value in Greek nature-culture mythology, and Odysseus' type of culture heroism certainly represents this, in contrast to Achilles, who pollutes rivers and "offends the earth" (*Il.* 24.54). The end result of this symbolic series, and particularly its vital link of the living tree with the constructed dwelling, is to give a vivid sense that Odysseus has created a system in which raw vitality flows from the earth up through the marriage bed and then through the *oikos* and everything it represents.

The life of the tree is obviously enough a "*sēma*" of the vitality of Odysseus' relationship with Penelope, which after his stint with the dread god-

[28] One can detect the tree and pillar cult of Bronze Age religious iconography in all these episodes, especially since both Minoan and Mycenaean gems often portray the cult sanctuary from outside its low stone wall with the top of the sacred tree visible above it. For survivals, cf. W. Burkert, *Griechische Religion der archaïschen und klassischen Epoche* (Stuttgart, 1977), 93. On the "symbolic organization of space" in the *oikos*, cf. J.-P. Vernant, *Mythe et pensée chez les Grecs* (Paris, 1965), 97–143, esp. 116, 130. The "symbolic organization" of Eumaeus' steading would seem, now that F. Chamoux has worked out the references, to follow the pattern carefully ("La porcherie d'Eumée," *Revue des études grecques* 65 (1952), 281–88. Note esp. the wild pear tree *in* the wall (14.10), with Laertes' thorn-hedges (24.224), the perfect "raw" equivalents of the inner olive.

[29] Norman Austin, *Archery at the Dark of the Moon* (Berkeley and Los Angeles, 1975), 283. When Calypso brings woven articles for the raft's sail, he skillfully "works that too" (*ho d'eu technēsato kai ta*, 5.259): in the exotic world, he must cope with some women's work, for the divinely ordained complementarity he will practice with Penelope is not yet regained (cf. Xenophon, *Oeconomicus* 7.22–31). Note that in the Sirens' presence he imagistically *becomes* the mast, lashed bolt upright and "steady" (*empedon*) in the mast-dock (12.161f.). D. Gary Miller has argued on phonological grounds that the descriptions of both the bed and the oar *sēmeta* echo epigraphic language (where *sēma* = "tomb-marker") and thus remind us of Odysseus' identity as *hērōs*: *Homer and the Ionian Epic Tradition* (Innsbruck, 1982), 66–69.

desses may well be in question (as Penelope's loyalty never is, despite folk-tale variants to the contrary). His revelation, elicited by Penelope's artful probe of both his personal identity and his typological identity as competent institution-builder, ends with the indirect but heart-stopping question, "Is our bed still stable (*empedon*), wife, or has some other man dislodged it?" (23.203f.). When in answer she throws her arms about his neck the gesture has symbolic as well as emotional significance.[30]

In social terms, stability is an important element of vitality; here we have to appreciate the slight illogicality on the surface of Odysseus' opening gambit in the declaration-speech where he first uses the all important word that will recur at the end and in Penelope's references to its content:

> No (mere) mortal man living, no matter how vital (*hēbōn*)
> Could have pried this bed loose, since I built into it a great *sēma*.

> (23.187f.)

Obviously a pun on the more specific but equally resonant meaning of *sēma* is intended, indeed almost forced on us here by the surface illogicality, namely "(funeral) monument." But on the level of its meaning (implied between husband and wife) for their relationship, the key word also, of course, stresses the community of knowledge and cunning that "builds," as we say, the kind of relationship that here enjoys this stunning reunion.

To make this reunion possible, sexual loyalty had to be asserted, against the tension of folktale variants in which Penelope's was not maintained in her husband's absence as well as against the potential parallel of the Atreid saga (and whatever credit we give to the Suitors' claims that Penelope encouraged them, 2.91f.). That is the significance of the repeated *stathmos*-passages that begin in the first book of the poem:

> (Penelope) descended the high stairway of the home,
> Not alone, for two maidservants attended her.
> And she, when she came before the Suitors, this splendid woman,
> Took her stand before the column of the well-built roof,
> Holding up her glistening shawl before her face;
> And a true maidservant stood to either side.

> (1.330–335)

All this iconography—shawl (*krēdemnon*), maidservants, and lady-at-the-pillar—transmits a strong message of chastity that of course protects Pene-

---

[30]The detail recalls a *swayamvara* in which the Hindu princess puts a garland around the neck of her chosen lord—a motif to which this reunion is often compared; cf. Page, *Folktales*, 107–8. It has not been noticed, I think, that in the *Odyssey* no less than in the *Iliad* the determining action, set in the prehistory of each poem—respectively, the beginning of the Trojan War and the marriage of Odysseus and Penelope—is anachronistically recreated *within* the epic. Foley calls the latter a "recourtship" ("'Reverse Similes,'" 16). Compare also, on this important point, the view from the wall in *Il.* 3.

lope's appearance before the Suitors; in fact, it is an arresting scene, iconic for this whole issue in the *Odyssey*, as the picture of Menelaus ranging the battlefield in frustration while his rival is safely in bed with Helen encapsulates the causes of the Trojan war in the early part of the *Iliad*.[31] And this scene is the Suitors' final entrapment. When it occurs for the third time (18.206–13), every one of them wants to sleep with her, which completes their fatal structural parallel with the crew: the crew surprise Circe at her loom and are turned into animals; shortly after, on Thrinakia, they lose self-control (albeit over a slightly different temptation) and perish. The suitors surprise Penelope at *her* loom (2.109 = 24.145) and become "animals" in this scene, one of the few psychological descriptions of sexual desire in epic. It leads directly to their destruction; Penelope's next and last appearance in this Gestalt, 21.63–66, will be the bow test.

To appreciate the full power of this scene, we must go back to its mythological prototype, the display of the first woman before both gods and men when they shared a "pre-exilic" existence. In Hesiod's narrative this very event is obviously part of the great *krisis* that definitively divides men from the table and being of the gods.[32] The *Odyssey* parallel has a not dissimilar effect, for in contrast to his men Odysseus encounters, respectively, the exotic *daimones* and Penelope and survives, while both crew and suitors perish. They are ordinary humanity; he is a soon-to-be-immortalized *hēmitheos*, "demigod," or *hērōs*. The devastating effect of Penelope on the Suitors, a clear parallel of the effect of the love-goddess on the unwary and before that of primordial "woman" on hapless mankind, plays a key role in giving Odysseus that heroic identity by contrast.

While we have stressed Penelope's loyalty, it is balanced by the loyalty— after his heroic fashion—of Odysseus himself. His return from "moving" to

---

[31] *Il.* 3.448–61. For the iconography here, cf. *Spontaneity and Tradition*, chaps. 3 and 4, and the discussion there of chastity as attractant. My assertion that *thringkoisi*, "copings," at *Odyssey* 17.267 suggests Penelope's chastity and the well-being of the home (*Spontaneity and Tradition*, 62 and 89) gains strong support from the "new" Archilochus fragment, which uses the word in an explicitly sexual context; cf. esp. John Van Sickle, "The New Erotic Fragment of Archilochus," *Quaderni Urbinati di cultura classica* 20 (1975), 123–56. See also Euripides, *Helen* 70, again a context where sexual chastity is the issue. Finally, on the religious and political force of the imagined overthrow of the *oikos* wall here, cf. W. R. Connor, "The Razing of the House in Greek Society," *Transactions of the American Philological Association* 115 (1985), 75–102.

[32] *Theogony* 570–93. She is a *thauma idesthai* to all of them, but "*amēchanon* to mortals" (589). Between these scenes on the scale from primordial to heroic, we might compare the effect of Aphrodite on the gods when she and Ares are caught in the golden net Hephaestus has woven(!) over their bed, 8.335–43, and especially the effect of Helen at the wall on the old men of Troy, reenacting their utter downfall: *Il.* 3.154–58. Patricia Bulman reminds me that Penelope is often "like Aphrodite" in the second half of the poem; cf. also Uvo Hölscher, "Penelope vor dem Freiern" (translated in this vol., 133–40); *Homeric Hymn to Aphrodite* 187–90 with Boedeker, *Descent from Heaven*, 79; Page, *Folktales*, 87; A. M. Heidel's translation of *Gilgamesh*, 50ff. On the crew's unwariness versus Odysseus's caution, cf. 10.230f. and 312f., and Charles Segal, "Circean Temptations: Homer, Vergil, Ovid," *Transactions of the American Philological Association* 99 (1968), 419–42, in particular 425–27.

"stable" and from being outside in "raw" nature to operating a social institution (on natural power) depends on his ability to control sexual energy. This too was set up through symbolic structures in the exotic world (cf. Teiresias's words at 11.105); naturally, as the Siren episode establishes, his way is not to avoid temptation—in this exotic scene "ordinary humanity" errs in the opposite direction, stuffing wax in its ears—but to overcome it. "Heroic" success is defined as reaching the right context and using vital energy in sanctioned and inherently productive ways, which on the human level of the poem means returning to the loyalty that Penelope had symbolized all along.

On this level the still-living tree symbolizing the vitality of their relationship conveys a sense quite familiar in myth and literature that marriage involves a creative harnessing of vital, and particularly sexual, energy. John Finley has simply but well said that in the *Odyssey* "monogamy is central to the theme of home."[33] In an *oikos*-based civilization, however, there is much more to that theme of "home" than the word now conveys in modern English.

Recent work has made it very clear that the *oikos* represented the entire "minimal state" system of the Archaic period.[34] The primary social institution providing cohesion in this system is guest-bonding, *xenia*, which explains its ubiquitous importance in the *Odyssey*. The hero's mere appearance both in Scheria and Ithaca, though the surface reason is different in each case, precipitates a call-in of goods to the central *oikos* from surrounding households; in other words Odysseus automatically "stimulates the economy" of the *oikos* system, which was based on the movement of goods to the center for redistribution. He is not only the savior of *this oikos* (2.59 = 17.538), but of what we would call today a world order; he is indeed its personal symbol, or personification.

In a similar way, the bed-tree is its objective symbol. What Detienne has so well said about the "*consubstantialité du groupe politique et de l'olivier*," ("consubstantiality of the political group and the olive") which obtained in *polis* ideology in Attica because of the tree's hardiness and economic productivity, would seem to be already latent in this particular *olivier*, which is presented as the climax of a series of tree and pillar symbols at the center of the Ithacan social and geographical system.[35] Just as the tree-bed is, in de

[33] *Homer's Odyssey* (Cambridge. Mass., 1978), 188.

[34] H. Posner, "The Homeric Version of the Minimal State," *Ethics* 90 (1979), 27–46.

[35] M. Detienne, "L'Olivier: Un mythe politico-religieux," *Problèmes de la terre en Grèce ancienne*, ed. M. I. Finley (Paris and the Hague, 1973), 293–306. The words quoted appear on p. 295. See too Boedeker, *Descent from Heaven*, 116f. For the political dimension of the marital reunion, cf. Hans Strasburger. "Der Einzelne und die Gemeinschaft im Denken der Griechen," *Historische Zeitschrift* 177 (1954), 227–48; P. A. Albrecht, *Eros und die Ehe bei Homer* (Zurich, 1938), 4; and esp. K. Latte, "Zeitgeschichtliches zu Archilochus," *Hermes* 92 (1964), 387. On the tree as axis-symbol informing the physico-political concept of the *oikos*, cf. H. R. Ellis Davidson, *Gods and Myths of Northern Europe* (Harmondsworth, 1964–75), 190f.; see also 88,

Vries' words, *mit dem "Heil" der Familie verwachsen* ("intimately bound up with the well-being of the family") (*Altgermanische Religionsgeschichte*, note 27, above), so is it bound up (or grown into) the well-being of the social order. If that was true in the *polis* order, it was true *a fortiori* in the *oikos* world before state tensions conflicted with family loyalties. Thus the secret of the bed which only Penelope and Odysseus know is also a sign born in traditional poetic symbolism for their joint identity as generators of the social order. Their ability to decode the sign together is an active demonstration of their joint, typological, and social identity.

The most evident and basic step toward creation of social order is of course the begetting of legitimate children, or what Vernant calls in his happy expression the couple's ability "to engender a line of descent firmly rooted in the earth."[36] But it is fitting that one faithful household retainer has been let in on the secret, for she symbolizes the extension of the life-support system Odysseus and Penelope jointly establish to the wider household (see also the extension of family rights to Eumaios, 21.216), from which, primarily through *xenia* and marriage, order can move out, in theory at least, to the entire *ethnos*. Thus Penelope draws attention to the secret-sharer, Aktoris, within the ring composition that closes her acceptance speech by citing her husband's "accurate recitation of the *sēmata*" (23.225–28); knowledge of the code symbolizes community.

Whether or not we choose to see tension between the economy, organization, and values of the *oikos* and "*polis* ideology" in the epics, an issue of some controversy in Homeric scholarship, there is certainly an acute, pervasive tension between *oikos* values, which are essentially family values, and those that are mobilized in war by the fighting band, or *laos*. This ambivalent, partly protective but partly competitive "society," which is always in danger of deteriorating toward an anomic *Männerbund*, exemplifies the frightening tendency toward absolute disorder inherent in war, which Homer explores mythologically in book 21 of the *Iliad*.[37] As I have argued elsewhere, Homer seems pointedly to raise and then evade this issue when he remembers and then forgets that Odysseus bears on his body a much surer recognition sign that could have circumvented the need to go into the bed-building story altogether, namely the hunting-intiation scar.[38]

---

and the discussion by Whitman, *Euripides and the Full Circle of Myth* (Cambridge, Mass., 1974), 3.

[36] Jean-Pierre Vernant, "Between the Beasts and the Gods," in *Myth and Society in Ancient Greece*, tr. Janet Lloyd (rpt. New York, 1988), 181. Cf. the whole discussion here and in "Marriage," pp. 55–77 of the same volume, for more of the anthropological background.

[37] Gregory Nagy, *The Best of the Achaeans: Concepts of the Hero in Archaic Greek Poetry*, (Baltimore and London, 1979), 83 and 121f.; James Redfield, *Nature and Culture in the Iliad: The Tragedy of Hector* (Chicago and London, 1975), chap. 5, and Jeffrey Duban, "Miscellanea: The Whirlwind and the Fight at the River," *Eranos* 78 (1980), 187–92.

[38] Nancy Felson-Rubin and Wiliam Sale, "Meleager and Odysseus: A Structural and Cultural Study of the Greek Hunting-Maturation Myth," *Arethusa* 16 (1983), 137–71, and bibliogra-

It is undoubtedly the clash of these two ideologies, *oikos* and *laos*, home and warrior band, much more than the different competitive styles they represent, which reverberated throughout the tradition as an open antagonism between Odysseus and Achilles.[39] As far as the *Odyssey* is concerned, at any rate, it is not only Achilles, who stands outside family and society and "dishonors the dumb earth in his fury," but Agamemnon, who "sacrifices" family values to warfighting priorities in the person of Iphigeneia and, as we have seen, relates only to the negative value of loom and bed symbolism, who from their respective positions furnish foil to Odysseus' successful reconquest and management of the *oikos*.[40] These are the two heroes who appear even before the shades of the Suitors arrive to lament their own versions of failure in the dismal reverberation of the underworld (24.15–97).

Yet it would be an incomplete response to Homer's art if we regard Odysseus or Penelope *only* as vehicles for ideologies. As Virginia Woolf said, underneath its fairy tale surface the poem deals with real people, "crafty, subtle, and passionate."[41] In the midst of all the mythological and ideological resonance of their deeds and character is a struggle with real problems—like sexual control and loyalty—that faces every society and every individual.

This returns us to the question I have sought to raise by stressing the closeness in silhouette between Penelope and the dread goddesses, with their archetypal attributes. It is intuitively obvious to anyone seeing that connection that it must reflect a reverential regard on Homer's part for the "power of the feminine." Here, and not as a "confused vestige of the [historical] mother-right system," we will find for example explanation for Penelope's prerogative of bestowing rulership on whoever marries her, unless that rulership, whatever it was, had devolved on Telemachus along with the *oikos*.[42] As the bedpost puts mythic resonance behind Penelope's loyalty, its *Weltmantel* significance hints at the dimensions of her nurturing or "economic" importance. Here in the area of production and work—a very large

---

phy therein cited, to which add now M. Nagler, "Ethical Anxiety and Artistic Inconsistency: The Case of Oral Epic," in Mark Griffith and Donald J. Mastronarde, eds., *Cabinet of the Muses: Essays on Classical and Comparative Literature in Honor of Thomas G. Rosenmeyer* (Atlanta, 1990), pp. 225–39.

[39] Cf. Nagy, *Best of the Achaeans*, 23–25, to which the present argument is offered as supplement.

[40] If Burkert is correct, Iphigeneia's fate undoubtedly instantiates a maiden-sacrifice that preceded competitive and dangerous male undertakings, and since all such rituals reflect underlying social tensions, was as typological as, if not a part of, the Männerbund associations of Achilles (Walter Burkert, *Homo Necans* [Berlin, 1972], 70–85). On the relationship of sacrifice to group violence, see, of course, René Girard, *Violence and the Sacred* (Baltimore and London, 1977) and *Des choses cachées depuis la fondation du monde* (Paris, 1978).

[41] "On Not Knowing Greek," *The Common Reader* (New York, 1953), 39.

[42] Moses Finley, *World of Odysseus*, 97. Cf. also the discussion by Agathe Thornton, *People and Themes*, 109.

concern of the poem we have barely touched on—she is stable producer, balancing the "hunting and gathering" income of her husband to create what Xenophon called the divinely ordained complementarity of man and woman (Xenophon, *Oeconomicus* 7.22–31).[43]

In describing the distribution of social and economic roles in the poem, Marylin Arthur has written: "It was Homer, then, who was the first to formulate the promise of a position of worth and honor for women which even today is glorified by the defenders of the traditional separation of the sexes. Such hopes have been revealed as a sham for our own times, but for the Greeks of Homer's time the negative side of this ideal had not yet fully revealed itself."[44] I do not, however, think we are compelled to believe—and the point is crucial—that the negative side of the ideal, exploitation and devaluation, lies innate in any separation of roles. That the separation of roles has been turned into a cleavage plane for the organization of exploitation throughout the ages is undeniable; but in theory there is no reason why what Helene Foley calls a "natural and efficient" gender differentiation, provided both genders address it through complementarity and mutual respect, need invoke exploitation—any more than what we have been calling loyalty, which Foley more aptly calls "creative fidelity," should be perceived as a deprivation.[45]

The story of Odysseus's extrication from the outer world, which is marked as dangerous and counterproductive in strongest contrast to "home," may yield to interpretation as the building of a relationship based on these key values of loyalty and diversity. In human terms Charles Segal has already suggested this, standing at the end of a long "allegorical" interpretive tradition: "When Odysseus and Circe part without farewells . . . we see clearly and unsentimentally . . . the inevitable brevity of a purely physical liaison. We are thus turned again, subtly, to the very different bond Odysseus is seeking on Ithaca."[46] This formulation explains simply why, given the more than suggestive similarities between Penelope and the dread goddesses, Odysseus' relationship with the latter is so negative, why extrication

[43] See above, p. 154. Penelope's "cleverness" (2.116–22) is therefore much more than a character trait that makes her a good wife for Odysseus (see, e.g., Thornton, note 11, above); it is woman's *technē*, enabling her to contribute wealth to the *oikos*, applied in this poem specifically to defeating the Suitors and their efforts to treat her as (re-)movable property. Fittingly, through that skill she delays their project long enough to enable Odysseus to return and begin restoring the entire system.

[44] "Early Greece: The Origins of the Western Attitude toward Women," in J. Peradotto and J. P. Sullivan, eds., *Women in the Ancient World* (Albany, 1984), 16. But matters are also not this simple. On the difference between woman's "official" social status and her psychological influence, cf. Philip Slater, *The Glory of Hera* (Boston, 1968), 8.

[45] Foley, "'Reverse Similes'," 72 and 76. The question of diversity versus discrimination is extremely important in modern thought. Particularly cogent are the discussions of Mahatma Gandhi on the subject, conveniently collected by N. K. Bose, *Selections from Gandhi* (Ahmedabad, 1957), 263–69 and chap. 18.

[46] Segal, "Circean Temptations," 424; for the allegorists, cf. G. de F. Lord, *Homeric Renaissance* (New Haven, 1961).

from it is a condition of his return. Under the surface, Penelope and the goddesses of the outer world are similar, but in their respective settings they symbolize different *relationships* of the hero to the feminine. Odysseus' return from the world of pleasure to the world of work, constantly marked in the vocabulary of the poem as a process of trial (*peira*) and struggle, and in its mythology as a progressive return to the protection of Athena, on a practical level means, as the allegorists always maintained, a return from the state in which one sees woman as an object (the chief characteristic of man-in-*laos*) to that in which one can respect her as a partner in the great enterprise of nurturing life.

It seems psychologically perfect that Penelope has all the attributes of the dread goddess—as though she were what the hero was really searching for all along in Calypso, Circe, Nausicaa. If it would be anachronistic to say that Penelope was what he was seeking in them, at least he was seeking a way to make the potent attraction of woman socially productive, to make it the basis of a unity that can transcend time and space. This is the "mysterium" Günter Dietz referred to as symbolized by the shared secret of the marriage bed.[47]

The control of sexual energy and respect for gender complementarity (and diversity) present in the reverse similes and other symbolic codes seem to be, in Homer's vision, the two most important characteristics of this achievement. While acknowledging them and accepting the responsibility to form a stable, life-supporting network inevitably brings Odysseus into tension with the all-male system of raiding, competition, and warfare, we must be careful lest we ourselves fall into the judgmental framework modern feminists would call "patriarchal" in our final assessment of the picture Homer has created. We would be judgmental, I think, if we failed ourselves to recognize the human challenge at the heart of this order. It has been claimed that there is no such thing as a domestic hero.[48] But without any reference to the "Iliadic" violence Odysseus brings back to "purify" his megaron of the Suitors, there is an intense heroism in what he and Penelope must wrestle with in themselves to regain their relationship and to recreate Ithaca.[49] In both the usual and the technical sense of the word, Odysseus' homecoming is his most exotic adventure.

[47] "*Die personale Gemeinschaft zwischen den Liebenden ist ein Mysterium*" ("The personal community between lovers is a mystery"), Dietz (n. 27, above), 30.

[48] Cf. M. I. Finley, *World of Odysseus*, 116–17. The extraordinary difficulty Vietnam veterans experienced in returning to civilian life brings home the psychological difficulty of return even in a world where there were purificatory rituals (and war was perceived to be a legitimate, if deeply ambivalent, enterprise). Nonmilitary aspects of Odysseus' heroism emerge variously in later tradition; cf. W. B. Stanford, *The Ulysses Theme*, (Ann Arbor, 1968).

[49] The goal of this struggle is also called kleos and has "points of contact with the *Iliad*," as A. T. Edwards has most recently put it; cf. his *Achilles in the Odyssey* (Königstein, 1985), 81. Yet it goes beyond the Iliadic "*kleos* from deeds of violence" (ibid.) in requiring as well the loyalty and active cooperation of Penelope, her chastity toward the Suitors, and acceptance of the returned Odysseus.

· · ·

Penelope's Perspective

CHARACTER FROM PLOT

NANCY FELSON-RUBIN

PENELOPE in the *Odyssey* both weaves and interprets plots; she also takes pleasure in the plots she has woven. Yet the traditional view of Penelope limits her to a single plot, MARRIAGE-AVOIDANCE, and confines her to a single role, faithful and enduring wife.[1] This single plot belongs primarily to a larger plot schema: RETURN OF HUSBAND, RECOVERY OF WIFE AS BRIDE, VENGEANCE AGAINST FALSE SUITORS.[2] As a subordinate plot. it lacks autonomy, and its heroine seems to act more to suit her husband than out of personal desire.

This univalent Penelope whom Western tradition, since Homer, has taken for granted, can be seen to originate in the *Odyssey* itself. She specifically emerges from the remarks of Agamemnon's ghost when, in book 24, he couples praise of Penelope with blame of his own wife Klytaimestra, setting the two heroines in an opposition to one another that has persisted through the centuries.[3]

But how objective and how reliable is Agamemnon as a narrator of Ithakan and Argive events? Are his praise of Penelope and his blame of Klytaimestra convincing? Do they offset those doubts about her virtue raised by the same ghost figure in the first Nekyia of book 11? I shall contend that, on the contrary, the doubts of Agamemnon of book 11, once raised (regardless of who raised them, or under what circumstances[4]), re-

---

NOTE: Please refer to the Bibliography, pp. 239–52, for full citations of works referred to by author's name only.

[1] Penelope, despite rival traditions (notably, association with Pan and other love adventures; see E. Wüst, *s.v.* Penelope, Pauly-Wissowa, *Real-Encyclopädie*, vol. 19.1 [1937], 460–93, esp. c. 479–81), is popularly considered the paragon of the virtuous wife since Homer; cf. Wüst, ibid., col. 483.

[2] Cf. my list of plot-types on p. 165; the labels for Odysseus' plots are of only marginal interest to this study.

[3] For Nagy (1979, 36, n.1) this passage "reflects a formal tradition of praise poetry centering on the theme of Penelope, as distinguished by the contrasting blame poetry about Clytemnestra"; in his discussion of *psogoi* and *enkōmia* (255 n.1) Nagy cites 24.201–2 as "one of the clearest instances of blame as blame poetry."

[4] Agamemnon of book 11 is a creature fashioned by Odysseus to suit his purposes of winning safe and cautious convoy from the Phaiakians. It is in his interest, as teller of his own

main because the primary narrator never dispels them. Moreover, the Agamemnon of book 24 who affirms Penelope's virtue is conspicuously unreliable as a judge of female character; indeed, the primary narrator expressly undermines his evaluation of the two heroines by placing it in the context of a dead suitor's mistaken report of events in Ithaka. In explaining their slaughter, Amphimedon's shade includes this piece of misinformation:

> Then, in the craftiness of his mind, he urged his lady
> to set the bow and the gray iron in front of the Suitors,
> the contest for us ill-fated men, the beginning of our slaughter.[5]

(24.167–69)

The slain suitor, supposing that Penelope recognized her husband before the contest, mistakenly ascribed to Odysseus sole responsibility or blame for initiating that event.[6] Penelope thus earns praise from Agamemnon's ghost on false grounds: she is not held accountable for proposing the contest of the bow.

Other scenes too reveal a Penelope far more complex than the ghost of Agamemnon imagines. To recover some of that complexity, I examine passages that seem to indicate contradictory motives and inconsistent behavior and that are apt to keep the reader confused about Penelope's actual desires until that moment of clarity (for Penelope and reader) at 23.205–8, when Penelope finally embraces Odysseus as her husband.[7] Incidentally, such reasonable bewilderment has spawned numerous scholarly attempts to excise any passages that undermine the image of Penelope as unproblematically faithful.[8] I shall take a different route.

ADVENTURES, to make Agamemnon in the Underworld suspect even Penelope of potential betrayal.

[5] I use Lattimore's translation. All quotations from the *Odyssey* are from W. B. Stanford, *The Odyssey of Homer*, 2nd ed., 2 vols. (London, 1958–59).

[6] The observation that "dead Amphimedon's statement in the Second Nekyia . . . is his own inference" dates to the scholiast (Dindorf II.725.15) and is offered by Finley (1978, 14n.6) as one of several examples of the poet showing people's wrong ideas. It is baffling that Page (1955, chap. 5) takes the ghost so seriously and relies so heavily on this "inconsistency" in the Second Nekyia to argue for contamination by "the other version" in which Penelope recognized Odysseus before the setting of the contest.

[7] I see this moment, when Penelope's knees loosen, as a *lusis*, or "release," for the reader as well, perhaps even a *lusis* of the plot in the Aristotelian sense of "denouement," as opposed to *desis*, "complication" (Aristotle, *Poetics* 1455b24–1456a10). Until 23.205 even the knowing reader feels suspense as to whether Penelope and Odysseus will ever happily reunite. Note how, though we know (from 1.76–79) that Odysseus will return, we are never directly informed that Penelope will have waited for him, and the references to her possible inconstancy form a virtual leitmotif.

[8] For a summary and discussion of the Analytic position vis-à-vis the so-called Continuation of the *Odyssey* (Page's term), which includes the Second Nekyia, see Page (1955, chap. 5), Kirk (1962, 245–48), Moulton (1974b, esp. 154n.7), and Wender (1978, 10–18).

To the arguments made by Erbse (1972), Moulton (1974b), Finley (1978), and others against the Analyst assertion that the first and second Nekyiai are incompatible, we can add a narratological observation. The First Nekyia, as Odysseus' "creation," need not be compatible

I propose to show that Homer, by withholding information from Penelope until 23.205, offers her no rational solution to her dilemma of whether to await Odysseus or not. In plot language, he assigns her roles in two incompatible types of plot: in BRIDE-CONTEST and MARRIAGE-AVOIDANCE (with each plot-type further specified for a maiden or widow and for a matron).

The multiple plots that Penelope weaves, seen from the perspective of various male characters (particularly Odysseus, the Suitors, and Agamemnon), constitute the following plot-types: BRIDE-PRIZE, ADULTERY, FRIGIDITY AND TEASE, and LOYALTY AND CUNNING. In BRIDE-PRIZE suitors desire to marry, select a potential bride, and compete in a contest for her hand. In ADULTERY a wife betrays her husband and takes a lover. In FRIGIDITY AND TEASE, a potential bride thwarts her suitors' desires, leading them on and tormenting them, all the while not intending to marry. Finally, in LOYALTY AND CUNNING, a wife cunningly holds eager suitors at bay until her husband returns. The second and fourth plot-types unfold from the absent husband's point of view, the first and third from that of the Suitors.

From her own female-centered perspective, Penelope weaves and participates in the following, corresponding four plot-types, some virtually indiscernible from those seen by the male characters: COURTSHIP AND MARRIAGE; DALLIANCE AND INFIDELITY; DISDAIN AND BRIDE OF DEATH; and PATIENCE AND CUNNING. In COURTSHIP AND MARRIAGE, a maiden or widow enjoys male attention and/or desires to marry; she accepts courtship and sets herself up as bride-prize in a contest. In DALLIANCE AND INFIDELITY, a wife (her husband away) enjoys courtship and/or engages in a (playful?) act of infidelity. In DISDAIN AND BRIDE OF DEATH, a maiden or widow disdains unworthy suitors and prefers virginal death to any marriage. Finally, in PATIENCE AND CUNNING a wife cunningly (indeed heroically) withstands seduction and awaits her husband's return.

Though I do not use all of these terms equally, I present them here because it is important for us to know that the bride has her own story, even when it is not presented in full.[9] The second group takes into account the maiden or matron's own desires and attitudes toward her actions (to the extent that we can observe them). Note how the same sequences of action acquire a different shade of meaning and a different label depending on whether they are "focalized"[10] from a male or female center. In what follows, I pay special attention to female-focalized plots, which are often overlooked in readings of the *Odyssey*.

By keeping Penelope ignorant as to her marital status and by representing

---

with the second, Homer's, since Odysseus as a character-teller need not be either omniscient or truthful.

I dismiss issues concerning the genesis of the text, because my concern is rather with its impact on the reader, given its form.

[9]For the comparable observation that the witch in fairy tale has her story too, see Gilbert and Gubar (1979, esp. 79). The notion of female-centered plots was suggested to me by Gilbert and Gubar and by Miller (1980, xi).

[10]An illuminating discussion of the concept of focalization appears in Bal (1985, 100–114). The term comes from Genette (1980, pp.185–210, "Perspective," and pp. 212–62, "Voice").

her as uncertain as to which of her several plots she is at any moment involved in, Homer gives a legitimacy and reasonableness to her multiplicity of purposes (which in turn engenders our legitimate perplexity). Much of her behavior becomes intelligible to us if we consider that she is unremittingly vexed by the question, "Am I moving toward new union or toward reunion?" Behavior shameful if her husband lives is normal if he has perished at sea.[11]

Homer has Penelope, in this state of ignorance, set up the contest. She takes this step uncertain whether Odysseus will return in time, mistrusting omens and the statements of seers or beggars. Nor does she propose the contest relying, as some have thought, on her intuition that Odysseus is home already.[12] Certainly, on the one hand, she feels she has exhausted her strategies for deferring the decision; she hopes, on the other, that her husband will arrive in time. Additional sentiments can be adduced as influencing her move: an attraction to the stranger, loneliness,[13] ripeness for eros,

---

[11]Emlyn-Jones (1984, 12) interprets her "inability to make an end" (16.126–27) as referring "not to her personal preferences or to some 'feminine' weakness but to the social situation," since "the exact situation with regard to Penelope's prerogatives in this matter is confused." On the topic of Penelope's prerogatives, particularly the "lack of agreement on who is her *kurios*" (the person in charge of her), see Lacey (1966, 62ff.) and references in Emlyn-Jones (17, notes 51 and 52) and in Marquardt (1984, esp. 43f. and n. 12). In my opinion, Odysseus' parting words (18.259–70) define Penelope's prerogatives more than do social pressure, customs of the times, etc. (See note 27, below).

[12]This position has become increasingly popular. It emerged out of the ingenious but overstated proposal by Harsh (1950) that Odysseus and Penelope communicate by code. Critiquing Harsh, Amory (1963) suggested that Penelope intuits the presence of her husband "intermittently." For Austin (1975, 232), the "spiritual harmony between the two, shown in their understanding of each other's language, makes it hardly credible that no recognition has taken place." Austin (1975) and Russo (1982) support Amory's notion of intuition. Emlyn-Jones (1984) faults all these "Intuitionists" (including Harsh) for ignoring certain passages, but mainly he is ideologically and/or temperamentally opposed to "psychologizing" (see note 13 below, where I defend and locate this form of criticism).

Both Amory and Austin give full analyses of the feeling state of Penelope from the time she first encounters the stranger. Neither makes enough, in my opinion, of Penelope's self-interest, and both (together with Harsh) overestimate what she knows. Amory's Penelope emerges as an unconscious and unreflective being, very "female" in an old sense of the word but not so very "like-minded" to Odysseus. Austin perhaps overromanticizes the level of communication achieved by the pair.

My reconsideration of Penelope passages is meant to provide an alternative to the hypothesis that Penelope based her decision to set up the contest on intuition alone, and an alternative as well to the model of total communication between a husband and wife, even a couple such as Odysseus and Penelope whose relationship rests on *homophrosynē*.

[13]Devereux (1957) gives a convincing psychoanalytic portrait of Penelope's lonely state, as indicated in her dream; Russo, too (1982, 6 and 9), offers a psychological interpretation of the dream of book 19. Another sensitive psychological interpreter, Van Nortwick (1979), links Penelope's divided mind in books 18 and 19 with Homer's portrayal of Nausikaa. Others cite Devereux with apparent approval.

Emlyn-Jones (1984), on the other hand, vehemently opposes postulating any "psychological 'sub-text'" for understanding characters in the *Odyssey*; he prefers a genetic explanation. In my

her son's coming of age.[14] None of these, however powerful, changes the fact that by setting up the contest now she risks infidelity.[15]

To these several possible motivations we may add an explanation from plot. What if Penelope, weaver of plots (as her name, from *pēnē*, "woof" or "web," suggests),[16] calculated her move to fit simultaneously into several possible plots? What if, indeed, she is complicitous with her author in that she willingly takes up several strands of plot simultaneously?

We can learn much about her character by posing this question, even if we eventually discard it as overstated.[17] We then ask **how** Penelope weaves plots, and whether she interprets plots she has woven. Is she a character who, like Odysseus, aims to control events as they happen but, inevitably, sometimes falls short, due to obstacles unforeseen and results unintended? Does she preview and rehearse imagined sequences of events and retrospectively formulate them in a coherent narrative, like Odysseus when he "spoke to his own great-hearted spirit" (5.465–73) or "plotted out the destruction of the overmastering suitors" with Athene (13.373ff.; also 20.37ff.) or with Telemachos (16.235–39)?[18] In narrating her life events, does she select and reshape with the freedom of a storyteller? In short, is she a "plotting" character? Perhaps we can envision a scale for describing characters, from unwitting agents who act within whatever plot is given to them, on the one hand, to supreme plotters who seemingly control their fictional lives, on the other. Would we not place Penelope and Odysseus closer to the latter pole than the former?

---

view, the locus for a psychological interpretation is in the interpreter, who may legitimately base such inferences about Penelope's psyche on clues in the text. The problem with eschewing this whole approach is that one is left only with genetic explanations, which, even when ingenious, do not account for literary impact.

[14] Among scholarly explanations that account for COURTSHIP or indeed DALLIANCE, the appeal to plot needs is prominent. Woodhouse (1930), who names his tenth chapter "Penelopeia's Collapse," states (84f.) that "a new departure on the part of Penelopeia is the only way of overcoming the deadlock" and this explains her "sudden resolve" that is "without motive, without justification, and apparently runs counter to the epithet of 'sensible' or 'wise'." Tolstoi (1934) and Hölscher (1967b [this volume, 133–40]) take the coming-of-age of Telemachos, a folktale motif, as determining the moment of Penelope's decision to hold the contest. While admiring all these ingenious contributions, I do not find that they "explain" Penelope's decision on the level that here concerns me, namely, that of the psychological plausibility and consequent intelligibility to the reader of the character Penelope.

[15] See note 2, above: I mean not only adultery and infidelity, but ADULTERY and INFIDELITY as plot-types.

[16] On the derivation of Pēnelopeia from *pēnē*, "woof" or "loom," cf. E. Wüst, "Penelope," esp. c. 461. Wüst refers to Didymos in the scholion to *Od.* 4.797 and to Eustathius on *Od.*1.343ff. as ancient sources for this etymology. Of course, name puns, to be effective, need not rely on *valid* etymologies, as Howard N. Porter pointed out to me long ago.

[17] Consider, in Vaihinger (1968), the expediency of fictions in furthering understanding. My proposal that Penelope is Homer's accomplice in weaving strands of plot is to be taken as such an "as if" proposal, in a spirit of useful play.

[18] On narration as cognition, see White (1970, 1) and Alter (1981, chap. 8, "Narration and Knowledge").

Whenever she previews her destiny in dreams and fantasies, and whenever she retrospectively interprets the plots she has spun, Penelope seems empowered (by Homer) to select and arrange events. Thus, like a narrator, she makes a *muthos* in Aristotle's sense, as a *synthesis pragmatōn*, "a putting together of deeds" (Aristotle, *Poetics* 1450a4–5).

Building up Penelope's features as a creator of plots requires that we know, at each plot moment, what she knows, what beliefs and convictions she holds, what she desires and fears, what actions she thinks are possible and permissible for her to take. In other words, we may treat her as if she were a character in real life, with a world of her own.[19] We ascribe to her a psychological coherence that, admittedly, we as readers construct. We are mute on the question of Homer's absolute intentionality, since we are focusing here on the impact of the text rather than on its production.

This study aims, then, to expand the interpretation of Penelope's most frequent epithet, *periphrōn*, "thinking all around," as well as the etymological pun on her name as "weaver." From our analysis *periphrōn Pēnelopeia* finally emerges as a character aware of the plots she creates and, like Odysseus, cunning in securing her own best interests in terms of survival, duty, and pleasure. Thus she acts for her own sake as well as for the limited purpose that Agamemnon's ghost assigns her, namely, to assure Odysseus' glory and safety. Agamemnon's worldview is male focalized, whereas Homer offers us a larger perspective. Examining Penelope's character from plot leads us to supplement her traditional image as a patient, faithful, enduring wife with a fuller portrait—of a complex, problematic figure who ultimately remains faithful to her absent husband but comes dangerously close, and for good reasons, to an unintentional betrayal. And in the course of her life history, she participates in a multitude of plots.

PENELOPE AND PLOT

Penelope engages in the following actions: she offers words of encouragement and promises to each suitor; devises the trick of the web; appears before the Suitors and solicits gifts; dreams, ponders, scolds, weeps and prays; interviews the stranger and tells him her dream; sets up the contest of the bow; and eventually entraps her husband into divulging his secret knowledge of their marriage bed. Some of these activities she enacts before

---

[19] My approach was influenced at an early stage by several efforts by literary theorists to apply the philosophical concept (dating from Leibniz) of Possible Worlds to literary worlds, especially by Pavel (1986, chap. 3, "Salient Worlds"), Doležel (1976), Ryan (1985). Doležel uses the concept of modalities in a way that influenced my formulation of the questions we must ask about Penelope. Ryan, developing Pavel's notion of "character domain," has proposed a way to map out a world from the perspective of a character.

our eyes (mimesis); others a character recounts (diegesis).[20] I shall try to recover her motives and self-knowledge as she previews and makes her decisions and acts on them, and as she retrospectively evaluates her choices. The passages I treat are out of textual order; the first two demonstrate Penelope's sincerity in setting up the contest; the second and third are retrospections by Penelope, indicating her plot awareness; the remaining five indicate Penelope's participation in several plot-types as she makes her choices.

My analysis depends on the assumption, which the first two passages support, that Penelope is sincere in setting up the contest of the bow to determine whom she will marry, and that indeed she envisions her wedding taking place.

Tears

> She sat down, and laid the bow on her dear knees, while
> she took her lord's bow out of its case, all the while weeping
> aloud. But when she had sated herself with tears and crying,
> she went on her way to the hall to be with the lordly suitors.

(21.55ff.)

Penelope sheds these bitter tears in private when she has placed her husband's bow on her knees. Her mood in this passage is sombre: wanting to remain steadfast, she has run out of strategies. She weeps not only at the sight of the weapons, reminders of her absent husband, but also at the dire implications of her decision not to wait.[21]

---

[20] Plato (*Republic* 392d1–394c5) distinguishes three types of narration: simple diegesis (as in dithyramb), diegesis through mimesis (as in drama), and a mixture of the two (as in epic). His discussion has influenced narratologists, notably Genette (1980, pp. 162–85), where he treats the question of the relation of the narration to its own materials ("Distance"). In this study I have merely marked a passage as mimetic or diegetic without drawing implications.

[21] Hölscher (1967b [this volume, 133–40]) and Finley (1978) both see the importance of Penelope's tears in establishing her sincerity.

Combellack (1973, 38) convincingly shows that Penelope's earlier tears, after the interview (19.603), and Penelope's second prayer to Artemis (20.61–90) are "completely incompatible with the Harsh-Amory woman who knows that Odysseus is asleep downstairs." Then, following Whallon (1961, 128), he asserts that Penelope believed the Suitors would certainly fail in the contest. This "solution" is, however, inharmonious with Penelope's tears when she takes out the weapons for the contest. Thornton's idea (1970), that Penelope's decision proves her "utter loyalty to Odysseus" since she is obeying his instructions, gets us back to a univalent Penelope. Van Nortwick's (1983, 24–25) Penelope has indeed decided "to bury Odysseus and her old life with him by remarrying, while Athena plots the resumption of their marital happiness." Wife and goddess are at cross purposes: Penelope weeps for the loss of Odysseus while at the same time, as a tool of Athene, she unwittingly works for his return. The coexistence of these two levels of intentionality generates irony.

Another proposal, that Penelope uses the contest as a divining test (Amory [1963], followed by Austin [1969 and 1975]), gives us a Penelope who passively allows her fate to rest "on the laps of the gods." Consider Zeus' statement in the council of book 1: would Penelope be the

Penelope's mournful behavior as she collects the weapons belongs, if she is a matron, not to a successful marriage-avoidance plot (LOYALTY and CLEVERNESS; PATIENCE) but to a failed one, a remarriage, which is equivalent to ADULTERY/INFIDELITY.

Helen Apology

Penelope also reveals her sincerity in setting up the contest when, in retrospect, she tacitly acknowledges to her husband how close she had come to adultery. This is the problematic Helen passage that many consider an interpolation but that in fact illuminates the complexity of Penelope.[22]

> Do not be angry with me, Odysseus, since, beyond other men,
> you have the most understanding. . . . Then do not now be angry with me
>   nor blame me, because
> I did not greet you, as I do now, at first when I saw you.
> For always the spirit deep in my very heart was fearful
> that some one of the mortal men would come my way and deceive me
> with words. For there are many who scheme for wicked advantage.
> For neither would . . . Helen of Argos
> have lain in love with an outlander . . .
> if she had known that the warlike sons of the Achaians would bring her
> home again to the beloved land of her fathers.
> It was a god who stirred her to do the shameful thing she
> did, and never before had she had in her heart this terrible
> wildness, out of which came suffering to us also.
> But now, since you have given me accurate proof . . .
> so you persuade my heart, though it has been very stubborn.

(23.209–30)

Penelope's attitude toward Helen is unusually empathetic. Her remark that Helen would not have lain with a foreigner had she known that the sons of the Achaians would bring her home again, suggests that it is not the betrayal itself, but ignorance about the future that is ruinous folly (*atē*). Penelope implies that, had she yielded to the stranger claiming to be Odys-

---

sort of character, like Aigisthos, to blame the gods if things did not turn out favorably? It seems unlikely. Consider as well Athene-Mentes' statement to Telemachos (1.203–5) that Odysseus will find a way home, since he is a man of many resources (*epei polumēchanos estin*). Why would we expect Penelope to be different?

[22] For a summary of the arguments in favor of athetesis, see van der Valk (1949, 194–95). He claims that the lines are no interpolation "but in fact they show us very clearly the inner emotion of Penelope" (195) because "Penelope has for a long time wavered and actually failed to recognize her husband. . . . It is obvious she is afraid of Odysseus' reaction and wrath."

Beye too anticipates my point when he comments (1974, 97) that Penelope defends Helen "on the ground that chastity is a very chancey thing," and that "within one human heart exist several desires or reactions, but some of them, while they can be acknowledged, must be suppressed." His brief study uncovers many dimensions of Penelope's character, through parallels to Helen, Klytaimestra, even Kirke.

seus or married a suitor, she too would have been subject to reproach; since she did not, she ought to be absolved from blame.[23] Thus, by exonerating Helen she hopes to exonerate herself for not immediately embracing her husband and for nearly causing a Trojan War!

Accentuating the similarity between their two situations leads Penelope to veil one conspicuous distinction, namely that Helen abandoned Menelaos out of sheer desire. Penelope's principle, that any woman might unwittingly betray her husband, hardly applies to Helen. This distortion of the comparison, for her argument's sake, reveals the degree to which Penelope understands how dangerously close she came to marrying a suitor, with her husband already nearby!

Here Penelope comes closest to reflecting on the theme of infidelity. Her worst possible scenario would have been marriage to a stranger or a suitor followed by Odysseus' return. This, she now realizes, would have earned her ill repute for all time and made her indistinguishable from Helen. Except here, she never alludes to such a possibility or hints at second thoughts about proposing the contest. Now, for the first time, she begins to minimize her near-betrayal by indirectly defending the legitimacy of a bride-contest if a woman thinks herself a widow. Her insistence on Helen's ignorance (as if Menelaos were permanently missing when Helen departed with Paris) causes me, as reader, not to object to the passage, but, relying on it, to add a dimension to my own sense of Penelope's complexity and plot-awareness as she asks her husband for double pardon.

Penelope's Tale

A second retrospection that gives us a sense of Penelope as a spinner of plots is her account to Odysseus after lovemaking. The narrator tells how Penelope, herself as narrator, reduced her plots to a single type:

> When Penelope and Odysseus had enjoyed their
> lovemaking, they took their pleasure in talking, each one telling his story.
> She, shining among women, told of all she had endured
> in the palace, as she watched the Suitors, a ravening
> company, who on her account were slaughtering many oxen
> and fat sheep, and much wine was being drawn from the wine jars.

$$(23.300–305)$$

This is the story of holding the Suitors at bay until Odysseus' return. It is LOYALTY and CLEVERNESS, or PATIENCE, and it has no affinity with ADULTERY or INFIDELITY. Penelope's story corresponds to Odysseus' adventures seen only as obstacles to return—without reference to any pleasure the adventurer took in his travels. Each spouse/storyteller, now at last out of

---

[23] It is an argument *a fortiori* (cf. Aristotle, *Rhetoric* 1358a14–17 and 1397b12–29): if Helen acted thus, and is absolved, why cannot I, who almost committed a less severe breach of faith, be forgiven? Thus Penelope distorts factual truth for her argument's sake.

danger, interprets all prior events in terms of REUNION. Moreover, by depicting the Suitors as villains who attacked Odysseus' household and by focusing solely on their misdeeds, Penelope's story helps justify their slaughter. Though she blithely dismisses the other side of the story, we as readers cannot: her encouragement of them and indeed her enjoyment of their attention lessen their criminal culpability, and her omission of this aspect from what she tells Odysseus helps launder her image for posterity.

We turn now to Penelope's behavior before she embraces Odysseus in 23.205, in five passages that together disclose a multivalent Penelope.

Encouragements, Promises, and Ambivalence

The text is unrelenting in informing us, always diegetically, that Penelope encouraged the Suitors. Telemachos (1.245–51; cf. 16.122–28) and Amphimedon (24.126–28) state that "she would not refuse the hateful marriage, nor would she bring it about"; Amphimedon adds, "But she was planning our death and destruction with this other stratagem of her heart's devising." Thus he connects the ruse of the loom to Penelope's noncommittal behavior toward them. The suitor Antinoos (2.85–128) and the goddess Athene (13.379–81) observe that she raised the Suitors' hopes and made promises to each, but "her mind had other intentions" (noos de hoi alla menoinai; 2.92 and 13.381).

The Shroud of Laertes

In the Second Nekyia the ghost of Amphimedon quotes Penelope's proposal of the ruse of the loom:

> "Young men, my suitors now that the great Odysseus has
> perished, wait, though you are eager to marry me, until
> I finish this web, so that my weaving will not be
> useless and wasted. This is a shroud for the hero
> Laertes.'"

> (24.131–34)

Then he tells of her servant's betrayal that led the Suitors to discover Penelope "in the act of undoing her glorious weaving" so that "against her will and by force, she had to finish it" (24.145–46). Finally, "she displayed the great piece of weaving that she had woven. She had washed it, and it shone like the sun or the moon" (24.147–48).

Earlier, describing to the stranger-Odysseus her treatment of the Suitors (19.137–56), Penelope recalled how she was weaving her own wiles (137) and how some spirit (tis daimōn) "put the idea of the web in my mind" (138). She quoted herself announcing the project to her suitors and urging them to wait to marry her until she finished weaving the shroud (141–47).

This promise, however deceitful, contributed to the complaints the Suitors Antinoos (book 2) and Amphimedon (book 24) harbored against her.[24] It also keeps us as readers perplexed as to Penelope's real intentions.

Words of encouragement and secret promises would not in themselves prove a heightened interest in the Suitors or a turning toward men for attention, since these actions could be part of a stratagem to placate oppressive suitors (PATIENCE). Other passages contribute to our sense of an increasingly sensuous Penelope who participates actively in COURTSHIP.[25]

Solicitation of Gifts

It is Athene who prodded Penelope to appear before the Suitors:

> But now the goddess, gray-eyed Athene, put it in the mind
> of the daughter of Ikarios, circumspect Penelope,
> to show herself to the Suitors, so that she might all the more
> open their hearts, and so that she might seem all the more precious (timēessa)
> in the eyes of her husband and son even than she had been before this.
> She laughed, in an idle way. and spoke to her nurse and named her:
> "Eurynome, my heart desires, though before it did not,
> to show myself to the Suitors, although I still hate them."

(18.158–65)

Though the purpose clauses introduced by hopōs express the goddess's intentions in putting this idea in Penelope's mind, the expression "my heart desires" (164: thumos moi eeldetai) suggests to me that Athene's "intervention" does not lessen Penelope's responsibility for her decision.[26] We can assume

---

[24] Penelope is viewed by the Suitors as a bewitcher, almost a Kirke figure. Her web is an entrapment for them, much like Kirke's island for Odysseus' men. See the excellent discussion of Penelope as a Kirke figure in Beye (1974).

[25] The ancient tradition was as ambivalent on the topic of Penelope's sensuality as modern scholars (see E. Wüst, note 1 above). Some, wanting an uncomplicated Penelope, align themselves with the character Agamemnon: they tend to excise whatever violates their image of the heroine. Others, using the *Odyssey* as social history, explain Penelope's actions as reactions to social constraints. Marquardt (1984), e.g., who collects and treats all these passages and anticipates my case for a complex Penelope (48), vitiates her own argument by underestimating Penelope's autonomy. For example, she concludes (35 and 33) that Penelope "goes through the motions of encouraging courtship" because of social constraints and obligations on her to remarry once there is no realistic hope of Odysseus' return. She sees no evidence of choice on Penelope's part, though Odysseus' parting words (quoted by Penelope at 18.259–70)—if we accept the quotation as "authentic" and not Penelope's *ad hoc* invention—make it clear that it is her decision to proceed with marriage plans or not. If we contrast Penelope's situation with that of Klytaimestra (3.267–68: "a man was there, a singer, whom Agamemnon, when he went to Troy, had given many instructions to keep watch on his wife"), we can imagine that the social fabric reflected in the *Odyssey* admitted at least these two different sorts of marital relationship.

[26] For Athene as the plan and guiding hand of the poet, see Reinhardt (1960b, 45). If this is

that Athene could only influence Penelope in accord with Penelope's own character and disposition. Thus Athene's purpose, planted in Penelope's mind (*epi phresi thēke*), becomes Penelope's even though it contradicts her dominant set of feelings, hatred for the Suitors, a hatred explicit in her earlier wish for their demise (4.681ff.).

Appearance before suitors is a standard courtship motif, and Homer shows us a Penelope allowing herself to be courted. Which men does she aim to impress? Clearly, the hated suitors. Indeed, her embarrassed laugh is a sign of her own discomfort at the incongruity between her actions and this dominant, negative emotion;[27] at the same time, the laughter invites us to think of the laughter-loving goddess Aphrodite, whose influence suggests coquetry. Penelope conceals such coquetry from her nurse Eurynome, who (as an embodiment of propriety) might well disapprove of her mistress's flirtation.

Penelope's appearance has its intended impact on the Suitors (18.212–13). This, in turn, impresses Odysseus (18.281–83), who is happy "because she beguiled gifts out of them and enchanted their spirits with blandishing words, though her own mind had other intentions." That last formulaic clause reflects Odysseus' assessment of her motivations, along with the narrator's. Compare Athene's reassurances to Odysseus at 13.381, using the same formula. How accurate an assessment is it in this passage? Is the narrator totally cognizant of his own character's intentions? Does he allow Penelope to take pleasure in the Suitors as she beguiles them and possibly to overlook the cost of that pleasure, namely a plot moving rapidly toward remarriage? Is Penelope's behavior with the Suitors incautious in the same way as Odysseus' with Polyphemos?

Odysseus is not offended when he sees his wife winning male attention. He values the economic gains, which will help replenish the household. As a tactician himself, he respects her tactics. Moreover, as one of her attentive males, he is not threatened by his competition. Rather, he expects to (re-)claim Penelope, and her value for him is enhanced by the need to compete for her. For the reader, this scene emphasizes the husband's recovery of

---

so, which plots does the goddess, in the poet's stead, further? She knows Penelope is a matron, so that eliminates all maiden plots. BRIDE-CONTEST (MATRON) (which appears to the Suitors as BRIDE-CONTEST [maiden] and is therefore a *dolos*, or "deceit") is an expedient plot for her to support; so is MARRIAGE-AVOIDANCE (MATRON). To make Penelope *timēessa mallon . . . ē paros*, "more cherished than before," is a way of goading husband and son toward competing through the bride-contest for her hand (with the son helping win her for his father—an unusual situation in bride-contests). That is, Athene increases the intensity of competition among men for a beautiful woman. The scene is archetypally powerful.

[27]Levine (1983) argues that, besides representing her confusion, Penelope's laughter expresses her cunning: she "laughs at the notion of fooling the Suitors because she knows she can succeed." I link her laughter to coquetry and a new awareness of eros. Cf. the similarly arresting laughter of Earth and the Sea just before Persephone plucks the narcissus (a proleptic symbol of her loss of virginity) in *Hymn to Demeter* 14: *gaia te pas' egelasse kai halmuron oidma thalassēs*.

his wife as bride; i.e., it is BRIDE-CONTEST for a matron, where suitor = husband and bride = wife. Relevant here is a scene on the brooch that Penelope gave Odysseus when he departed twenty years earlier (19.225–31). The scene itself suggests an erotic conquest: the capture of a fawn by a hound who "preyed on the fawn and strangled it and the fawn struggled with his feet as he tried to escape." Odysseus is the hound pursuing Penelope, and her flirtations with others (a resistance of sorts) stimulate him rather than incurring his wrath.[28]

Dream and Contest

The interview of Penelope with the stranger begins with Odysseus' compliment to Penelope (19.107–14) and his elaborate, persuasive lie (165ff.). It culminates with his mention of her departure gift to her husband (225–31) and with his prediction that Odysseus will presently come home (270 and 306–7). Penelope offers the stranger a bath and addresses him as "Dear friend" (350). But at the crucial point when Eurykleia recognizes Odysseus by his scar (467–77) and turns to Penelope for affirmation, Athene averts her perception (478–79).[29]

Shortly thereafter Penelope begins to share her innermost thoughts with the stranger. First, she confides her sharp anxieties over Telemachos (516–34),[30] and soon her dream of the eagle and the geese.[31]

> But come listen to a dream of mine and interpret it for me.
> I have twenty geese here about the house, and they feed on
> grains of wheat from the water trough. I love to watch them.
> But a great eagle with crooked beak came down from the mountain,
> and broke the necks of them all and killed them. So the whole twenty
> lay dead about the house, but he soared high in the bright air.
> Then *I began to weep*—that was in my dream—*and cried out*
> *aloud*, and around me gathered the fair-haired Achaian women
> *as I cried out sorrowing* for my geese killed by the eagle.
> But he came back again and perched on the jut of the gabled
> roof. He now had a human voice and spoke aloud to me:

[28] The brooch is a complicated symbol, since it conveys meaning both as an object and as an object decorated with images. As a departure gift from wife to husband, it binds Odysseus, reminding him of Penelope's claims. Its decorations symbolize the erotic chase, perhaps even the first capture of Penelope by Odysseus. But the chase itself is not unambiguously "male captures female." Consider Penelope's trick of the marriage bed—a sort of verbal trap in which she ensnares her husband, an entrapment that the chase scene on the brooch may anticipate.

[29] It is here that Page (1955) and others place the recognition of husband by wife in the earlier version.

[30] See Marquardt's (1984) convincing analysis of the simile of the daughters of Pandareos.

[31] On the irony produced by the polyphony of voices in the narration of Penelope's dream, see Delrieu, Hilt and Létoublon (1984, 192). Odysseus, the narrator, Eurykleia, and the audience know that the liar is Odysseus, and that he is already home; Penelope asserts that the dream is false but believes (perhaps) that the stranger is the Cretan Aithon.

"Do not fear, O daughter of far-famed Ikarios.
This is no dream, but a blessing real as day. You will see it
done. The geese are the Suitors, and I, eagle, have been
a bird of portent, but now I am your own husband, come home,
and I shall inflict shameless destruction on all the Suitors."
So he spoke, and then the honey-sweet sleep released me,
and I looked about and saw the geese in my palace, feeding
on their grains of wheat from the water trough, just as they had been.

(19.535–53)

To this confidence the stranger Odysseus replies:

Lady, it is impossible to read this dream and avoid it
by turning it another way, since Odysseus himself has told you
its meaning, how it will end. The suitors' doom is evident
for one and all. Not one will avoid his death and destruction.

(19.555–58)

Penelope's response is to deny the validity of the dream. She offers an allegory of two gates through which dreams pass: this one, she insists, passed through the gate of ivory and cannot be believed (19.560–69); it is helplessly ineffectual (*amēchanos*) and difficult to decipher (*akritomuthos*). Penelope suddenly announces her plan to hold the bride-contest (570–72).

Aside from depicting her pleasure as she watches the Suitors and her grief as she previews their death,[32] the central portion of the dream reveals a Penelope awaiting her husband's return yet reluctant to relinquish her attachment to the Suitors. The careful construction of the dream precludes our inferring that Penelope is ambivalent toward Odysseus' homecoming, or that she would continue her attachment to the Suitors if she knew Odysseus was home. For she does not mourn in her dream once eagle-Odysseus tells her, "Now I am your own husband, come home." And yet with things as she supposes them to be at this juncture, the Suitors' presence is her sole pleasure, though a mixed one. Should Odysseus not return, she desires a continuation of that pleasure, naturally disguising this from herself by expressing her grief for dead suitors in terms of grief over pet geese. At this moment, she is not the consummate "weaver of plots," for she presents herself to Odysseus in all her vulnerability.

Penelope awakens to experience a jarring discrepancy between the dream events and reality. When she finds her geese still alive, she feels the dream message doubly annulled. That is, the presence in her palace of literal geese eating from the trough undermines the dream figure's equation between

---

[32] Penelope mourns their death as geese in the dream as she will never mourn them later, in reality, as suitors. Dream-Penelope's grief for the Suitors is emphasized by triple repetitions (19.541–43):

> Then *I began to weep*—that was in my dream—and *cried out
> aloud,* and around me gathered the fair-haired Achaian women
> *as I cried out sorrowing* for my geese killed by the eagle.

geese and suitors—asserting, visually, that geese are geese and, further, that *her* geese are still alive. Moreover, if she means to sustain the dream metaphor and use "geese" to designate her suitors (a possibility that the text leaves indeterminate), then the presence in her palace of the Suitors eating like animals is incongruent with the vivid dream image of suitors slain.[33] Perhaps Penelope denies that equation by saying "geese are geese" and denies the death of the Suitors by saying "my suitors are still feeding."[34]

Penelope's predominant reaction against the gentle, dreamed suggestion that Odysseus is home and that she forego her attachment to the Suitors ("Do not fear . . . ") is to affirm COURTSHIP by setting up the bride-contest.

If we grant that Penelope takes pleasure in her suitors/geese, and now look back to the ruse of the web, that event (which Amphimedon's ghost saw as purely deceitful) takes on new ambiguities. The deferral tactics of Penelope the weaver serve two functions: they enable her, first, to hold off the Suitors for some years to give her husband a chance to return home in time to rescue her (i.e., prolonging the courtship for *his* sake) and second, to defer the remarriage so that *she* can take pleasure as long as possible in "watching her pet geese" (i.e., prolonging the courtship for *her own* sake). The one plot is LOYALTY and CLEVERNESS and PATIENCE, the other COURTSHIP; if, however, Penelope suspects that Odysseus is home and still enjoys COURTSHIP, the plot-type is DALLIANCE—a weak or incompleted form of INFIDELITY.

The weaving itself as a physical process is double-edged: she weaves by day (moving toward remarriage) and unweaves by night (undoing her day's progress).[35] She has told the Suitors to defer their suit until she finishes the shroud, insinuating that she will marry one of them eventually. Like her messages of encouragement to each, the project itself entices and allures and indeed entraps them. But this allurement is aimed not only at their destruc-

---

[33] Scholarly debate remains inconclusive as to Penelope's meaning when she says, "and I looked about and saw the geese in my place, feeding on their grains of wheat from the water trough, just as they had been." Marquardt (1984, 43n.12) reviews the literature and then sides with the Literalists as opposed to the Psychological Critics (Russo, Devereux, Van Nortwick).

For me Penelope's remark is provocatively enigmatic, as we cannot know whether or not she accepts the equation geese = suitors offered by the dream-figure Odysseus and affirmed by the stranger. It feels like a teasing gesture from the poet.

[34] The dream is an explicit portent of the future. Nevertheless, to the dreamer herself the presence of the geese-suitors in waking life seems to contradict the dream message. In the dream proper the death of the geese (= suitors) is vividly felt.

On augury in the *Odyssey*, particularly in connection with this passage, see Podlecki (1967); on the possibility that Penelope used the contest as a form of divination, see Amory (1963, 109ff.), followed by Austin (1975, 235ff. and 278n.28); and on the force of conditions in prophecy, see Peradotto (1974, 822–24), who develops a typology for prophecies in the *Odyssey*.

[35] This scene has contributed to the archetypal image of Penelope as virtuous wife. Scholars rarely notice that the loom deceit contains an encouragement to the Suitors.

For a different view of Penelope's weaving as part of an argument for a solar/lunar interpretation of the courtship of Odysseus and Penelope, see Austin (1975, esp. 252–53).

tion, should Odysseus return, but at prolonging their wooing as well. It perpetuates COURTSHIP *for her sake*. In short, the web for Laertes' shroud reveals and symbolizes Penelope's full ambivalence toward the Suitors and toward her situation. All the while that she weaves she is saying yes to them, but it is an outward yes, contradicted by a secret no at night. The Suitors legitimately accuse her of leading them on (TEASE); their anger has grounds. Telemachos too is aware of this coquettish side of Penelope's behavior, and it angers him as well.

Odysseus accepts a complex Penelope who laments over her geese. He consoles her in the dream but at present, in real life, he can give her only limited consolation. He cannot repeat his assurance to her that her geese are as good as dead or that Odysseus is as good as home. He must leave her in a state of ignorance as to whether or not Odysseus will return and kill all the Suitors.

Without such consolation (Odysseus has not returned, as far as she can tell), Penelope reacts to her disappointment by reaffirming COURTSHIP and MARRIAGE. She prefers this plot to no action at all. She is not ready (as her dream shows) to give up the attention of the Suitors and the possibility of marrying one of them—until she has sure knowledge that Odysseus has arrived.

Note that the idea for the contest comes to Penelope suddenly, like the brainstorm of the web. Both ideas have several facets and reflect the complexity of Penelope. The bow contest, from Penelope's focalization at the moment she proposes it, could be an event in COURTSHIP and BRIDE-PRIZE (for a widow); it could also fit into LOYALTY and CLEVERNESS. Penelope would not see it as an event in ADULTERY and INFIDELITY—the Argos plot. Like a skilled chess player, Penelope knows when she proposes the contest that she is choosing a move that will fit into more than one strategy or plot trajectory.

Compare in this connection Antinoos' comment to Telemachos that Penelope "is winning a great name (*kleos*) / for herself, but for you she is causing much loss of substance" (2.125–26). He sees Penelope's flirtations and encouragements of the Suitors as bringing her some gain. Consider, too, the sustained parallelism between her and Odysseus:[36] just as he enjoys his ad-

---

[36] For "like-mindedness" (*homophrosynē*) as a principle of marriage, the often-cited passage from Odysseus' prayer for Nausikaa is worth quoting in full:

> May the gods give you everything that your heart longs for;
> may they grant you a husband and a house and sweet agreement
> in all things, for nothing is better than this, more steadfast
> than when two people, a man and his wife, keep a harmonious
> household; a thing that brings much distress to the people who hate them
> and pleasure to their well-wishers, and for them the best reputation.

(6.180–85)

The reciprocity suggested by *homophrosynē* is evident in the Penelope-Odysseus relation, in their mutual sharing of *muthoi* in the marriage bed and in Homer's allotting them parallel, multiple plots.

ventures even though they delay his homecoming, so she "loves to watch" (*iainomai eisoroōsa*) her pet geese.

Odysseus and Penelope each have plots obstructing REUNION and plots that lead to it. Odysseus' ADVENTURES, if for the sake of learning (1.3),[37] retard his homecoming. Similarly, Penelope's COURTSHIP is not at all for the sake of, nor does it facilitate, her husband's safe return (though if she had antagonized the Suitors, they might have become destructive). Neither of these two plots moves rapidly toward closure; part of our fascination with the *Odyssey* is seeing them leisurely unfold. Either her husband's return or her marriage to a suitor will put an end to the pleasurable COURTSHIP of Penelope, unless she is wanton enough to keep it going even once she knows Odysseus is home (DALLIANCE).

Prayer for Sudden Death

This prayer echoes Penelope's earlier wish on the occasion of tempting the Suitors (18.202–5) that "chaste Artemis would give me a death so / soft, and now, so I would not go on in my heart grieving / all my life, and longing for love of a husband excellent / in every virtue, since he stood out among the Achaians." Here, for a second time, she prays for death as a better alternative than hateful remarriage:

> Artemis . . . how I wish
> that with the cast of your arrow you could take the life from inside
> my heart, this moment, or that soon the stormwind would snatch me
> away, and be gone, carrying me down misty pathways,
> and set me down where the recurrent Ocean empties
> his stream; as once the stormwinds carried away the daughters
> of Pandareos. The gods killed their parents, and they were left there
> orphaned in the palace, and radiant Aphrodite
> tended them and fed them with cheese, and sweet honey, and pleasant
> wine; and Hera granted to them, beyond all women,
> beauty and good sense, and chaste Artemis gave them stature,
> and Athene instructed them in glorious handiwork.
> But when bright Aphrodite had gone up to tall Olympos
> to request for these girls the achievement of blossoming marriage,
> from Zeus who rejoices in the thunder . . .
> meanwhile the seizing stormwinds carried away these maidens
> and gave them over into the care of the hateful Furies.
> So I wish that they who have their homes on Olympos
> would make me vanish, or sweet-haired Artemis strike me, so that
> I could meet the Odysseus I long for, even under the hateful
> earth, and not have to please the mind of an inferior
> husband. Yet the evil is endurable, when one . . . sleeps . . .

[37] Cf. Cavafy's "Ithaca" as an interpretation of the adventures along this line.

But now the god has sent the evil dreams thronging upon me.
For on this very night there was one who lay by me, like him
as he was when he went with the army, so that my own heart
was happy. I thought it was no dream, but a waking vision.

(20.61–90)

In this long and complex prayer, Penelope asks for death as a new way of
avoiding remarriage. Though we know little about the myth of the daughters of Pandareos from other sources, clearly the four goddesses (Aphrodite,
Hera, Artemis, and Athene) intended that marriage, not death, culminate
the tale.[38] Moreover, we find no hint of the maidens' reluctance to marry
nor joy at their "rescue." Unincorporated, the *muthos* was a tale not of
DISDAIN, like the myths of Io, Daphne, Cassandra, the Danaids, and
others, but rather of negative COURTSHIP and MARRIAGE—of marriage
interrupted by tragic and premature death.

Penelope reverses the positive and negative in her use of the tale for
her own purposes, which nevertheless retains the language of violent abduction.[39] Instead of a villainous abductor or his agent,[40] Penelope imagines a
beneficent rescuer (gods or Artemis) answering her plea. Furthermore, she
fantasizes that her rescuer will, in a second act of kindness, reunite her, in
death, with her husband. Preferring death to the upcoming remarriage, she
prays not for union but reunion. The language of marriage suits her fantasy:
she will become a bride of sorts. Thus MARRIAGE-AVOIDANCE (for a
widow) becomes BRIDE OF DEATH in Penelope's prayer. She has relin-
quished PATIENCE, with husband returning in the nick of time—despite
assurances by Theoklymenos and the stranger that Odysseus will soon return.

The language describing the readiness for marriage of the daughters of
Pandareos is sensuous and alluring, whereas Penelope casts their alternative
destiny, delivery over to the hateful Furies, in violent, harrowing terms.
Nonetheless, she prays for a similar rescue and death, with a twist: that she
will die only to reunite with Odysseus in the Underworld. As virtual BRIDE
OF DEATH she is comparable to Persephone, but, unlike Persephone, Pene-

---

[38] Cf. Pandora's preparation by the goddesses in Hesiod, *Works and Days* 59–82 in anticipa-
tion of her marriage to Epimetheus.

[39] For the persistence of the language of violent abduction, cf. lines 66, *anelonto thuellai*, and
77, *harpuiai anēreipsanto*, two parts of a ring composition framing the simile. The parallel lines
in the comparant (61–62: *Artemi . . . balous' ek thumon heloio* and 63: *m'anarpaxasa thuella*)
also suggest violence and unwillingness.

For the language of rape, cf. *Hymn to Demeter* 19–20 (*harpaxas d'aekousan . . .
olophuromenēn*) and for the victim's own description of the force-feeding (an analogue of rape)
and the abduction, cf. 413 (*akousan de biēi me prosēnankasse pasasthai*) and 431–32 (*pherōn . . .
poll' aekazomenēn*).

[40] The figure is villainous especially (and perhaps only) when focalized by the virgin; cf.
Persephone's account to her mother of the force-feeding and violent abduction by Hades (see
above, note 39).

lope requests this gloomy outcome. She disdains marrying a live but inferior Suitor. Thus she expands the traditional plot-type by coupling PA-
TIENCE with DISDAIN, and by adding BRIDE OF DEATH.[41] And she has
invented a new pattern, a hybrid of COURTSHIP/MARRIAGE and PA-
TIENCE—a resumption, in death, of her present marriage, a reunion in the
Underworld with her husband. In this hybrid plot, she fuses two otherwise
antithetical types of plot.

The sensuous language describing the virginal maidens and their pending
marriage anticipates the sensuality surrounding Penelope as she moves toward an uncertain future. Whatever happens, this future will be different
from the state of chastity and sexual limbo in which she has lived for twenty
years. Penelope's language suits her fantasy of a reunion with Odysseus in
the Underworld. For her, "blossoming marriage" may turn out to be marriage to a suitor, reunion with an Odysseus who has returned and reclaimed
her, reunion in death with Odysseus, or even union with the stranger.

Penelope wants Artemis to help her avoid not only an unwanted marriage, but betrayal and infidelity as well. Her dilemma, reflected keenly in
the prayer, is the need to be mindful simultaneously of Artemis as goddess
of chastity and Aphrodite as goddess of sexuality: neither should she be
adamantly virginal, nor should she succumb to the wrong union at the
wrong time, nor hold back from Odysseus should he return. The passage
anticipates her identification with Helen in book 23. As she prepares to
remarry, it is easier and emotionally safer to consider Odysseus dead than
about to arrive in Ithaca too late.

The interplay of Artemis and Aphrodite in the character Penelope underscores her complexity. The presence of both goddesses is often felt.[42]
Whether she will turn to Artemis or to Aphrodite is a key question raised
early in the text and sustained until the moment of embrace. Penelope is
herself as uncertain of her divine affinities as are other characters (Telemachos, Odysseus, the Suitors). Even we cannot yet know whether Penelope will remain chaste for Odysseus or not.[43]

A network, then, of passages that can be understood as part of Penelope's plan
to hold out against the criminal-Suitors, also reveals a sensuous Penelope under the influence of Aphrodite as well as Artemis. Ambiguity as to Penelope's
intentions is deliberately sustained for the reader until 23.205: the release for
Penelope in that passage, as her knees give way, is a release (*lusis*) for us as
well; her unchanneled eroticism had felt dangerous to any of us willing to
imagine that she might turn out to be a Helen or even a Klytaimestra.

[41] This is the Peleus/Thetis or Pandora/Epimetheus subtype, wherein divinities adorn the
bride.
[42] Cf. 18.193 and 202 just before Penelope descends to solicit gifts from the Suitors; 19.54
as she comes to her interview with the stranger "looking like Artemis or like golden Aphrodite"; and 20.60–61 and 68–69 as she prays to Artemis.
[43] Artemis oversees Penelope's chastity, I suggest, because Penelope is like a virgin bride.

Curiously, once she is safe and knows she is safe, Penelope turns playful. In a bold move she flagrantly alludes to the possibility of infidelity. This is the famous deceit of the marriage bed. The possibility to which she alludes is one that she barely managed to avoid: the intrusion of some other man into the sanctity of her marriage-bed. Only in the safety of her husband's presence, in the safety of knowing that he is back, can a playful and erotic Penelope tease him on so serious a subject as adultery.

The bold taunt admits to their discourse a theme that Folktale might have handled much more openly and crudely: the chastity test of the wife whose husband has just returned from a long journey.[44] The marriage-bed test, anticipated much earlier in Telemachos' question to Eumaios (16.33–35: "whether my mother endures still in the halls, or whether / some other man has married her, and the bed of Odysseus / lies forlorn of sleepers with spider webs grown upon it"), is at once a husband test and a chastity test, the latter in that by suggesting she was unfaithful—that someone moved their bed—Penelope affirms her fidelity. For Odysseus, rage at the prospect of a faithless Penelope melts into joy at full knowledge that she has waited for him and endured. Via the bed-ruse she reveals to him, on her own initiative and of her own accord, that she has chosen to be his faithful wife.[45]

CONCLUSION: A COMPLEX PENELOPE

In book 24 Agamemnon, lacking Odysseus's subtlety, misses the mark in his assessment of two heroines, Penelope and Klytaimestra. His is a male-centered view: a woman either is or is not faithful. Any suggestion that Penelope encouraged the Suitors would have activated a misogynist condemnation, as Odysseus' characterization of Agamemnon in book 11 makes plain. As readers, we are more privileged with information than was he: the network of passages discussed above indicate a side of Penelope not entirely consonant with the side he celebrates. We are therefore faced with reconciling conflicting evidence about her state of mind. Unlike Agamemnon and Amphimedon, we know that it was she, and not Odysseus, who decided to set the contest when she did. We know she flirted and held on to COURTSHIP and MARRIAGE when Odysseus was urging her (in his interpretation of her dream) to relinquish her attachment to the Suitors. In short, we find her far more prudent about her own security and attentive to her own pleasures than others (both characters and critics) have acknowledged.

Our *periphrōn Pēnelopeia* is the creator of several plots that we can label

---

[44] These are listed under MARRIAGE TESTS (H300–499, esp. H360, 400, 430, and 460) in Stith Thompson's *Motif-Index* (1955). Woodhouse (1930) is particularly interesting in his analyses of such folktale elements, though I find his labels idiosyncratic.

[45] Compare Alcestis' attempt (Euripides, *Alcestis* 280ff.) to explain to Admetos that she chose to die on his behalf despite knowing that she had other options.

from her own female-centered perspective: COURTSHIP and MARRIAGE, DALLIANCE, DISDAIN and BRIDE OF DEATH, and PATIENCE. She dreaded INFIDELITY and wanted to avoid it at all cost. At crucial moments of decision, she showed an awareness of all these plots and, in her decisions, she fulfilled her epithet *periphrōn*, "circumspect," for she took into account her own safety and well-being along with that of her family. Her greatest challenge was recognition of her own desires, and her apologia for Helen illustrates the extent to which she realized, in retrospect, how close to a disastrous decision she had come.

The Refusal of Odysseus

JEAN-PIERRE VERNANT
(translated by Vincent Farenga)

BEGINNING with the opening lines of the *Odyssey*, the nymph Kalypso makes her appearance and takes center stage. It is through her that the poet begins his story: when book 1 opens,[1] Odysseus has been trapped for seven years on the island where this goddess is keeping him, and he has lost all hope of seeing his home again. On Olympus Athena denounces Kalypso before the assembled gods as the one responsible for the sufferings of her protégé. And it is to Kalypso that Zeus dispatches Hermes as a messenger notifying her of his order to let the hero take to sea again and return home. Owing to its position at the outset of the narrative and its recurrence many times in the course of the text,[2] the entire episode—the figure of Kalypso, the goddess's love for a mortal, the long captivity alongside her that she imposes on Odysseus[3]—imparts to the wanderings of the king of Ithaka their true significance. It reveals what is at stake throughout the entire Odyssean adventure: the question whether the hero will return by way of his homeland to the world of mortals.[4]

Then all the others, as many as fled sheer destruction,
were at home now. . . .
This one alone, longing for his wife and his homecoming,
was detained by the queenly nymph Kalypso, bright among goddesses,

---

[1] *Od.*1.11–15. These same lines are repeated in the text at the start of book 5, where they serve, as in book 1, to introduce the assembly of the gods and to realize the decision taken earlier in book 1 to send Hermes to Kalypso as a messenger transmitting the order to release Odysseus. Concerning the episode's duplication and its importance in the poem's narrative chronology, cf. E. Delebecque, *Construction de l'Odyssée* (Paris, 1980), 12–13.

[2] 1.11–87; 4.555–58; 5.13–302; 7.244–66; 8.450–53; 9.29–30; 12.389 and 447–50; 17.140–44; 23.333–37.

[3] Odysseus has stayed seven years with Kalypso, as he himself makes clear when answering a question from Arete, queen of the Phaiakes (7.259–61). This seven-year period, out of a total span we can calculate of eight or nine years' wandering from the end of the Trojan War to the return to Ithaka, indicates the importance of this stay in the circuit of the voyage as a whole.

[4] On this point cf. P. Vidal-Naquet, "Land and Sacrifice in the *Odyssey*: A Study of Religious and Mythical Meanings," in *The Black Hunter: Forms of Thought and Forms of Society in the Greek World*, trans. A. Szegedy-Maszak (Baltimore, 1986), 15–38. [this vol., 33–53]

in her hallowed caverns, desiring that he should be her husband.

(1.11–15; repeated in book 5)

Kalypso's name, taken from *kaluptein*, "to hide," has a transparency that gives away the secret of the powers the goddess incarnates. Deep in her caverns, she is not simply "the hidden one"; she is also, or especially, "the one who hides." But to "hide" Odysseus, as do Thanatos and Eros (Death and Love[5]), Kalypso did not have to abduct him or ravish him. On this point she is different from the divinities she invokes for Hermes as examples to justify her situation, for they satisfied their passionate love for human beings by abducting them into the "beyond," making them suddenly disappear, when alive and well from the face of the earth.[6] In this way Eos "ravished" Tithonos, or Hemera Orion.[7] But on this occasion it is a shipwrecked Odysseus who arrived on his own at the limits of the West at the end of the world. He is stranded here with Kalypso in her rocky lair, this "navel of all the waters,"[8] which is a place beautified with woods, delightful springs, and soft meadows, and which calls to mind the erotic, macabre meadow where the Sirens sing to enchant and undo those who listen.[9]

---

[5] When it takes hold of mortals, death wraps them in a dark cloud, covers over their faces with night, and hoods them in darkness. Eros does not operate differently. In both cases this action of "hiding" is expressed by the verb *amphikalyptein*; for death, cf. *Il.* 5.68 and 16.350; for Eros, *Il.* 3.442.

[6] *Od.* 5.121ff. On this sudden "abduction" by a supernatural power, cf. *Il.* 6.346–47; *Od.* 7.61; and esp. *Homeric Hymn to Aphrodite* 202–38.

[7] In his *Homeric Problems* (68.5) Heraclitus interprets the loves of Hemera and Orion as allegories and underscores the connection between Thanatos and Eros: "When a young man of noble family and great beauty died, his funeral procession at daybreak was euphemistically called an 'abduction by Hemera,'" as though he were not dead at all but had been ravished as the object of erotic passion.

[8] Even though it is situated in the west at the farthest boundary of the world, the island is nevertheless called *omphalos thalassēs*, "navel of the sea" (1.50, repeated in book 5). It is also referred to as *nēsos ōgygiē*, "ogygian island" (1.85), an adjective Hesiod applies to the waters of the Styx, the river of Hades flowing *under* the earth and through black night, down to the bottom of Tartaros (*Theogony* 806). Hesiod locates Atlas, Kalypso's father, in the same subterranean place, "staunchly upholding the wide heaven upon his head and with arms unwearying [he] sustains [it] (*Theogony* 746–48; translation from *Hesiod*, tr. Richmond Lattimore [Ann Arbor, 1959]). Hesiod here goes against the tradition, which places Atlas at the farthest point west. When Homer speaks of the "navel of the sea" in reference to the island where Kalypso resides, he does so in order to invoke immediately the goddess's father, the "malignant Atlas, who has discovered / all the depths of the sea," and who at the same time "sustains the towering / columns which bracket earth and sky and hold them together" (*Od.* 1.50–54). In his role as a cosmic pillar rooted at the deepest point and ascending to heaven through the earth, Atlas can just as easily appear in the Greeks' mythical geography all the way to the west, at the very bottom, or at the navel of the world. These are all ways of saying that he is not *in* the world known to humans. Likewise, the island where Kalypso lives is all the way to the east, ogygian like the Styx, and at the navel of the sea: it has no place in human space but is a figure of the other world.

[9] Soft meadows, *leimōnes malakoi*, where Kalypso dwells: *Od.*5.72; a meadow in bloom,

This island where man and nymph dwell together, cut off from everything and everyone, alone in amorous confrontation and in a solitude made for two, is located in a sort of marginal space as a place apart, far from the gods and far from humans.[10] It is a world located elsewhere: neither that of the ever-youthful immortals (even though Kalypso is a goddess[11]), nor that of human beings subject to old age and death (even though Odysseus is a mortal man), nor that of the dead under the Earth in Hades. Odysseus has disappeared, without leaving a trace, into a sort of no-place where he lives a parenthetical existence.

Like the Sirens, Kalypso charms Odysseus—she can herself sing with a beautiful voice—as she pours forth endless litanies of sweet love: *aiei de malakoisi kai haimulioisi logoisi / thelgei. Thelgei*: she enchants and bewitches him so that he might forget Ithaka, *hopōs Ithakēs epilēsetai*.[12]

For Odysseus, forgetting Ithaka means cutting the ties that still connect him to his life and his own people, and to those loved ones who for their part remain attached to his memory, whether they hope against hope for him to return alive or whether they are ready to erect the funerary *mnēma* for a dead Odysseus. But so long as he remains secluded and hidden with Kalypso, Odysseus' state is neither that of the living nor that of the dead. Although still alive, he is already (and ahead of time) like someone blotted our from human memory. To repeat Telemachus's words at 1.235, he alone of all men has become by will of the gods invisible, *aistos*. He has disappeared "out of sight, out of knowledge," *aistos, apustos*—beyond reach of human eye or ear. If at least, the young boy adds, he died normally, under Troy's walls or in the arms of his comrades-in-misfortune, "all the Achaians would have heaped a grave mound over him / and he would have won great fame, *mega kleos*, for himself and his son hereafter" (1.239-40). But the Harpies have carried him off: the living have nothing more to do with him, as a man belonging nowhere bereft of remembrance, he no longer has fame; vanished, obliterated, he has disappeared without glory, *akleiōs*.[13] For the

---

leimōn anthemoeis, where the Sirens dwell: *Od.*12.159. For the erotic value of *leimōn*, which can refer to the female genitals, cf. André Motte, *Prairies et jardins de la Grèce antique* (Brussels, 1973), 50–56 and 83–87. For its funerary or macabre value, ibid. 250–79. The flowering meadow where the enticing Sirens station themselves is strewn with bones and with human remains whose flesh is decaying (*Od.* 12.45–46).

[10] For the "faraway" nature of the island, cf. *Od.* 5.55; far away from the gods: 5.80 and 100; far away from humans: 5.101–2.

[11] The nymph is on several occasions called *thea* or *theos*, "goddess" (1.14 and 51; 5.78; 7.255; esp. 5.79, where the two *theoi* are the pair Kalypso-Hermes; 5.118, where Kalypso includes herself in the group of goddesses who have fallen in love with a mortal; 5.138, where before yielding she grants that no [other] god can opppose the will of Zeus; 5.192–94, where the pair Kalypso-Odysseus refers to a *god* and a man, *theos* and *anēr*).

[12] *Od.*5.61 and 1.56–57 (repeated in book 5).

[13] *Od.*1.241.

hero whose ideal is to leave behind a *kleos aphthiton*, an "undying glory," could there be anything worse than disappearing this way, *akleiōs*, without glory?[14]

What then does Kalypso's seduction offer Odysseus to make him "forget" Ithaka? First of all, naturally, escape from the challenges of the return, the miseries of seafaring, and all the pains that she as a goddess knows in advance will aflict him before he finally regains his native land.[15] But these are still mere trifles. The nymph has much more to offer him: If he agrees to remain with her, she promises to make him immortal and to spare him forever from old age and death. He will live in her company as a god, immortal, in the permanent bloom of youth, for never to die and never to know the decrepitude of old age are what one stands to gain from love shared with the goddess.[16] But there is a price to pay in Kalypso's bed for this escape beyond the borders that mark the universal human condition. Sharing divine immortality in the nymph's arms would constitute for Odysseus a renunciation of his career as an epic hero. Were he no longer to figure as a model of endurance in a text that, like the *Odyssey*, sang his trials, he would have to allow his memory to be erased in the minds of humans and his posthumous fame to be taken from him; and though still alive, he would have to allow himself to sink into the depths of oblivion. Ultimately, he would have to accept an obscure, anonymous immortality—as anonymous as the death of those humans who could not take on a heroic fate and form in Hades the indistinct mass of the "nameless," the *nōnumnoi*.[17]

The Kalypso episode presents, for the first time in our literary tradition, what might be called the heroic refusal of immortality. For the Greeks of the archaic period, Odysseus could not really claim as a personal achievement this eternal afterlife shared with Kalypso, since no one on earth would know of it, nor would anyone remember the name of the hero from Ithaka to celebrate it. Unlike us, Homer's Greeks could not attribute importance to the absence of death—in their eyes an absurd hope for mortals—but in a tradition based on memory, they would value the unbounded endurance among the living of a glory acquired in life, at the cost of life, throughout an existence where life and death cannot be separated.

On the shore of this isle where immortality hangs on a single word, Odysseus sits on a rock, staring at the sea, bemoaning and sobbing his lot all day long. He is melting, liquifying, into tears. His *aiōn*, or "life force,"

---

[14] Cf. J.-P. Vernant, "La Belle Mort et le cadavre outragé," in *La Mort, les morts dans les sociétés anciennes*, ed. G. Gnoli and J.-P. Vernant (Cambridge and Paris, 1982); 45–76.

[15] *Od.* 5.205ff.

[16] *Od.* 5.136; 209; 7.257; 8.453; 23.336.

[17] Hesiod, *Works and Days* 154. In the context of archaic Greek culture, where the category of the individual is very different from the "ego" of today, only the posthumous glory of death can be called "personal." The immortality of an "invisible and unknown" being remains outside of what for the Greeks constitutes a subject's individuality—i.e., essentially his renown; cf. J.-P. Vernant, "La Belle Mort" (above, note 14), 12 and 53.

saps out of him continuously (*kateibeto aiōn*) in *pothos*, or "sorrowful regret," for his mortal life. Likewise, at the other end of the world, Penelope is for her part consuming her *aiōn* in tears of regret for the vanished Odysseus.[18] She weeps for a living man who is perhaps now dead; he, on an isle of immortality that cuts him off from life as though he were dead, weeps for his existence in life as a creature destined to die.

Gripped by nostalgia for the fleeting, ephemeral world to which he belongs, our hero no longer relishes the charms of the nymph.[19] If he comes at night to sleep with her, it is because he must. He joins her in bed—she with desire, he without.[20]

It is for these reasons, then, that Odysseus rejects this immortality granted by a woman's favor; by removing him from what constitutes his life, it leads him at last to find death desirable. Gone is *erōs*, gone is *himeros*, gone is love or desire for the nymph with the lovely hair. Now, *thanein himeiretai*, "he longs to die" (1.59).

Nostos, his return; *gynē*, Penelope, his wife; Ithaka, his homeland, son, aging father, faithful companions; and then *thanein*, to die. These are all those things toward which Odysseus' power to love, his nostalgic desire, and his *pothos* yearn because he has wearied of Kalypso and has refused a non-death that is also a non-life. His is a yearning for life, precarious and mortal; for trials; for wanderings renewed time and again without end; and for a fate of heroic endurance which he must accept in order to become himself, Odysseus. For this is Odysseus of Ithaka, whose name the text of the *Odyssey* still sings today as it recounts his returns and celebrates his undying glory. But of this man the poet would not have had a word to say— and we not a word to hear—had he remained far from his own people, immortal, and "hidden" with Kalypso.[21]

---

[18] Odysseus' tears: *Od.* 1.55; 5.82–83, 151–53, and 160–61; Penelope's tears: 19.204–9; 262–65.

[19] *Od.* 5.153: Odysseus' vitality is drained out in tears "since the nymph was no longer pleasing to him," *epei ouketi hēndane nymphē*.

[20] At night Odysseus goes back to Kalypso of necessity, *anankē*; against his wishes because she wishes it: 5.154–55.

[21] It is proverbial that, once an exploit has been accomplished, it must not remain hidden (*kalypsai*) in silence. What is needed is the divine melody of praise poetry (Pindar, *Nemean* 9.6–7).

The Song of the Sirens

PIETRO PUCCI

Come this way, honored Odysseus, great glory of the Achaians,
and stay your ship, so that you can listen here to our singing;
for no one else has ever sailed past this place in his black ship
until he has listened to the honey-sweet voice that issues
from our lips; then goes on, well pleased, knowing more than ever
he did; for we know everything that the Argives and Trojans
did and suffered in wide Troy through the gods' despite.
Over all the generous earth we know everything that happens.

(*Od.* 12.184–91)

THE SIRENS invite Odysseus to stop his ship and to listen to their voice so that he may enjoy their song and return wiser. For they know the god-sent toils the Argives and the Trojans suffered in war and they know each time whatever has happened in the world (*Od.* 12.184–91).

The most remarkable feature of this text is that its diction "reproduces"—so to speak—the diction of the *Iliad* in such a way that it should be recognized as different from that of the *Odyssey*. The first noun-epithet that the Sirens address to Odysseus (184),

honored Odysseus, great glory of the Achaians

(*poluain' Oduseu, mega kudos Achaiōn*)

is found only here in the *Odyssey*, while it occurs twice in the *Iliad* in passages that narrate important deeds of Odysseus: the Embassy (9.673) and the Doloneia (10.544). It is indeed customary to consider both these parts as late, but recent critics have forcefully argued that often what is labeled as late or interpolated contains on the contrary the key for interpreting "older" passages.[1] Even the first part of the whole noun-epithet phrase, *poluain' Oduseu*, occurs only in the *Iliad* and in a reversed order, in a passage in which Odysseus is momentarily the center of the action (11.430). The

This paper is part of a larger study on the poetics of the two epics, the *Iliad* and the *Odyssey*, on which I am currently working. I wish to thank Gregory Nagy for his friendly discussion on some points of my argument. I have read a first draft of this paper at Johns Hopkins, Stanford, and USC, where I reaped interesting contributions from the discussions with colleagues and students.

[1] See the whole argument in G. Nagy's *The Best of the Achaeans* (Baltimore, 1979).

compound adjective *poluainos* is a fixed, exclusive epithet for Odysseus, and characterizes him as the one who uses stories for his success and survival.[2] Yet, oddly enough, this epithet appears only here in the *Odyssey*, while in the *Iliad* it occurs on three important occasions for the hero. The Sirens' purpose in choosing this epithet cannot leave any doubt: they identify Odysseus as the warrior at Troy rather than the hero of the *Odyssey*. They call him also *mega kudos Achaiōn* ("great glory of the Achaians") which, though not exclusively an epithet for Odysseus, is never used in the *Odyssey* to refer to Odysseus except in this passage. The Sirens make their purpose clearer as they continue to speak. In line 187,

> until he has listened to the honey-sweet voice that issues from our lips

> *prin g' hēmeōn meligērun apo stomatōn op' akousai*

two remarkable features attract our attention. First the traditional phrase, *op' akousai*, occurs in the *Odyssey* only to indicate listening to the Sirens' voice (*Od.* 12.52, 160, 185, 187), while in the *Iliad* it refers to the voices of different people (gods, 7.53; Agamemnon, 11.137; and Achilles, 21.98). As concerns the digamma of *opa*, only in *Od.* 12.52 and 160 among the examples quoted above, is it metrically guaranteed.

Coming to the second feature, we note the extraordinary precision of the expression *apo stomatōn* (from our lips), for *stoma* (literally, "mouth") in Homer is rarely connected with the production of the voice, *glōssa* (tongue) being used to denote the source of the voice (see, for instance, *Il.* 1.249: *apo glōssēs . . . rheen audē*, "from his tongue . . . flowed the sound"). Yet *stoma* is connected with the voice four times: three times in the *Iliad* and only once in the *Odyssey*, in the song of the Sirens. The analysis of the Iliadic passages is rewarding, for in *Il.* 2.489, *stoma* is used by the poet to indicate his own mouth as producing the song, while in *Il.* 2.250 and 14.91, this word is used by Odysseus. The Sirens, then, while inviting Odysseus to listen to their song, pick a usage that in the *Iliad* characterizes only the poet's and Odysseus' diction.

Line 188 offers surprising new evidence that the diction of the Sirens has been poetically edited in order to show its Iliadic marks that characterize Odysseus as one of the important heroes of that poem. For the phrase of line 188, *kai pleiona eidōs* (knowing more than ever) is a *hapax* in the *Odyssey* (and yet what appeal could be more alluring for the Odysseus of the *Odyssey* than that of "knowing more"?), while the same phrase is repeated four

---

[2]On the meaning of *poluainos* "having many *ainoi* (fables)," see K. Meuli, "Herkunft und Wesen des Fabel," *Schweizerische Gesellschaft für Volkskunde* 50 (1954), 65–88 = his *Gesammelte Schriften* (Basel, 1975), vol. 2, 731–56, who translates by "fabelreich." In note 2 (742–43), Meuli accounts for the two possible meanings of the word, "storyteller" and "object of many praises," on which modern scholars are still disagreeing, and he makes the important point that the epithet implies neither "Sagenkundig" nor "Causeur": Odysseus' *ainoi* are means for fighting and rescue, just like his *mēchanē*. On *ainos* and its connection in Homer with gifts, see P. Pucci, *Hesiod and the Language of Poetry* (Baltimore, 1977), 76n. 3.

times in the *Iliad*. The analysis of the Iliadic passages is most rewarding. This phrase (*kai pleiona oida, ēdē,* etc.)—which shows respect for the digamma—is used by the poet to single out Zeus as stronger and wiser than Poseidon (*Il.* 13.355), and later it is used by Poseidon himself to exhibit the grounds of his superiority over Apollo (21.440). In both cases the phrase is part of a larger expression that says "I" or "he" was born first and know(s) more:

$$\ldots proteros \quad {genomai \atop genomēn} \quad kai\ pleiona \quad {ēdē \atop oida}$$

Now in *Il.* 19.219, when Odysseus begins to advise Achilles, he recognizes Achilles' military superiority, but he asserts that he surpasses Achilles in counsel, since "I was born first and know more":

proteros genomēn kai pleiona oida.

The Sirens know their hero well: they pick up this bold expression used by Odysseus to emphasize that he is superior to Achilles in wisdom just as Zeus is superior to Poseidon and Poseidon to Apollo.[3]

Line 188 is also crucial to the Sirens' message, for they utter two promises of great significance in this context. First they promise joy to their listener, and then they specify that he will return home. As we know, Circe had warned Odysseus that the Sirens' listener fails to return home, but the Sirens deny that claim. However, I shall comment on this point later.

Lines 189–190 are also most surprising, because the obvious Odyssean color exposes more forcefully the Iliadic mark, once it is perceived. The phrase

> everything that the Argives and Trojans
> did and suffered in wide Troy through the gods' despite.

hos' eni Troiēi eureiēi
Argeioi Trōes te theōn iotēti mogēsan,

at first looks typically Odyssean, since the expression *theōn iotēti mogēsan* (they did and suffered . . . through the gods' despite) at the end of the line occurs exclusively in the *Odyssey*: 7.214 and 17.119 (= 12.190). But this impression must be corrected by noting that here the Sirens use the word *iotēti* in accordance with the exclusive usage or grammar of the *Iliad*. It has been noticed by P. Krarup, ("Verwendung von Abstrakta in den direkten Reden bei Homer," *Classica et Medievalia* 10 (1948), 1–17, in particular p. 12) that this word appears exclusively in dialogue both in the *Iliad* and in the *Odyssey*; but no one has noticed that, in the *Iliad*, only gods use that

---

[3] The last Iliadic example of the expression *kai pleiona oida* occurs in *Il.* 23.312: it is somehow different from the other examples we have reviewed, for it is used negatively: *oude,* with the plural *isasi,* and, therefore, also in a different place in the line. Finally, it concerns the superiority of horse racers.

expression (5.874; 15.41; 18.396; 19.9) while in the *Odyssey* (where the word occurs seven times) only mortals use it with the single exception of the Sirens, who, therefore, follow the grammar of the *Iliad*.

Even the common phrase "over all the generous earth" (*epi chthoni poulu-boteirēi*), with which the Sirens close their song, is Iliadic: six times in the *Iliad* and only here in the *Odyssey*! One should nevertheless add that a slight modification of that phrase, *poti chthoni pouluboteirēi*, occurs in *Od.* 8.378 and that the simple dative is found four more times in the *Iliad*.

So far I have analyzed only large phrases, formulaic expressions—the dictional material, so to speak, of which the Homeric mosaic is composed. But it is possible to argue that the Sirens obey the grammar of the *Iliad*, even in the minutiae: *nōiterēn* (our) in line 185 is a *hapax* in the *Odyssey*, though it is a *hapax* in the *Iliad* too (15.39);[4] *ou gar pō* (for never yet) in the opening of line 186 is essentially Iliadic, for in that poem these words open the line six times out of seven occurrences, while in the *Odyssey* the same words most often occupy the middle part of the line.[5] There is, finally, not one line in the Sirens' utterance that does not contain conspicuous formulae or expressions that are, for us, exclusively or almost exclusively Iliadic.

The Sirens' conspicuous use of Iliadic traditional phrases can hardly be an accident; on the contrary it forces the listener to the realization that they mean to define Odysseus as the Odysseus of the *Iliad*. A certain degree of uniqueness in the composition of the text and the cumulative evidence I have gathered discourage the sort of explanation that would justify the Iliadic color of the text on mechanical grounds. It would be possible to argue, for instance, that line 184,

Come this way, honored Odysseus, great glory of the Achaians

deur' ag' iōn, poluain' Oduseu, mega kudos Achaiōn,

owes its composition to the fact that the only vocative formula that the poet has at hand to cover the part of the line after *deur' ag' iōn* (come this way) is precisely this one; but to argue in this way would imply that the poet chooses a traditional, fixed beginning, *deur' ag' iōn*, and then attaches to it the only possible noun-epithet. But *deur' ag' iōn* itself is not traditional in our epic unless in the limited forms of *deur' ithi* or *deur' itō* (come this way) that may begin the line. It is therefore created uniquely for this occasion. It looks, then, as if the only fixed part of the line is the noun-epithet and that therefore, even based on the Parryan principle of economy, this is the part

---

[4] E. Risch, *Wortbildung der homerishe Sprache*[2] (Berlin, New York, 1974), 346, shows the formation of *nōiteros* from the dual *nōi*.

[5] More precisely, *ou gar pō* occurs five times in the *Odyssey* and seven in the *Iliad*. Out of seven Iliadic examples, only once (4.331) does *ou gar pō* occur in the second colon of the verse, whereas out of the five Odyssean examples, only in 12.186 and 19.365 does the expression occur at the beginning of the verse.

on behalf of which the first part of the line has been composed.[6] In other terms, given the uniqueness of the beginning of this line, and of the next one, the poet could have arranged the expressions in many different ways had he wanted the Sirens to address Odysseus by a different noun-epithet phrase.

This argument indicates that the poet used a certain degree of compositional freedom in order to choose the noun-epithet phrase and confirms therefore the results of the cumulative evidence. No doubts should remain about the intention of the passage: its diction points insistently at Iliadic phrases, selecting them in such a way that, while they are common and repeated in the *Iliad*, they are *hapax legomena* in the *Odyssey*. This intention is consonant with a series of facts and implications that we are now able to look at in their full signficance. First of all, the Iliadic color of the Sirens' portrayal of Odysseus is consistent with their claim to be able to sing the deeds of the Trojan war. The toils Odysseus suffered at Troy—and that the Sirens are ready to sing about—must be identified with the themes of that epic tradition that for us is represented by the *Iliad*. The Sirens' stylistic and formulaic appropriation of that tradition proves that the epic songs about the Trojan war were already fixed in closed-up, immutable forms or compositions, namely, in what we call "texts." For, without the existence of these fixed compositions, the sort of allusions we have discovered would be unthinkable. Of all those texts we possess only the *Iliad*, and the argument that the *Iliad* must have already been a fixed text is therefore also applicable in this case. We may speculate whether the typical Iliadic features of the Sirens' song are common characteristics of the whole tradition of which the *Iliad* is part; it remains, however, clear and certain that the Sirens' song alludes also to the *Iliad*, to the text of the *Iliad*. The deeds that the Sirens are ready to sing are also part of the Iliadic themes.[7]

It is therefore correct to say that Odysseus can be appealed to as a "literary" character of the *Iliad* and that Odysseus is indeed seduced by this idea

[6]Notice also that the beginning of the next line (186), *nēa katastēson,* is not traditional: in fact it is a *hapax* and confirms the large freedom of composition in these two lines of the Sirens' song. Had the poet wanted the Sirens to address Odysseus with an Odyssean noun-epithet-phrase, he had many choices.

[7]In accordance with Nagy's view, the tradition may have already been fixed into two (or more) "genres," each of them endowed with specific scenes and therefore with specific language and formulae. A certain vagueness of the term *tradition*, however, and its affiliation with the romantic aesthetic convince me to use the word *text* instead of tradition. Obviously I do not mean by *text* the "original creation" by one or several authors, the expression and mirror of his (or their) intentions, the place of a fixed and closed-up meaning whose truth is deciphered by the most careful reading uncovered from under the veneer of historical dust and corruption.

All these philological cares are indeed necessary, but the text will not give what it has not. For the text emerges through the passivity and dissemination of language—in this case, of the epic tradition: activity, meaning, authorial force and passivity, dissemination of meaning and of the author's intentions coexist in the mode of a specific "repetition" that "creates" our poems and that embodies in its own way the difference and the deferral of language.

and longs to listen to this song that presents him as an important character. The Sirens expose Odysseus' awareness of being such a character and consequently their invitation to listen to their song means in reality an urging— to put it bluntly—to stop the ship, to disembark from the ship that takes him on the Odyssean wanderings, and to remain with them; in other words, they invite him to change poet and poem, and to return to be the character of the *Iliad*. The poet of the *Odyssey* ironically exposes Odysseus' readiness to leave the wandering of the *Odyssey* in favor of the splendid toils of the *Iliad*. But he preempts Odysseus' longing by making sure, with the help of Circe, that Odysseus will not be able to stop the ship, and by warning him (and explaining to us) that this longing means death. The text of the *Odyssey* has already presented to us various examples of the possible truth of this. Odysseus asks the bard Demodocus to sing about Odysseus' last glorious deed and the final assault against Troy (*Od.* 8.499ff.) and in response Odysseus weeps and cries just as one of the captive women whose husband the conquering soldiers have killed (*Od.* 8.521ff.). The "reverse simile" indicates a specific intention in the Odyssean text, namely to show that the song about glory or glorious deeds (*kleos* and *klea*) elicits an irresistible cry, a sort of funereal weeping rather than boasting and confidence. Odysseus, the sacker of Troy, weeps just like one of the victims of his victorious action.[8] Menelaos' inability to turn his mind from the past proves the same point. A sort of self-destructive nostalgia compels these old heroes to dwell in the memory of their splendid and grievous past. The Sirens with their specific Iliadic diction appeal both to Odysseus' literary complacency and to his nostalgia for his glorious deeds: that is why the Sirens' song would bring Odysseus out of the *Odyssey* to rot on their island.

But the poet of the *Odyssey* watches over his Odysseus and does not allow him to leave the ship, smart though he is. He even arranges for Odysseus to listen to the Sirens' song, but he has doctored the hero (and us) to such an extent that neither he nor we can listen to it impartially. An extraordinary dialogue between the poet of the *Odyssey* and that of the *Iliad* takes place in this scene. The Sirens look like Muses and speak with the diction of the *Iliad*: the implication is obviously that the poet of the *Odyssey* considers the divine inspirers of the *Iliad* to possess the attributes of the Sirens rather than the attributes generally granted to the Muses. The poet of the *Odyssey* presses the point that the inspirers of the *Iliad* are turned toward an irretrievable and remote *kleos* and grief, whose song indeed fascinates the listeners; yet the memory of that *kleos* and grief spells only death. In this way,

---

[8] On the "reverse similes," see H. Foley, "'Reverse Similes' and Sex Roles in the *Odyssey*," *Arethusa* 11 (1978), 7ff. (with bibliography). On the particular reverse simile we are commenting on, see C. Diano, "La poetica dei Feaci," *Belfagor* 18 (1963), 403ff. = *Saggezza e Poetiche degli Antichi* (Venezia, 1968), 185ff., who interprets Odysseus' crying as moved by pity (206): "Certo è il poeta che piange su Troia, e quella Ulisse, perchè il cuore del poeta è il cuore stesso di Ulisse." The analysis that follows reveals a depth in Diano's thought that is not made apparent in this short quotation and cannot be reproduced without long argument.

by incorporating their Iliadic song into the poem, the *Odyssey* appropriates the *Iliad* with a gesture of disavowal.

We do not need to refer to the brilliant assumptions and arguments formulated by E. Buschor in his book *Die Musen des Jenseits* (Munich, 1944) to realize that in their song to Odysseus, the Sirens ascribe to themselves the attributes of Muses. The Sirens define themselves as melodious singers, as bestowers of pleasurable song, and as being omniscient. These traits indeed identify the Muses as we know them from the epic texts and in particular from *Iliad* 2.484ff.; *Odyssey* 8.63, 73ff., 24.60ff.; Hesiod, *Theogony* 97ff.; etc. The Sirens emphasize their omniscient knowledge and, to some extent, rightly so, for they recognize Odysseus *at sight*, whereas other goddesses or divine beings, such as Circe and Polyphemus, for instance, fail to do so. The Sirens must really know what happened in Troy, if they know personally and recognize at sight who is who. They therefore have the same power of presence as do the Muses or Apollo, who inspire Demodocus when he sings the truth about Troy (*Od.* 8.488–91):

> Either the Muse, daughter of Zeus, taught you, or Apollo
> taught you, for you sing the doom of the Achaeans so accurately
> and what the Achaeans did and suffered and what they endured,
> as though either yourself were present there or you heard it from another.[9]

Furthermore the Sirens "know each time all things that (*idmen d' hossa*) have happened on the bountiful earth," or "things that shall happen on the bountiful earth."[10] Their omnniscience equates the Sirens with the Muses of *Il.* 2.484ff., who know all things (*panta*) since they are ever present:

> For you, who are goddesses, are there, and you know all things
>
> *humeis gar theai este pareste te iste te panta.*

[9] Notice, however, that the Sirens do not speak of *kleos* or *klea* but use the verb *mogeō* (*panth' hos . . . mogēsan* ["what they endured"]). One might be tempted to give relevance to the exclusion of *kleos*, but we must remember that in the *Iliad* itself *kleos* can be a very ambivalent notion (see for instance *Il.* 2.486). On *kleos* in the Odyssey, see C. Segal, "*Kleos* and Its Ironies in the *Odyssey*" (*L'Antiquite classique* 52 (1983), 22–47) [this volume, pp. 201–21].

The interpretation that I am suggesting would help to explain that strange epithet that Odysseus uses in *Od.* 23.326 to describe the Sirens: *ēd' hōs Seirēnōn hadinaōn phthongon akousen. Hadinos*, which has baffled interpreters, is a common epithet for funeral lamentations in the *Iliad*: *hadinou . . . gooio* (*Il.* 22.430; 18.366, etc.), and see *Od.* 4.721, 24.317, etc. As singers of deeds that spell death, the epithet is appropriate to the Sirens.

[10] The interpretation of the aorist subjunctive *genētai* in line 191 is not certain. Ameis-Hentze takes it to be an *iterative* subjunctive and translates "alles was jedesmal geschieht." But C. J. Ruijgh, *Autour de "te" épique* (Leiden, 1971), 561n.10, remarks that it could represent a permanent fact with a distributive-iterative subjunctive with a futural meaning, "that which shall happen." The distributive-iterative subjunctive is rare with these relatives: one case with *hossa* in *Il.* 3.66 (with *ken*), one case with *hoion* in *Od.* 18.137.

The repetition of the verb *idmen* at the beginning of the two lines, 189 and 191, reminds us of the repeated *idmen* that the Muses utter in Hesiod, *Theogony* 27 and 28.

As concerns the pleasure, the *terpnos* that the Sirens bestow—a fixed element in the epic description of the song, or of the Muses—the Sirens are explicit:

> He shall return home, when he has gotten his pleasure and with greater knowledge

> *all' ho ge terpsamenos neitai kai pleiona eidōs.*

Finally they are outspoken about the beauty of their song: they term their voice *meligērun*, "sweetly singing," a *hapax* in the *Iliad*, *Odyssey*, and all of Hesiod. The word is picked up by *Hymn to Apollo* 519 to define the *aoidē*, the song that the Muse inspires.[11]

All these connotations prove that the Sirens present themselves to Odysseus as melodious, sweet singers who possess the same attributes (power of memory, omniscience, and pleasure) that the epic Muses possess. But, as I have already suggested, the Sirens' subjective view of themselves is framed by the ruse of the poet. For, at the time in which we listen to their song, Odysseus has already been warned by Circe about the danger that the Sirens present for him (*Od.* 12.158–64). A synchronic analysis of these three scenes (to which one should add the quick but revealing mention in *Od.* 23. 326) would be rewarding, but it is too long to be presented here.[12]

By an amusing stroke the poet has Circe interpreting and framing the Sirens for Odysseus and for us. Circe, the sensual magician, who possesses the same destructive power of *thelgein* (*Od.* 10.213, 291, 318, 326) that she attributes to the Sirens, emerges as a savior of Odysseus against powers who are so similar to herself. The irony, of course, is manifold: not the least because the Sirens are so unaware of the plot that frames and preempts their

---

[11] *Meligērus* is composed of *meli*, "honey," and the theme of *gērusasthai* ("to voice") a word of high tone, used by the Muses themselves in Hesiod, *Theogony* 28 where they say:

idmen d' eut' ethelōmen alēthea gērusasthai.

[12] This synchronic analysis should take into account both the personality of the narrators and the strategy of the narrative. For we cannot neglect the fact that the song of the Sirens is described and termed a ruinous "enchantment" by three masters of incantation and magic: first Circe, the magician, expert in spells that transform men into pigs; second, Odysseus, who here casts his spells on the Phaeacians (*Od.* 11.334 = 13.2) with his stories; and third, the poet of the *Odyssey*, who knows that the poet always enchants (*Od.* 1.337, 17.518–21).

The narrative strategy is complex: in the three narratives in which the Sirens are described (*Od.* 12.39ff., 158ff., 181ff.), some details are new and some are left aside, probably in order to enhance the mystery of the Sirens and to make the narrative and the narrator, Odysseus, more appealing. Some of these changes are easy to understand. It is reasonable that Odysseus fails to describe the huge pile of bones as he sees the Sirens on their meadow. The mention of bones and death would have detracted from the charm Odysseus felt and wanted to describe. Yet the question remains, Did a huge pile of bones in fact lie around the Sirens?

success. These omniscient singers fail to see what happens before their eyes, for it escapes them that Odysseus is bound fast to the ship's mast and they do not know that his companions hear neither him nor their song. The Sirens, who claim to know each time everything that has happened on the surface of this world, show a pathetic blindness to what is present and so visible.

At any rate Circe has already characterized the Sirens' pleasing song as a powerful incantation that creates confusion and paralyzes the will (*thelgein*): no one, she says, returns home from their island, and a huge heap of bones proves her claim.[13] Yet the Sirens themselves assert that their listener will return home, and no mention of bones occurs when Odysseus sees their meadow. Who is right? We, of course, will never know.

If the Sirens, however, are really the polemical embodiment of what for the poet of the *Odyssey* is wrong in the *Iliad*, then we know the reason for this ruse and irony. The Sirens must sound like Muses, inspirers of the *Iliad*, in order to be truthful singers of Odysseus' past toils: therefore they establish the genuine identity of the Odyssean hero with the *Iliad* by enhancing his glorious literary pedigree: but since Odysseus must not abandon the ship that the singer of the *Odyssey* leads through his poetic wanderings, then the Sirens must be made to appear destructive and a little bit pathetic in that their innocence is so adroitly baffled by the poet of the *Odyssey*.

Finally the Sirens prove to be blind to what occurs before their eyes: these singers that have the same knowledge as the Muses of the *Iliad* are really turned to the past, live in a spatial and temporal remoteness that is frightening since their musean memory becomes forgetfulness of the present and spells only grief, pity, and death. Against this Iliadic song, the *Odyssey* asserts a memory that fulfills the present, grants successful knowledge, and ensures earthly, though controlled, pleasures.

---

[13] As concerns the etymology of Sirens (*Seirēnes*) there is no agreement among scholars. Chantraine, *Dictionnaire étymologique de la langue grecque* (Paris, 1968–80), 993–94, with his characteristic self-restraint refers to various hypotheses without being convinced by any one. Within Greek itself the word *Seirēn* has been connected with *seira*, "rope": in this case the *Seirēnes* would be those who "tie up"; or with *seirios* the Dog Star, and the Sirens would be daimons of the South and of the sea stillness (K. Latte, *Kleine Schriften* [Munich, 1968], 106–21). W. Brandenstein (*Kratylos* 6 [1961], p. 169), V. Pisani (*Rheinisches Museum* 100 [1957], 391 and *Paideia* 23 [1968], 377), and M. Durante (*Sulla preistoria della tradizione poetica greca*, vol. 1 [Rome, 1971], 158) opt for a Thracian origin of the word: *Zeirēnē*, as already Hesychius testifies, means "Aphrodite" in Macedonian and can be connected with Greek *chairō*. The Sirens therefore would be the "desiring" ones.

Both Chantraine and Frisk are silent on the possibility that *Seirēn* may be connected with semitic *Sir*, "song," on which see K. Maròt, *Die Anfänge der griechischen Literatur* (Budapest, 1960) and the remarks of G. K. Gresseth, "The Homeric Sirens," *Transactions of the American Philological Association* 101 (1970), 205 and note 5.

Kleos and Its Ironies in the *Odyssey*

CHARLES SEGAL

For Gabriel Germain, *in memoriam*

I

HEROIC GLORY, *kleos*, occupies a central place not only in Greek epic, but in the entire Indo-European epic tradition.[1] In the *Iliad* a warrior's *kleos* is more important than life itself, as Achilles' ultimate choice makes clear. In a shame-culture, like that of the society depicted in Homer, where esteem depends on how one is viewed and talked of by one's peers, *kleos* is fundamental as a measure of one's value to others and to oneself.[2] Both of the Homeric poems, however, while based on this value sytem, also comment on it and even explore its limits. Achilles does this explicitly in *Iliad* 9.[3] The *Odyssey*, too, rather more indirectly, also questions heroic values and the concept of *kleos* which lies at the center. The complexities and ironies in the *Odyssey*'s view of *kleos* form the subject of this essay.

The *Odyssey* is remarkable for its self-consciousness about the social function of heroic poetry, the contexts in which such poetry is performed, and the rapport between the bard and his hearers.[4] On three occasions situations

---

[1] See R. Schmitt, *Dichtung und Dichtersprache in indogermanischer Zeit* (Wiesbaden, 1967), 61–102; Schmitt, ed., *Indogermanisch Dichtersprache* (*Wege der Forschung*, 165 [Darmstadt, 1968]), 337–39; M. Durante, "La terminologia relativa alla creazione poetica," in *Rendiconti dell' Accademia Nazionale dei Lincei* 15 (1960), 244–49 (= Schmitt, 1968, 283–90, in German translation); A. Pagliaro, "Aedi e rapsodi," in *Saggi di critica semantica*[2] (Messina-Florence, 1961), 11–13; E. Benveniste, *Le Vocabulaire des institutions indo-européennes* (Paris, 1969), vol 2, 58f.; Zs. Ritoók, "Stages in the Development of Greek Epic", in *Acta Antiqua Academiae Scientiarum Hungaricae* 23 (1975), 137; G. Nagy, *Comparative Studies in Greek and Indic Meter* (Cambridge, Mass., 1974), 229–61, and *The Best of the Achaeans* (Baltimore, 1979) chaps. 1 and 6. The motif of *kleos* also plays a role in the Gilgamesh epic: see Tablet IV.vi.29–41 (Gilgamesh's speech to Enkidu before the attack on Humbaba) in J. B. Pritchard, ed., *Ancient Near Eastern Texts Relating to the Old Testament*[2] (Princeton, 1955), 82.

[2] See E. R. Dodds, *The Greeks and the Irrational* (Berkeley and Los Angeles, 1951), 17f.; J. Russo and B. Simon, "Homeric Psychology and the Oral Epic Tradition," *Journal of the History of Ideas* 29 (1968), 483–98, esp. 487f.; M. I. Finley, *The World of Odysseus* (rev. ed. New York, 1965), 125ff.

[3] See *Iliad* 9.318ff.; C. Whitman, *Homer and the Heroic Tradition* (Cambridge, Mass., 1958), 188ff.

[4] See H. Fränkel, *Dichtung und Philosophie des frühen Griechentums*[2] (Munich, 1962), 8ff.; W.

of bardic recitation are described in detail: the song of Phemius in book 1, the songs of Demodocus in book 8, and the *apologoi* recited by Odysseus himself, especially in book 11. When he introduces the disguised Odysseus into the the palace, Eumaeus also compares his storytelling skill to that of a bard (17.518–21). These passages help relate the values of heroic *kleos* directly to the bardic tradition that keeps it alive: they show that tradition operating before our eyes (and in our ears) in the songs about great deeds of the past that poets sing and people "hear" from generation to generation.

In the first two of these situations, the songs of Phemius and Demodocus, a curious reversal takes place: instead of the *terpsis*, the joy or delight that song should bring,[5] these songs bring grief, pain, and tears (1.336–52; 8.62ff.; 11.333–69). When Odysseus tells his tale, moreover, he is compared explicitly to a bard by King Alcinoos (11.368). Shortly before, the effects of his song were remarked in third-person narrative: he held everyone in silence, just like Phemius in book 1 (11.333 = 1.339). His song, like Phemius', casts a spell or enchantment (*kēlēthmos*, 11.334: cf. *thelktēria*, 1.337).[6] Alcinoos compliments him not only on his skill in general (*epistamenos*, 11.368), but also specifically on the beauty of his verbal expression as well as on the wisdom or good sense of its contents (11. 367: "You have a grace upon your words, and there is sound sense within them").[7] Now, a hero or bard may sing of the "glorious deeds of men," the *klea andrōn*, as Achilles does in *Iliad* 9 or Demodocus in *Od.* 8.73.[8] But what elicits Alcinoos' praise here (as more naturally Arete's in 11.336–41) is a tale about women. This interruption of Odysseus' narrative, the only one that occurs, follows immediately on the "Catalogue of Heroines."

Marg, *Homer über die Dichtung: Der Schild des Achilleus*[2] (Münster, 1971), 11ff.; W. Schadewaldt, "Die Gestalt des homerischen Sängers" (1943), in *Von Homers Welt und Werk*[3] (Stuttgart, 1959), 54–86; G. Germain, *Genèse de l'Odyssée* (Paris, 1954), 583ff.

[5] For the importance of *terpsis* in Homeric song, see Schadewaldt (above, note 4), 83f.; G. Lanata, *Poetica Pre-Platonica, testimonianze e frammenti* (Florence, 1963), 8f. with the references there cited. See also below, note 34. Phemius, the bard of Ithaca, has the patronymic Terpiades, 22.330, and see W. B. Stanford, ed., *The Odyssey of Homer*[2] (London, 1961, 1965), on 22.330–32. Parallel to Odysseus's weeping on Scheria is Telemachus's weeping at Sparta, 4.113–16. Menelaus's tales are not bardic song, but the motif of weeping at a postprandial entertainment is a thematic link between the Telemacheia and Odysseus' *nostos*.

[6] On the importance of poetry's "spell" in Homer, see Lanata (above, note 5), 16f., with the references there cited. Circe's combination of song, magical spells, and love also brings together the "magic" of poetry and the seductive magic of love's power, with a suggestion of the danger inherent in both; see C. Segal, "Eros and Incantation: Sappho and Oral Poetry," in *Arethusa* 7 (1974), 142–44.

[7] For the theme of Odysseus as a bard, see K. Rüter, *Odysseeinterpretationen* [ed. K. Matthiessen, *Hypomnemata* 19 (Göttingen, 1969)], 237f. B. Seidensticker, "Archilochus and Odysseus," in *Greek, Roman and Byzantine Studies* 19 (1976), 14f., also touches on this topic, but primarily in Odysseus' role as a paradigm for the later poet and without exploring its significance for the *Odyssey*.

[8] For the *kleos andrōn*, "der vornehmste und vorzüglichste Gegenstand der epischen Dichtung," see Schmitt (1967; above, note 1), 93–95 and Schmitt (1968; above, note 1), 341–43. Cf. also Hesiod, *Theogony* 10 and the remarks of E. M. Bradley, "On King Amphidamas' Funeral and Hesiod's Muses," *La Parola del passato* 163 (1975), 285–88.

This inversion in the hero's "bardic" role as a singer of the *klea andrōn* takes on a broader significance in the light of the passage in which Odysseus announces his heroic identity at the beginning of his tale (9.19–20):

> I am Odysseus son of Laertes, known before all men
> for the study of crafty designs, and my fame (*kleos*) goes up to the heavens.

These lines have several noteworthy features. First, with one partial exception to be discussed later, this is the only place in the *Odyssey* where a character speaks of his own *kleos*. It is also the only place in Homer where *melō*, common in the third person in this sense, "be a concern to," occurs in the first person.[9] The closest parallel in this association of *melei* ("is a concern to") with enduring fame, or *kleos*, is Circe's brief allusion to the Argo as *pasi melousa* ("in all people's minds," *Od.* 12.70), a usage appropriate to a ship famed in legend and probably already celebrated in epic song. In using the verb in the first person here in book 9, Odysseus calls attention to the fact that he is, in a sense, singing a *kleos* that normally would be recited *about* him in the third person.

The Homeric hero is generally unreticent about his own achievements.[10] His *kleos*, however, the fame that is "heard" among mortals (cf. *Il.* 2.486), lives in the mouths of the bards, not of the hero himself. As Walter Marg puts it, "Ruhm, weiter und dauernder, über den Tod hinaus, ist das grosse Verlangen der homerischen Helden. Ihn gibt vor allem der Sanger, der die Kunde befestigt und weiterträgt."[11] This *kleos* is for others to sing, for "strangers to carry around the wide world," as Penelope says (*Od.* 19.333), or to spread "wide over Greece and the midlands of Argos" (1.344 = 4.816), or for gods to embody in "graceful song among mortals who live on the earth" (24.196–98; cf. *Il.* 6.357f.). As the parallels in the Indic epic tradition suggest, *kleos aphthiton* ("imperishable glory") is not merely a creation of humans, but something akin to the eternal elements of the world, possessed of an objective existence in the lives of societies and their traditions.[12]

In the *Iliad* it is rare for a hero to speak of "my glory," *emon kleos*, in the first person. A hero may talk of "winning *kleos* for myself," as Hector does when he boasts of his martial prowess (*Il.* 6.444–46):

> And the spirit will not let me, since I have learned to be valiant
> and to fight always among the foremost ranks of the Trojans,
> winning for my own self great glory, and for my father.

[9] The closest parallel is Theognis 245. Song can be the subject of *melei*, but always, of course, in the third person: *Od.* 1.159, 358f.; Hesiod, *Theogony* 61f.; *Hymn to Hermes* 451. Cf. also the proper name Astymeloisa, in Alcman, frag. 3.64, 73 (D. Page, ed., *Poetae Melici Graeci* [Oxford, 1962]).

[10] See Stanford (above, note 5), on 9.19–20.

[11] Marg (above, note 4), 20.

[12] See Nagy, *Comparative Studies* (above, note 1), 241ff.

Even here *kleos* is something to be won and is closely associated with the father as well as the individual hero.

Parallels to Odysseus' phrasing occur at two moments of special heroic intensity in the *Iliad*. Achilles in 9.412–16 contrasts the *kleos aphthiton* that he will win if he fights at Troy with long life and loss of *kleos* (*ōleto moi kleos esthlon*: "the excellence of my glory is gone," 9.415). Even here, where *emon* is not actually used, the hero's *kleos* is not something achieved and final. Quite the contrary, it seems remote and beyond his direct control. Hector's challenge to the Greek army in *Iliad* 7 offers a closer parallel: his opponent will die, Hector boasts, "but my *kleos* will not perish" (*Il.* 7.91: *to d' emon kleos ou pot' oleitai*). Here, too, as in *Iliad* 6.446 above, the hero is in the process of creating that *kleos*. Similarly, Achilles in *Iliad* 9.415 stands at a moment of crucial decision that will determine whether or not that *kleos* will exist in the future.

The situation of Odysseus at *Od.* 9.19–20 is very different. He is not involved in action or decision. He is, in fact, far from the heroic world, safe among the soft, luxury-loving Phaeacians. He is not creating that *kleos* by fighting, but rather recreating it by the "Ich-Erzählung" of the long, bard-like narrative that is to occupy the next four books.[13] Both hero and bard, he is in the unique position of being the singer of his own *kleos*. His *kleos*, in other words, gains both a subjective and an objective aspect. The interlude in book 11 makes this double function explicit.

The anomalous position of Odysseus as the reciter of his own *kleos*, in other words, brings together two aspects of *kleos* which are usually kept separate. First, as Nagy has recently suggested, *kleos* is "the formal word which the Singer himself (*aoidos*) used to designate the songs which he sang in praise of gods and men, or, by extension, the songs which people learned to sing from him."[14] Second, *kleos* is also the objectification of the hero's personal survival in epic song, the "imperishable fame" that lives among mortals and keeps alive the hero's name. Thus, as Nagy points out, the usual translation of *kleos* as "fame" is inadequate, for "fame" indicates only the "consequences rather than the full semantic range," whereas in fact the relation between the actual "fame" of the hero and the medium that preserves that "fame" is more complex: "The actions of gods and heroes gain fame through the medium of the Singer, and the Singer calls his medium *kleos*."[15]

By removing Odysseus far from the locus of his great heroic achievements at Troy and even from the adventures of the more recent past, the poet views *kleos* retrospectively. It is already fixed as part of a heroic tradition. That tradition can itself be held up for reflection, examination, criticism. Odysseus' encounters with the Cyclops and with Scylla, for example, reveal

---

[13] See K. Reinhardt, "Die Abenteuer der *Odyssee*" (1948), in *Tradition und Geist*, ed. C. Becker (Göttingen, 1960), 58ff. [tr. in this vol., 73ff.]

[14] Nagy, *Comparative Studies* (above, note 1), 248; see in general 245–52.

[15] Ibid., 250.

the inappropriateness of the traditional heroic response of straightforward battle in this strange world of fabulous monsters (*Od.* 9.299–306; 12.226–33).[16]

Aware of the increasing discrepancies between the heroic world of the epic cycle and the contemporary world of his audience, the poet of the *Odyssey* calls attention to the fact that the glory of heroic deeds exists only through song: it is truly *kleos* in the sense of tales that humans know by hearsay (*kleos oion akouomen*: "we hear only the rumor of it," *Il.* 2.486). The great deeds of the past, in other words, are now especially designated as a part of heroic song *qua* song. Their "objective" existence as unquestioned events that the audience accepts when it is under the "spell" of the poet's magic (*thelxis, kēlēthmos*) yields momentarily to an awareness of the form that makes possible that spell. The magic of the singer is necessary to call these deeds into being and give them their life. The "message" appears, for a moment, as the creation of its "medium." Hesiod, looking at the epic tradition from a certain distance, can even go so far as to suggest that the poet's Muses can speak falsehood that resembles "truth" (*Theogony*, 27 f.):[17]

> We know how to say many false things that seem like true sayings,
> but we know also how to speak the truth when we wish to.

Odysseus, able to tell tales with the skill of a bard in book 11, can also tell stories that make falsehood seem like truth after the manner of Hesiod's Muses: "He knew how to say many false things that were like true sayings" (*Od.* 19.203).

The *Iliad* offers a few brief glimpses of *kleos* self-consciously denoted as a creation of bardic tradition. Helen reflects on the fame in song (*aoidimoi*) that she and Paris will have in the songs of mortals of later time (*Il.* 6.356–58). Achilles, at a crucial point for his own *kleos*, sings the *klea andrōn* (*Il.* 9.189). On the other hand a later poet like Ibycus is quite overt about the distinction and the interdependence between the objective *kleos* of heroes that the poet transmits and the personal "fame" that the medium confers (Ibycus, frag. 282.47 Page).[18]

II

Odysseus' formulation of his *kleos* in 9.19–20 has yet another anomaly. His *kleos* derives not from heroic deeds achieved in the forefront of battle, like Hector's in *Il.* 6.446, but from their opposite, *doloi* ("trickery"). A syntactical ambiguity accompanies the ambiguity of the *kleos*:

---

[16] See Reinhardt (above, note 13), 59 [in tr., this volume, pp. 73–74] and Whitman (above, note 3), 300, on the inappropriateness or ineffectuality of the heroic stance against Scylla.

[17] On these lines and their problems, see P. Pucci, *Hesiod and the Language of Poetry* (Baltimore, 1977), chap. 1, with the bibliography there cited; Lanata (above, note 5), 24f.

[18] See the paraphrase of this poem in Nagy, *Comparative Studies* (above, note 1), 250.

I am Odysseus son of Laertes, who am known to all humans (*pasi . . . anthrōpoisi*)

for the study of all ruses (*pasi doloisin*), and my fame (*kleos*) goes up to heaven.

Pasi is so placed that it can go either with *anthrōpoisi* ("humans") or with *doloisin* ("ruses").[19] Odysseus' *kleos* can be a universal fame ("all humans") or a fame won for the thoroughness of his trickery, the totality of his immersion in unheroic guile ("all ruses").

Odysseus' description of himself here is to be connected with the sinister side of himself contained in his name: identity as "the man of pains" (*odunai*) or the man "doomed to odium" (*odus(s)omai*; cf. *Od.* 1.62; 5.340, 423; 19.275, 406–9).[20] Odysseus' very name, as Dimock, Austin, and others have pointed out, so deliberately concealed or revealed, associates him with the ambiguous practices of trickery and his descent from the trickster Autolycus. That ambiguity is perhaps also present in *melō*, whose unique Homeric occurrence in the first person I have already noted. *Melō* can mean "I am a concern to humans in song," but also "I am a care to humans," i.e., a "worry," "concern," or "problem" to humans in a more negative sense (cf. *Od.* 5.6).

Odysseus' representation of himself as an ambiguous hero of *dolos* is all the more striking in the light of Penelope's very different view of him and his *kleos* at the end of book 4. She fears the loss of her noble and courageous husband

who among the Danaans excelled in all virtues (*aretēisi*),
a brave man, whose fame (*kleos*) goes wide through Hellas and the midst of Argos.

(4.725f. = 4.815f.)[21]

Viewing Odysseus nostalgically from the needy perspective of Ithaca, Penelope endows him with the traditional heroic *aretai* and the traditional widespreading *kleos*. Odysseus himself, fighting his way out of the strange fairyland world of his sea travels, sojourning among the unwarlike Phaeacians, has come to experience and value a very different aspect of himself. Encounters with monsters like Polyphemus, soon to be described, have taught him the futility of the Danaan *aretai* that Penelope praises and the emptiness of the *kleos* that spreads far over Hellas and the midst of Argos. Here he needs

[19] See Stanford (above, note 5), *ad loc.* Rüter (above, note 7), 254, sees in *pasi doloisi* a reference to the Trojan horse sung by Demodocus, as well as to the *doloi* that the hero will exhibit again on Ithaca, the whole constituting a self-conscious praise of the *Odyssey* and the *Odyssey*-poet.

[20] See Stanford (above, note 5), on 1.52 and his article "The Homeric Etymology of the Name Odysseus," in *Classical Philology* 47 (1952), 209–13; G. E. Dimock, "The Name of Odysseus," in *Hudson Review* 9 (1956), 52–70; N. Austin, "Name Magic in the *Odyssey*," in *California Studies in Classical Antiquity* 5 (1972), 1–19.

[21] Austin (above, note 20) comments on some of the peculiarities of *Od.* 4.725f. = 815f. but does not connect them with the anomalies of 9.19f.

a larger, more universal, more convertible form of *kleos*. He must also exercise skills that have an ambiguous value among the warriors at Troy.

Odysseus' formula here, *kleos ouranon hikei*, reflects another peculiarity of his *kleos*. Fame being as central as it is to both epics, one would expect this formula to be of frequent occurrence.[22] In fact it occurs only once in the *Iliad*, significantly of a solid, durable, but not otherwise particularly famous object, Nestor's shield (*Il.* 8.192). It occurs only three times in the *Odyssey*, here in 9.20 and also in 8.74 and 19.108. It is striking that neither of the other two instances describes the martial glory of a traditional epic hero. *Odyssey* 8.73f. does not refer to a warrior at all, but to song: the muse inspires Demodocus to sing a "lay whose *kleos* mounts to the wide heaven."

The other occurrence is more striking still. It describes Penelope whom Odysseus, disguised as a beggar, addresses for the first time in the darkened halls of his palace (19.108–9):

> Your fame goes up into the wide heaven
> as of some blameless king.

One of several "reverse similes" applied to Penelope,[23] this one too places heroic *kleos* in a new and unfamiliar light. A noble queen keeping her fidelity to her absent lord in the palace has *kleos* as well as does a warrior facing his enemies on the open field of the battle. Though nothing overt is said, a situation is created in which each recognizes and begins to revivify the obscured *kleos* of the other. Here the threatened queen, beset by dangers, approaching desperation, lacking a firm protector in her house, receives this formula of heroic honor from the king in the guise of a starving, homeless beggar. Not only is he without *kleos* at this point, but he is even without name. He explicitly asks Penelope not to inquire about his lineage or his homeland, for that would fill him with grief and painful memory (*Od.* 19.116–18):

> But do not ask who I am, the name of my country,
> for fear you may increase in my heart its burden of sorrow
> as I think back; I am very full of grief.

The situation utterly reverses heroic practice. The traditional warrior who guards his *kleos* as his most precious possession proudly boasts his name, his race, his origins, and his native land, as for instance Glaukos does in his

---

[22] See the useful brief survey by W. Marg, "Das erste Lied des Demodokos," in *Navicula Chiloniensis (Festschrift für Felix Jacoby)* (Leiden, 1956), 27, note 3. Though the formula describes physical movements into the sky frequently in the *Iliad*, it is used of *kleos* only in *Il.* 8.92. Marg suggests that its usage in the *Odyssey* reflects the poet's self-conscious attempt to claim a place of honor for his work beside the *Iliad* (pp. 27f.), an idea developed by Rüter (above, note 7) 254. At the other end of the vertical scale, the "deep *kleos*" of Indic epic, used by Pindar (*Olympian* 7.53), seems not to have appealed to the Homeric poet: it occurs only in the proper name, *Bathyklēs*, at *Il.* 16.594: see Schmitt (1967, above, note 1), 75f.

[23] See H. P. Foley, "'Reverse Similes' and Sex Roles in the *Odyssey*," in *Arethusa* 11 (1978), 7–26, esp. 11ff.

encounter with Diomedes in *Iliad* 6.150ff. Penelope makes the appropriate reply; here, for the only time in the poem besides 9.19f., a character speaks of *kleos* in the first person. Repeating lines she had used to the suitor Eurymachos in the previous book, she says that her *kleos* would be greater only if Odysseus should return and care for her (*Od.* 19.127f. = 18.254f.):

> If he were to come back to me and take care of my life, then
> my reputation (*kleos . . . emon*) would be more great and splendid.

Now, she continues, instead of the *kleos* that should give joy, she has only *achos*, "grief" (19.129 = 18.256, *nun d' achomai*). In the speech in book 18, she spoke mournfully of the difficulty of Odysseus' return and complained of the Suitors' behavior, but here she tells the story of her web (19.137–56). Her tale reveals that her *kleos*, like Odysseus' in 9.19f., has its basis in *doloi* ("ruses"); and in fact she precedes her account of "weaving" the shroud with her "weaving of guile" (19.137): *egō de dolous tolupeuō* ("and I weave ruses").

This combination of *dolos* and the highest heroic *kleos* again points up the paradoxes and contradictions in Odysseus' "heroism." A woman can be expected to use *doloi* for her *kleos*, but a hero should win his *kleos* in fair fight on the battlefield. Yet for the woman too, *dolos* is ambiguous: it can lead to the exact opposite of *kleos*, namely "shame" and "disgrace," *aischunē* or *aischos*. The notorious example of this latter is Clytaemnestra, whose "guileful" planning (*dolomētis*, 11.422) and fashioning of guile (*dolon ērtue*, 11.439) "poured down shame (*aischos*) on herself and on all women after her" (11.433f.). Both Penelope and Odysseus tread a fine line where *dolos* leads to "glory," not "shame." In this respect, as in so many others, Odysseus and Penelope complement and parallel one another.

This complementarity of *dolos* and *kleos* for them both is especially clear in the second Nekyia. Amphimedon tells Agamemnon the full account of Penelope's "guile" (note *dolos* in 24.128 and 141, cf. *polukerdeiai*, 24.167). Agamemnon at once contrasts her with Clytaemnestra (24.196–202). He praises her "great *aretē*" and "good sense" and declares that "the glory of her *aretē* will never perish" (*to hoi kleos ou pot' oleitai / hēs aretēs*, 196f.) The gods will make her a subject of "lovely song" (*aoidēn chariessan*), whereas Clytaemnestra will be a subject of "hateful song" and bring ill fame to women (*stugerē aoidē*; *chalepēn phēmin*, 200, 201).[24] Penelope can use *dolos* but still win the *kleos* and *aretē* that are diametrically opposite to Clytaemnestra's *aischos* and *stugerē aoidē*. Odysseus, on the other hand, master of disguise and trickery, nevertheless fights a heroic battle of sorts (24.178–90), whereas lordly Agamemnon dies "a most pitiable death" (11.412), unable

---

[24] Note *aoidē*, not *kleos* here: see Nagy, *Comparative Studies* (above, note 1), 260f.; *Best of the Achaeans* (above, note 1), 36–39; Rüter (above, note 7), 233, note 9. Note the repetition 24.202 = 11.434: the same contrasts are implicit in both passages, but the full contrasts between Penelope and Clytaemnestra, Odysseus and Agamemnon are spelled out only here.

even to get his hands on the heroic weapon (11.423–25). This last scene contrasts with the heroic exertion of Odysseus' son at the crucial moment of battle:

> but I lifted my hands and with them beat on
> the ground as I died upon the sword . . .

(11.423f.)

> and closed his own hand over his spear . . .

(21.433)

Agamemnon's heroism cannot cope with a woman's *doloi*; Odysseus, meeting Penelope on her own ground, can enlist their separate *doloi* jointly in the reestablishment, rather than the destruction, of their house and their *kleos*. At the crucial transition between fairyland and Ithaca in his landing on Scheria, Odysseus has praised the "good fame" that husband and wife enjoy when they live together in "harmony of spirit," *homophrosunē* (6.180–85): *malista de t' ekluon autoi* ("and for them the best reputation," 6.185). That remote prayer for Nausicaa and her prospective husband now becomes relevant for Penelope and himself, fulfilled in the reaffirmed *kleos* of his Ithacan wife.[25]

The poem defines heroism through a series of symmetries and inversions: Odyssean *doloi* contrast with Agamemnon's *kleos*, the success of the one with the failure of the other. The house-destroying *dolos* of Clytaemnestra also contrasts with the house-preserving *dolos* of Penelope, as *aischos* contrasts with *kleos*. Simultaneously, the *kleos* of Odysseus, paradoxically achieved through *dolos*, parallels the *kleos* of Penelope: she is a woman who weaves guile (19.137), but, woman though she is, still gains the *kleos* usually reserved for male heroes. He, a hero of the Trojan war, possessing the masculine *kleos* of the warrior, wins that *kleos* through *dolos* and, in this poem, through a deed executed in the interior space of the house, the realm usually associated with women. The Iliadic warrior at once announces his name to his antagonist: Odysseus wins his major triumphs by circumspectly (and often unheroically) hiding his name.

III

Odysseus' "fame" that "reaches to the heavens" in 9.20 recurs later in that same book in an exploit that contains one of his most brilliant *doloi* and forms one of the most important parts of his *kleos*. In 9.251ff. he has his first face-to-face encounter with the monstrous Cyclops. He addresses him, for the first time, as follows (9.259–66):

[25] On the importance of *homophrosunē* in the *Odyssey*, see Norman Austin, *Archery at the Dark of the Moon* (Berkeley and Los Angeles, 1975), 202ff.

> We are Achaians coming from Troy, beaten off our true course
> by winds from every direction across the great gulf of the open
> sea, making for home, by the wrong way, on the wrong courses.
> So we have come. So it has pleased Zeus to arrange it.
> We claim we are of the following of the son of Atreus,
> Agamemnon, whose fame now is the greatest thing under heaven,
> such a city was that he sacked and destroyed so many people.

Odysseus here presents himself in terms both of his helpless wanderings on the vast sea and of the heroic glory of his Trojan exploits, the capture and destruction of a great city which constitute the "greatest *kleos* under the heavens" of his leader (264f.). That same configuration, wanderings and capturing Troy, introduces Odysseus as the hero of the poem in its very first lines (1.1f.):

> Tell me, Muse, of the man of many ways, who was driven
> far journeys, after he had sacked Troy's sacred citadel.

Far from Troy and Trojan heroism, however, this *megiston hupouranion kleos* ("greatest *kleos* under the heavens") has little meaning. It certainly makes little impression on the Cyclops, who "with pitiless spirit" dismisses his appeal for suppliant rights (9.272–80). Odysseus replies with *doliois epeessin* ("crafty words," 9.282): one may hark back proudly to martial deeds at Troy, but in this post-Trojan world, the hero will have to achieve *kleos* by new means.[26]

The narrative context of the wide *kleos* of 9.264 contains another irony. "The greatest distance possible," Norman Austin remarks apropos of the spatial field of Homer's world, "Homer expresses in the proportion: Agamemnon's glory is as widely dispersed beneath the sky as the city was great which he destroyed."[27] Odysseus borrows from his leader at Troy a *kleos* that embraces the sky and the earth. But Odysseus speaks of the great void of the sea (*mega laitma thalassēs*, 260) and of his vast *kleos* under the heavens at the point when he is trapped in a cave that, though "wide" (9.237), is nevertheless a dark and rather crowded (219–23) enclosure (cf. *muchon antrou*, 236). He is dwarfed by the giant who towers above him (cf. 9.257) and uses his massive strength to seal that enclosure with a rock that not even twenty-two wagons could budge (9.240–43). The rock both makes the enclosure definitive and renders futile traditional heroic battle with the sword (9.299–305).

There is one further irony. Odysseus invokes with pride and confidence the *kleos* of a leader whose death, as he will relate in the Nekyia of book 11,

---

[26] At his first meeting with Polyphemus, Odysseus addresses him only with "words," *epessin*, without a modifier, 9.258: there would seem to be a progression to the "guileful words" and then the "insults" of 9.282 and 474, respectively.

[27] Austin, *Archery* (above, note 25), 89. It is interesting that the definition of *kleos* by its breadth (*euru*) occurs only in the *Odyssey*, though it is well established in the Indo-European epic tradition: see Schmitt (1967; above, note 1), 72f.

was anything but glorious (11.406–34). Agamemnon illustrates the failure and inadequacy of the traditional *kleos* in this world. Citing him, Odysseus will also find an alternative.

To defeat the Cyclops, Odysseus has to resort to the extreme form of *dolos*, temporarily negating his personal identity and becoming *outis-mē tis*, "No Man" (9.366), which is also the *mētis* of his guile or *dolos*.[28] The pun associates the abandonment of heroic identity with the guile on which he has increasingly to rely in this strange world. Later he resumes the traditional heroic stance and boasts like an Iliadic warrior over a defeated enemy. He makes the mistake here of addressing the Cyclops "with insults" (*kertomioisi*, 9.474) rather than with "guile" (9.282). The result is disastrous (9.504f.): in possession of his enemy's name, the Cyclops can call down the curse of Poseidon against him (9.530f., cf. 504f.).[29]

In this passage Odysseus assumes the heroic, warrior epithet, "sacker of cities," *ptoliporthion*. He thereby identifies himself with the Iliadic *kleos* of his leader in whose name he introduced himself to the Cyclops in 9.265, *dieperse polin*. May one speculate that by the time Odysseus has reached Alcinoos' court he is more aware of the incongruity of that martial epithet in this marine realm? By now he has learned to regard himself less as a "sacker of cities" than as a man of guile and tricks:

> I am Odysseus son of Laertes, known before all humans
> for the study of crafty designs, and my fame goes up to the heavens.
>
> (9.19f.)[30]

In achieving the final restoration of his heroic status too, Odysseus will need *doloi* more than the martial prowess of a "sacker of cities."

The converse of Odysseus' inappropriately heroic address to the Cyclops occurs in the next book. Landing on another unknown island, Odysseus confesses his disorientation (10.189–97): he does not know the celestial coordinates of east and west, sunrise and sunset, and finds himself at a loss for his usual *mētis* (10.192f.):

> then let us hasten our minds and think, whether there is
> any course (*mētis*) left open to us. But I think there is none.

[28] See A. J. Podlecki, "Guest Gifts and Nobodies in *Odyssey* 9," in *Phoenix* 15 (1961), 125–33; Austin, "Name Magic" (above, note 20), 13ff.; C. P. Segal, "The Phaeacians and the Symbolism of Odysseus' Return," in *Arion* 1.4 (1962), 34f.

[29] See C. S. Brown, "Odysseus and Polyphemus: The Name and the Curse," in *Comparative Literature* 18 (1966), 193–202, especially 196; see also Austin, "Name Magic" (above, note 20), 3f.

[30] The notion that Odysseus' narrative reflects a retrospective interpretation and understanding of his previous actions is interestingly developed by E. M. Bradley, "'The Greatness of his Nature': Fire and Justice in the *Odyssey*," *Ramus* 5 (1976), 137–48, especially 144: "When he reaches Phaeacia Odysseus is, in significant ways, a different man from what he was during the course of his travels from Troy. A measure of that difference is indicated by the hero's ability to narrate critically his adventures to the Phaeacians, as he analyzes the causes and effects of his own behavior and that of his men." See also Segal, "Phaeacians" (above, note 28), 23f.

At this declaration his men's spirit is broken as they remember the violence (*biē*) of the Cyclops and Laestrygonians (10.198–200), and they weep miserably (201f.). Not only is there an antithesis of *mētis* and *biē*, as acted out in the Polyphemus episode, but the absence of Odysseus' *mētis*, closely akin to his *dolos*, results in a loss of speech: his men can only "wail shrilly" and lament (10.201f.): *klaion de ligeōs thaleron kata dakru cheontes.* "Guileful words," *dolia epea*, are the saving device of Odysseus' *mētis* against brute force (9.282). Shortly before, his "honeyed words" of encouragement (*meilichia epea*, 10.173) kept his men from grieving about death (10.172–78). Now, in the absence of his *mētis*, words give way to inarticulate and helpless grief ("but there came no advantage to them for all their sorrowing," 10.202). Soon afterward, these dispirited companions, lacking the guidance of Odysseus' *mētis*, lose their human voice (*phōnē*, 10.239) and in their bestial transformation by Circe are penned up "wailing" (*klaiontes*, 10.241).

IV

In 9.19f., as we have seen, Odysseus' formal declaration of his heroic identity has associations with the bardic view of *kleos* as something past and definitively formed: he sings as his own a *kleos* that ought to come from another's mouth. In book 11 Odysseus actually performs as a bard who skillfully sings a warrior's deeds. From the Phaeacian perspective of aesthetic distance, martial exploits and painful suffering appear only as art.[31] But when Odysseus faces his great deed of restoring order on Ithaca and regaining name and kingdom, he sets up just the reverse relation of art and action. No longer the soldier doing the work of a bard, but a beggar in disguise, he elicits from his regal weapon the sound that is music to the warrior's ears. Holding the great bow, finally, in his hands, he handles it as a poet handles a lyre (21.406–11):

> As when a man, who well understands the lyre and singing,
> easily, holding it on either side, pulls the strongly twisted
> cord of sheep's gut, so as to slip it over a new peg,
> so, without any strain, Odysseus strung the great bow.
> Then plucking it in his right hand he tested the bowstring,
> and it gave him back an excellent sound (*aeise*) like the voice of a swallow.

---

[31] Marg (above, note 4), 16f. and 20; Lanata (above, note 5), 17. Rüter (above, note 7), 243 and also 237) makes the point that Odysseus, unlike Demodocus, moves more deeply into his grief as he sings, yet also gains a certain distance from it that he had not had before; all the while the Phaeacian audience enjoys his tale as if it were merely the song of a bard. W. Burkert, "Das Lied von Ares und Aphrodite," in *Rheinisches Museum* 103 (1960), 141–43, also stresses the contrast between the light Olympian world depicted by the Phaeacian bard and the serious side of Olympus shown in the *Iliad*.

Tried by Odysseus, the bow "sings beautifully" like a swallow—or as the verb *aeise* also suggests, like a bard (21.410f.).[32] The order, aesthetic and social, implied by song now begins once more to approximate the moral and political order reestablished by the return of the king. Disorder in Mycenae, we recall, included the banishment of the bard whom Agamemnon left to guard his queen (3.267–72).[33]

Among the Phaeacians Odysseus could recreate his heroic past and its *kleos* only in song. Here on Ithaca he is a warrior who brings back to the palace the joy and rightful celebration of heroic deeds that earlier could only be evoked by bards whose tales made the listeners weep. The joyful songs of Phemius and Demodocus on Scheria caused private grief to Penelope and Odysseus but gave public "joy" (*terpsis*) to the rest of the audience (cf. 1.342, 347; 8.91f., 536–43; 9.3–15). The "song" of the bow gives public "grief" (*achos*) to the audience at large (21.412, above) but private "rejoicing" to Odysseus (21.414): "Hearing this, long-suffering great Odysseus was happy." This inversion of joy and grief now refers not merely to the quiet, interior bardic situation when Odysseus was isolated in the house of strangers, but also to the heroic situation on the battlefield, where the bow brings a living *kleos* to one and "grief" (*penthos*) to the other in actual deeds, not their reflection in song. We may compare the wounding of Menelaus in *Iliad*, 4.196–97 = 206–7:

> whom someone skilled in the bow's use shot with an arrow,
> Trojan or Lykian, glory (*kleos*) to him, but to us a sorrow (*penthos*).[34]

When Odysseus sang like a bard on Scheria, heroic *kleos* was a fossilized vestige in the amber of the Phaeacians' unheroic hedonism (cf. 8.246–55). In this setting a heroic declaration of *kleos*, like that of 9.19–20 or like the reaction to a taunt about a more trivial *kleos* in an athletic, not a martial, competition (8.152–57), could appear only as incongruous (8.146–47). Now, at the brink of heroic battle once more, the hero uses a bardic metaphor not merely to state in words, but to enact in deeds, what it meant to win *kleos* at Troy.

V

This perspective on heroic song also casts fresh light on the episode of the Sirens. They are described in the vocabulary of the bard: their song casts a spell (*thelgousi*, 12.40; *ligurēi thelgousin aoidēi*, "by the melody of their sing-

---

[32] For other aspects of the simile of the bow as lyre see Segal, "Phaeacians" (above, note 28), 51; Austin, "Archery" (above, note 25), 247, 251; D. J. Stewart, *The Disguised Guest: Rank, Role, and Identity in the Odyssey* (Lewisburg, Pa., 1976), 158f.

[33] For the importance of the bard in *Od.* 3, see Rüter (above, note 7), 234, note 12.

[34] For the contrast of "joy" and "grief" in the bardic tradition as reflected in Homer, see Nagy, *Comparative Studies* (above, note 1), 255–61; *Best of the Achaeans* (above, note 1), chap. 5.

ing they enchant him," 12.44), like that of Phemius (*thelktēria*, 1.337; cf. 11.334), a vocabulary that links them with the ambiguous and seductive magic (also called *thelxis*) of Circe (10.291, 318). Their power depends emphatically on hearing (12.41, 48, 49, 52, 185, 187, 193, 198). Their "voice" is itself a "song" (*aoidē*, 12.44, 183, 198) that is "clear sounding" (*ligurē*, 12.44, 183) or "honey-voiced" (*meligērus*, 187; hence the homeopathic magic of the "honey-sweet" wax, *meliēdēs*, 12.48, of the antidote). It also brings the "joy" or "delight," *terpsis*, associated with bardic song (*terpomenos*, 12.52; *terpsamenos*, 12.188; cf. 1.342, 347).[35] The song's material is the epic tradition, the efforts at Troy as well as "what passes on the wide-nurturing earth" (12.189–91).

The Sirens' rendering of the heroic tradition, however, is akin, in a certain way, to the bardic song of Scheria: it shows heroic adventure as something frozen and crystallized into lifeless, static form, something dead and past, a subject for song and nothing more. For this reason, perhaps, they are the first adventure of Odysseus after Hades (12.39, "You will come first of all to the Sirens"). Thus they stand in close proximity to that dead world of purely retrospective heroism. Yet when Odysseus had related his adventure among the dead—with the Siren-like "spell" and the art of a bard, to be sure (11.334, 368)—those shades were still a living part of his past, directly related to his *nostos* ("return", 11.100, 196).[36] What he hears in the Underworld stirs grief or arouses indignation (11.435–39, 465f.) and thus reinforces that longing for mother, father, and wife which is essential to his return (cf. 11.152–334). What the Sirens sing is remote from any experience. The magical charm of their sweet voice on the windless sea is epic *kleos* in the abstract—lovely but somehow dehumanized (cf. the vast generality of "over all the generous earth we know everything that happens," 12.191).

As the past of which the Sirens sing has the deathly vacuity of what is long dead and without flesh (cf. 12.45f.), so they themselves are characterized by motionlessness. As Odysseus and his men draw near, a windless calm forces them to take oars (12.167–72). These Sirens, unlike their later descendants in Greek art, do not fly[37] but "sit" (*hēmenai en leimōni*, 12.45) and ask Odysseus to "stop the ship" (*nēa katastēson*, 12.185) in order to hear their voice. They claim that no one "has ever yet passed by (*parēlase*) in his

---

[35] For the Sirens' attributes of epic song, see Fränkel (above, note 4), 10; Reinhardt (above, note 13), 60–62 [this vol., 75–76]. Cf. P. Pucci, "The Song of the Sirens," in *Arethusa* 12 (1979), 121–32, esp. 126ff. [this volume, pp. 191–99, esp. 195ff.].

[36] See J. H. Finley, Jr., *Homer's Odyssey* (Cambridge, Mass., 1978), 130f.: "His [Odysseus'] curiosity might have been thought satisfied in the Underworld. But that revelation surrounded or concerned his own past and future; the Siren song has no tie with him. . . . He will reach home by what he learned in the Underworld, this other, complete, impersonal song ends a man's hope of wife and children. . . . The famous song expresses one side of a myth of which homecoming expresses the other; the two sides are not quite compatible."

[37] See J. Pollard, *Seers, Shrines, and Siren* (New York and London, 1965), 137–45. On the change from the flowery meadow of Homer to the cliffs of later painters and writers, see also Reinhardt (above, note 13), 61 [this vol., 75–76].

black ship / before hearing the honey-voiced speech from our mouths" (12.186f.). Escape from them, therefore, consists in keeping active, moving, passing by (*parex elaan*, 12.47: *parēlasan*, 12.197).

Not only do the Sirens know of the exploits at Troy, but they also address Odysseus by the heroic epithet *mega kudos Achaiōn*, "great glory of the Achaeans" (12.184). This is the only place in the poem where he is so titled. This epithet occurs seven times in the *Iliad*. It has only two other occurrences in the *Odyssey*, here and in the formulaic line by which Telemachus twice addresses the aged Nestor in book 3 (3.79 = 202). Well might the inexperienced youth at his first direct contact with the glories of Troy address the oldest of the Achaean warriors in these terms, terms that perhaps remind us that Nestor, more than any other Homeric character, lives in the past.

Odysseus, however, will continue his journey and effect a return to the living past and living *kleos* that await him on Ithaca, not at Troy. He must therefore resist the blandishment of the heroic tradition as frozen into this spell-binding but lifeless song. What the Sirens know is too general and too remote to help him in his quest to recover Ithaca. To remain and listen to their song would be to yield to the seduction of a heroic tradition rendered in its most elegant, attractive, and deadly form, devoid of reality for the tasks that await this hero of *dolos*. The Nekyia and, in a different way, the lives of Nestor and Menelaus have shown this danger in lived example. The Sirens cast that danger of entrapment by the past specifically into the form of poetic song and the fascination it exercises. Were he to heed it, he too would be frozen into a sterile past, one of those rotting skeletons on the island. His task, therefore, is not to listen but to "pass by."

Rather than preserving fame by the remembering Muse of true epic song (*Muse*, after all, is probably etymologically akin to "memory"),[38] the Sirens bring forgetfulness of home and loved ones (12.42f.). Pindar told how golden "charmers" (*Kēlēdones*), akin to these Sirens, perched atop a mythical temple of Apollo at Delphi and sang so sweetly that the visitors "perished there apart from wives and children, their souls suspended at their honeyed voice" (*Paean* 8.75–79 Snell).[39] For Odysseus thus to perish obscurely on the rock to which the magic of the Sirens' song draws him would be to forget the "return" (*nostos*) on which in fact his *kleos* rests.

In this temptation of "forgetting the return," the Sirens' magical spell has affinities not only with Circe, but also with the Lotos-Eaters. There too a man "forgets his return" (*nostoio lathētai*, 9.97 and 102: cf. *oikade nostēsanti*,

---

[38] For the Muse and "memory," see Lanata (above, note 5), 3 with references there cited; Pucci (above, note 17), 22–24; M. Detienne, *Les Maîtres de vérité dans la Grèce archaïque*[2] (Paris, 1973), 13ff.

[39] *Athenaeus*, 7.36 (p. 290E), cited by B. Snell, ed., *Pindari Carmina cum Fragmentis*[3] (Leipzig, 1964), on frag. 52i, points out the affinity between these "Charmers" and the Sirens in this "forgetting" of home and loved ones.

12.43). The victims of the Lotos, like Odysseus in book 12, have to be bound forcibly in the ship (9.99 and 12.196). The Sirens inhabit a "flowery meadow" (*leimōn' anthemoenta*, 12.159): the lotos is a "flower-like food" (*anthinon eidar*, 9.84).

The abode of the Sirens is characterized by death and decay. Circe describes the bones of "rotting men" near their meadow (*andrōn pythomenōn*, 12.46), and Odysseus warns his men of the danger in terms of dying or avoiding death ("knowing all we may either / die, or turn aside from death and escape destruction," 12.156f.). Epic song and the memory that it preserves, however, confer a victory over death. Its "imperishable fame," *kleos aphthiton*, is the exact antithesis of the Sirens' rot and decay. As Nagy has shown, *aphthiton*, whose root, *phthi-*, "occurs frequently in the context of plants" (cf. the *aphthitoi ampeloi* of *Od.* 9.133), has associations with the vital liquids or substances that overcome death: "From the present survey of all the Greek epic nouns (except *kleos*) which are described by *aphthito-*, we may posit a least common denominator in the context: an unfailing stream of water, fire, semen, vegetal extract (wine). By extension, the gods representing these entities may also have the epithet *aphthito-*, as well as the things that they own or make.[40] True epic song counters the decay to which mortal things are subject with a *kleos* seen as close to the very essence of life, akin to the vital fluids that sustain the life of mortals and the natural world.

In the Siren episode, song not only is a ghostly imitation of epic but even becomes its own negation. This song brings death, not life. It does not go out over the broad earth among mortals. Those who succumb to it remain closed off from mortals, becalmed on a nameless sea, their bodies rotting in a flowery meadow. The Sirens know the secrets of the past, but it is a past that has no future life in the "remembering" of successive generations. Here the hero forgets his loved ones among whom his *kleos* might live on after his death (cf. 12.42f.). The epic bard, aided by the goddess of memory, makes the past live in the present and bridges over the void between the sunless realm of the dead and the bright world of the living,[41] as Odysseus himself does in the Nekyia of book 11; the Sirens' song entraps the living in the putrefaction of his own hopelessly mortal remains.

Though fundamentally different in many ways, the Sirens have certain resemblances to the Harpies, "Seelenvogel," "snatchers" of the soul from life

---

[40] See Nagy, *Comparative Studies* (above, note 1), 244; *Best of the Achaeans* (above, note 1), chap. 10.

[41] See J.-P Vernant, "Mythical Aspects of Memory" (1959) in, *Myth and Thought among the Greeks*, no translator named (London and Boston, 1983, pp. 75–80, in particular 80: "By eliminating the barrier that separates the present from the past it throws a bridge between the world of the living and that beyond to which everything that leaves the light of the day must return. . . . The privilege that Mnemosyne confers upon the bard is the possibility of contacting the other world, of entering and returning from it freely. The past is seen as a dimension of the beyond." See also Detienne (above, note 38), chap. 2, esp. 20ff.

to death.[42] In the case of Homer's Sirens, the song that should immortalize ironically brings oblivion. Where the *Odyssey* mentions these "snatchers" in relation to Odysseus, there is an interesting overlap with the Sirens, for *harpuiai* negate his *kleos* (1.240f. = 14.370f.):

> And he would have won great fame for himself and his son hereafter.
> But now ingloriously (*akleiōs*) the stormwinds (*harpyiai*) have caught and carried him away.

Closely related to this negation of Odysseus' *kleos* is Penelope's lament as she imagines the death not only of a husband but also of a son, the latter also "snatched" away (4.725–28):

> and who [sc., Odyssey] among the Danaans surpassed in all virtues,
> and great, whose fame goes wide through Hellas and midmost Argos;
> and now again the stormwinds (*thuellai*) have caught away my beloved
> son, without trace, from the halls, and I never heard when he left me.

Such a death is analogous to the doom of the Sirens' island in book 12. The "harpies" who snatch a man away "without *kleos*" to the remote corners of the world on the winds of the storm deprive him of the *kleos* that would be "heard" as people in a civilized community sing of a death by glorious deeds, witnessed by his comrades and commemorated by a funeral monument (1.239 = 14.369, "So all the Achaeans would have heaped a grave mound over him"). Lost in the obscure reaches of the wild, he would necessarily perish *akleiōs* ("ingloriously"), in the anonymity of nature's violence, just as the victims of the Sirens in book 12 rot in nameless heaps in a remote, mysterious ocean, reclaimed entirely by nature's elemental processes of putrefaction and decay.

The Sirens have the *terpsis* of the epic bard, but no contact with the *kleos* through which he conquers death. The verb that repeatedly describes the "hearing" of their song is *akouein* (eight times: see above, never *kluein*.[43] As their voice does not go beyond the nameless "island" (12.201) where they sit, so the "hearing" (*akouein*) of their song is entirely literal, not the symbolical "imperishable *kleos*" that leads from death to life. As their victims succumb to the physical decay of their physical remains and are reduced to the rotting flesh of mere body, so a purely physical blocking of the ears as the corporeal organ of hearing suffices to defeat them. Indeed Homer dwells concretely on the physical details of placing wax, a substance also used to preserve, in the ears (12.47f., 177).

[42] For similarities and differences between Sirens and Harpies, see U. von Wilamowitz-Moellendorff, *Der Glaube der Hellenen*[3] (Darmstadt, 1959), vol. 1, 263f. with note 1, 264; Sittig, "Harpyien," in Pauly-Wissowa, *Real-Encyclopädie* 7.2 (1912), c. 2422; Zwicker, "Sirenen," in Pauly-Wissowa, 3 A.1 (1927), c. 293f.

[43] *Akouein* is also the verb Odysseus uses for "hearing" the Sirens when he relates this episode to Penelope, 23.326, *Seirēnōn hadinaōn phthongon akousen.*

Like Hesiod's Muses, the Sirens speak in the language of "knowing" (*id-men . . . idmen*, 12.189, 191: cf. *Theogony* 27f.), but no word of "memory" or "remembering" characterizes their song. All the basic elements of this song, then, its knowledge, pleasure, and "hearing," form a perversion of true heroic song. Whoever heeds it is caught by the fatal "spell" of empty "delight" in a purely physical "hearing" that will isolate him far from the living memory of future generations. Here he will rot away obscurely, his remains indistinguishable in a heap of rotting skin and bones, not the whole forms of the active figures of heroes who breathe and move in their deeds when the epic bard awakens the *klea andrōn*.

Seen in this perspective, the episode of the Sirens is not just another fantastic adventure of Odysseus' wanderings. Through his characteristic form of mythic image, the traditional singer here finds symbolic expression for the implicit values and poetics of epic song and epic *kleos*.

VI

Odysseus' last words in book 21 are an ironical invocation of the nonheroic scenes of feasting and song that have occurred throughout the poem. With grim humor he suggests that it is now the time "to make merry with song and the lyre, for these are the accompaniments of the feast" (21.428–30):

> Now is the time for their dinner to be served the Achaeans
> in the daylight, then follow with other entertainment,
> the dance and the lyre; for these things come at the end of the feasting.

We recall the first feast and the first song in book 1, when Odysseus seemed hopelessly far away and the Suitors controlled the palace and forced the bard to sing (1.145–55; 1.152, cf. 21.430; 22.352f.).[44] But now, as the equation of lyre to bow in the similes of 405 and 411 changes from trope to action, so the ironical invitation to feasting and song in 21.428–30 changes to heroic combat in the military formulas that close the book (21.433f.):

> and [Telemachus] closed his own hand over his spear, and took his position
> close beside him and the next chair, all armed in bright bronze.

Now too the "contests" that accompanied those feasts as part of Phaeacian levity (cf. the *aethloi* and *kleos* of 8.145–48) have higher stakes as Odysseus opens a grimmer "contest" (22.5 ~ 21.91, "Here is a task that has been achieved, without any deception")[45] and aims "at a target which no one ever

---

[44] Stanford (above, note 5) on 21.428–30 notes the parallelism between the *anathēmata daitos* of 21.430 and 1.152.

[45] If *aaatos* means "blameless," as some have thought (see Stanford, *ad loc.*), then the phrase will be ironic. For the special nature of this contest and its possible ritual associations, see Germain (above, note 4), chap. 1.

yet hit" (22.6). Odysseus no longer has to use the bardlike "charm" (*thelxis*) of his lies to win his way into the palace, as he does through the tales that Eumaeus singles out when he introduces him to Penelope for the first time (17.518–21). Making good his rightful place within the palace by a "song" of a very different kind, Odysseus performs a final bardlike act that both completes and supersedes all his previous skillful manipulation of words.

The end of book 21 resonates in still a different register when the great deed is really accomplished and Odysseus has purged the enemies from his halls. Still reflecting on the practical exigencies of the situation, Odysseus orders a bath and fresh clothes and then gives instructions that "the inspired singer take his clear-sounding lyre, and give us the lead for festive dance, so that anyone / who is outside . . . / . . . will think we are having a wedding. . . . " (23.133–36). His commands are promptly obeyed: soon "the inspired / singer took up his hallowed lyre and stirred up within them / the impulse for the sweetness of song and the stately dancing" (23.143–45). Now Odysseus, not the Suitors, commands song. He is indeed celebrating a wedding, in a sense, for he and Penelope, the obstacles removed, are on the verge of their reunion, the next major event in the poem (23.152–288). The motif of the wedding celebration, however, appears with a twist of bitter irony: the "suitors" of the new "bride" are lying dead, and the festivity is the extension of the deed of killing them. The occasion for the song here in 23.133ff. contrasts both with Phemius' singing in book 1 and, more immediately, with his frightened holding of his lyre in the fear of death in 22.330ff. (22.332b = 23.133b). Phemius' song here also contrasts with the song of Demodocus in book 8. The stated aim of song in book 23 is not joy (*terpsis*) per se, though Phemius' patronymic is Terpiades (22.330), but rather the dangerous circumstances of battle and the prospect of facing still more uneven odds (23.118–22). Not a scene of happy conviviality, but a speech about the martial virtues of valor and loyalty introduces the order that the "divine bard" play on his lyre (23.124–28). The purpose of this song, finally, is not to proclaim and perpetuate *kleos*, but the opposite, to *prevent* the "wide fame" of a great deed from going out into the world (23.137f.):

> Let no rumor go abroad in the town that the Suitors
> have been murdered.

Thus even when Odysseus accomplishes his great exploit, the usual terms of heroic *kleos* are inverted.

The comparison of the bow to the bard's lyre in the former passage (21.404ff.) not only introduces the long-anticipated scene of heroic combat and heroic *kleos* but also brings together the two sides of Odysseus' role in the poem. By subordinating song to action (for in book 21 the bardic associations are figurative only), the similes implicitly reassert Odysseus' full return to the heroic world and to the *kleos*, rightfully his, that has been so problematical in the poem. He may owe that *kleos* to "trickery," *dolos*, as lines 9.19f. suggest; yet this hero of *mētis*, *mechanē*, and *polukerdeiai* is also capable of heroic battle against great odds.

At the same time an important ambiguity remains, parallel to the ambiguities of Odysseus' *kleos*. The slaughter of the Suitors has, to be sure, some of the appurtenances of heroic battle: Athena-Mentor is there to exhort Odysseus by his valor at Troy (22.226–30). Yet this deed is hardly a heroic exploit on the Iliadic scale. From the Suitors' point of view, given a full hearing in the second Nekyia, it is guile and murder. When the slain suitor Amphimedon describes the deed, he begins with the deceit of a woman (24.125ff.), stresses the craftiness of Odysseus (24.167, *polukerdeiai*), and implies that he and his companions never had a fair chance. The heroic detail of the "lovely armor" (*perikallea teuchea*, 24.165) figures only as part of the hopeless odds against which he and his companions had to contend. Like Agamemnon in book 11, he views his death not as a proud heroic end on the field of battle, but as "a wretched doom" (*kakon telos*, 24.124; cf. 11.412, *oiktistōi thanatōi*). As we have already seen, his speech completes the symmetries and contrasts between Odysseus and Agamemnon, Penelope and Clytaemnestra, *kleos* and *dolos*, *kleos* and *aischos*.

The peculiarities in the language of *kleos* which we have studied here suggest that the poet of the *Odyssey* was aware of the ambiguities attaching to his hero "of many turns." He deliberately plays off against one another different perspectives on the heroic tradition. Composing, probably, at a time when the heroic ideal is itself undergoing change and redefinition, and when, possibly, epic language is becoming more and more fluid, he uses traditional elements in new ways and refashions a hero and a style where nonheroic values and fresh social, ethical, and aesthetic currents make themselves felt.

From distanced, self-conscious, and ironic reflection on *kleos*, Homer returns us in the last three books of the epic to full participation in the making of *kleos*. Odysseus' reassertion of his heroic persona and his restoration to wife, house, and kingship consist precisely in this movement from singer to actor. He (re-)creates *kleos* in song when he recites the *apologoi* to Alcinoos' court skillfully like a professional bard, but he finally wins *kleos* in deeds when he makes the warrior's bow sing like the poet's lyre. Both in song and in action, Odysseus' task is to restore order—domestic, civic, and cosmic. He reestablishes song and feasting as a sign of that order in his palace when the bard, spared from death by the grim warrior-king (22.330ff.), can once more play the accompaniment to joyful dancing and merriment as king and queen are about to be united (23.143–45, 22.332b = 23.133b).[46]

With its characteristic openness toward what is new, changing, and dan-

---

[46] It is part of the sustained contrast between Odysseus and Agamemnon that the latter, describing the slaughter of his men at his failed *nostos*, compares them to swine being slaughtered at a great man's house in preparation for a wedding (*gamos*, 11.415).

gerous as well as what is firm and traditional in life, the poem's last scene is not the songful feast of a reunited house in a celebratory *hieros gamos*, as one might have expected, but a scene of battle. Odysseus' last address to his son is the admonition (24.506–9),

> Telemachus, you yourself, stepping forth (to battle) where men fight
> and the best are separated out, shall learn not to shame (*kataischunein*)
> the race of your fathers, for in valor and
> in manliness we are distinguished over the whole earth.

Is this a final realism beneath the poet's apparently happy ending? What the wily and much-enduring hero bequeathes to his son for the future is not only the visible proof of his own *kleos* (here defined by its opposite, non-*aischos*), but also the necessary experience of war.[47]

---

[47] I wish to thank Professors Gregory Nagy and William Wyatt for friendly criticism and advice.

Composition by Theme and the *Mētis* of the *Odyssey*

LAURA M. SLATKIN

WHY is the narrative structure of the *Odyssey* so complicated? Although the plot of the poem is perfectly straightforward—Aristotle observed that it was the imitation of a single action—nevertheless the ordering of its narrative is elaborately nonlinear. The *Iliad* gets under way with a question from which ensues a linear, chronological account of the events the poem presents: so much so that, for example, even material that one might have expected to be presented in a flashback—the identification and history of the Greek leaders and their relationship to Helen—is told by her in the *Teichoskopia*, in a present continuous with that of the ongoing narration of events. The *Iliad* demarcates its subject—the wrath of Achilles—at the outset and organizes its story from the onset of the wrath to Achilles' renunciation of it in book 19 and the consequent episodes of the death and ransoming of Hector, according to the literal order in which those events take place.

The *Odyssey*, by contrast—to summarize what is familiar—begins in the proem with a proleptic reference to Odysseus' loss of his companions and to the specific episode of the eating of the cattle of Helios, then appeals to the Muse to begin *hamothen ge*—"from somewhere"[1]; and the response is to locate Odysseus on Calypso's island, where we will not actually meet him until book 5. The action then proceeds with Poseidon going off to the Aethiopians, while the rest of the gods hold a council on Olympus in which Odysseus is not the first order of business: Agamemnon, Orestes, and Aegisthus are. Once Athena enjoins the Olympians to turn their attention to Odysseus, Zeus is immediately willing, asserting that he hasn't forgotten Odysseus. But the latter's way home, explains Zeus, has been barred by Poseidon, who maintains his grievance over the blinding of his son the Cyclops—another of a number of allusions to an episode that the poem treats as past history although it is in the future from the narrative's standpoint. The narrative then takes up events in the human sphere on Ithaca, and the Telemachia takes the hero's son to Pylos and as far as Sparta in search of information about his father. In book 5 the poem at last introduces us to its hero—with, in effect, another beginning, another discussion on Olympus—but *not* in fact at his last stop, as we might have assumed

---

[1] See J. S. Clay, "The Beginning of the *Odyssey*," *American Journal of Philology* 97 (1976), 313–26.

from the council of the gods in book 1. Rather, Odysseus is only at the penultimate stage of his return home, so that the narrative will then move forward chronologically for a while—books 5–8—before turning backward in book 9. Thus we discover eventually, for example, that by the time Odysseus rejects the immortality Calypso offers, he has already been to the underworld, has seen death, and has heard Achilles' evaluation of it.

Telemachus' journey, moreover, frames books 5–15. The narrative, leaving Odysseus' son after his first day in Sparta in book 4, proceeds from Calypso on Ogygia to the Phaeacians on Scheria, where we hear the whole retrospective account of Odysseus' travels, covering the past ten years. The Phaeacians then return Odysseus to Ithaca, where he makes his way to Eumaios' hut and converses with him—at which point, at the opening of book 15, we return to Telemachus, just waking up on Sparta: for him, only one night has passed. And the vacuum created by Odysseus' absence in books 1–4 is filled by stories about him in which the past—a past extended for us by the memories of those in Ithaca, Pylos, and Sparta to include at least a second decade: that of the Trojan War with its antecedent events and immediate aftermath—is recalled against and vividly contrasted with a shadowy and enigmatic present.

As this brief summary illustrates, the *Odyssey*, as it moves back and forth, gives us the simultaneous perspective of many time-frames: the limitless framework of the gods, the lifetime of Odysseus (Penelope pointedly establishes this in book 23, reflecting that "the gods begrudged that we should spend our youth together"[2]), the protracted return, the sudden maturation of Telemachus. The narrative sequence of the remainder of the poem, though more strictly chronological, displays a complementary virtuosity of concentration, counterpointing discretion and disclosure in the actions of Odysseus and Penelope until the *Odyssey*'s ultimate closure is achieved in the crucial convergence of events on a single day.[3]

How are we to understand the significance of the complex structure sketched here? Tz. Todorov, in a well-known essay, cites the *Odyssey* as the best means of dispelling illusions about the transparent simplicity of "primitive narrative": "Few contemporary works reveal such an accumulation of 'perversities,' so many methods and devices which make this work anything and everything but a simple narrative."[4] In recent years, indeed, the *Odyssey* has found a special place in influential writings on narrative theory aimed, as a rule, at modern fiction. In G. Genette's study of "narrative discourse," for example, the *Odyssey*, notably, is the paradigm that serves to introduce the defining terms by which the author establishes categories of a systematic theory of narrative at the same time as he develops an analysis of Proust's formidable masterpiece.

[2] 23. 210–11.
[3] See J. H. Finley, Jr., *Homer's Odyssey* (Cambridge, Mass., 1978), esp. chap. 7.
[4] Tzvetan Todorov, *The Poetics of Prose* (Ithaca, 1977), 53.

In order to proceed from basic distinctions among the possible meanings of the word *narrative*, Genette offers the *Odyssey* to illustrate how "narrative" can be used to refer to 1) "the narrative statement that undertakes to tell of an event or a series of events: thus we would term '*narrative of Ulysses*' the speech given to the Phaeacians in Books ix–xii of the *Odyssey*, and also these four books themselves"; 2) "the succession of events, real or fictitious, that are the subjects of this discourse . . . : an example would be the adventures experienced by Ulysses from the fall of Troy to his arrival on Calypso's island"; and 3) an event, "not, however, the event that is recounted, but the event that consists of someone recounting something: the act of narrating taken in itself. We thus say that Books ix–xii of the *Odyssey* are devoted to the narrative of Ulysses in the same way that we say that book xxiii is devoted to the slaughter of the Suitors." These separate denotations among which the *Odyssey* allows such lucid discrimination enable an analysis "which constantly implies a study of relationships: on the one hand the relationship between a discourse and the events that it recounts (narrative in its second meaning), on the other hand the relationship between the same discourse and the act that produces it, actually (Homer) or fictively (Ulysses) (narrative in its third meaning)."[5]

It is a fundamental perception that any narrative is relational: that it both represents, and itself constitutes, a set of flexible, nonstatic interrelations, involving narrator (actual or fictive), audience (actual or fictive), process of communication, and substance of communication. To the configurations fruitfully identified by Genette, however, any discussion of the *Odyssey* must contribute an additional component, if its aim is not simply to view Homeric epic as illustrative background material but to bring the *Odyssey* itself into focus. This element is the relationship of an oral poem to the poetic tradition—the tradition of discourse, in Genette's terms—in which it participates: the tradition in which it was shaped and which it transmits.

Since the pioneering studies of Milman Parry, the traditional basis of oral poetry has received much meticulous scrutiny. Beyond the level of inherited meter, diction, and phraseology, however, a facet of the relationship between the epic and its tradition that bears particularly on the question of narrative complexity is that of "theme," elucidated by the work of Parry and especially by that of Albert Lord, where considerations of theory and practice intersect.

Lord uses the term *theme* to designate "a recurrent element of narration or description."[6] Based on his and Parry's fieldwork, Lord demonstrates that

---

[5] Gérard Genette, *Narrative Discourse: An Essay in Method*, tr. J. Lewin (Ithaca, 1980), 25–27.

[6] See, for example, "Composition by Theme in Homer and Southslavic Epos," *Transactions of the American Philological Association* 82 (1951), 73, as well as *The Singer of Tales* (Cambridge, Mass., 1960), 68. Lord's terminology follows Parry, who used "theme" to refer to "repeated incidents or descriptive passages."

the theme serves as crucial a function as the formula in developing the oral poet's technique of composition in performance.

> Although the themes lead naturally from one to another to form a song which exists as a whole in the singer's mind with Aristotelian beginning, middle, and end, the units within this whole, the themes, have a semi-independent life of their own. The theme in oral poetry exists at one and the same time in and for itself and for the whole story. This can be said both for the theme in general and also for any individual singer's form of it. His task is to adapt and adjust it to the particular song that he is recreating.[7]

As the accomplished oral poet regenerates the tradition in which he sings, his use of recognizable themes allows him—indeed, requires him—to situate his song in the context of other narratives on the same subject, within the same genre.

> [The theme] does not have a single "pure" form either for the individual singer or for the tradition as a whole. Its form is ever changing in the singer's mind because the theme is in reality *protean* [italics mine]; in the singer's mind it has many shapes, all the forms in which he has ever sung it. It is not a static entity, but a living, changing, adaptable artistic creation. Yet it exists for the sake of the song. And the shapes that it has taken in the past have been suitable for the song of the moment. *In a traditional poem, therefore, there is a pull in two directions: one is toward the song being sung and the other is toward previous uses of the same theme.* [italics mine][8]

The oral poem, therefore, continuously repositions itself with respect to a tradition made up of alternative narrative possibilities: "The substitution of one multiform of a theme for another, one kind of recognition scene for another kind, for example one kind of disguise for another is not uncommon as songs pass from one singer to another."[9] This means that there will inevitably be diverse "versions" and "variants" of a single song which exist, as it were, in an implicit dialogue with each other.[10]

Each performance-composition of a song must necessarily reflect, and participate in, the evolution of possible alternatives to the version it actually presents. We know that there were other treatments of Odysseus' return to Ithaca, as the *Theogony*[11] suggests and the *Telegony* reminds us[12] and, more-

---

[7] *Singer of Tales*, 94.

[8] Ibid.

[9] Ibid., 119.

[10] "In some respects the larger themes and the song are alike. Their outward form and their specific content are ever-changing. Yet there is a basic idea or combination of ideas that is fairly stable. We can say, then, that a song is the story about a given hero, but its expressed forms are multiple, and each of these expressed forms or tellings of the story is itself a separate song in its own right, authentic and valid as a song unto itself." (*Singer of Tales*, 100)

[11] *Theogony* 1011–18.

[12] For a general argument on the archaic provenance of the epic cycle, see W. Kullmann, *Die*

over, that there were other *nostoi*, which the epic cycle also preserves, and which the *Odyssey* itself refers to. The *Odyssey*, therefore, needs to be approached in the context of a tradition of singing about the return of the hero, a tradition comprised of multiforms—equal thematic variants, which do not presuppose an Ur-form—that interact with each other on the level of theme, of story-pattern, and of narrative arrangement.

In the light of these observations, the *Odyssey* can be seen to have assimilated patterns of other return-stories to its own cast of characters and its own set of concerns. The evidence of traditional patterns, as demonstrated by the South Slavic material, indicates that in return stories the hero's son plays a limited role, although he is essential in revenge stories of the Agamemnon-Orestes type.[13] The *Odyssey* has combined two distinct (though overlapping) structural arrangements into one: the pattern of the son avenging the father, central to the Agamemnon-Orestes story, is modulated into the rescue and return of the imprisoned hero—the fundamental scheme of the *Odyssey*, whose hero returns not in the company of his son, but alone and in disguise.[14]

What I wish to draw attention to in this context is that the *Odyssey* acknowledges the Agamemnon story not just as a parallel set of events but precisely as an *alternative narrative model*. It does this from the very outset, when book 1 opens the action with Zeus saying, in effect,[15] "I can't help thinking about the Agamemnon story, especially the part about the foolish suitor upon whom the hero's son took vengeance." To which Athene replies, in effect, "Yes, that certainly is a *model story*" and adds, "Let all foolish suitors perish *in the same way*"—*hōs*—that is, at the hands of the hero's son.[16] Athene, later in the same book, adduces Orestes as an example of established heroic renown, a model to Telemachus of what his story might be. Orestes is a son whose *kleos*—epic fame—already has wide circulation.[17] In book 3 Telemachus confirms explicitly that he has taken the point. On hearing another injunction to him—this time from Nestor—to achieve fame like that of Orestes, Telemachus agrees that Orestes certainly did punish the murderous suitor and avenge his father, and that this will be an epic song for posterity. "But the gods," he asserts (to paraphrase 3.208–9), "haven't spun such fortune for me as to be able to punish the Suitors and have an

---

Quellen der Ilias (*Troischer Sagenkreis*) (Wiesbaden, 1960). R. Sacks has convincingly demonstrated the presence of traditional material in the *Telegony* in an unpublished paper presented to the Columbia University Seminar on Classical Civilization, entitled "Ending the *Odyssey*: Odysseus Traditions and the Homeric *Odyssey*." On the indications within the *Odyssey* of other return possibilities for Odysseus, see S. R. West, "An Alternative *Nostos* for Odysseus," *Liverpool Classical Monthly* 6–7 (1981), 169–75.

[13] Lord, *Singer of Tales*, 159ff.
[14] Ibid., 121.
[15] I am paraphrasing here to refer in summary to *Od.* 1.32–41.
[16] To paraphrase 1.45–47.
[17] 1.298ff.

Orestes-like story." The story the gods have spun for Telemachus, although it might have proceeded like that of Orestes—that is, they have themes in common—takes a different turn.

The juxtaposition of different narrative models is identified as such by the *Odyssey* itself, which even alludes to other representations, other versions and treatments, of its own subject matter. We can go a step further, to emphasize that the *Odyssey*'s overt acknowledgment of alternative story-patterns is part of a larger strategy by means of which the poem insists on the complexity of its own narrative structure and thereby draws attention to the very *process* of singing tales, of generating and regenerating epic song. The *Odyssey* may be said to treat narrative, or narrative discourse, as a subject in itself.

Albert Lord writes:

> While recognizing the fact that the singer knows the whole song before he starts to sing (not textually, of course, but thematically), nevertheless, at some time when he reaches key points in the performance of the song, he finds that he is drawn in one direction or another by the similarities with related groups [of songs] at those points. The intensity of that pull may differ from performance to performance, but it is always there, and the singer always relives that tense moment.[18]

My point is that the *Odyssey* incorporates an explicit awareness of the creative tension of composition, an awareness of the existence of possibilities that could become other songs; and this implies a claim that alternative treatments have been rejected and that the path taken to create *this* song, the one being sung—our *Odyssey*—is the ultimate and preemptive path.

The *Odyssey* underscores these issues as a poem of audiences in a post-Iliadic world, audiences for whom the preeminent narrative is the narrative of Troy. Telemachus attests to this when, lamenting his father's disappearance, he asserts that if Odysseus had been celebrated for his exploits like the heroes who perished fighting at Troy, the grief of his survivors would have been lessened. It is in part the *Odyssey*'s relationship to the epic about Troy, as the *Odyssey* represents it, that returns the poem continually to the issue of narrative. For in the Odyssean world of audiences, every new song must presuppose the existence of songs about Troy—of an *Iliad*—whose prestige is the narrative ideal.

In this context the *Odyssey* poses the question, "What kind of song can be sung about Odysseus?" by creating an internal audience for whom the answer is a matter of urgent suspense. In *Odyssey* 1, the bard Phemius entertains the Suitors with a return-song of the Achaean heroes. Penelope interrupts

---

[18] *Singer of Tales*, 123. Lord continues, "Even though the pattern of the song he intends to sing is set early in the performance, forces moving in other directions will still be felt at critical junctures, simply because the theme involved can lead in more than one path."

him, objecting that this song is always too painful for her to listen to. Telemachus, even as he argues with her, specifies Penelope's objection: that there is no place for Odysseus in a *nostos*-song. The unvoiced corollary remains: Might there be a *kleos*-epic about Odysseus? Athene complicates the answer: in the guise of Mentes, she first assures Telemachus that his father is still alive, casts doubt on this information shortly thereafter, and ends by sending Telemachus in search of *either* the *kleos* or the *nostos* of his father. Will the song about him be correspondingly complicated?

The *Odyssey*'s own audience knows things that Telemachus does not—his father's whereabouts and Athene's plan, for example. Yet the multiple audiences within the *Odyssey* allow its listeners to reflect on what it means to be in the position of audience. There are many narrators; from the opening of the poem, in the absence of Odysseus, and before the poem has even introduced him directly, he is variously represented by narratives from a range of sources. Different Odysseus stories are delivered by Nestor, by Menelaos, by Helen, by Athene as Mentes and Mentor; the Suitors have their recollections, and Telemachus his secondhand version. Menelaos and Helen, who claim to be telling the same story but offer diametrically conflicting ones, make it clear that it is not easy for an audience to get a straight story, to discriminate among stories, or even to know what a straight story is.

By putting the story of Odysseus' return finally into the mouth of the hero, the *Odyssey* highlights the audience's role as active participants in the creation of the narrative, collaborators in the opening of alternative narrative paths and the pressures of tradition, which are the conditions of poetic composition. The demands that are subtly integrated in the production of narrative emerge as Odysseus recites his return-story to the Phaeacian connoisseurs of the epic of Troy, temporarily disrupting and displacing the epic perspective before rejoining and being reincorporated into it; so that the *Odyssey*'s assertion of superiority is expressed in part by allowing us to see the transitions it absorbs—that is, its use of the traditional operations of selection and combination of themes—but also by contrast to Odysseus' own recitation, or, to put it another way, in answer to Odysseus' challenge to the epic viewpoint.

Odysseus' recital is incomplete when he terminates it at 11.332. Alkinoos encourages him to continue by offering an approving assessment of the story that compares Odysseus explicitly to an *aoidos*, although he admits an audience's susceptibility to the seductiveness of false tales deceptively intended. It has been observed that one function of the proposed pause in the tales is to underscore the larger-than-life scale of the *Odyssey* itself, which far surpasses that of an evening's entertainment.[19] Alkinoos' expressed readiness to stay awake all night, listening to the end, confirms that the quality of the story matches its extraordinary length.

---

[19] See G. Nagy, *The Best of the Achaeans: Concepts of the Hero in Archaic Greek Poetry* (Baltimore and London, 1979), 18–20.

But the "intermezzo" provides a commentary on other aspects of the procedure of epic storytelling (performance-composition) as well. Alkinoos' remarks address the content (composition) in addition to the form (performance) of Odysseus' "song." We remember that in book 8, Odysseus praised Demodokos in the context of asking him to change the *content* of his singing. He requested a song—of the Trojan horse—that would attest to the singer's access to the Muses. As the *Odyssey*'s audience perceives, Odysseus himself could provide confirmation of this.[20] Now Alkinoos' praise of Odysseus as *aoidos* prefaces his request for a different kind of song. Alkinoos says, "You're like an *aoidos*"—and asks for a song about the heroes who died at Troy, that is, for a *kleos*-song. Odysseus' tales until this point have made only peripheral mention of Troy and have included no account of the *klea* of the heroes in the Trojan war. Instead, the encounters in uncharted territory that Odysseus has so far described are intriguing but alien; although *like* what an *aoidos* would sing, they are outside the conventional repertory of heroic experience, and equally that of epic song.

Alkinoos' reminder to Odysseus of the *topoi* of the Trojan heroes both acknowledges a conventional hierarchy of subjects within epic and reverts to it as a touchstone of poetic truth. Demodokos, responding to Odysseus' challenge to sing *kata moiran* about the episode of the Trojan horse, will prove whether he sings the *truth*; similarly, recounting stories of the heroes at Troy will authenticate, for Alkinoos and the Phaeacians, Odysseus' claims about himself—and, by extension, his unprecedented adventures outside the Trojan sphere (that is, outside the realm of common human history). But the premise that assigns value to verifiable authenticity based on conventional expectations of canonical, recognizable *topoi*, or familiar representations, is called into question by the implications of the interruption itself: by Odysseus' ending and resuming his recitation, taking up his tale again with precisely what Alkinoos has asked for, incorporating the transition into the narrative without a break, as though it were a feature of the story; by his elision and abridgment of the recitation, the *Odyssey* alerts *its* audience to question the idea of a "fixed or authentic version" of a story, reminds listeners of the multiformity of themes, and invites them to think about the role of ambiguity, multiplicity of tradition, revision, and point of view in telling (and hearing) stories. Alkinoos' invoking of the poetic process in the context of what turns out to be an interruption, an artificial ending and re-beginning, draws the audience's attention to the actual ending of Odysseus' tales and possibly to the actual beginning as well. When Odysseus brings his recitation to a close at the end of book 12, is this the real ending or is it another pause? Could there be more to tell? These questions are brought to the fore by the way Odysseus breaks off at that point, after a mere two and a half lines on his adventure with Calypso. The half line is suggestive, because Odysseus seems to stop in midsentence, where more might have fol-

[20] Ibid., 100ff.

lowed, in order to ask why he should *muthologeuein* a story he has told the previous day?

His reference here is to the remarks addressed to Arete at book 7.244–66 in which he summarized his stay on Ogygia—an abbreviated enough passage; but even more fleeting is the two-line, passing allusion to Calypso at the outset of book 9 that occurs in the course of Odysseus' reflection on the preciousness of one's own homeland. This initiates a kind of inverted ringstructure around books 9–12, ending with the two and a half "broken" lines on Calypso noted above. It is an inverted one in that both passages, rather than enclosing Odysseus' "bardic" recitation of the adventures, have their backs to it, as it were—opening outward to a frame of reference external to Odysseus' own account of this episode.

The version in book 7, which the abruptly truncated mention of the Calypso story at the end of book 12 refers us to, offers in itself a kind of false start. Arete has asked Odysseus who he is and where he comes from, and his answer's opening phrase, *Ōgugiē tis nēsos*, is misleadingly like the conventional introduction to an account of one's origins. As has been observed, it is deceptively like Eumaios telling Odysseus where he comes from (*nēsos tis Suriē* . . . 15.403), or Odysseus telling Penelope that he comes from Crete (*Krētē tis gai' esti* . . . 19.172).[21] In other words, it looks as though Odysseus is about to lie, thus confirming the suspicions of Arete, who thinks he has already lied. Just where the ironies reside in this exchange can be discerned, of course, solely by the Homeric audience. In a precisely parallel way, it is apparent only to the Homeric audience just how partial and limited Odysseus' version of the encounter with Calypso is—because only they have heard book 5. Odysseus' tales are displayed to the audience of the *Odyssey* as dazzling yet perhaps inadequate: incomplete by the standard that the *Odyssey* itself has set for us.

These versions of the Calypso story constitute a unique instance of the inner narrative of Odysseus' first-person recitation referring to the outer narrative of the epic. When Odysseus reminds the Phaeacians that they have heard this episode before, he links together for the poem's audience its two disparate experiences of his adventure on Ogygia. With the version of the Calypso episode as Odysseus tells it, we are aware of a story that is not only attenuated but actually fails in some of its information, although its literal audience, the Phaeacians, cannot realize this. Odysseus, at 7.262–63, says that Calypso let him go but that he doesn't know why. The *outer* epic narrative, however, has put *us*, as *its* listeners, in a position to know the entire sequence of events from Olympus on down.

The effect of presenting this disparity is to accord to the outer Homeric narrative the authority of absolute reality. The *Odyssey* becomes the intrinsic standard of validity by which we perceive the fictive potential of Odysseus' tales. To put it another way, Homeric poetics urges the paradoxical unre-

---

[21] B. Fenik, *Studies in the Odyssey* (Wiesbaden, 1974), 16–17.

liability of the first-person eyewitness, the need for interpretation—and also the shifting perspectives that inhere in the relation between singer and audience and stand to be exploited by narrative virtuosity.

Alkinoos' request expresses an audience's assumption that what will authenticate a story is what the audience can recognize: that is, the piece of the puzzle they already possess. But the *Odyssey* compels us to acknowledge the limitations of this point of view, although we are led to understand it from the inside and to sympathize with it. The *Odyssey* encourages us to see that one's involvement inherently precludes one's seeing the whole picture—that, in a sense, you are the last person who can tell your own story. Far closer to Alkinoos than the heroes of Troy is the prophecy from Nausithoos, which he quotes at the end of book 7: that Poseidon will someday be angry with the Phaeacians and end their seafaring. Odysseus then proceeds to describe, over the course of three books, how and why *he* is Poseidon's bitterest enemy; at the end of which Alkinoos, with considerable naïveté, wishes the Phaeacians conveying Odysseus back to Ithaca smooth sailing. Correspondingly, Odysseus fails to recognize and hence cannot communicate Athene's agency behind his return home; moreover, the same Odysseus who has told Alkinoos that one's homeland is the sweetest thing in life to see (and that he has spent years on Calypso's island picturing Ithaca to himself) wakes up on Ithaca with no idea where he is or what he is looking at. The view that can reorient the audience and establish appropriate bearings for determining the poem's proper sphere is not one that reverts to the Trojan war—as Alkinoos does, or as Odysseus describes Aiolos doing at 10.14–15. It is rather the view that the poem assigns to Athene in 13 when she answers the mystified Odysseus' inquiry about his surroundings by saying:

> You are naive, stranger, or you have come from far away,
> if you really are asking about this country. It is not
> so very nameless after all. A great many people know it,
> whether all who live eastward toward the dawn
> or those who dwell toward the shadowy west.
>
> . . . .
>
> so the name of Ithaca has reached even to Troy,
> which they say is far from Achaean land.

(13.237–41 . . . 248–49)

"You must be very ignorant if you ask about Ithaca. It is hardly obscure. . . . In fact, Ithaca is such a distinguished place that its fame has reached to Troy—which they say is very far away."[22] Decisively, the focus has shifted.

These questions posed by the *Odyssey* about authenticity, about point of

---

[22] 13.237–39, 248–49.

view, about the integrity of the discourse, about which tradition is the relevant one, are raised in part formally—by the juxtaposition of the many endings and beginnings—and in part by the poem's recurrent themes of deception, disguise, and recognition.[23] They are questions to be answered by the *totality* of the epic itself, built up of many perspectives beyond what the various audiences can request or the multiple eyewitnesses can report. The *Odyssey* encompasses them all, both involved and uninvolved, including that of the Olympians. It can integrate a multiplicity of traditions and can lay claim to an encompassing authority.

I observed above that the interruption of Odysseus' recitation and the invitation by Alkinoos to resume draws the audience's attention to the *actual* ending of the tales and perhaps to their actual beginning as well. Odysseus begins his story in the first place in answer to Alkinoos' request that he identify himself. In the course of the *Odyssey*, we remember, many people ask Odysseus who he is and where he is from; but the question that initiates the telling of the tales is a special one, with special diction. Alkinoos inquires at the end of book 8:

> Come then, tell me this and recount accurately,
> in what direction you were driven off course and what places you came to
> belonging to humans, both them and their well-inhabited cities—
> as many as were savage and violent, and without justice,
> and those who were hospitable to strangers with a god-fearing mind.

> (8.572–76)

"Tell me, where were you driven off course, and which men and cities did you come to, and what were their minds?"

Here we are emphatically recalled not only to the beginning of the recitation but to the beginning of the *Odyssey*:

> Tell me, Muse. of the man of many turns, who was driven
> far and wide, after he sacked Troy's sacred citadel;
> many were those whose cities he saw, whose minds he learned of.

> (1.1–3)

For the synthesis of perspectives and traditions that these questions demand can be answered only by the Muse—which is to say, only by the epic as a whole.

With this passage we also double back to recognize the echoed diction of Telemachus' speech about Orestes—"the gods haven't spun such fortune for me as to have *kleos* and *aoidē* like that of Orestes"—in that Alkinoos' speech at the end of book 8 not only returns us to the beginning of the poem overall

---

[23] On these subjects see especially S. Murnaghan, *Disguise and Recognition in the Odyssey* (Princeton, 1987).

but, a little further on, makes a statement about the imperative of epic song as the motivator of human events. The king here asks Odysseus why he weeps and laments to hear the fate of the Greeks and of Troy. "Don't you know," says Alkinoos, "that the gods have spun this so that it might be a subject of song for mortals to come?" If the *Odyssey* chooses epic narrative as a subject, it is for no lesser reason than the view voiced by Alkinoos: epic is itself the justification for human endeavor and suffering.

That the threads of human suffering spun by the gods become the fabric of epic song is reinforced by the distribution of diction that joins spinning or weaving[24] and poetic composition in an image of artisan production that complements the convention of the *aoidos* as divinely inspired.[25] This artisan aspect can, moreover, coexist with a vision of the singer as divinely affiliated and may have done so for a long time. Not only is there a divine craftsman among the Olympians[26], but even in an archaic cosmogony like that of Alcman the primordial creative power is a demiurge (specifically a metalworker).[27] Certainly the association of weaving and poetic composition is ancient.[28] Not only do we see it elsewhere in early Greek—as in *Iliad* 3, where Helen weaves the *klea andrōn*; in the Hesiodic fragment 357 Merkelbach-West; in Sappho, Bacchylides, and Pindar—but it has been shown to have an Indo-European provenance.[29]

These interpenetrating associations are particularly resonant in the *Odyssey*, however, because the *Odyssey* gives weaving special prominence. Penelope's weaving and unweaving of the shroud for Laertes—the account of which is given, remarkably, three times in the poem—is the intricate device, or device of intricacy, by which Penelope manipulates the Suitors' attention and keeps them under control; it is the ruse by which time can be turned back and brought forward again. This ploy, proclaimed by the Suitors themselves (after the fact) as assuring Penelope's *kleos*, is the stratagem that Penelope refers to as her *mētis* (19.158).

We remember here that in the *Odyssey* the word *mētis* occurs formulaically in conjunction with *huphainō* in expressions that mean "to weave a scheme." When, for example, at book 13.303, Athena, having asserted the bond of *mētis* between herself and Odysseus, declares:

---

[24] Spinning and weaving are treated interchangeably by the two Homeric poems; in the *Odyssey* the *klōthes*, the spinsters themselves, are said to *weave* with thread.

[25] This image may represent the *craft* of learning performance-composition. Lord, *The Singer of Tales*, 13–29, has described the conditions and the stages of developing singing techniques among modern-day singers that may not have been very different for those of an earlier era.

[26] See F. Frontisi-Ducroux, *Dédale: Mythologie de l'artisane en Grèce ancienne* (Paris, 1975), on Olympian craftsmen.

[27] Alcman fr. 5 (Page).

[28] For a valuable discussion of the association of weaving and singing in archaic poetry, see J. M. Snyder, "The Web of Song: Weaving Imagery in Homer and the Lyric Poets," *Classical Journal* 76 (1980–81), 193–96.

[29] See R. Schmitt, *Dichtung und Dichtersprache in indogermanischer Zeit* (Wiesbaden, 1967), 298–301.

> Now again I am here, to weave a scheme with you,

to which Odysseus responds at 13.386:

> Come then, weave a scheme, the way I will pay [the Suitors] back,

these expressions confirm the appropriateness of Penelope's use of *mētis* to denote the weaving scheme. As, in the literal act of weaving[30], material and design emerge simultaneously from a single process, so with Penelope the action of weaving and unweaving does not fashion a device but constitutes the device itself.

The dual movement of Penelope's scheme—weaving and unweaving— leads us to look more closely at the properties of *mētis*, an element crucial to the working out of events in the *Odyssey* and fundamental to its values. The meaning and role of *mētis*, as it is represented from Hesiod and Homer through late antiquity, have been illuminated by M. Detienne and J.-P. Vernant in their study *Les Ruses de l'intelligence: La Métis des grecs* (1974).[31] Examining the structure and operations of *mētis* as it is presented on a variety of levels and in a wide range of contexts from archaic poetry to the second century A.D. treatises on fishing and hunting ascribed to Oppian, they point out that the terminology associated with *mētis* has regularly to do with techniques of weaving, especially weaving nets, plaiting ropes or coils, fitting together traps—verbs like *huphainō, plekein, tektainesthai, strephein*— and they distinguish a number of its essential and consistent features, especially its mobility, flexibility, multiplicity, and diversity.[32]

Mētis is naturally attributed to such shape-shifters as Proteus, Nereus, and Thetis; according to Apollodorus, the divinity Metis herself has the power of metamorphosis. Zeus, therefore, observe Detienne and Vernant, "masters Metis by turning her own weapons against herself. These are premeditation, trickery, the surprise attack, the sudden assault."[33] Similarly, Menelaos has to outmaneuver Proteus by becoming a shape-shifter himself, temporarily: pretending to be a seal in order to get the better of the clever old fellow.

---

[30] Frontisi-Ducroux, *Dédale*, chap. 3, 52ff.

[31] References below are to the English translation published under the title *Cunning Intelligence in Greek Culture and Society*, tr. J. Lloyd (Sussex and Atlantic Highlands, 1978).

[32] Detienne and Vernant write (20):

Why does *mētis* appear as multiple (*pantoiē*), many-colored (*poikilē*), shifting (*aiolē*)? Because its field of application is the world of movement, of multiplicity, and of ambiguity. It bears on fluid situations which are constantly changing and which at every moment combine contrary features and forces that are opposed to each other. In order to seize upon the fleeting *kairos*, *mētis* had to make itself even swifter than the latter. In order to dominate a changing situation, full of contrasts, it must become even more supple, even more shifting, more polymorphic than the flow of time: it must adapt itself constantly to events as they succeed each other and be pliable enough to accommodate the unexpected so as to implement the plan in mind more successfully.

[33] *Cunning Intelligence*, 21.

In the world of natural history, *mētis* is the property of such creatures as the octopus, with its polymorphy and its capacity for disguise through camouflage. The fox is called the most scheming of animals, considered a master of *mētis* especially, it seems, in its ploy of reversing its own position.[34] It is said to *epistrephein*—to reverse itself suddenly, to turn back on itself to capture its unsuspecting prey or to escape from adversaries. This "secret of reversal" possessed by the fox is said to be "the last word in craftiness."[35] Another creature deserves to be singled out: a fish, aggrandized with the name of "fox-fish" because of its behavior, which is described as follows by Plutarch: "It generally avoids bait (*dolos*), but if it is caught it gets rid of it. Thanks to its energy and flexibility (*hugrotēta*), it is able to change its body (*metaballein to sōma*) and turn it inside out (*strephein*) so that the *interior* becomes the *exterior* [italics mine]: the hook falls out (*hōste ton entos ektos genomenon apopiptein angkistron*)."[36] And more from Aelian: "It unfolds its internal organs and turns them inside out, divesting itself of its body as if it were a shirt"; or as Vernant and Detienne put it, "This fish turns itself inside out like a glove."[37]

The tricks of reversal exhibiting the *mētis* of these creatures have clear affinities not only with Penelope's weaving and unweaving the web, but with the ingenious stroke of that supreme figure of *mētis*, Hermes, who in the Homeric *Hymn to Hermes*, when he wants to effect the theft of the cattle of Apollo and elude discovery, drives the herd backward so that their tracks will look as though they had gone the other way; he turns them *prosthen opisthen*, as the Hymn says.[38] These few indications suggest some of the qualities of Odysseus, the ultimate man of *mētis*. Eustathius actually calls him an octopus.[39]

Polumētis is Odysseus' most frequently occurring distinctive epithet and *mētis* his preeminent attribute, which Athene, the daughter of Metis, enthusiastically endorses and claims as the source both of their unity and of their *kleos*. She declares:

> For you are far the best of all mortals
> in planning and speaking, and I among all the gods
> am famous for cleverness and schemes.

> (13.297–99)

Odysseus the dissembler, the man who assumes many identities, is called superior in *mētis* to all mortals—and is the only mortal bearer of the epithet *polumētis* in the Homeric corpus, the others being the crafty Hermes (once)

---

[34] Detienne and Vernant (ibid., 36) quote Aelian, *On the Nature of Animals* 6. 24.
[35] Detienne and Vernant, 36.
[36] *On the Cleverness of Animals* 977b, as quoted ibid., 37.
[37] Ibid., 37, quoting Aelian, *On the Nature of Animals* 9.12.
[38] Homeric *Hymn to Hermes* 77–78.
[39] Eustathios 1381.36ff., cited by Detienne and Vernant, 39, 52n.91.

and the craftsman Hephaistos (once). Odysseus succeeds through *mētis amumon*, as he himself calls it, in outwitting the Cyclops—and this of course is underscored by the pun through which that *mētis* consists of *mē tis*.

The narrative of the *Odyssey*—which Albert Lord has called protean in its fundamental properties[40]—embodies, in its many weavings, its reversals, its twisting of time, a *mētis* of its own. The epic song, and it alone, can see from all the angles, comprehend many points of view and many strands of tradition, even incorporating allusions to incompatible ones. It alone can disclose the identity of its hero, although it alone has not created him. More precisely, only the epic song can control that identity and that disclosure, whereas for all Odysseus' skill at disguising himself, he cannot have sufficient perspective on himself, on his own defining features, to anticipate or circumvent Eurykleia's recognition of him or to perceive that Penelope is testing *him* when she volunteers to have his bed moved. The narrative of the *Odyssey* asserts its own supremacy and justifies the assertion by inviting its audience to reflect on the process of storytelling. Like the fox-fish, it has turned its outside inside and made its framework its focus. As Detienne and Vernant observe, "The only way to get the better of a *polumētis* one is to exhibit even more *mētis*."[41] The singer of his own story, Odysseus, is indeed *polumētis*; the traditional song that encompasses him and *all* his stories is *pan-mētis*.[42]

[40] See above, 226–28.

[41] Detienne and Vernant, 30.

[42] A version of this paper was given at the Annual Meeting of the American Philological Association in December 1981, and the present version at a Homer symposium organized by Peter Bing at the University of Pennsylvania in March 1984. In the intervening years, numerous innovative directions in the study of Homeric narrative have been discovered. Although text and notes here have not been updated to include work published since this paper was originally delivered (with the exception of Sheila Murnaghan's study [above, n.23], which I had seen at an earlier stage), I hope that at least the questions offered here will be found compatible with those so illuminatingly posed by Homerist colleagues and others over the subsequent decade.

This paper was intended initially—and still is—as a tribute to the work of the late Albert B. Lord. As always, I benefited from the insights of Richard Sacks, Seth Schein, Amy Johnson, Gregory Nagy, and in particular Nelly Oliensis and the late Steele Commager.

Albrecht, P. A. 1938. *Eros und die Ehe bei Homer*. Zurich.

Allen, T. W., ed. 1917–19. *Odyssea. Homeri Opera*. Vols. 3 and 4. 2nd edition. Oxford.

Alter, R. 1981. *The Art of Biblical Narrative*. New York.

Amory, A. 1966. "The Gates of Horn and Ivory." *Yale Classical Studies* 20: 3–57.

———. 1963. "The Reunion of Odysseus and Penelope." *Essays on the Odyssey: Selected Modern Criticism*. Edited by C. H. Taylor. 100–121. Bloomington.

Anderson, W. S. 1958. "Calypso and Elysium." *Classical Journal* 54: 2–11. [Reprinted 1963. *Essays on the Odyssey: Selected Modern Criticism*. Edited C. H. Taylor. 73–86. Bloomington.]

Armstrong, J. I. 1958. "The Arming Motif in the *Iliad*." *American Journal of Philology* 79: 337–54.

Arthur, M. 1973. "Early Greece: The Origins of the Western Attitude toward Women." *Arethusa* 6: 7–58. (Reprinted 1984. *Women in the Ancient World: The Arethusa Papers*. Edited by J. Peradotto and J. P. Sullivan. 7–58. Albany.)

Asheri, D. 1966. *Distribuzioni di terre nell' antica Grecia. Memorie dell' Accademia delle scienze di Torino*. Turin.

Austin, N. 1981. "Odysseus *Polytropos:* Man of Many Minds." *Arche* 6: 40–52.

———. 1975. *Archery at the Dark of the Moon: Poetic Problems in Homer's Odyssey*. Berkeley, Los Angeles, London.

———. 1972. "Name Magic in the *Odyssey*." *California Studies in Classical Antiquity* 5: 1–19.

———. 1969. "Telemachos *Polymechanos*" *California Studies in Classical Antiquity* 2: 45–63.

Bal, M. 1985. *Narratology: Introduction to the Theory of Narrative*. Translated by C. van Boheemen. Toronto.

Benveniste, E. 1969. *Le Vocabulaire des institutions indo-européennes*. 2 vols. Paris. [*Indo-European Language and Society*. Translated by E. Palmer. Miami Linguistics Series, no. 12. Coral Gables 1973.]

———. 1966. *Problèmes de linguistique générale*. vol. 1. Paris. [*Problems in General Linguistics*. Translated by M. E. Meek. Miami Linguistics Series, no. 8. Coral Gables, 1971.]

Bérard, V. 1924. *Introduction à l'Odyssée*. 3 vols. Paris.

Bergren, A. 1983. "Odyssean Temporality: Many (Re)turns." *Approaches to Homer*. Edited by C. Rubino and C. Shelmerdine. 38–73. Austin and London.

———. 1979–80. "Helen's Web: Time and Tableau in the *Iliad*." *Helios* 7: 19–34.

Bethe, E. 1924. "Die griechische Dichtung." *Handbuch der Literaturwissenschaft*. Edited by O. Walzel. 1–86. Wildbad-Potsdam.

———. 1922a. *Die Gedichte Homers. Wissenschaft und Bildung*, no. 180. Leipzig.

———. 1922b. *Homer: Dichtung und Saga*. Vol. 2: *Odyssee, Kyklos, Zeitbestimmung*. Leipzig and Berlin [2nd edition 1929].

Beye, C. R. 1974. "Male and Female in the Homeric Poems." *Ramus* 3: 87–101.

———. 1968. *The Iliad, the Odyssey, and the Epic Tradition*. New York.

Boedeker, D. 1984. *Descent from Heaven: Images of Dew in Greek Poetry and Religion*. American Classical Studies, no. 13. Chico, Ca.

——. 1974. *Aphrodite's Entry into Greek Epic. Mnemosyne* Supplement, no. 31. Leiden.

Bolte, J., and G. Polivka. 1915. *Anmerkungen zu den Kinder- und Hausmärchen der Brüder Grimm.* Leipzig [2nd edition Hildesheim, 1963].

Bornemann, E. 1953. *Odyssee-Interpretationen.* Frankfurt am Main.

Bose, N. K., ed. 1957. *Selections from Gandhi.* Ahmedabad.

Bradley, E. M. 1976. "'The Greatness of his Nature': Fire and Justice in the *Odyssey*." *Ramus* 5: 137–48.

——. 1975. "On King Amphidamas' Funeral and Hesiod's Muses." La Parola del passato 163: 285–88.

Brehm, A. E. 1914. *Brehms Tierleben: Allgemeine Kunde des Tierreichs,* vol. 11. 4th edition, edited by O. zur Strassen. Leipzig and Vienna.

Bremer, J. M., I.J.F. de Jong, and J. Kalff, eds. 1987. *Homer: Beyond Oral Poetry.* Amsterdam.

Brémond, C. 1968. "Postérité américaine de Propp." *Communications* 11: 147–64. [Reprinted in 1973. *Logique du récit.* Paris. 59–80.]

——. 1964. "Le Message Narratif." *Communications* 4: 4–32. [Reprinted in 1973. *Logique du récit.* Paris. 11–47].

Brown, C. S. 1966. "Odysseus and Polyphemus: The Name and the Curse." *Comparative Literature* 18: 193–202.

Büchner, W. 1940. *Die Penelopeszenen in der Odyssee.*" *Hermes* 75: 129–67.

Buffière, F. 1956. *Les Mythes d'Homère et la pensée grecque.* Paris.

Burkert, W. 1977. *Griechische Religion der archaischen und klassischen Epoche.* Stuttgart. [1984. *Greek Religion.* Translated by J. Raffan. Cambridge, Mass.]

——. 1972. *Homo Necans.* Berlin and New York. [Translated by P. Bing. 1983. Berkeley, Los Angeles, London.]

——. 1969. "Das Proömium des Parmenides und die Katabase des Pythagoras." *Phronesis* 14: 1–30.

——. 1960. "Das Lied von Ares und Aphrodite: Zum Verhältnis von *Odyssee* und *Ilias*." *Rheinisches Museum* 103: 130–44.

Buschor, E. 1944. *Die Musen des Jenseits.* Munich.

——. 1941. *Meermänner. Sitzungsberichte der Bayerischen Akademie der Wissenschaften,* Phil.-hist. Abt., Bd. 2, Heft 1. Munich.

Butler, S. 1967 [1897]. *The Authoress of the Odyssey.* 3rd edition. Chicago.

Butterworth, E.A.S. 1970. *The Tree at the Navel of the Earth.* Berlin.

Calame, C. 1976. "Mythe grec et structure narratives: Le Mythe des Cyclopes dans l'*Odysée*." *Živa Antika* 26: 311–28.

Casabona, J. 1966. *Recherches sur le vocabulaire des sacrifices.* Aix-Gap.

Chamoux, F. 1952. "La Porcherie d'Eumée." *Revue des études grecques* 65: 281–88.

Chantraine, P. 1968–80. *Dictionnaire étymologique de la langue grecque.* Paris.

——. 1933. *La Formation des noms en Grec ancien.* Paris.

Clark, R. J. 1979. *Catabasis: Vergil and the Wisdom Tradition.* Amsterdam.

Clarke, H. W. 1967. *The Art of the Odyssey.* Englewood Cliffs, N.J.

Clay, J. S. 1983. *The Wrath of Athena: Gods and Men in the Odyssey.* Princeton.

——. 1980. "Goat Island: *Od.* 9.116–141." *Classical Quarterly* 30: 261–64.

——. 1976. "The Beginning of the *Odyssey*." *American Journal of Philology* 97: 313–26.

Cohen, B., ed. 1995. *The Distaff Side: Representing the Female in Homer's Odyssey.* New York and Oxford.

Cole, T. 1967. *Democritus and the Sources of Greek Anthropology.* American Philological Association Monographs, no. 25. Ann Arbor.

Combellack, F. M. 1973. "Three Odyssean Problems." *California Studies in Classical Antiquity* 6: 17–46.

Connor, W. R. 1985. "The Razing of the House in Greek Society." *Transactions of the American Philological Association* 115: 75–102.

Crane, G. 1988. *Calypso: Backgrounds and Conventions of the Odyssey. Beiträge zur klassischen Philologie,* no. 191. Frankfurt am Main.

Davidson, H.R.E. 1964–75. *Gods and Myths of Northern Europe.* Harmondsworth.

Delebecque, E. 1980. *Construction de l'Odysée.* Paris.

Delrieu, A. D., D. Hilt, and F. Létoublon. 1984. "Homère à plusiers voix: Les Techniques narratives dans l'épopée grecque archaïque." *LALIES: Actes des sessions de linguistique et de littérature.* 177–94.

Detienne, M. 1979. *Dionysos Slain.* Translated by L. and M. Muellner. Baltimore and London. [First publication 1977. *Dionysos mis à mort.* Paris]

———. 1977. *The Gardens of Adonis: Spices in Greek Mythology.* Translated by J. Lloyd. Sussex and Atlantic Highlands, N.J. [First publication 1972. *Les Jardins d'Adonis.* Paris.]

———. 1973. "L'Olivier: Un mythe politico-religieux,'" in *Problèmes de la terre en Grèce ancienne.* Edited by M. I. Finley. Paris and the Hague.

———. 1967a. *Les Maîtres de vérité dans la Grèce archaïque.* Paris [2nd edition Paris, 1973].

———. 1967b. "La Mémoire du poète." *Les Maîtres de vérité.* 9–27.

Detienne, M., and J.-P Vernant. 1989. *The Cuisine of Sacrifice in Ancient Greece.* Translated by P. Wissing. Chicago and London [First publication 1979. *La Cuisine du sacrifice en pays grec.* Paris].

———. 1978. *Cunning Intelligence in Greek Culture and Society.* Translated by J. Lloyd. Sussex and Atlantic Highlands, N.J. [First publication 1974. *Les Ruses de l'intelligence: La Métis des grecs.* Paris].

Devereux, G. 1957. "The Character of Penelope." *Psychoanalytic Quarterly* 26: 378–86.

Diano, C. 1968. *Sagezza e Poetiche degli Antichi.* Venice.

———. 1963. "La poetica dei Feaci." *Belfagor* 18: 403–24.

Diels, H., and W. Kranz, eds. 1934. *Die Fragmente der Vorsokratiker.* 5th ed. Berlin.

Dietz, G. 1971. "Das Bett des Odysseus." *Symbolon* 7: 9–32.

Dimock, G. 1989. *The Unity of the Odyssey.* Amherst.

———. 1956. "The Name of Odysseus." *Hudson Review* 9: 52–70 [Reprinted 1962. *Homer: A Collection of Critical Essays.* Edited by G. Steiner and R. Fagles. 106–121. Englewood Cliffs; 1963. *Essays on the Odyssey: Selected Modern Criticism.* Edited by C. H. Taylor. 54–72. Bloomington.]

Dindorf, W. 1855. *Scholia Graeca in Homeri Odysseam.* 2 vols. Oxford (Reprinted Amsterdam, 1962).

Dirlmeier, F. 1967. "Die schreckliche Kalypso." *Lebende Antike: Festschrift für R. Sühnel:* 20–26. Edited by H. Meller and H.-J Zimmermann. Berlin.

Dodds, E. R. 1951. *The Greeks and the Irrational.* Berkeley.

Doherty, L. E. 1995. *Siren Songs: Gender, Audiences, and Narrators in the Odyssey.* Ann Arbor.

———. 1993. "Tyro in *Odyssey* 11: Closed and Open Readings." *Helios* 20: 3–15.

———. 1992. "Gender and Internal Audiences in the *Odyssey.*" *American Journal of Philology* 113: 161–77.

———. 1991. "The Internal and Implied Audiences of *Odyssey* 11." *Arethusa* 24: 145–76.

———. 1990. "Joyce's Penelope and Homer's: Feminist Reconsiderations." *Classical and Modern Literature* 10: 343–49.

Doležel, L. 1976. "Narrative Modalities." *Journal of Literary Semantics* 5: 5–14.

Dombrowski, D. 1984. *The Philosophy of Vegetarianism.* Amherst, Mass.

Duban, J. 1980. "Miscellanea: The Whirlwind and the Fight at the River." *Eranos* 78: 187–92.

Dumézil, G. 1973. *Mythe et épopée.* Vol. 3. Paris.

Dunbar, H. 1962. *A Complete Concordance to the Odyssey of Homer.* Revised by B. Marzullo. Hildesheim.

Durante, M. 1971-76. *Sulla preistoria della tradizione poetica greca.* 2 vols. Rome.

———. 1960. "Ricerche sulla preistoria della lingua poetica greca: La terminologia relativa alla creazione poetica." *Rendiconti della Classe di Scienze morale, storichi e filologiche dell'Accademia dei Lincei* 15: 231–49.

Edwards, A. T. 1985. *Achilles in the Odyssey. Beiträge zur klassischen Philologie,* no. 171. Königstein.

Eisenberger, H. 1973. *Studien zur Odyssee.* Wiesbaden.

Eisler, R. 1910. *Weltmantel und Himmelszelt.* Vol. 2. Munich.

Eitrem, S. 1938. "Phaiaker." *Paulys Real-Encyclopädie der classischen Altertumswissenschaft.* Vol. 19. 2. Cols. 1518–34.

———. 1915. *Opferritus und Voropfer der Griechen und Römer. Videnskapsselskapets Skrifter:* Hist.-Phil. Kl., no. 2: 1. Kristiania.

———. 1904. *Die Phaiakenepisode in der Odyssee. Videnskapsselskapets Skrifter:* Hist.-Phil. Kl., no. 2. Kristiania.

Emlyn-Jones, C. 1984. "The Reunion of Odysseus and Penelope." *Greece & Rome* 31: 1–18.

Erbse, H. 1972. *Beiträge zum Verständnis der Odyssee.* Berlin.

Felson-Rubin, N. 1994. *Regarding Penelope: From Character to Poetics.* Princeton.

———. 1987. "Penelope's Perspective: Character from Plot." *Homer: Beyond Oral Poetry.* Edited by J. M. Bremer, I.J.F. de Jong, and J. Kalff. 61–83. Amsterdam. [Reworked and expanded in this volume, pp. 163–83, and in *Regarding Penelope,* pp. 15–43.]

Felson-Rubin, N., and W. Sale. 1983. "Meleager and Odysseus: A Structural and Cultural Study of the Greek Hunting-Maturation Myth." *Arethusa* 16: 137–71.

Fenik, B. 1974. *Studies in the Odyssey. Hermes Einzelschriften,* no. 30. Wiesbaden.

Festugière, A. J. 1949. "A propos des arétalogies d'Isis." *Harvard Theological Review* 42: 209–34 [Reprinted 1972. *Etudes de religion grecque et hellénistique.* 138–63. Paris].

Finley, J. H., Jr. 1978. *Homer's Odyssey.* Cambridge, Mass.

Finley, M. I.. 1967. "Utopianism Ancient and Modern." *The Critical Spirit: Essays in Honor of Herbert Marcuse.* 3–20. Boston. [Reprinted 1975. *The Use and Abuse of History.* 178–93. New York.]

———. 1955. "Marriage, Sale and Gift in the Homeric World." *Revue internationale des droits de l'antiquité* 3: 167–94. [Reprinted 1981. *Economy and Society in Ancient Greece.* Edited by B. D. Shaw and R. P. Saller. 233–45. New York and London.]

———. 1954. *The World of Odysseus.* New York. [Revised edition, 1965. New York and London. Newly revised edition, 1978. New York and London.]

Focke, F. 1943. *Die Odyssee.* Stuttgart-Berlin.

Foley, H. P. 1978. "'Reverse Similes' and Sex Roles in the *Odyssey*." *Arethusa* 11: 7–26. [Reprinted 1984. *Women in the Ancient World: The Arethusa Papers.* Edited by J. Peradotto and J. P. Sullivan. 59–78. Albany.]

Ford A. 1992. *Homer: The Poetry of the Past*. Ithaca, N.Y., and London.

Frame, D. 1978. *The Myth of Return in Early Greek Epic*. New Haven and London.

Fränkel, H. 1962. *Dichtung und Philosophie des frühen Griechentums*. 2nd edition. Munich. [*Early Greek Poetry and Philosophy*. Translated by M. Hadas and J. Willis. Oxford. 1973]

———. 1921. *Die Homerischen Gleichnisse*. Göttingen. [Reprinted 1977. Göttingen.]

Frobenius, L. 1904. *Das Zeitalter des Sonnengottes*. Berlin.

Frontisi-Ducroux, F. 1975. *Dédale: Mythologie de l'artisane en Grèce ancienne*. Paris.

Garlan, Y. 1968. "Fortifications et histoire grecque." *Problèmes de la guerre en Grèce ancienne*. Edited by J.-P Vernant. 245–60. Paris and The Hague.

Genette, G. 1980. *Narrative Discourse*. Translated by J. Lewin. Ithaca, N.Y., and London.

Germain, G. 1960. *Homer*. Translated by R. Howard. London.

———. 1954a. *Genèse de l'Odyssée: Le Fantastique et le sacré*. Paris.

———. 1954b. *Homère et la mystique des nombres*. Paris.

Gernet, L. 1968. *Anthropologie de la Grèce antique*. Paris. [*The Anthropology of Ancient Greece*. Translated by J. Hamilton and B. Nagy. Baltimore and London, 1981.]

Gilbert, S. M., and S. Gubar. 1979. *The Madwoman in the Attic*. New Haven and London.

Girard, R. 1978. *Des choses cachées depuis la fondation du monde*. Paris.

———. 1977. *Violence and the Sacred*. Baltimore and London. [First publication 1972: *La Violence et le sacré*. Paris.]

Goold, G. P. 1960. "Homer and the Alphabet." *Transactions of the American Philological Association* 91: 272–91.

Gordon, R. L., ed. 1981. *Myth, Religion and Society: Stucturalist Essays by M. Detienne, L. Gernet, J.-P. Vernant and P. Vidal-Naquet*. Cambridge and Paris.

Gresseth, G. K. 1970. "The Homeric Sirens." *Transactions of the American Philological Association* 101: 203–18.

Grimm, W. 1857. *Die Sage von Polyphem. Abhandlung der königlichen Akademie der Wissenschaften*. Berlin.

Güntert, H. 1921. *Von der Sprache der Götter und Geister*. Halle.

———. 1919. *Kalypso: Bedeutungsgeschichtliche Untersuchungen auf dem Gebiet der indogermanischen Sprachen*. Halle.

Hansen, W. F. 1977. "Odysseus' Last Journey." *Quaderni Urbinati di cultura classica* 24: 27–48.

———. 1972. *The Conference Sequence: Patterned Narration and Narrative Inconsistency in the Odyssey*. Berkeley and Los Angeles.

Harsh, P. W. 1950. "Penelope and Odysseus in *Odyssey* XIX." *American Journal of Philology* 71: 1–21.

Haussleiter, J. 1935. *Der Vegetarismus in der Antike*. Berlin.

Havelock, E. A. 1963. *A Preface to Plato*. Cambridge, Mass. and Oxford. [Reprinted New York, 1967.]

———. 1957. *The Liberal Temper in Greek Politics*. London.

Heidel, A. 1963. *The Gilgamesh Epic*. Chicago.

Hexter, R. 1993. *A Guide to the Odyssey: A Commentary on the Translation by Robert Fitzgerald*. New York.

Hirvonen, K. 1968. *Matriarchal Survivals and Certain Trends in Homer's Female Characters*. Helsinki.

Hölscher, U. 1989. *Die Odyssee: Epos zwischen Märchen und Roman*. Munich.

———. 1978. "The Transformation from Folk-Tale to Epic." *Homer: Tradition and Innovation*. Edited by B. Fenik. 51–67. Leiden.

———. 1972."Die Erkennungsszene in 23. Buch der *Odyssee*." *Griechisch in der Schule*. Edited by Egon Romisch. 156–65. Frankfurt am Main.

———. 1967a. "Die Atridensage in der *Odyssee*." *Festschrift für Richard Alewyn*. Edited by H. Singer and B. von Wiese. 1–16. Cologne-Graz.

———. 1967b. "Penelope vor den Freiern." *Lebende Antike: Symposium für Rudolph Sühnel*. Edited by H. Meller and H.-J Zimmermann. 27–33. Berlin [This volume, 133–40].

———. 1939. *Untersuchungen zur Form der Odyssee. Hermes Einzelschriften*, no. 6. Berlin.

Householder, F., and G. Nagy. 1972. "Greek." *Current Trends in Linguistics* 9: 735–816.

Jacoby, F. 1923-. *Die Fragmente der griechischen Historiker*. 15 vols. Leiden.

Kahn, L. 1981. "Ulysse." *Dictionnaire des mythologies*. Edited by Y. Bonnefoy. Vol. 2. 517–20. Paris [*Dictionary of Mythologies*. Translated under the Direction of W. Doniger. Vol. 1. 494–98. Chicago, 1991].

———. 1980. "Ulysse, la ruse et la mort." *Critique* 393: 116–34.

Kahn, L., and N. Loraux. 1981. "Mort. Les Mythes Grecs." *Dictionnaire des mythologies*. Ed. Y. Bonnefoy. Vol. 2. 117–24. Paris [*Dictionary of Mythologies*. Translated under the Direction of W. Doniger. Vol. 1. 405–12. Chicago, 1991].

Kaschnitz, M. L. 1947. *Griechische Mythen*. Hamburg.

Katz, M. A. 1991. *Penelope's Renown*. Princeton.

Kirchoff, A. 1879. *Die Homerische Odyssee und ihre Entstehung*. 2nd edition. Berlin.

———. 1869. *Die Composition der Odyssee*. Berlin.

Kirk, G. S. 1970. *Myth: Its Meaning and Functions in Ancient and Other Cultures*. Berkeley and Los Angeles.

———. 1962. *The Songs of Homer*. Cambridge.

Klingner, F. 1944. *Über die vier ersten Bücher der Odyssee. Sitzungsberichte der Sachsischen Akademie der Wissenschaften*, Phil.-Hist. Klasse., no. 96, 1. Leipzig.

Kranz, W. 1915. "Die Irrfahrten des Odysseus." *Hermes* 50: 93–112.

Krarup, P. 1948. "Verwendung von Abstrakta in den direkten Rede bei Homer." *Classica et Medievalia* 10: 1–17.

Kron, U. 1976. *Die zehn attischen Phylenheroen: Geschichte, Mythos, Kult und Darstellung*. Berlin.

Kuhn, A. 1855. "Die Sagen von der weise Frau." *Zeitschrift für deutsche Mythologie und Sittenkunde* 3: 368–99.

Kullmann, W. 1956. *Die Quellen der Ilias (Troischer Sagenkreis.). Hermes Einzelschriften*, no. 14. Wiesbaden.

Lacey, W. K. 1966. "Homeric *hedna* and Penelope's *Kurios*." *Journal of Hellenic Studies* 86: 55–68.

Lanata, G. 1963. *Poetica Pre-Platonica, testimonianze e frammenti*. Florence.

Lang, M. L. 1969. "Homer and Oral Techniques." *Hesperia* 38: 159–68.

Latte, K. 1968a. *Kleine Schriften*. Munich.

———. 1968b. "Die Sirenen." *Kleine Schriften*. 106–11.

———. 1964. "Zeitgeschichtliches zu Archilochus." *Hermes* 92: 385–90.

Lattimore, R. 1965. *The Odyssey of Homer*. New York.

———. 1959. *Hesiod*. Ann Arbor.

———. 1951. *The Iliad of Homer*. Chicago.

Lee, D.J.N. 1964. *The Similes of the Iliad and Odyssey Compared*. Melbourne.

Levine, D. 1983. "Penelope's Laugh: *Odyssey* 18.163." *American Journal of Philology* 104: 172–77.

Levy, H. 1963. "The Odyssean Suitors and the Guest-Host Relationship." *Transactions of the American Philological Association* 94: 145–53.

Leyen, F. von der. 1925. *Das Märchen: Ein Versuch.* 3rd edition. *Wissenschaft und Bildung*, no. 96. Leipzig. [4th edition Heidelberg, 1958.]

Liddell, H. G., and R. Scott. *A Greek-English Lexicon.* 9th ed. with supplement rev. H. S. Jones. Oxford, 1968.

Loraux, N. 1978. "Sur la race des femmes et quelques-unes de ses tribus." *Arethusa* 11: 43–87. [Reprinted 1981 in *Les Enfants d'Athéna: Idées athéniennes sur la citoyenneté et la division des sexes.* 75–117. Paris. English translation 1993. *The Children of Athena: Athenian Ideas about Citizenship and the Division between the Sexes.* Translated by C. Levine. 72–110. Princeton.]

Lord, A. B. 1960. *The Singer of Tales.* Cambridge, Mass. [Reprinted 1965. New York.]

———. 1951. "Composition by Theme in Homer and Southslavic Epos." *Transactions of the American Philological Association* 82: 71–80.

Lord, G. de F. 1961. *Homeric Renaissance.* New Haven.

Lovejoy, A. O., and G. Boas. 1935. *Primitivism and Related Ideas in Antiquity.* Baltimore.

Marg, W. 1971. *Homer über die Dichtung: Der Schild des Achilleus.* 2nd edition. Münster.

———. 1956. "Das erste Lied des Demodokos." *Navicula Chiloniensis: Festschrift für Felix Jacoby.* 16–29. Leiden.

Marienstras, R. 1965. "Prospéro ou le Machiavélisme du bien." *Bulletin de la Faculté des lettres de Strasbourg* 42: 899–917.

Maròt, K. 1960. *Die Anfänge der griechischen Literatur: Vorfragen.* Budapest.

Marquardt, P. 1984. "Penelope *Polutropos.*" *American Journal of Philology* 106: 32–48.

Martin, R. P. 1989. *The Language of Heroes.* Ithaca, N.Y., and London.

Mattes, W. 1958. *Odysseus bei den Phäaken.* Würzburg.

Merkelbach, R., and M. L. West, eds. 1967. *Fragmenta Hesiodea.* Oxford.

Meuli, K. 1954. "Herkunft und Wesen des Fabel" (*Schweizerische Gesellschaft für Volkskunde* 50: 65–88 [Reprinted in his *Gesammelte Schriften.* Vol. 2. 731–56. Basel-Stuttgart, 1975].

———. 1942. *Schweizermasken.* Zurich.

———. 1935. "Scythica." *Hermes* 70: 121–76.

———. 1921. *Odysee und Argonautika.* Berlin.

Millard, A. R. 1964. "Gilgamesh X: A New Fragment." *IRAQ* 26: 99–105.

Miller, D. G. 1982. *Homer and the Ionian Epic Tradition.* Innsbruck.

Miller, N. K. 1980. *The Heroine's Text: Readings in the French and English Novel, 1722–1782.* New York.

Monro, D. B. 1901. *Homer's Odyssey: Books XIII–XXIV.* Oxford.

Monro, D. B., and T. W. Allen, eds. 1920. *Homeri Opera.* 3rd edition. Vols. 1 and 2, *Iliad.* Oxford.

Morson, G. S., and C. Emerson. 1990. *Mikhail Bakhtin: Creation of a Prosaics.* Stanford.

Mossé, C. 1980. "Ithaque ou la naissance de la cité." *Annali del seminario di studi del mondo classico, Istituto universitario orientale, Napoli* 2: 7–19.

Most, G. 1989. "The Structure and Function of Odysseus' *Apologoi.*" *Transactions of the American Philological Association* 119: 15–30.

Motte, A. 1973. *Prairies et jardins de la Grèce antique. Mémoires de la classe de Lettres de l'Académie royale de Belgique.* 2nd series, no. 66. Brussels.

Moulton, C. 1977: *Similes in the Iliad and Odyssey. Hypomnemata,* no. 49. Göttingen.

———. 1974a. "Similes in the *Iliad.*" *Hermes* 102: 381–97.

———. 1974b. "The End of the *Odyssey.*" *Greek, Roman and Byzantine Studies* 15: 153–69.

Mühll, P. von der. 1976. *Ausgewählte kleine Schriften.* Edited by B. Wyss. *Schweizerische Beiträge zur Altertumswissenschaft,* 12. Basel.

———. ed. 1946. *Homeri Odyssea. Bibliotheca Scriptorum Graecorum et Romanorum Teubneriana.* 3rd edition 1962. Stuttgart [reprinted 1984].

———. 1940a. "*Odyssee.*" *Paulys Real-Encyclopädie der classischen Altertumswissenschaft. Supplementband* 7. Cols. 696–768 [Reprinted in *Ausgewählte Kleine Schriften,* 27–121].

———. 1940b. "Die Dichter der *Odyssee.*" *Jahrbuch des Vereins Schweizer Gymnasiallehrer* 68: 80–103 [Reprinted in *Ausgewählte kleine Schriften,* 122–47].

Murnaghan, S. 1990. Review of U. Hölscher, *Die Odyssee: Epos zwischen Märchen und Roman. American Journal of Philology* 111: 271–74.

———. 1987. *Disguise and Recognition in the Odyssey.* Princeton.

———. 1986. "Penelope's *Agnoia:* Knowledge, Power, and Gender in the *Odyssey.*" *Helios* 13: 103–15.

Mutschmann, H., ed. 1958. *Sextus Empiricus. Pyrrhoneiōn hypotyposeōn libri tres.* Revised by I. Mau. Leipzig.

Nagler, M. 1990a. "Ethical Anxiety and Artistic Inconsistency: The Case of Oral Epic." *Cabinet of the Muses: Essays on Classical and Comparative Literature in Honor of Thomas G. Rosenmeyer.* Edited by M. Griffith and D. J. Mastronarde. 225–39. Atlanta.

———. 1990b. "Odysseus: The Proem and the Problem." *Classical Antiquity* 9: 335–56.

———. 1988. "Toward a Semantics of Ancient Conflict: *Eris* in the *Iliad.*" *Classical World* 82: 81–90.

———. 1980. "Entretiens avec Tirésias." *Classical World* 74: 89–108.

———. 1977. "Dread Goddess Endowed with Speech." *Archaeological News* 6: 77–85 [Revised and expanded in this volume, 141–61].

———. 1974. *Spontaneity and Tradition: A Study in the Oral Art of Homer.* Berkeley and Los Angeles.

Nagy, G. 1990. *Pindar's Homer: The Lyric Possession of an Epic Past.* Baltimore and London.

———. 1983. "*Sema and Noesis:* Some Illustrations." *Arethusa* 16: 35–55.

———. 1979. *The Best of the Achaeans: Concepts of the Hero in Archaic Greek Poetry.* Baltimore and London.

———. 1974. *Comparative Studies in Greek and Indic Meter.* Harvard Studies in Comparative Literature, no. 33. Cambridge, Mass.

———. 1973. "Phaethon, Sappho's Phaon, and the White Rock of Leukas." *Harvard Studies in Classical Philology* 77: 137–77.

Niles, J. D. 1978. "Patterning in the Wanderings of Odysseus." *Ramus* 7: 46–60.

Norden, E. 1927. *Vergils Aeneis, Buch 6.* 3rd edition. Berlin.

Olson, S. D. 1990. "The Stories of Agamemnon in Homer's *Odyssey.*" *Transactions of the American Philological Association* 120: 57–71.

Ong, W. J. 1982. *Orality and Literacy*. London and New York.

Page, D. 1973. *Folktales in Homer's Odyssey*. Cambridge, Mass.

———. ed. 1962. *Poetae Melici Graeci*. Oxford.

———. 1955. *The Homeric Odyssey*. Oxford.

Pagliaro, A. 1961. "Aedi e rapsodi." *Nuovi saggi di critica semantica*. 3–62. Messina-Florence. [First publication 1951. "La terminologia poetica di Omero e l'origine dell'epica.," *Ricerche Linguistiche* 12: 1–46.]

Parry, A. 1966. "Have We Homer's *Iliad?*" *Yale Classical Studies* 20: 175–216. [Reprinted 1978. *Essays on the Iliad: Selected Modern Criticism*. Edited by J. Wright. 1–27, 128–34. Bloomington and London.

Parry, M. 1971. *The Making of Homeric Verse: The Collected Essays of Milman Parry*. Edited by A. Parry. Oxford.

Pauly, A., G. Wissowa, et al., eds. 1893–1980. *Real-Encyclopädie der classischen Altertumswissenschaft*. Stuttgart.

Pavel, T. 1986. *Fictional Worlds*. Cambridge, Mass.

———. 1980. "Narrative Domains." *Poetics Today* 1: 105–14.

Peabody, B. 1975. *The Winged Word*. Albany.

Pearson, A. E. 1917. *The Fragments of Sophocles*. 3 vols. Cambridge.

Pease, A. S. 1937. "Ölbaum." *Paulys Real-Encyclopädie der classischen Altertumswissenschaft*. Vol. 17.2. Cols. 1998–2022.

Pembroke, S. G. 1979. "The Early Human Family: Some Views 1770–1870." *Classical Influences in Western Thought A.D. 1650–1870*. Edited by R. R. Bolgar. Cambridge 275–91.

———. 1967. "Women in Charge: The Function of Alternatives in Early Greek Tradition and the Ancient Idea of Matriarchy." *Journal of the Warburg and Courtauld Institutes* 30: 1–35.

Peradotto, J. 1990. *Man in the Middle Voice: Name and Narration in the Odyssey*. Martin Classical Lectures. New Series, no. 1. Princeton.

———. 1974. "*Odyssey* 8.564-71: Verisimilitude, Narrative Analysis, and Bricolage." *Texas Studies in Literature and Language* 15: 803–32.

Pfeiffer, R. 1928. Review of E. Schwartz, *Die Odyssee,* and U. von Wilamowitz-Moellendorff, *Die Heimkehr des Odysseus*. *Deutsche Literaturzeitung* 49: cols. 2355–2372 [Reprinted 1960 in his *Ausgewählte Schriften*. 8–25. Munich].

Podlecki, A. 1971. "Some Odyssean Similes." *Greece & Rome* 18: 81–90.

———. 1967. "Omens in the *Odyssey*." *Greece and Rome* 14: 12–23.

———. 1961. "Guest Gifts and Nobodies in *Odyssey* 9." *Phoenix* 15: 125–33.

Pollard, J. 1965. *Seers, Shrines, and Sirens*. New York and London.

Porter, H. 1962. "Introduction", to *Homer: The Odyssey*. Translated by G. H. Palmer, Edited by H. Porter. 1–20. New York.

Posner, R. A. 1979–80. "The Homeric Version of the Minimal State." *Ethics* 90: 27–46.

Powell, B. B. 1991. *Homer and the Origin of the Greek Alphabet*. Cambridge.

———. 1977. *Composition by Theme in the Odyssey*. Meisenheim am Glan.

———. 1970. "Narrative Patterns in the Homeric Tale of Menelaus." *Transactions of the American Philological Association* 101: 419–31.

Pratt, L. H. 1993. *Lying and Poetry from Homer to Pindar: Falsehood and Deception in Archaic Greek Poetics*. Ann Arbor.

Pritchard, J. B. 1969. *Ancient Near Eastern Texts Relating to the Old Testament*. 3rd edition with Supplement. Princeton.

Propp, V. 1968. *Morphology of the Folk Tale*. 2nd edition. Translated by L. Scott. *Bibliographical and Special Series of the American Folklore Society*, no. 9. Austin and London.

Pucci, P. 1987. *Odysseus Polutropos: Intertextual Readings in the Odyssey and Iliad*. Ithaca, N.Y., and London.

———. 1979. "The Song of the Sirens." *Arethusa* 12: 121–32 [This volume: 191–99].

———. 1977. *Hesiod and the Language of Poetry*. Baltimore and London.

Radermacher, L. 1915. *Die Erzählungen der Odyssee. Sitzungsberichte der Kais. Akademie der Wissenschaften in Wien*, Phil.-Hist. Kl., Bd. 1. Vienna.

Rankin, A. V. 1962. "Penelope's Dreams in Books XIX and XX of the *Odyssey*." *Helikon* 2: 617–24.

Redfield, J. 1982. "Notes on the Greek Wedding." *Arethusa* 15: 181–201.

———. 1975. *Nature and Culture in the Iliad: The Tragedy of Hector*. Chicago and London.

Reinhardt, K. 1966. *Vermächtnis der Antike: Gesammelte Essays zur Philosophie und Geschichtsschreibung*. Göttingen.

———. 1960a. "Die Abenteuer der *Odyssee*." *Tradition und Geist: Gesammelte Essays zur Dichtung*. Edited by C. Becker. 47–124. Göttingen. [First publication 1948. *Von Werken und Formen*. 52–162. Godesberg. This volume, 63–132].

———. 1960b. "Homer und die Telemachie." *Tradition und Geist: Gesammelte Essays zur Dichtung*. Edited by C. Becker. 37–46. Göttingen [First publication 1948. *Von Werken und Formen*. 37–51. Godesberg].

Richardson, S. 1990. *The Homeric Narrator*. Nashville.

Richter, W. 1968. *Die Landwirtschaft im homerischen Zeitalter*. Göttingen.

Risch, E. 1974. *Wortbildung der homerische Sprache*. 2nd edition. Berlin and New York.

Ritoók, Zs. 1975. "Stages in the Development of Greek Epic." *Acta Antiqua Academiae Scientiarum Hungaricae* 23: 127–40.

Robinson, D. M. 1931. "Bouzyges and the First Plough on the Krater of the Painter of Naples Hephaistos." *American Journal of Archaeology* 35: 152–60.

Rohde, E. 1901. *Kleine Schriften*. 2 vols. Tübingen-Leipzig.

Roisman, H. R. 1987. "Penelope's Indignation." *Transactions of the American Philological Association* 117: 59–68.

Rudhardt, J. 1958. *Notions fondamentales de la pensée religieuse et actes constitutifs du culte dans la Grèce classique*. Geneva.

Ruijgh, C. J. 1971. *Autour de te épique*. Leiden.

Russo, J. 1982. "Interview and Aftermath: Dream, Fantasy, and Intuition in *Odyssey* 19 and 20." *American Journal of Philology* 103: 4–18.

———. 1968. "Homer against His Tradition." *Arion* 7: 275–95.

Russo, J., and B. Simon. 1968. "Homeric Psychology and the Oral Epic Tradition." *Journal of the History of Ideas* 29: 483–98 [Reprinted 1978. *Essays on the Iliad: Selected Modern Criticism*. Edited by J. Wright. 41–57, 137–39. Bloomington and London].

Rüter, K. 1969. *Odysseeinterpretationen: Untersuchungen zum ersten Buch und zum Phauakis*. Edited by K. Matthiessen. *Hypomnemata*, no. 19. Göttingen.

Ryan, M.-L. 1985. "The Modal Structure of Narrative Universes." *Poetics Today* 6: 717–55.

Sacks, R. 1987. *The Traditional Phrase in Homer: Two Studies in Form, Meaning and Interpretation*. Columbia Studies in the Classical Tradition, no. 14. Leiden.

———. 1982. "Ending the *Odyssey:* Odysseus Traditions and the Homeric *Odyssey.*" Unpublished paper presented at the Columbia University Seminar in Classical Civilization.

Saïd, S. 1979. "Les Crimes des prétendants, la maison d'Ulysse et les festins de l'*Odyssée.*" *Etudes de littérature ancienne.* 9–49. Paris.

Schadewaldt, W. 1965. *Von Homers Welt und Werk.* 4th edition. Stuttgart.

———. 1959. *Neue Kriterien zur Odyssee-Analyse. Die Widererkennung des Odysseus und der Penelope. Sitzungsberichte der Heidelberger Akademie der Wissenschaften,* Phil.-Hist. Kl. Heidelberg [Reprinted 1970. *Hellas und Hesperien: Gesammelte Schriften zur antike und zur neueren Literatur.* 2nd edition. Vol. 1, 58–77. Zurich and Stuttgart].

Schein, S. L. 1984. *The Mortal Hero: An Introduction to Homer's Iliad.* Berkeley, Los Angeles, London.

———. 1970. "Odysseus and Polyphemus in the *Odyssey.*" *Greek, Roman and Byzantine Studies* 11: 73–83.

Scheinberg, S. 1979. "The Bee Maidens of the Homeric Hymn to Hermes." *Harvard Studies in Classical Philology* 83: 1–28.

Schmiel, R. 1972. "Telemachus in Sparta." *Transactions of the American Philological Association* 103: 463–72.

Schmitt, R., ed. 1968. *Indogermanische Dichtersprache. Wege der Forschung,* no. 165. Darmstadt.

———. 1967. *Dichtung und Dichtersprache in indogermanischer Zeit.* Wiesbaden.

Schwartz, E. 1924. *Die Odyssee.* Munich.

Scott, W. C. 1974. *The Oral Nature of the Homeric Simile. Mnemosyne* Supplement, no. 28. Leiden.

Segal, C. 1994. *Singers, Heroes, and Gods in the Odyssey.* Ithaca, N.Y.

———. 1983. "*Kleos* and Its Ironies in the *Odyssey.*" *L'Antiquité classique* 52: 22–47 [This volume, 201–21].

———. 1974. "Eros and Incantation: Sappho and Oral Poetry." *Arethusa* 7:139–60.

———. 1968. "Circean Temptations: Homer, Vergil, Ovid." *Transactions and Proceedings of the American Philological Association* 98: 419–42.

———. 1967. "Transition and Ritual in Odysseus' Return." *La parola del passato* 116: 321–42.

———. 1962. "The Phaeacians and the Symbolism of Odysseus' Return." *Arion* 1: 17–64.

Seidensticker, B. 1978. "Archilochus and Odysseus." *Greek, Roman and Byzantine Studies* 19: 5–22.

Seligo, I. 1938. *Zwischen Traum und Tat.* Frankfurt am Main.

Sellschopp, I. 1934. *Stilistische Untersuchungen zu Hesiod.* Ph.D. dissertation. Hamburg.

Sickle, J. V. 1975. "The New Erotic Fragment of Archilochus." *Quaderni Urbinati di cultura classica* 20: 123–56.

Sittig, E. 1912. "Harpyien." *Paulys Real-Encyclopädie der classischen Altertumswissenschaft.* Vol. 7.2. Cols. 2417–31.

Slater, P. 1968. *The Glory of Hera.* Boston.

Slatkin, L. M. 1991. *The Power of Thetis: Allusion and Interpretation in the Iliad.* Berkeley, Los Angeles, Oxford.

Snell, B., ed. 1964. *Pindari Carmina cum Fragmentis.* 3rd edition. Leipzig.

Snyder, J. M. 1980–81. "The Web of Song: Weaving Imagery in Homer and the Lyric Poets." *Classical Journal* 76: 193–96.

Solmsen, F., ed. 1970. *Hesiodi Theogonia, Opera et Dies, Scutum*, with *Fragmenta Selecta*, ed. R. Merkelbach and M. L. West. Oxford.

Stanford, W. B. 1958–59. *The Odyssey of Homer*. 2 vols. 2nd edition. London [Both volumes frequently reprinted, with addenda through 1971].

———. 1954. *The Ulysses Theme*. Oxford [Second edition, Oxford, 1963; reprinted Ann Arbor, 1968].

———. 1952. "The Homeric Etymology of the Name Odysseus." *Classical Philology* 47: 209–13.

Steinberg, M. 1981. "Ordering the Unordered: Time, Space, and Deceptive Coherence." *Yale French Studies* 61: 60–88.

Stewart, D. J. 1976. *The Disguised Guest: Rank, Role, and Identity in the Odyssey*. Lewisburg, Pa., and London.

Strasburger, H. 1954. "Der Einzelne und die Gemeinschaft im Denken der Griechen." *Historische Zeitschrift* 177: 227–48.

Taylor, C. H., ed. 1963. *Essays on the Odyssey: Selected Modern Criticism*. Bloomington.

Thalmann, G. 1992. *The Odyssey: An Epic of Return*. New York.

———. 1984. *Conventions of Form and Thought in Early Greek Epic Poetry*. Baltimore and London.

Thompson, Stith. 1955. *Motif-Index of Folk-Literature. A Classification of Narrative Elements in Folktales,* . . . 2nd edition. 6 vols. Bloomington, Ind.

Thornton, A. 1970. *People and Themes in Homer's Odyssey*. London.

Tièche, E. 1945. "Atlas als Personifikation der Weltachse." *Museum Helveticum* 2: 64–83.

Todorov, Tz. 1977. *The Poetics of Prose*. Translated by R. Howard, Ithaca, N.Y.

———. 1967. "Le Récit primitif." *Tel Quel* 30: 47–55.

Tolstoi, J. 1934. "Einige Märchenparallelen zur Heimkehr des Odysseus." *Philologus* 89: 261–74.

Vaihinger, H. 1968. *The Philosophy of "As If."* Translated by C. K. Ogden. New York.

Valk, M.H.A.L.H. van der. 1949. *Textual Criticism of the Odyssey*. Leiden.

Van Nortwick, T. 1983. "Penelope as Double Agent." *Classical World* 77: 24–25.

———. 1979. "Penelope and Nausikaa." *Transactions of the American Philological Association* 109: 269–76.

Vernant, J.-P. 1983a. *Myth and Thought among the Greeks*. London and Boston [First publication: 1965. *Mythe et pensée chez les Grecs*. Paris].

———. 1983b. "Hesiod's Myth of the Races: An Essay in Structural Analysis." *Myth and Thought:* 3–32.

———. 1982a. "La Belle Mort et le cadavre outragé." *La Mort, les morts dans les sociétés anciennes*. Edited by G. Gnoli and J.-P. Vernant. 45–76. Paris [Reprinted in his *L'Individu, la mort, l'amour: Soi-même et l'autre en Grèce ancienne*. 41–79. Paris, 1989. Translated by A. Szegedy-Maszak in *Mortals and Immortals: Collected Essays*. Edited by F. I. Zeitlin. 50–74. Princeton, 1991].

———. 1982b. "Le Refus d'Ulysse." *Le Temps de la réflexion* 3: 13–18 [This volume, 185–89].

———. 1981. "Death with Two Faces." Translated by J. Lloyd in *Mortality and Immortality: The Anthropology and Archaeology of Death*. Edited by S. C.

Humphries and H. King. London: Academic Press. 285–91 [This volume, 55–61].

———. 1980a. *Myth and Society in Ancient Greece*. Translated by J. Lloyd. Brighton and Atlantic Highlands, N.J. [Reprinted New York, 1988. First publication 1974. *Mythe et société en Grèce ancienne*. Paris].

———. 1980b. "The Myth of Prometheus in Hesiod." *Myth and Society*. 168–85.

———. 1977. "Sacrifice et alimentation humaine: A propos du Prométhée d'Hésiode." *Annali della Scuola Normale Superiore di Pisa* 3: 905–40.

Vester, H. 1968. "Das 19. Buch der *Odyssee*." *Gymnasium* 75: 417–34.

Vidal-Naquet, P. 1986. *The Black Hunter: Forms of Thought and Forms of Society in the Greek World*. Translated by A. Szegedy-Maszak. Baltimore and London.

———. 1986b. "Land and Sacrifice in the *Odyssey*: A Study of Religious and Mythical Meanings." In *The Black Hunter*. 15–38. Baltimore = 1981. *Myth, Religion and Society: Structuralist Essays by M. Detienne, L. Gernet, J.-P. Vernant, and P. Vidal-Naquet*. Edited by R. L. Gordon. Cambridge-Paris. [First publication 1970. "Valeurs religieuses et mythiques de la terre et du sacrifice dans l'*Odyssée*." *Annales E.S.C.* 25: 1278–97 = 1973. *Problèmes de la terre en grèce ancienne*. Edited by M. I. Finley. 269–92. The Hague. = 1981. *Le Chasseur noir: Formes de pensée et formes de société dans le monde grec*. 39–68. Paris.] [This volume: 33–53]

———. 1986c. "Slavery and the Rule of Women in Tradition, Myth, and Utopia." *The Black Hunter*. 205–23.

Vries, J. de. 1957. *Altgermanische Religionsgeschichte*. Vol. 2. Berlin.

Wade-Gery, H. T. 1952. *The Poet of the Iliad*. Cambridge.

Watkins, C. 1970. "Language of Gods and Language of Men: Remarks on Some Indo-European Metalinguistic Traditions." *Myth and Law among the Indo-Europeans*. Edited by J. Puhvel. 1–17. Berkeley and Los Angeles.

Weicker, G. 1915. "Seirenen." *Ausführliches Lexikon der griechischen und römischen Mythologie*. Edited by W. Roscher. Vol. 4. Cols. 601–39. Leipzig.

Wender, D. 1978. *The Last Scenes of the Odyssey*. Mnemosyne Supplement, no. 52. Leiden.

West, S. R. 1981. "An Alternative *Nostos* for Odysseus." *Liverpool Classical Monthly* 6–7: 169–75.

Whallon, W. 1961. "The Homeric Epithets." *Yale Classical Studies* 17: 97–142.

White, H. 1981. "The Value of Narrativity in the Representation of Reality." *On Narrative*. Edited by W.J.T. Mitchell. Chicago.

Whitman, C. H. 1974. *Euripides and the Full Circle of Myth*. Cambridge, Mass.

———. 1958. *Homer and the Heroic Tradition*. Cambridge, Mass.

Wiedemann, A. 1906. *Altägyptische Sagen und Märchen*. Leipzig.

Wilamowitz-Moellendorff, U. von. 1931. *Der Glaube der Hellenen*. 2 vols. Berlin [Reprinted Darmstadt, 1959].

———. 1927. *Die Heimkehr des Odysseus*. Berlin.

———. 1884. *Homerische Untersuchungen*. Berlin.

Willcock, M. M. 1970. "Some Aspects of the Gods in the *Iliad*." *Bulletin of the Institute of Classical Studies in London* 17: 1–10 [Reprinted 1978. *Essays on the Iliad: Selected Modern Criticism*. Edited by J. Wright. 58–69, 139–42. Bloomington and London].

Winkler, J. J. 1990. "Penelope's Cunning and Homer's." *The Constraints of Desire*. 129–61. New York and London.

Woodhouse, W. J. 1930. *The Composition of Homer's Odyssey*. Oxford [Reprinted Oxford, 1969].

Woolf, V. 1953. "On Not Knowing Greek." *The Common Reader: First Series*. 24–39. New York [First publication London, 1925].

Wright, J., ed. 1978. *Essays on the Iliad: Selected Modern Criticism*. Bloomington and London.

Wüst, E. 1937. "Penelope." *Paulys Real-Encyclopädie der classischen Altertumswissenschaft*. Vol. 19.1. Cols. 460–93.

Ziehen, L. 1939. "Opfer." *Paulys Real-Encyclopädie der classischen Altertumswissenschaft*. Vol. 18.1. Cols. 579–627.

Zwicker, J. 1927. "Sirenen." *Paulys Real-Encyclopädie der classischen Altertumswissenschaft*. Vol. 3A.1. Cols. 288–308.

VINCENT FARENGA, who translated Jean-Pierre Vernant's "The Refusal of Odysseus," is Associate Professor of Classics and Comparative Literature at the University of Southern California. He has written on Greek lyric poetry and is now completing a book on "State Formation and Cultural Development in Archaic and Classical Greece."

NANCY FELSON-RUBIN is Professor of Classics at the University of Georgia. She has written *Regarding Penelope: From Character to Poetics* (Princeton, 1994) and is the author of many articles on early Greek epic and lyric poetry and literary theory. In addition, she edited the special issue of *Arethusa,* vol. 16.1–2 (1983), entitled *Semiotics and Classical Studies.*

HARRIET I. FLOWER, who translated Karl Reinhardt's "The Adventures in the *Odyssey,*" is Assistant Professor of Classics at Franklin and Marshall College, Lancaster, Pennsylvania. She has written on Greek historiography and recently completed *Masks of Ancestors and Aristocratic Power in Roman Culture* (forthcoming, Oxford, 1996).

UVO HÖLSCHER is Professor Emeritus of Greek at the University of Munich. His distinguished publications include *Untersuchungen zur Form der Odyssee* (Berlin, 1939), *Empedokles und Hölderlin* (Frankfurt am Main, 1965), *Die Chance des Unbehagens: Drei Essays zur Situation der klassischen Studien* (Göttingen, 1965), *Anfängliches Fragen: Studien zur frühen griechischen Philosophie* (Göttingen, 1968), and *Die Odyssee: Epos zwischen Märchen und Roman* (Munich, 1989). In addition he edited Karl Reinhardt's posthumously published *Die Ilias und ihr Dichter* (Göttingen, 1961).

JANET LLOYD, who translated J.-P. Vernant's "Death with Two Faces," is a teacher and translator of French.

MICHAEL N. NAGLER is Professor Emeritus of Classics and Comparative Literature at the University of California, Berkeley. He has written *Spontaneity and Tradition: A Study in the Oral Art of Homer* (Berkeley, Los Angeles, London, 1974), *America Without Violence* (Covalo, Ca. 1982), and essays on Homeric epic, oral poetry, and pacifism.

PIETRO PUCCI is Professor of Classics at Cornell University. He has written *Hesiod and the Language of Poetry* (Baltimore and London, 1977), *The Violence of Pity in Euripides' Medea* (Ithaca and London, 1980), *Odysseus Polutropos: Intertextual Readings in the Odyssey and the Iliad* (Ithaca and London, 1987), *Oedipus and the Fabrication of the Father: Oedipus Tyrannus in*

Modern Criticism and Philosophy (Baltimore and London, 1992), and numerous articles on archaic and classical Greek literature. In addition he edited *Language and the Tragic Hero: Essays on Greek Tragedy in Honor of Gordon M. Kirkwood* (Atlanta, 1988).

KARL REINHARDT (1886–1957), whose work reflects both traditional classical scholarship and modern hermeneutics, was for many years Professor of Greek at the J. W. Goethe University in Frankfurt am Main. His numerous publications on ancient Greek literature and thought include *Sophokles* (Frankfurt am Main, 1933; 3rd edition, 1947; English translation by D. and H. Harvey, Oxford, 1979), *Aischylos als Regisseur und Theologe* (Berne, 1949), and *Die Ilias und ihr Dichter,* edited by Uvo Hölscher (Göttingen, 1961). His shorter studies are collected in two volumes, edited by Carl Becker: *Tradition und Geist: Gesammelte Essays zur Dichtung und Vermächtnis der Antike; Gesammelte Essays zur Philosophie und Geschichtsschreibung* (Göttingen, 1960 and 1966).

SIMON RICHTER, who translated Uvo Hölscher's "Penelope and the Suitors," is Assistant Professor of German at the University of Maryland, College Park. He works on the history of medicine and the history of sexuality and has written *Laocoön's Body and the Aesthetics of Pain* (Detroit, 1992).

SETH L. SCHEIN is Professor of Classics and Comparative Literature at the University of California, Davis. His writings, mainly on Homeric epic and Attic tragedy, include *The Iambic Trimeter in Aeschylus and Sophocles: A Study in Metrical Form* (Leiden, 1979) and *The Mortal Hero: An Introduction to Homer's Iliad* (Berkeley, Los Angeles, London, 1984).

CHARLES P. SEGAL is Professor of Classics at Harvard University. He has written *The Theme of the Mutilation of the Corpse in the Iliad* (Leiden, 1971), *Tragedy and Civilization: An Interpretation of Sophocles,* Martin Classical Lectures, vol. 26 (Cambridge, Mass, and London, 1981), *Interpreting Greek Tragedy: Myth, Poetry, Text* (Ithaca and London, 1986), *Language and Desire in Seneca's Phaedra* (Princeton, 1986), *Orpheus: The Myth of the Poet* (Baltimore and London, 1989), *Lucretius on Death and Anxiety* (Princeton, 1990), and *Singers, Heroes, and Gods in the Odyssey* (Ithaca and London, 1994), as well as many other books and articles on Greek and Latin poetry and literary theory. In addition he edited G. B. Conte's *The Rhetoric of Imitation: Genre and Poetic Memory in Virgil and Other Latin Poets* (Ithaca and London, 1980).

LAURA M. SLATKIN is Associate Professor of Classics at the University of Chicago. She has written *The Power of Thetis: Allusion and Interpretation in the Iliad* (Berkeley, Los Angeles, Oxford, 1992), as well as shorter studies of Homeric epic, Attic tragedy, Greek mythology, and oral poetics.

ANDREW SZEGEDY-MASZAK, who translated Pierre Vidal-Naquet's "Land and Sacrifice in the *Odyssey:* A Study of Religious and Mythical Meanings," is Professor of Classics at Wesleyan University. He has written *The Nomoi of Theophrastus* (New York, 1981) and previously translated Vidal-Naquet's *The Black Hunter: Forms of Thought and Forms of Society in the Greek World* (Baltimore and London, 1986) and François Lissarague's *The Aesthetics of the Greek Banquet* (Princeton, 1987).

JEAN-PIERRE VERNANT is Professor Emeritus of the Collège de France, where he held the Chair of Comparative Studies in Ancient Religions from 1975 to 1984. He was co-founder and first director of the Centre de Recherches Comparées sur les Sociétés Anciennes (now called Centre Louis Gernet) at the Ecole des Hautes Etudes en Sciences Sociales in Paris. He has written and edited many works on Greek history, literature, institutions, values, and *mentalité*. His most influential contributions (all translated into English) have been *Les Origines de la pensée grecque, Mythe et pensée chez les grecs, Mythe et société en Grèce ancienne, Mythe et tragédie en Grèce ancienne* (with Pierre Vidal-Naquet), and *Les Ruses de l'intelligence: La Métis des Grecs* (with Marcel Detienne). Recently he has published *L'Individu, la mort, l'amour,* most of which appears in *Mortals and Immortals: Collected Essays,* edited by Froma I. Zeitlin (Princeton, 1991), and *Figures, idoles, masques,* a collection of his annual reports for the Collège de France.

PIERRE VIDAL-NAQUET is Director of the Centre Louis Gernet (formerly the Centre de Recherches Comparées sur les Sociétés Anciennes), of which he was a co-founder, at the Ecole des Hautes Etudes en Sciences Sociales in Paris. He has written, edited, and introduced many works on Greek and modern history and historiography; Greek literature, institutions, and *mentalité*; Jews and Judaism in France; and French society. His best known and most influential works of classical scholarship have been *Le Chasseur noir: Formes de pensée et formes de société dans le monde grec* and *Mythe et tragédie en Grèce ancienne* (with Jean-Pierre Vernant), both translated into English, and *Clisthène l'Athénien* (with Pierre Lévêque). He wrote *Torture: Cancer of Democracy, France and Algeria 1954–62* (Harmondsworth and Baltimore, 1963) and *Assassins of Memory: Essays on the Denial of the Holocaust* (New York, 1992), translated mainly from essays in *Les Juifs, la mémoire et le présent,* 2 vols. (Paris, 1981, 1991). Recently he published *Mémoires 1: La Brisure et l'attente, 1930–1945* (Paris, 1995).

About the Author

SETH L. SCHEIN is Professor of Comparative Literature and Classics at the University of California, Davis. His books include *The Mortal Hero: An Introduction to Homer's "Iliad"* (University of California) and *The Iambic Trimeter in Aeschylus and Sophocles: A Study in Metrical Form* (E. J. Brill).